W9-BPJ-218

1001 Cupcakes, Cookies & other tempting treats

1001 Cupcakes, Cookies & other tempting treats

CONSULTANT EDITOR: **Susanna Tee**

This edition published in 2011
LOVE FOOD is an imprint of Parragon Books Ltd

Parragon
Queen Street House
4 Queen Street
Bath BA1 1HE, UK

www.parragon.com

ISBN: 978-1-4454-5588-4
Printed in China

Created and produced by Ivy Contract
Additional photography by Sian Irvine
Food styling by Jack Sargeson, Anna Irvine, and Maud Eden
New recipes by Susanna Tee with Sarah Banbery and Jacqueline Bellefontaine

Notes for the Reader
This book uses imperial, metric, and US cup measurements. Follow the same units of measurement throughout; do not mix imperial and metric. All spoon measurements are level: teaspoons are assumed to be 5 ml, and tablespoons are assumed to be 15 ml. Unless otherwise stated, milk is assumed to be whole, eggs and individual vegetables, such as potatoes, are medium, and pepper is freshly ground black pepper.

The times given are an approximate guide only. Preparation times differ according to the techniques used by different people and the cooking times may also vary from those given as a result of the type of oven used. Optional ingredients, variations, or serving suggestions have not been included in the calculations.

Recipes using raw or very lightly cooked eggs should be avoided by infants, the elderly, pregnant women, convalescents, and anyone with a chronic condition. Pregnant and breastfeeding women are advised to avoid eating peanuts and peanut products. People with nut allergies should be aware that some of the ready-made ingredients used in the recipes in this book may contain nuts. Always check the packaging before use.

Contents

Introduction 6

Cute Cupcakes 12

Crowd-Pleasing Cookies 64

Blissful Brownies and Bars 162

Marvelous Muffins 200

Tempting Treats 256

Index 300

Introduction

The cupcakes, cookies, and other tempting treats included in this book are easy and enjoyable to make, fun to eat, and great to share whatever the time of day. Every home should have a well-stocked jar of them waiting to be dipped into, and they are the perfect choice for a midmorning coffee or afternoon cup of tea, at a children's party, or on a festive occasion. Whatever the reason, you are sure to find what you are looking for among the 1,001 delicious goodies that have been gathered together in this comprehensive collection.

The making of cookies started in ancient Egypt with a mixture of flour and water that was baked on both sides on a griddle, resulting in a flat, hard cake. To this mixture, leaveners were added to make the cake rise, and then sugar to sweeten it. Wood-burning and coal-fired ovens were developed, and from these humble beginnings cookies and other treats such as pastries, cupcakes, muffins, bars, and brownies, have evolved. Today, every country has its own favorite recipe, be it chocolate chip cookies, biscotti, or oatcakes—the list is endless!

The star ingredients

Sugar, fat, eggs, flour, and a liquid are the basic ingredients that the majority of the recipes share.

Sugar

Superfine sugar is usually recommended because it dissolves more easily than granulated sugar. Nevertheless, granulated sugar can be used if necessary.

Fat

Butter is the fat that is suggested in most of the recipes, because it adds richness and produces the best flavor. However, margarine can be used as an alternative, and is less expensive. It is important, though, to use a margarine containing not less that 60 percent fat; choose a hard margarine that is described on the package as suitable for baking. The exception is when a recipe calls for a soft margarine. In this instance, all the ingredients are beaten together with an electric mixer until mixed.

Eggs

The size of eggs used in the recipes is medium unless otherwise stated. If possible, use eggs that are at room temperature because cold eggs can cause the mixture to curdle and will result in a less soft mixture.

Flour

The flour used in the recipes may be all-purpose or self-rising. Should you need self-rising flour but only have all-purpose, sift 2½ teaspoons of baking powder into every 1⅔ cups all-purpose flour.

Liquid

The liquid in the recipes is used to bind the ingredients together and is usually milk, eggs, butter, oil, water, or fruit juice.

Equipment & helpful techniques

To make any of the recipes in this book requires very little special equipment and, in many cases, improvisation can be helpful! Nevertheless, here are some suggestions that you may find useful:

- Use your hands! Dampen them slightly when shaping cookies into a ball.
- A hand-held electric mixer is useful for whisking and beating mixtures together but, failing this, use a balloon whisk for whisking and a wooden spoon for creaming.
- If you don't have a pan of the size that is specified in the recipe, you can often improvise. A quantity of batter designed for a square pan will fill a 1 inch/2.5 cm larger round pan and vice versa. When making bar cookies, recipes that specify a particular size of pan can equally be made in a pan with different dimensions but with the same capacity.
- Use a food processor for rubbing fat into flour, but when the eggs or liquid are added, make sure you blend them quickly, because overworked dough will be tough.
- When preparing a pan for baking brownies and bar cookies, especially one that is not shallow, line with parchment paper, letting it hang over the edge of the pan. This makes it easier when lifting and removing the brownies or cookies later.
- If a recipe asks for toasted nuts and you do not have any, you can toast them yourself (see right).

To toast nuts

Preheat the oven to 350°F/180°C. Spread the nuts in a single layer on a baking sheet and cook in the preheated oven for 5–10 minutes, turning and watching them carefully until golden brown.

To melt chocolate

In a bowl

Many of the recipes require you to melt chocolate in a heatproof bowl set over a saucepan of simmering water. This is the safest way to melt it because it will not overheat and become dry. Make sure the bowl does not touch the water.

In a microwave

Break the chocolate into a heatproof bowl and cook on Low until the chocolate is soft on top. As a guide, 3½ oz/100 g will take about 4 minutes. Check and stir every minute.

Assuring success

Almost all the recipes in the book are easy to make. Follow these useful suggestions and you will be guaranteed success every time you bake:

- Preheat the oven for 10–15 minutes before baking, even if the oven manufacturer's instructions suggest that this is not necessary. If you have a fan-assisted oven, reduce the temperature according to their instructions.
- It is important that ingredients are measured accurately, so it is worth investing in good-quality measuring cups and standard measuring spoons.
- Get into the habit of preparing baking sheets, paper cases, and pans before commencing preparation, because mixtures that contain self-rising flour start to activate once the liquid has been added to them and should therefore be baked as soon as possible after they have been prepared.
- When butter or hard margarine needs to be softened before blending with another ingredient, either remove it from the refrigerator and let stand at room temperature for about 1 hour, or cut into cubes, place in a bowl, and microwave on High for 10 seconds, until softened slightly. Be careful not to let it melt.
- It is not necessary to sift flour to facilitate even mixing unless you are combining several dry ingredients.
- After adding the flour to a cupcake or muffin batter, do not overbeat it because this will make the batter tough.
- Where dough has to be refrigerated to make it firmer and easier to handle, you can speed this up by wrapping the dough in parchment paper and placing in the freezer for a third of the time that you would normally refrigerate it.
- Do not overbeat brownie or bar cookie batters because this can make them rise too much and sink when they cool.
- Always place cookie dough on cold baking sheets to prevent the dough from spreading excessively and browning too much around the edges. When making a large quantity of cookies, let the baking sheet cool for a few minutes in between batches.
- Bake cookies on nonstick baking sheets or line them with parchment paper but, unless specified in the recipe, do not grease the sheets because the cookies will spread excessively, become too thin, and brown too quickly around the edges.
- Place cookies well apart on the baking sheet to allow room for them to spread during cooking. Unless they are particularly large, a gap of 2 inches/5 cm is usually enough.
- For even browning, position baking sheets of cupcakes, cookies, bars, or muffins on the middle rack of the oven.
- Unless otherwise stated, transfer cookies to a wire rack as soon as they are firm enough to handle, and cupcakes and muffins directly after they are removed from the oven, and let cool. This will let the steam evaporate and prevent them from becoming soggy.
- When baking cupcakes and muffins, try to resist the temptation to open the oven door during the first half of the cooking time as cold air can cause the batter to sink in the middle.

Bake & store

With a few exceptions, most of the cupcakes, cookies, and other tempting treats in this book will keep well in a pan or airtight container and, in the case of brownies and bar cookies, even in the baking pan in which they were cooked, if it is kept covered with foil. However, the following tips will also help:

- Ideally, store baked cupcakes, cookies, and muffins undecorated. Any item that is decorated with cream, cream cheese, or yogurt should be stored in the refrigerator.
- Store soft cookies separately from crisp varieties so that they don't all become soft, and don't store cookies and cakes together because the cookies will absorb moisture from the cakes and soften.
- Store different flavored cookies separately so that their flavors do not mix.
- Only store cookies when they are completely cold. If stored while still warm, they are liable to stick together.
- One or two sugar cubes added to a pan of cookies helps to keep them crisp.
- Most cupcakes, cookies, muffins, and pastries can be frozen and thawed at short notice, but most are best when just baked.

The presentation

Finally, when serving your cupcakes, cookies, or other tempting treats, presentation makes all the difference. Serve the delicate types on fine china or glass plates, or use cake stands and baskets lined with napkins, or even pans lined with parchment paper can be used.

The beautifully photographed recipes in this book will capture your imagination—and with 1,001 of them to choose from, you are really spoiled for choice!

The finishing touches

Basic icing

1 cup confectioners' sugar
1 tbsp cold water

Sift the sugar into a bowl and gradually add the water, then beat together until the icing coats the back of a spoon.

Variations

Orange or lemon icing: Replace the water with citrus juice.
Chocolate icing: Replace 2 tablespoons of the confectioners' sugar with 2 tablespoons of cocoa.
Coffee icing: Mix 1 teaspoon of instant coffee with 1 tablespoon of boiling water. Cool and mix with the confectioners' sugar as before.
Liqueur icing: Replace the water with 1 tablespoon of liqueur.
Orange flower or rose water icing: Add ½ tablespoon of orange flower or rose water to ½ tablespoon of water and mix with the sugar.
Mocha icing: Replace 2 tablespoons of the sugar with 2 tablespoons of cocoa and mix 1 teaspoon of instant coffee with 1 tablespoon of boiling water. Let cool and mix with the sugar and cocoa as before.

Buttercream

1 cup butter, softened
1 tbsp cream or milk
3 cups confectioners' sugar

Place the butter and cream in a bowl and beat together. Gradually sift in the confectioners' sugar and beat until smooth.

Variations

Orange or lemon buttercream: Substitute fresh orange or lemon juice for the cream and add a little orange or yellow food coloring.
Chocolate buttercream: Replace ½ cup of the sugar with ½ cup cocoa.
Coffee buttercream: Replace the cream with 1 tablespoon of cold strong espresso coffee and ¼ teaspoon of coffee extract.
Mocha buttercream: Replace ½ cup of the sugar with ½ cup cocoa and replace the cream with 1 tablespoon of cold espresso coffee.
Nut buttercream: Beat ¾ cup butter with the sugar, then add ¼ teaspoon of vanilla extract, ¼ cup smooth peanut or almond butter, and ⅔ cup chopped pecans to the finished frosting and beat well.

Royal icing

Crème au beurre

2 egg yolks
¾ cup butter, softened
scant 1 cup superfine sugar
4 tbsp water

Place the egg yolks in a bowl and whisk lightly. Place the butter in a separate bowl and beat until fluffy. Place the sugar and water into a saucepan and heat gently until the sugar has dissolved, then bring to a boil and boil for 2–3 minutes, or until the temperature reads 225°F/107°C on a sugar thermometer. Whisking all the time, pour the syrup into the egg yolks in a thin stream and continue to whisk the mixture until it is thick and cold. Gradually beat the egg mixture into the butter until combined.

Variations

Chocolate crème au beurre: Add 1½ tablespoons of chocolate extract to the finished frosting.
Coffee crème au beurre: Add 1½ tablespoons of coffee extract to the finished frosting.
Mocha crème au beurre: Mix 1 tablespoon of chocolate extract with ½ tablespoon of coffee extract. Add to the finished frosting and beat well to combine.
Orange or lemon crème au beurre: Stir 2 tablespoons of juice and 1 teaspoon of finely grated rind of either lemon or orange into the frosting and beat well to combine.
Strawberry or raspberry crème au beurre: Add 2 tablespoons of strawberry or raspberry syrup to the frosting and beat well to combine.

Royal icing

3 large egg whites
4 ⅓ cups confectioners' sugar
1 tsp liquid glycerin

Place the egg whites in a large bowl and gradually sift in 1¾ cups confectioners' sugar, stirring in between each addition until the mixture is thick. Whisk the mixture, gradually adding the remaining sugar. Whisk for 10 minutes, or until it is stiff. Stir in the glycerin until smooth.

Fondant

4 ⅓ cups confectioners' sugar
1 large egg white
2 tbsp liquid glycerin
1 tsp vanilla extract or almond extract

Sift the confectioners' sugar into a large bowl and gradually beat in the egg white until the mixture is thick and smooth. Beat in the glycerin and vanilla extract.

Almond paste

1½ cups confectioners' sugar, plus extra for dusting
scant 1 cup superfine sugar
2 large eggs, plus 1 large egg yolk
½ tsp almond extract
1 tsp lemon juice
heapng ⅓ cup ground almonds

Sift the confectioners' sugar into a heatproof bowl and stir in the superfine sugar. Whisk the 2 eggs with the egg yolk and stir into the sugar. Place the bowl over a saucepan of simmering water and whisk for 10–12 minutes, or until thick and pale. Sit the bottom of the bowl in cold water. Whisk in the almond extract and lemon juice and whisk until cool. Stir in the almonds and beat to form a paste. Roll the almond paste to the desired size on a work surface dusted with confectioners' sugar.

Apricot glaze

½ cup smooth apricot jam
½ cup superfine sugar
1 cup water

Sift the apricot jam into a saucepan and stir in the sugar and water. Heat gently to simmering point and stir until clear. Let cool.

Fudge frosting

Fudge frosting

½ cup superfine sugar
⅓ cup evaporated milk
3 tbsp butter
¼ tsp vanilla extract

Place the sugar and evaporated milk into a saucepan and stir, then heat gently until the sugar has dissolved. Bring to a boil, then reduce the heat and simmer for 5–6 minutes. Remove from the heat and add the butter and vanilla and whisk until smooth. Let cool, cover, and chill for 2 hours until thick.

Variations

Coffee fudge: Replace the vanilla extract with 1 tablespoon of coffee extract.
Chocolate fudge: Add 4 oz/115 g chopped semisweet chocolate with the butter and stir until melted.
Coconut fudge: Add 2 tablespoons of grated creamed coconut with the butter and stir.
Nut fudge: Stir in ⅔ cup chopped toasted pecans to the frosting.

Butterscotch frosting

4 tbsp butter
½ cup light brown sugar
pinch of salt
⅓ cup evaporated milk
2 cups confectioners' sugar
½ tsp vanilla extract

Place the butter, brown sugar, salt, and evaporated milk in a saucepan and heat until the sugar has dissolved, then stir until smooth. Let cool slightly. Sift in the confectioners' sugar and vanilla and beat well. Let cool completely.

Cream cheese frosting

9 tbsp butter, softened
1 cup cream cheese
scant 4 cups confectioners' sugar
1 tsp vanilla extract

Place the butter and cheese in a bowl and beat until light and fluffy. Gradually sift in the sugar, add the vanilla, and beat until smooth.

Vanilla frosting

2 tbsp butter, softened
1 vanilla bean
2 cups confectioners' sugar
3-4 tbsp heavy cream

Place the butter in a bowl and beat until fluffy. Split the vanilla bean lengthwise and add the seeds to the butter, then sift in the confectioners' sugar and beat until smooth. Add the cream and beat again until creamy.

Chocolate frosting

3½ oz/100 g semisweet chocolate, chopped
scant ⅔ cup butter, softened
1¼ cups confectioners' sugar
½ tsp chocolate extract

Place the chocolate in a heatproof bowl, set the bowl over a saucepan of gently simmering water, and heat until melted. Let cool. Place the butter in a bowl and beat until fluffy, then sift in the sugar and beat until smooth. Add the cooled chocolate and chocolate extract and beat until combined.

American frosting

1⅛ cups superfine sugar
4 tbsp water
¼ tsp cream of tartar
½ tsp vanilla extract
1 large egg white

Place the sugar, water, and cream of tartar into a saucepan and heat gently until the sugar has dissolved. Add the vanilla and heat (without boiling), stirring until the temperature reads 250°F/120°C on a sugar thermometer. Let cool slightly. Whisk the egg white in a large bowl until stiff, then continue whisking as you add the syrup in a thin stream and continue to whisk until smooth and thick.

Seven-minute frosting

1 large egg white
pinch of salt
1½ cups superfine sugar
5 tbsp water
¼ tsp cream of tartar
1 tsp vanilla extract

Place the egg white in a heatproof bowl and add the salt, sugar, water, and cream of tartar. Beat together, then place the bowl in a double-boiler over boiling water and whisk for 7 minutes, until stiff peaks form. Remove from the heat, add the vanilla, and beat until smooth.

Chocolate ganache

5½ oz/150 g semisweet chocolate, chopped
⅔ cup heavy cream

Place the chocolate in a heatproof bowl. Pour the cream into a pan and bring gently up to simmering point. Pour the hot cream over the chocolate and mix until smooth.

Crème au beurre

Cute Cupcakes

01 Iced cupcakes

MAKES 16

8 tbsp butter, softened
½ cup superfine sugar
2 eggs, lightly beaten
heaping ¾ cup self-rising flour

TOPPING
1¾ cups confectioners' sugar
about 2 tbsp warm water
a few drops of food coloring (optional)
sugar flowers, colored sprinkles, candied cherries, and/or chocolate strands, for decorating

Preheat the oven to 375°F/190°C. Line two 12-hole muffin pans with 16 paper liners. Place the butter and sugar in a large bowl and beat together until light and fluffy, then gradually beat in the eggs. Sift in the flour and fold into the mixture. Spoon the batter into the paper liners.

Bake in the preheated oven for 15–20 minutes. Transfer to a wire rack to cool completely.

To make the frosting, sift the confectioners' sugar into a bowl and stir in just enough warm water to mix to a smooth paste that is thick enough to coat the back of a wooden spoon. Stir in a few drops of food coloring, if using, then spread the frosting over the cupcakes and decorate, as liked.

02 Orange cupcakes

Add the grated rind of ½ orange to the cake batter after beating in the eggs. Use orange juice instead of water when making the frosting.

03 Lemon cupcakes

Add the grated rind of ½ lemon to the cake batter after beating in the eggs. Use lemon juice instead of water when making the frosting.

04 Chocolate cupcakes

Replace 2 tablespoons of the flour with 2 tablespoons of cocoa and add 2 teaspoons of cocoa to the confectioners' sugar when making the frosting.

05 Coffee cupcakes

Dissolve 2 tablespoons of instant coffee in 3 tablespoons of boiling water. Add about two thirds to the cake batter after beating the eggs. Add the remainder to the confectioners' sugar when making the frosting.

06 Mocha cupcakes

Dissolve 1 tablespoon of instant coffee in 2 tablespoons of boiling water and beat in after adding the eggs. Add 1 tablespoon of cocoa to the flour and fold in. For a mocha frosting, add 1 teaspoon of cocoa to the confectioners' sugar. Dissolve 1 teaspoon of instant coffee in 1 tablespoon of boiling water and stir into the confectioners' sugar mixture with enough water until smooth.

07 Almond cupcakes

Add 1 teaspoon of almond extract after beating in the eggs. Replace 2 tablespoons of the flour with ground almonds.

08 Nutty cupcakes

Add ¼ cup finely chopped walnuts, pecans, or toasted hazelnuts before folding in the flour.

09 Candy-topped vanilla cupcakes

MAKES 18

generous 8 tbsp butter, softened, or soft margarine
¾ cup superfine sugar
1½ tsp vanilla extract
2 large eggs, lightly beaten
scant 1½ cups self-rising flour

TOPPING
1 quantity buttercream (page 10)
a selection of classic small candies, such as jelly beans, for decorating

Preheat the oven to 375°F/190°C. Line two 12-hole muffin pans with 18 paper liners. Place the butter and sugar in a large bowl and beat together until light and fluffy, then beat in the vanilla extract. Gradually beat in the eggs, then sift in the flour and fold into the mixture. Spoon the batter into the paper liners.

Bake in the preheated oven for 12–15 minutes, or until golden and springy to the touch. Transfer to a wire rack to cool completely.

Place the buttercream in a pastry bag fitted with a small star tip and pipe the buttercream on top of each cake. Arrange the candies on top to decorate.

10 Candy-topped chocolate cupcakes

Reduce the vanilla extract to ½ teaspoon. Melt 2½ oz/70 g semisweet chocolate, broken into pieces, and stir into the cake batter after beating in the eggs. Decorate with chocolate buttercream (page 10) and small chocolate candies.

11 Birthday party cakes

MAKES 24

1 cup butter, softened, or soft margarine
heaping 1 cup superfine sugar
4 eggs
1⅔ cups self-rising flour

TOPPING
¾ cup butter, softened
3 cups confectioners' sugar
a variety of candies and chocolates, sugar-coated chocolates, dried fruits, edible sugar flower shapes, cake decorating sprinkles, silver or gold dragées, colored sprinkles, various tubes of colored decorating icing, and candles and candleholders (optional), for decorating

Preheat the oven to 350°F/180°C. Line two 12-hole muffin pans with 24 paper liners. Place the butter, sugar, eggs, and flour in a large bowl and beat together until just smooth. Spoon the batter into the paper liners.

Bake in the preheated oven for 15–20 minutes, or until well risen, golden brown, and firm to the touch. Transfer to a wire rack to cool.

To make the frosting, place the butter in a bowl and beat until fluffy. Sift in the confectioners' sugar and beat together until smooth. When the cakes are cold, spread the frosting on top of each cake, then decorate as you like and place a candle in the top of each, if using.

12 Citrus almond party cakes

For more grown-up party cakes, replace heaping ⅓ cup of the flour with ground almonds and fold in ¼ cup finely chopped candied peel. Decorate with sugared almonds.

13 Chocolate butterfly cakes

Makes 12

1 oz/25 g semisweet chocolate, broken into pieces
9 tbsp butter, softened
⅔ cup superfine sugar
heaping 1 cup self-rising flour
2 large eggs
2 tbsp unsweetened cocoa
confectioners' sugar, for dusting

LEMON BUTTERCREAM
7 tbsp butter, softened
2 cups confectioners' sugar
grated rind of ½ lemon
1 tbsp lemon juice

Preheat the oven to 350°F/180°C. Line a 12-hole muffin pan with 12 paper liners. Place the chocolate in a heatproof bowl, set the bowl over a saucepan of gently simmering water, and heat until melted, then let cool slightly.

Place the butter, sugar, flour, eggs, and cocoa in a large bowl and beat together until the mixture is just smooth. Beat in the melted chocolate. Spoon the batter into the paper liners.

Bake in the preheated oven for 15 minutes, or until springy to the touch. Transfer to a wire rack to cool completely.

To make the frosting, place the butter in a bowl and beat until fluffy, then gradually sift in the confectioners' sugar and beat to combine. Beat in the lemon rind, then gradually beat in the lemon juice. Cut the top off each cake, then cut the top in half. Pipe the buttercream over the cut surface of each cake and push the 2 cut cake pieces into the frosting to form wings. Dust with sifted confectioners' sugar.

14 Chocolate orange butterfly cakes

Add the grated rind of ½ orange and 2 tablespoons of orange juice to the cake batter. For the frosting, replace the lemon juice and rind with orange juice and rind and decorate the completed cakes with very fine strips of orange rind, if liked.

15 Chocolate nut butterfly cakes

Add ¼ cup finely chopped hazelnuts to the cake batter. Sprinkle a few chopped toasted hazelnuts on the top to decorate.

16 White chocolate butterfly cakes

Replace the melted semisweet chocolate with melted white chocolate. Decorate the cakes with chocolate buttercream (page 10).

17 Honey & spice cakes

MAKES ABOUT 24

heaping ½ cup butter
½ cup brown sugar
¼ cup honey
scant 1½ cups self-rising flour
1 tsp ground allspice
2 eggs, lightly beaten
24 whole blanched almonds

Preheat the oven to 350°F/180°C. Line two 12-hole muffin pans with 24 paper liners. Place the butter, sugar, and honey in a large saucepan and heat gently, stirring, until the butter is melted. Remove the pan from the heat. Sift together the flour and allspice and stir into the mixture in the saucepan, then beat in the eggs until smooth.

Spoon the batter into the paper liners and place an almond on top of each one. Bake in the preheated oven for 20–25 minutes, or until well risen and golden brown. Transfer to a wire rack to cool completely.

18 Pecan & maple spice cakes

Replace the honey with maple syrup and the allspice with cinnamon. Decorate each cake with a pecan instead of an almond.

19 Nutmeg & hazelnut cakes

Add 1 tablespoon of finely chopped toasted hazelnuts to the honey and butter mixture. Replace the allspice with nutmeg and decorate each cake with a hazelnut instead of an almond.

20 Jumbo chocolate chip cupcakes

Makes 8

7 tbsp butter, softened
½ cup superfine sugar
2 large eggs
¾ cup self-rising flour
½ cup semisweet chocolate chips

Preheat the oven to 375°F/190°C. Line a 12-hole muffin pan with 8 paper liners.

Place the butter, sugar, eggs, and flour in a large bowl and beat together until just smooth. Fold in the chocolate chips. Spoon the batter into the paper liners.

Bake in the preheated oven for 20–25 minutes, or until well risen and golden brown. Transfer to a wire rack to cool completely.

21 Choc & nut cupcakes

Replace the semisweet chocolate chips with ⅓ cup milk chocolate chips and ⅓ cup chopped hazelnuts.

22 Sugar-coated chocolates cupcakes

Replace the semisweet chocolate chips with sugar-coated chocolates.

23 Queen's cakes

MAKES 18

8 tbsp butter, softened, or soft margarine
½ cup superfine sugar
2 large eggs, lightly beaten
4 tsp lemon juice
1¼ cups self-rising flour
¾ cup raisins
2–4 tbsp milk, if necessary

Preheat the oven to 375°F/190°C. Line two 12-hole muffin pans with 18 paper liners. Place the butter and sugar in a large bowl and beat together until light and fluffy. Gradually beat in the eggs, then beat in the lemon juice with 1 tablespoon of the flour. Fold in the remaining flour and the raisins. If necessary, add a little milk to create a soft dropping consistency. Spoon the batter into the paper liners.

Bake in the preheated oven for 15–20 minutes, or until well risen and golden brown. Transfer to a wire rack to cool completely.

24 Orange queen cakes

Replace the lemon juice with orange juice and add the grated rind of ½ orange with the juice.

25 Iced queen cakes

Sift 1⅓ cups confectioners' sugar into a small bowl and stir in about 4 teaspoons of lemon juice. Mix to a smooth icing that will coat the back of a wooden spoon. Spread the icing over the cakes so that you can just see the edges of the cake.

26 Rose petal cupcakes

MAKES 12

8 tbsp butter, softened
½ cup superfine sugar
2 eggs, lightly beaten
1 tbsp milk
few drops of extract of rose oil
¼ tsp vanilla extract
1¼ cups self-rising flour
silver dragées, for decorating

CRYSTALLIZED ROSE PETALS
12–24 rose petals
lightly beaten egg white, for brushing
superfine sugar, for sprinkling

FROSTING
6 tbsp butter, softened
1½ cups confectioners' sugar
pink or purple food coloring (optional)

To make the crystallized rose petals, gently rinse the petals and dry well with paper towels. Using a pastry brush, paint both sides of a rose petal with egg white, then coat well with superfine sugar. Place on a tray and repeat with the remaining petals. Cover the tray with foil and leave overnight.

Preheat the oven to 400°F/200°C. Line a 12-hole muffin pan with 12 paper liners.

Place the butter and sugar in a large bowl and beat together until light and fluffy, then gradually beat in the eggs. Stir in the milk, rose extract, and vanilla extract, then fold in the flour. Spoon the batter into the paper liners.

Bake in the preheated oven for 12–15 minutes, or until well risen and golden brown. Transfer to a wire rack to cool completely.

To make the frosting, place the butter in a large bowl and beat until fluffy. Sift in the confectioners' sugar and mix well together. Add a few drops of pink or purple food coloring to match the rose petals, if liked.

When the cupcakes are cold, spread the frosting on top of each cake. Top with 1–2 crystallized rose petals and sprinkle with silver dragées to decorate.

27 Sticky gingerbread cupcakes

MAKES 16

¾ cup all-purpose flour
2 tsp ground ginger
¾ tsp ground cinnamon
1 piece preserved ginger, finely chopped
¾ tsp baking soda
4 tbsp milk
6 tbsp butter, softened
⅓ cup dark brown sugar
2 tbsp blackstrap molasses
2 eggs, lightly beaten
1 piece preserved ginger, sliced, for decorating

FROSTING
6 tbsp butter, softened
1½ cups confectioners' sugar
2 tbsp ginger syrup from the preserved ginger jar

Preheat the oven to 325°F/160°C. Line two 12-hole muffin pans with 16 paper liners. Sift the flour, ground ginger, and cinnamon together into a bowl. Add the chopped ginger and toss in the flour mixture until it is well coated. Place the baking soda and milk in a separate bowl and stir to dissolve.

Place the butter and sugar in a large bowl and beat together until light and fluffy.

Beat in the blackstrap molasses, then gradually mix in the eggs. Beat in the flour mixture and gradually add the milk. Spoon the batter into the paper liners.

Bake in the preheated oven for 20 minutes, or until well risen and golden brown. Transfer to a wire rack to cool competely.

To make the frosting, place the butter in a bowl and beat until fluffy. Sift in the confectioners' sugar, add the ginger syrup, and beat together until smooth and creamy.

When the cupcakes are cold, spread the frosting on top of each cake, then decorate with pieces of the preserved ginger to decorate.

28 Sticky gingersnap cupcakes

Add ¼ cup finely chopped walnuts or pecans with the chopped preserved ginger. Decorate with chopped nuts.

29 Dark & white fudge cakes

MAKES 20

generous ¾ cup water
6 tbsp butter
½ cup superfine sugar
1 tbsp dark corn syrup
3 tbsp milk
1 tsp vanilla extract
1 tsp baking soda
1⅔ cups all-purpose flour
2 tbsp unsweetened cocoa

TOPPING
1¾ oz/50 g semisweet chocolate, broken into pieces
4 tbsp water
3½ tbsp butter
1¾ oz/50 g white chocolate, broken into pieces
3 cups confectioners' sugar
3½ oz/100 g semisweet chocolate shavings and 3½ oz/100 g white chocolate shavings, for decorating

Preheat the oven to 350°F/180°C. Line two 12-hole muffin pans with 20 paper liners. Place the water, butter, sugar, and syrup in a saucepan and heat gently, stirring, until the sugar has dissolved. Bring to a boil, reduce the heat, and cook gently for 5 minutes. Let cool.

Meanwhile, place the milk and vanilla extract in a bowl. Add the baking soda and stir to dissolve. Sift the flour and cocoa into a separate bowl and add the syrup mixture. Stir in the milk mixture and beat until smooth, then spoon the batter into the paper liners.

Bake in the preheated oven for 20 minutes, or until well risen and firm to the touch. Transfer to a wire rack to cool completely.

To make the frosting, place the semisweet chocolate in a small heatproof bowl, add half the water and half the butter, set the bowl over a saucepan of gently simmering water, and heat until melted. Stir until smooth and then let stand over the water. Repeat with the white chocolate and remaining water and butter. Sift half the confectioners' sugar into each bowl and beat until smooth and thick.

When the cupcakes are cold, top alternately with each frosting, then let set. Decorate with chocolate shavings.

30 Pecan fudge cupcakes

Stir ¼ cup chopped pecans into the flour and cocoa mixture before adding the syrup. Sprinkle chopped nuts instead of chocolate shavings on top of the frosting.

31 Frosted peanut butter cupcakes

MAKES 16

4 tbsp butter, softened,
or soft margarine
heaping 1 cup light brown sugar
½ cup crunchy peanut butter
2 eggs, lightly beaten
1 tsp vanilla extract
1⅔ cups all-purpose flour
2 tsp baking powder
generous ⅓ cup milk

FROSTING
heaping ¾ cup soft cream cheese
2 tbsp butter, softened
2 cups confectioners' sugar

Preheat the oven to 350°F/180°C. Line two 12-hole muffin pans with 16 paper liners. Place the butter, sugar, and peanut butter in a bowl and beat together for 1–2 minutes, or until well mixed. Gradually beat in the eggs, then add the vanilla extract. Sift in the flour and baking powder, then fold them into the mixture, alternating with the milk. Spoon the batter into the paper liners.

Bake in the preheated oven for 25 minutes, or until well risen and golden brown. Transfer to a wire rack to cool completely.

To make the frosting, place the cream cheese and butter in a large bowl and beat together until smooth. Sift the confectioners' sugar into the mixture, beat together until well mixed, then spread the frosting on top of each cupcake.

32 Peanut butter & jam cupcakes

Spoon half the batter into the paper liners then place about ½ teaspoon of strawberry or raspberry jam into the center of each. Carefully spoon the remaining batter into the paper liners so that it completely encloses the jam. Sprinkle with a little raw brown sugar and bake as before.

33 Chocolate peanut butter cupcakes

Spoon half the batter into the paper liners then place about ½ teaspoon of chocolate spread into the center of each. Carefully spoon the remaining batter into the paper liners so that it completely encloses the chocolate spread. Bake as before. Cool and spread with extra chocolate spread.

34 Moist walnut cupcakes

Makes 12

heaping ¾ cup walnuts
4 tbsp butter, softened, cut into small pieces
½ cup superfine sugar
grated rind of ½ lemon
½ cup self-rising flour
2 eggs
12 walnut halves, for decorating

FROSTING
4 tbsp butter, softened
¾ cup confectioners' sugar
grated rind of ½ lemon
1 tsp lemon juice

Preheat the oven to 375°F/190°C. Line a 12-hole muffin pan with 12 paper liners. Place the walnuts in a food processor and pulse until finely ground. Be careful not to overgrind, or the nuts will turn to oil.

Add the butter, sugar, lemon rind, flour, and eggs and blend until the mixture is evenly combined. Spoon the batter into the paper liners.

Bake in the preheated oven for 20 minutes, or until well risen and golden brown. Transfer to a wire rack to cool completely.

To make the frosting, place the butter in a bowl and beat until fluffy. Sift in the confectioners' sugar, add the lemon rind and juice, and mix well together. When the cupcakes are cold, spread the frosting on top of each cupcake and top with a walnut to decorate.

35 Sticky orange & walnut cupcakes

For the cupcakes, replace the lemon rind with orange rind. Instead of the frosting, heat 6 tablespoons of orange juice with 2 tablespoons of superfine sugar, stirring until the sugar dissolves, then boil until syrupy. Spoon the syrup over the hot cakes and let cool before serving.

36 Moist pecan cupcakes

Replace the walnuts with pecans and the lemon rind and juice with orange rind and juice.

37 Feathered-iced coffee cupcakes

Makes 16

1 tbsp instant coffee granules
1 tbsp boiling water
8 tbsp butter, softened, or soft margarine
½ cup light brown sugar
2 eggs
heaping ¾ cup self-rising flour
½ tsp baking powder
2 tbsp sour cream

ICING
2 cups confectioners' sugar
4 tsp warm water
1 tsp instant coffee granules
2 tsp boiling water

Preheat the oven to 375°F/190°C. Line two 12-hole muffin pans with 16 paper liners. Place the coffee granules in a cup or small bowl, add the boiling water, and stir until dissolved. Let cool slightly. Place the butter, sugar, and eggs in a large bowl. Sift in the flour and baking powder and beat until smooth. Add the dissolved coffee and sour cream and beat until mixed. Spoon the batter into the paper liners.

Bake in the preheated oven for 20 minutes, or until well risen and golden. Cool on a wire rack.

To make the frosting, sift ¾ cup of the confectioners' sugar into a bowl and add enough warm water to mix until thick enough to coat the back of a wooden spoon. Dissolve the coffee in the boiling water. Sift the remaining confectioners' sugar into a bowl and stir in the dissolved coffee. Frost the cakes with the white frosting, then pipe the coffee frosting in parallel lines on top. Draw a skewer across the piped lines in both directions. Let set.

38 Feathered-iced mocha cupcakes

Replace the sour cream with 2 oz/55 g melted semisweet chocolate.

39 Feathered-iced chocolate cupcakes

Replace the coffee granules for the cake batter with unsweetened cocoa. To complete the cakes, melt 6 oz/175 g milk chocolate and 1 oz/25 g white chocolate in separate bowls and spoon the white chocolate into a pastry bag fitted with a piping tip. Spread the milk chocolate over the top of the cakes, then quickly pipe the white chocolate in lines across the cakes. Drag a skewer across the piped lines in both directions to feather the chocolate.

40 Coconut cherry cupcakes

Makes 12

8 tbsp butter, softened, or soft margarine
½ cup superfine sugar
2 tbsp milk
2 eggs, lightly beaten
⅔ cup self-rising flour
½ tsp baking powder
¾ cup dry unsweetened coconut
4 oz/115 g candied cherries, quartered

TOPPING
1 quantity buttercream (page 10)
12 whole candied, maraschino, or fresh cherries, for decorating

Preheat the oven to 350°F/180°C. Line a 12-hole muffin pan with 12 paper liners.

Place the butter and sugar in a large bowl and beat together until light and fluffy. Stir in the milk and then gradually beat in the eggs. Sift in the flour and baking powder and fold them in with the coconut. Gently fold in most of the quartered cherries.

Spoon the batter into the paper liners and scatter the remaining quartered cherries evenly on top.

Bake in the preheated oven for 20–25 minutes, or until well risen, golden brown, and firm to the touch. Transfer to a wire rack to cool completely.

When the cupcakes are cold, place the buttercream in a pastry bag fitted with a large star tip. Pipe the buttercream on top of each cupcake, then add a cherry to decorate.

41 Iced coconut cherry cupcakes

When cooled, cover the cupcakes with basic icing (page 10). Cut 12 candied cherries in half and arrange two halves on each cake. Melt 2 oz/55 g semisweet chocolate and spoon it into a pastry bag fitted with a plain piping tip, then pipe cherry stems on the icing to join the cherries in a bunch.

42 Almond cherry cupcakes

Replace the coconut with ground almonds.

43 Carrot & orange cupcakes

Makes 12

8 tbsp butter, softened, or soft margarine
heaping ½ cup light brown sugar
juice and finely grated rind of 1 small orange
2 large eggs, lightly beaten
heaping 1 cup grated carrot
¼ cup walnut pieces, coarsely chopped
1 cup all-purpose flour
1 tsp ground pumpkin pie spice
1½ tsp baking powder

FROSTING
1¼ cups mascarpone cheese
4 tbsp confectioners' sugar
grated rind of 1 large orange

Preheat the oven to 350°F/180°C. Line a 12-hole muffin pan with 12 paper liners.

Place the butter, sugar, and orange rind in a bowl and beat together until light and fluffy, then gradually beat in the eggs. Squeeze any excess liquid from the carrots and add to the mixture with the walnuts and orange juice. Stir until well mixed. Sift in the flour, pumpkin pie spice, and baking powder and fold in. Spoon the batter into the paper liners.

Bake in the preheated oven for 25 minutes, or until risen, firm to the touch, and golden brown. Transfer to a wire rack to cool completely.

To make the frosting, place the mascarpone cheese, confectioners' sugar, and orange rind in a large bowl and beat together until they are well mixed.

When the cupcakes are cold, spread the frosting on top of each cupcake, swirling it with a round-bladed knife.

44 Carrot & lemon cupcakes

Replace the orange rind and juice in the cakes with lemon rind and juice. Instead of the frosting, sift 1½ cups confectioners' sugar into a large bowl and beat in enough lemon juice to make a smooth icing. Spread on top of the cakes and leave plain or decorate with lemon candy slices.

45 Chocolate carrot cupcakes

Add 3 oz/85 g semisweet chocolate chips along with the carrot. Beat 2 oz/55 g melted semisweet chocolate into the mascarpone frosting before spreading on the cupcakes.

46 Chocolate cupcakes with cream cheese frosting

Makes 18

6 tbsp butter, softened, or soft margarine
½ cup superfine sugar
2 eggs, lightly beaten
2 tbsp milk
⅓ cup semisweet chocolate chips
1⅔ cups self-rising flour
¼ cup unsweetened cocoa

TOPPING
8 oz/225 g white chocolate, broken into pieces
⅔ cup low-fat cream cheese
chocolate curls, for decorating

Preheat the oven to 400°F/200°C. Line two 12-hole muffin pans with 18 paper liners.

Place the butter and sugar in a large bowl and beat together until light and fluffy, then gradually beat in the eggs. Add the milk, then fold in the chocolate chips. Sift in the flour and cocoa, then fold into the batter. Spoon the batter into the paper liners and smooth the tops.

Bake in the preheated oven for 20 minutes, or until well risen and springy to the touch. Transfer to a wire rack to cool completely.

To make the frosting, place the chocolate in a small heatproof bowl, set the bowl over a saucepan of gently simmering water, and heat until melted. Let cool slightly. Place the cream cheese in a separate bowl and beat until softened, then beat in the slightly cooled chocolate.

When the cupcakes are cold, spread a little of the frosting over the top of each cupcake, then let chill in the refrigerator for 1 hour before serving. Decorate with a few chocolate curls, if liked.

47 White chocolate cupcakes

Replace the semisweet chocolate chips with ½ cup white chocolate chips. Omit the cocoa and increase the flour to 1¾ cups. Decorate with white chocolate curls made with a vegetable peeler.

48 With chocolate mascarpone frosting

For the frosting, replace the cream cheese with mascarpone and decorate with milk chocolate curls.

49 Lemon butterfly cakes

Makes 12

heaping ¾ cup self-rising flour
½ tsp baking powder
8 tbsp butter, softened
heaping ½ cup superfine sugar
2 eggs
finely grated rind of ½ lemon
2 tbsp milk
confectioners' sugar, for dusting

LEMON BUTTERCREAM
6 tbsp butter, softened
1½ cups confectioners' sugar
1 tbsp lemon juice

Preheat the oven to 375°F/190°C. Line a 12-hole muffin pan with 12 paper liners.

Sift the flour and baking powder into a large bowl, add the butter, sugar, eggs, lemon rind, and milk, and beat together until smooth. Spoon the batter into the paper liners.

Bake in the preheated oven for 15–20 minutes, or until well risen and golden brown. Transfer to a wire rack to cool completely.

To make the frosting, place the butter in a bowl and beat until fluffy. Sift in the confectioners' sugar, add the lemon juice, and beat together until smooth and creamy. When the cupcakes are cold, cut the top off each cake then cut the top in half.

Spread or pipe a little of the lemon frosting over the cut surface of each cupcake, then gently press the 2 cut cake pieces into it at an angle to resemble butterfly wings. Dust with sifted confectioners' sugar before serving.

50 Orange butterfly cakes

Replace the lemon rind and juice with orange rind and juice.

51 Vanilla butterfly cakes

Omit the lemon rind from the cake batter and replace the lemon juice in the frosting with 1 teaspoon of vanilla extract. Decorate with sugar sprinkles, if liked.

52 Banana & pecan cupcakes

MAKES 24

1⅔ cups all-purpose flour
1¼ tsp baking powder
¼ tsp baking soda
2 ripe bananas
8 tbsp butter, softened, or soft margarine
heaping ½ cup superfine sugar
½ tsp vanilla extract
2 eggs, lightly beaten
4 tbsp sour cream
heaping ⅓ cup pecans, coarsely chopped

TOPPING
8 tbsp butter, softened
1 cup confectioners' sugar
1 tbsp pecans, finely chopped

Preheat the oven to 375°F/190°C. Line two 12-hole muffin pans with 24 paper liners. Sift together the flour, baking powder, and baking soda. Place the bananas in a separate bowl and mash with a fork.

Place the butter, sugar, and vanilla extract in a large bowl and beat together until light and fluffy, then gradually beat in the eggs. Stir in the mashed bananas and sour cream. Fold in the flour mixture and chopped nuts. Spoon the batter into the paper liners.

Bake in the preheated oven for 20 minutes, or until well risen and golden brown. Transfer to a wire rack to cool completely.

To make the topping, place the butter in a bowl and beat until fluffy. Sift in the confectioners' sugar and mix together well. Spread the frosting on top of each cupcake and sprinkle with the pecans before serving.

53 Banana & date cupcakes

Omit the pecans from the cakes and the topping and add 2 oz/55 g chopped dates, folding in with the flour.

54 Banana & chocolate cupcakes

Replace the pecans with 3 oz/85 g semisweet or milk chocolate chips. Decorate the tops of the cakes with chocolate curls or chocolate sugar strands.

55 Banana & butterscotch cupcakes

Replace the pecans with 3 oz/85 g butterscotch-flavored chips. Decorate the tops with a few more butterscotch chips, if liked.

56 Cranberry cupcakes

Makes 14

$5\frac{1}{2}$ tbsp butter, softened, or soft margarine
$\frac{1}{2}$ cup superfine sugar
1 large egg, lightly beaten
2 tbsp milk
$\frac{3}{4}$ cup self-rising flour
1 tsp baking powder
heaping $\frac{3}{4}$ cup cranberries, frozen

Preheat the oven to 350°F/180°C. Line two 12-hole muffin pans with 14 paper liners.

Place the butter and sugar in a large bowl and beat together until light and fluffy, then gradually beat in the egg and stir in the milk. Sift in the flour and baking powder and fold into the mixture. Gently fold in the frozen cranberries. Spoon the batter into the paper liners.

Bake in the preheated oven for 15–20 minutes, or until well risen and golden brown. Transfer to a wire rack to cool completely.

57 Frozen blueberry cupcakes

Replace the frozen cranberries with frozen blueberries.

58 Cherry cupcakes

Replace the frozen cranberries with canned black cherries. Drain well and halve each cherry before adding to the batter.

59 Apple streusel cupcakes

Makes 14

½ tsp baking soda
10 oz/280 g jar applesauce
4 tbsp butter, softened, or soft margarine
½ cup raw brown sugar
1 large egg, lightly beaten
1¼ cups self-rising flour
½ tsp ground cinnamon
½ tsp freshly ground nutmeg

TOPPING
⅓ cup all-purpose flour
¼ cup raw brown sugar
¼ tsp ground cinnamon
¼ tsp freshly grated nutmeg
3 heaping tbsp butter, cut into small pieces

Preheat the oven to 350°F/180°C. Line two 12-hole muffin pans with 14 paper liners.

First, make the topping. Place the flour, sugar, cinnamon, and nutmeg in a large bowl. Add the butter and rub it in with your fingertips until the mixture resembles fine breadcrumbs. Set aside until required.

To make the cupcakes, add the baking soda to the jar of applesauce and stir until dissolved. Place the butter and sugar in a large bowl and beat together until light and fluffy, then gradually beat in the egg. Sift in the flour, cinnamon, and nutmeg and fold into the batter, alternating with the apple sauce.Spoon the batter into the paper liners. Scatter the reserved topping over each cupcake to cover the tops and press down gently. Bake in the preheated oven for 20 minutes, or until well risen and golden brown. Leave the cakes for 2–3 minutes in the pans before serving warm, or transfer to a wire rack to cool completely.

60 Apricot streusel cupcakes

Drain 10 oz/280 g canned apricots, reserving the juice. Chop the apricots and mix a little of the juice with 1 teaspoon of cornstarch. Place the apricots in a saucepan with the juice and bring to a boil. Add the cornstarch mixture, and cook over low heat, stirring, until thickened. Let cool, then complete as before, replacing the applesauce with the apricot mixture.

61 Cranberry streusel cupcakes

Replace the applesauce with cranberry sauce.

62 Cherry streusel cupcakes

Replace the applesauce with 7 oz/200 g canned cherry pie filling.

63 *Warm molten-centered chocolate cupcakes*

MAKES 8

4 tbsp butter, softened,
or soft margarine
¼ cup superfine sugar
1 large egg
⅔ cup self-rising flour
1 tbsp unsweetened cocoa
2 oz/55 g semisweet chocolate
confectioners' sugar, for dusting

Preheat the oven to 375°F/190°C. Line a 12-hole muffin pan with 8 paper liners.

Place the butter, sugar, egg, flour, and cocoa in a large bowl and beat together until just smooth. Spoon half of the batter into the paper liners. Using a teaspoon, make an indentation in the center of each cake. Break the chocolate into 8 even squares and place a piece in each indentation, then spoon the remaining cake batter on top.

Bake in the preheated oven for 20 minutes, or until well risen and springy to the touch. Leave the cupcakes in the pan for 2–3 minutes before serving warm, dusted with sifted confectioners' sugar.

64 *White chocolate-centered cupcakes*

Replace the semisweet chocolate with squares of white chocolate.

65 *Vanilla & chocolate cupcakes*

Increase the flour to ¾ cup and omit the cocoa. Add ½ teaspoon of vanilla extract to the butter and sugar, and use milk chocolate instead of the semisweet chocolate.

66 *Chocolate cherry cupcakes*

MAKES 12

1¾ oz/50 g semisweet chocolate,
broken into pieces
4½ tbsp butter
⅓ cup cherry jam
⅓ cup superfine sugar
2 large eggs
¾ cup self-rising flour

TOPPING
4 tsp Kirsch liqueur
⅔ cup heavy cream
12 fresh, candied, or
maraschino cherries
chocolate curls, for decorating

Preheat the oven to 350°F/180°C. Line a 12-hole muffin pan with 12 paper liners. Place the chocolate and butter in a saucepan and heat gently, stirring continuously, until melted. Pour into a large bowl, then stir until smooth and let cool slightly. Add the jam, sugar, and eggs to the cooled chocolate and beat together. Add the flour and stir together until combined. Spoon the batter into the paper liners.

Bake in the preheated oven for 20 minutes, or until firm to the touch. Let cool in the pan for 10 minutes, then transfer to a wire rack to cool completely.

When the cupcakes are cold, sprinkle the Kirsch over the tops of each and let soak for at least 15 minutes.

When ready to decorate, place the cream in a bowl and whip until soft peaks form. Spread the cream on top of the cupcakes with a knife to form the cream into peaks. Top each cupcake with a cherry and decorate with chocolate curls.

67 *Chocolate strawberry cupcakes*

Replace the cherry jam with strawberry jam and sprinkle the cold cupcakes with brandy instead of Kirsch. Decorate each cupcake with a small whole strawberry.

68 *Warm strawberry cupcakes baked in a teacup*

MAKES 6

8 tbsp butter, softened, plus extra for greasing
4 tbsp strawberry preserve
heaping ½ cup superfine sugar
2 eggs, lightly beaten
1 tsp vanilla extract
heaping ¾ cup self-rising flour
6 whole strawberries, for decorating
confectioners' sugar, for dusting

Preheat the oven to 350°F/180°C. Grease six ¾-cup capacity heavy round teacups with butter. Spoon 2 teaspoons of the strawberry preserve into the bottom of each teacup.

Place the butter and sugar in a large bowl and beat together until light and fluffy. Gradually add the eggs, beating well after each addition, then add the vanilla extract. Sift in the flour and fold into the batter. Spoon the batter into the teacups.

Stand the cups in a roasting pan, then pour in enough hot water to come one third up the sides of the cups. Bake in the preheated oven for 40 minutes, or until well risen and golden brown, and a skewer, inserted in the center, comes out clean. If overbrowning, cover the cupcakes with a sheet of foil. Let the cupcakes cool for 2–3 minutes, then carefully lift the cups from the pan and place them on saucers.

Top each cupcake with a strawberry, then dust them with sifted confectioners' sugar. Serve warm with the remaining strawberries on the side.

69 *Warm raspberry cupcakes*

Replace the strawberry preserve with raspberry preserve and decorate with fresh raspberries.

70 *Warm peach cupcakes*

Replace the strawberry preserve with a few well-drained, canned peach slices and decorate with extra peach slices.

71 *Tropical pineapple cupcakes*

MAKES 12

2 slices canned pineapple in natural juice
6 tbsp butter, softened, or soft margarine
½ cup superfine sugar
1 large egg, lightly beaten
⅔ cup self-rising flour

FROSTING
2 tbsp butter, softened
½ cup soft cream cheese
grated rind of 1 lemon or lime
heaping ¾ cup confectioners' sugar
1 tsp lemon juice or lime juice

Preheat the oven to 350°F/180°C. Line a 12-hole muffin pan with 12 paper liners. Drain the pineapple, reserving the juice.

Finely chop the pineapple slices. Place the butter and sugar in a large bowl and beat together until light and fluffy, then gradually beat in the egg. Add the flour and fold into the mixture. Fold in the chopped pineapple and 1 tablespoon of the reserved pineapple juice. Spoon the batter into the paper liners. Bake in the preheated oven for 20 minutes, or until well risen and golden brown. Transfer to a wire rack to cool completely.

To make the frosting, place the butter and cream cheese in a large bowl and beat together until smooth, then add the lemon or lime rind.

Sift the confectioners' sugar into the mixture and beat together until well mixed. Gradually beat in the lemon or lime juice, adding enough to form a spreading consistency.

When the cupcakes are cold, spread the frosting on top of each cake, or fill a pastry bag fitted with a large star tip and pipe the frosting on top.

72 *Pina colada cupcakes*

Add ¼ cup dry unsweetened coconut and an extra ½ tablespoon of pineapple juice to the cake batter. For the frosting, beat 2 tablespoons of dry unsweetened coconut into the frosting and replace the lemon or lime juice with rum.

73 Shredded orange cupcakes

MAKES 12

6 tbsp butter, softened, or soft margarine
½ cup superfine sugar
1 large egg, lightly beaten
⅔ cup self-rising flour
heaping ¼ cup ground almonds
grated rind and juice of 1 small orange

TOPPING
1 orange
¼ cup superfine sugar
1 tbsp toasted slivered almonds

Preheat the oven to 350°F/180°C. Line a 12-hole muffin pan with 12 paper liners. Place the butter and sugar in a large bowl and beat together until light and fluffy, then gradually beat in the egg. Add the flour, ground almonds, and orange rind and fold into the mixture, then fold in the orange juice. Spoon the batter into the paper liners.

Bake in the preheated oven for 20–25 minutes, or until well risen and golden brown.

Meanwhile, make the topping. Using a citrus zester, pare the rind from the orange, then squeeze the juice. Place the rind, juice, and sugar in a saucepan and heat gently, stirring, until the sugar has dissolved, then let simmer for 5 minutes.

When the cupcakes are cooked, prick them all over with a skewer and spoon the warm syrup and rind over each cake.

Scatter the slivered almonds on top and transfer to a wire rack to cool completely.

74 Shredded lemon cupcakes

Replace the orange rind and juice with lemon rind and juice.

75 Lime & coconut cupcakes

Replace the orange rind and juice in the cake with the rind and juice of 1½ limes. Add ¼ cup dry unsweetened coconut to the batter. For the topping, use the pared rind of 1 lime and the juice of 2 limes in place of the orange. Replace the almonds with toasted dry unsweetened coconut.

76 Mocha cupcakes with whipped cream

MAKES 20

2 tbsp instant espresso coffee powder
6 tbsp butter
½ cup superfine sugar
1 tbsp honey
generous ¾ cup water
1⅔ cups all-purpose flour
2 tbsp unsweetened cocoa
1 tsp baking soda
3 tbsp milk
1 large egg, lightly beaten

TOPPING
1 cup whipping cream
unsweetened cocoa, for dusting

Preheat the oven to 350°F/180°C. Line two 12-hole muffin pans with 20 paper liners. Place the coffee powder, butter, sugar, honey, and water in a saucepan and heat gently, stirring, until the sugar has dissolved. Bring to a boil, then reduce the heat and let simmer for 5 minutes. Pour into a large heatproof bowl and let cool. When the mixture has cooled, sift in the flour and cocoa. Place the baking soda and milk in a bowl and stir to dissolve, then add to the mixture with the egg and beat together until smooth. Spoon the batter into the paper liners.

Bake in the preheated oven for 15–20 minutes, or until well risen and firm to the touch. Transfer to a wire rack to cool completely.

For the topping, place the cream in a bowl and whip until it holds its shape. Spoon heaping teaspoonfuls of cream on top of each cake, then dust lightly with sifted cocoa.

77 Mocha walnut cupcakes

Add ¼ cup chopped walnuts to the batter. For the topping, dissolve 2 teaspoons of coffee powder in 1 tablespoon of boiling water and let cool. Lightly whip the cream until it begins to hold its shape, then add the coffee and 2 tablespoons of confectioners' sugar and whip until soft peaks form. Spread on the cakes and decorate with walnut halves.

78 Peaches 'n' cream cupcakes

MAKES 12

14 oz/400 g canned peach slices in fruit juice
8 tbsp butter, softened
heaping ½ cup superfine sugar
2 eggs, lightly beaten
heaping ¾ cup self-rising flour
⅔ cup heavy cream

Preheat the oven to 350°F/180°C. Line a 12-hole muffin pan with 12 paper liners. Drain the peaches, reserving the juice. Set aside 12 small slices and finely chop the remaining slices.

Place the butter and sugar in a large bowl and beat together until light and fluffy. Gradually beat in the eggs. Sift in the flour and fold into the mixture. Fold in the chopped peaches and 1 tablespoon of the reserved juice. Spoon the batter into the paper liners.

Bake in the oven for 25 minutes, or until golden brown. Let the cupcakes cool in the pan for 10 minutes, then transfer to a wire rack to cool completely.

When ready to decorate, place the cream in a bowl and whip until soft peaks form. Spread the cream on top of the cupcakes, using a knife to form the cream into peaks. Place the reserved peach slices on top to decorate.

79 Apricot cream cupcakes

Use 8 apricot halves in fruit juice instead of the peach slices. Slice 4 halves into 3 slices each and set aside for decoration. Finely chop the 4 remaining apricot halves and add to the batter with 1 tablespoon of juice from the can.

80 Dried apricot cupcakes

Replace the can of peach slices with ½ cup finely chopped plumped dried apricots and add 1 tablespoon of orange juice to replace the fruit juice from the can. To decorate, dust lightly with sifted confectioners' sugar.

81 24-carrot gold cupcakes

MAKES 12

¾ cup butter, softened, or soft margarine
heaping ½ cup superfine sugar
2 eggs, lightly beaten
heaping 1½ cup grated carrot
½ cup walnuts, finely chopped
2 tbsp orange juice
grated rind of ½ orange
1¼ cups self-rising flour
1 tsp ground cinnamon
12 walnut halves, for decorating

FROSTING
½ cup cream cheese
2 cups confectioners' sugar
1 tbsp orange juice

Preheat the oven to 350°F/180°C. Line a 12-hole muffin pan with 12 paper liners. Place the butter and sugar in a large bowl and beat together until light and fluffy, then gradually beat in the eggs. Fold in the grated carrot, walnuts, and orange juice and rind. Sift in the flour and cinnamon and fold into the batter until just combined. Spoon the batter into the paper liners.

Bake in the preheated oven for 15–20 minutes, or until golden and springy to the touch. Transfer to a wire rack to cool completely.

To make the frosting, place the cream cheese, confectioners' sugar, and orange juice in a bowl and beat together. Spread over the top of the cakes, then decorate with walnut halves.

82 9-carrot gold cupcakes

Use ¾ cup grated carrot and ½ cup grated zucchini, and replace the walnuts with ⅓ cup golden raisins. Decorate the top of each cake with a pecan.

83 Pure indulgence almond cupcakes

MAKES 12

7 tbsp butter, softened
½ cup superfine sugar
2 eggs, lightly beaten
¼ tsp almond extract
4 tbsp light cream
1¼ cups all-purpose flour
1½ tsp baking powder
¾ cup ground almonds

TOPPING
8 tbsp butter, softened
2 cups confectioners' sugar
few drops of almond extract
¼ cup toasted slivered almonds

Preheat the oven to 350°F/180°C. Line a 12-hole muffin pan with 12 paper liners. Place the butter and sugar in a large bowl and beat together until light and fluffy. Gradually beat in the eggs, then add the almond extract and cream. Sift in the flour and baking powder and fold into the batter, then fold in the ground almonds. Spoon the batter into the paper liners.

Bake in the preheated oven for 25 minutes, or until golden brown and firm to the touch. Let the cupcakes cool in the pan for 10 minutes, then transfer to a wire rack to cool completely.

To make the frosting, place the butter in a large bowl and beat until creamy. Sift in the confectioners' sugar. Add the almond extract and beat until smooth. Spread the frosting on top of each cake, using a knife to form the frosting into swirls. Sprinkle the almonds over the top.

84 Ice-cream cone cupcakes

MAKES 8

¾ cup butter, softened, or soft margarine
1 cup superfine sugar
1 tsp vanilla extract
3 eggs, lightly beaten
⅔ cup ground almonds
heaping 1 cup self-rising flour

TOPPING
1 quantity buttercream (page 10)
8 mini chocolate bars
sugar sprinkles
seedless raspberry jam (optional)

Preheat the oven to 350°F/180°C. Line a 12-hole muffin pan with 8 paper liners. Place the butter and sugar in a large bowl and beat together until light and fluffy, then beat in the vanilla extract. Gradually beat in the eggs, then fold in the almonds and flour. Spoon the batter into the paper liners, peaking the batter slightly in the middle.

Bake in the preheated oven for 20–25 minutes, or until golden and springy to the touch. Transfer to a wire rack to cool completely.

Spoon the buttercream into a pastry bag fitted with a large star tip and pipe the frosting over the cakes to peak like an ice-cream cone. Press a chocolate bar into each cake and scatter a few sprinkles on top. Warm the raspberry jam and drizzle a little over each cake, if liked.

85 Chocolate ice-cream cone cupcakes

Replace 2 tablespoons of flour with cocoa. Decorate with chocolate buttercream (page 10), chocolate sugar strands, and a drizzle of chocolate sauce.

86 Buttermilk & orange cupcakes

MAKES 12

¾ cup dark brown sugar
heaping 1 cup butter, softened
2 eggs, lightly beaten
scant 1½ cups all-purpose flour
¾ tsp baking powder
½ tsp baking soda
½ cup buttermilk

FROSTING
2 cups confectioners' sugar
finely grated rind of 2 oranges, plus 1 tbsp juice

Preheat the oven to 350°F/180°C. Line a 12-hole muffin pan with 12 paper liners. Place the brown sugar and heaping ½ cup of the butter in a large bowl and beat together until light and fluffy, then gradually beat in the eggs. Sift in the flour, baking powder, and baking soda and fold into the batter, then fold in the buttermilk and grated orange rind of 1 orange. Spoon the batter into the paper liners.

Bake in the preheated oven for 30 minutes, or until firm to the touch. Let the cupcakes cool in the pan for 10 minutes, then transfer to a wire rack to cool completely.

To make the frosting, place the remaining butter in a large bowl and beat until fluffy. Sift in the confectioners' sugar. Add the remaining orange rind and the juice and beat together until smooth.

When the cupcakes are cold, spread the frosting on top, using a knife to form the frosting into swirls.

87 Chocolate chip cupcakes

MAKES 12

7 tbsp butter, softened
½ cup superfine sugar
2 large eggs
¾ cup self-rising flour
heaping ½ cup semisweet chocolate chips

Preheat the oven to 375°F/190°C. Line a 12-hole muffin pan with 12 paper liners. Place the butter, sugar, eggs, and flour in a large bowl and beat together until just smooth. Fold in the chocolate chips. Spoon the batter into the paper liners.

Bake in the preheated oven for 15–20 minutes, or until well risen and golden brown. Transfer to a wire rack to cool completely.

88 Triple chocolate cupcakes

Reduce the flour to ⅔ cup and add 2 tablespoons of cocoa. Use a mixture of milk, white, and semisweet chocolate chips.

89 Butterscotch & peanut cupcakes

Replace the chocolate chips with butterscotch-flavored chips and add ¼ cup chopped peanuts to the batter.

90 With fudge frosting

To make the frosting, place 3 tablespoons of butter and 2 tablespoons of milk in a saucepan and heat, stirring, until the butter melts. Add 1⅔ cups confectioners' sugar and 1½ tablespoons of cocoa and beat until smooth. Let cool slightly, then use to cover the cupcakes.

91 Fresh raspberry cupcakes

MAKES 12

2¼ cups fresh raspberries
⅔ cup sunflower oil
2 eggs
¾ cup superfine sugar
½ tsp vanilla extract
2 cups all-purpose flour
¾ tsp baking soda

TOPPING
⅔ cup heavy cream
12 fresh raspberries
small mint leaves, for decorating

Preheat the oven to 350°F/180°C. Line a 12-hole muffin pan with 12 paper liners. Place the raspberries in a large bowl and crush lightly with a fork.

Place the oil, eggs, sugar, and vanilla extract in a large bowl and whisk together until well combined. Sift in the flour and baking soda and fold into the batter, then fold in the crushed raspberries. Spoon the batter into the paper liners.

Bake in the preheated oven for 30 minutes, or until golden brown and firm to the touch. Let the cupcakes cool in the pan for 10 minutes, then transfer to a wire rack to cool completely.

When ready to decorate, place the cream in a bowl and whip until soft peaks form. Spread the cream on top of the cupcakes, using a knife to smooth the cream. Top each cupcake with a raspberry and decorate with mint leaves.

92 Fresh strawberry cupcakes

Replace the raspberries with the same quantity of strawberries and add the grated rind of 1 small orange to the batter. If preferred, place the whipped cream into a pastry bag fitted with a large star tip, and pipe the cream on top of the cupcakes to decorate.

93 Blueberry cupcakes

MAKES 12

9 tbsp butter, softened
¾ cup superfine sugar
2 eggs, lightly beaten
1 cup all-purpose flour
½ tsp baking powder
¾ cup plumped dried blueberries
2 tbsp milk
confectioners' sugar, for dusting

Preheat the oven to 350°F/180°C. Line a 12-hole muffin pan with 12 paper liners. Place the butter and sugar in a large bowl and beat together until light and fluffy, then gradually beat in the eggs. Sift in the flour and baking powder and fold into the batter, then fold in the blueberries and milk. Spoon the batter into the paper liners.

Bake in the preheated oven for 25 minutes, or until golden brown and firm to the touch. Let the cupcakes cool in the pan for 10 minutes, then transfer to a wire rack to cool completely.

When the cupcakes are cold, dust with sifted confectioners' sugar.

94 Springtime cupcakes

MAKES 24

⅔ cup butter, softened, or soft margarine
¾ cup superfine sugar
1 tsp vanilla extract
2 large eggs, lightly beaten
1 cup self-rising flour
heaping ¼ cup cornstarch

FOR DECORATING
4 oz/115 g ready-to-roll fondant
yellow and green food colorings
2⅔ cups confectioners' sugar
about 3 tbsp cold water
colored sprinkles

Preheat the oven to 375°F/190°C. Line two 12-hole muffin pans with 24 paper liners. Place the butter and sugar in a large bowl and beat together until light and fluffy, then beat in the vanilla extract. Gradually beat in the eggs. Sift in the flour and cornstarch and fold into the batter. Spoon the batter into the paper liners.

Bake in the preheated oven for 12–15 minutes, or until golden and springy to the touch. Transfer to a wire rack to cool completely.

To decorate, divide the fondant in half and color one half pale yellow. Roll out both halves, then use the sides of a round cookie cutter to cut out white and yellow petal shapes. Set aside.

Sift the confectioners' sugar into a bowl and mix with the water until smooth. Place half of the icing in a small pastry bag fitted with a small plain tip. Divide the remaining icing in half and color one portion yellow and the other green.

Cover 12 cakes with yellow icing and 12 with green icing. Arrange white petals on top of the yellow icing to form flowers. Pipe a little blob of white icing into the center of each flower, then add a few colored sprinkles on top of the white icing to form the center of the flower. Arrange the yellow petals on the green icing and decorate in the same way. Let set.

95 Flower & bug cupcakes

MAKES 12

1¼ cups self-rising flour
1 tsp baking powder
1 cup superfine sugar
¾ cup very soft butter, cut into small pieces
3 eggs
1 tsp vanilla extract
2 tbsp milk

FOR DECORATING
1¾ cups confectioners' sugar
1 tbsp lemon juice
1–2 tbsp water
few drops of blue and green food coloring
white chocolate disks
white chocolate rainbow disks
jelly worm candies

Preheat the oven to 350°F/180°C. Line a 12-hole muffin pan with 12 paper liners. Sift the flour, baking powder, and sugar into a bowl. Add the butter, eggs, vanilla extract, and milk and beat together until creamy. Spoon the batter into the paper liners. Bake in the preheated oven for 15–20 minutes, or until risen and golden. Transfer to a wire rack to cool.

Place the confectioners' sugar, lemon juice, and water in a bowl and mix together until smooth. Color half of the icing blue and half of the icing green. Spread the icing over the cakes. For flower cakes, place a white chocolate disk in the center and the rainbow ones around it. For bug cakes, pipe a leaf with green icing on each cake and top with a gummy worm or bug.

96 Zoo animal cupcakes

MAKES 9

¾ cup butter, softened, or soft margarine
1 cup superfine sugar
1 tsp vanilla extract
3 eggs, lightly beaten
⅔ cup dry unsweetened coconut
heaping 1 cup self-rising flour

FOR DECORATING
1½ tsp unsweetened cocoa
½ cup confectioners' sugar
about 10½ oz/300 g ready-to-roll fondant
food coloring, such as pink, yellow, brown, and black

Preheat the oven to 350°F/180°C. Line a 12-hole muffin pan with 9 paper liners. Place the butter and sugar in a large bowl and beat together until light and fluffy, then beat in the vanilla extract. Gradually beat in the eggs, then fold in the coconut and flour. Spoon the batter into the paper liners. Bake in the preheated oven for 20–25 minutes, or until golden and springy to the touch. Transfer to a wire rack to cool completely.

To decorate, sift the cocoa and confectioners' sugar into a small bowl and add enough cold water to form a smooth, thick icing. Spoon into a small pastry bag fitted with a writing tip. Leave a small piece of fondant white and color a small piece pink. Divide the remainder into 2 large pieces and one smaller piece. Color one large piece gray, using a small amount of black food coloring, and the other yellow, and the small piece brown.

To make the elephants, roll out the gray frosting and cut out 3 circles to fit the tops of the cake. To make the ears, cut out 6 circles and cut away one third of each circle. Roll out the pink frosting and cut out 6 smaller circles, then cut away one third of each circle. Place on top of the gray circles, pinch in the center and sides, and fix to the cakes with a little water. Roll a little gray frosting into a sausage shape to make the trunks and secure on the cakes with a little water. With a little white frosting, make the eyes and tusks and secure to the cake. Pipe the eyes and eyebrows with the cocoa frosting.

To make the monkeys, roll and cut out 3 circles of brown frosting to fit the tops of the cake. Cut out the ears from brown frosting and make the centers of the ears with pink frosting. Secure to the cake by dampening with water. Cut out a circle of yellow frosting and cut out a small nick at the top, shape into the monkey's face, and secure to the cake. Make the eyes with a little white frosting and pipe on the remaining features.

To make the lions, cut out 3 circles of yellow frosting to fit the tops of the cake. Make the ears with brown and pink frosting and secure to the cakes. Make the nose with brown frosting and pipe on the features and the curly mane.

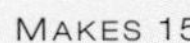

97 Animal lovers' cupcakes

MAKES 15

⅓ cup golden raisins
grated rind and juice of ½ orange
8 tbsp butter, softened, or soft margarine
heaping ½ cup superfine sugar
½ tsp vanilla extract
2 eggs, lightly beaten
1¼ cups self-rising flour
¼ quantity buttercream (page 10)

FOR DECORATING
2¼ cups confectioners' sugar, sifted
2–3 tbsp orange juice
sugar animal cake decorations

Preheat the oven to 350°F/180°C. Line two 12-hole muffin pans with 15 paper liners. Place the golden raisins in a saucepan with the orange rind and juice and gently heat until almost boiling. Remove from the heat and let cool.

Place the butter and sugar in a large bowl and beat together until light and fluffy, then beat in the vanilla extract. Gradually beat in the eggs, then fold in the golden raisins and the juice. Sift in the flour and fold into the batter. Spoon the batter into the paper liners.

Bake in the preheated oven for 15–20 minutes, or until golden and springy to the touch. Transfer to a wire rack to cool completely.

To make the basic icing, sift the confectioners' sugar in a bowl and add enough orange juice to mix to a smooth coating consistency. Cover the cakes with the icing and let set.

To decorate, pipe a rosette of buttercream on the cakes and top with a sugar animal decoration.

98 Bling & buy cupcakes

MAKES 10

¾ cup butter, softened, or soft margarine	*FOR DECORATING*
1 cup superfine sugar	*1 quantity buttercream (page 10)*
1 tsp vanilla extract	*pink, black, red, and yellow food coloring*
3 eggs, lightly beaten	*2–3 oz/55–85 g ready-to-roll fondant*
1¼ cups raspberries	*silver dragées*
1⅔ cups self-rising flour	*jelly candies*

Preheat the oven to 350°F/180°C. Line a 12-hole muffin pan with 10 paper liners. Place the butter and sugar in a large bowl and beat together until light and fluffy, then beat in the vanilla extract.

Gradually beat in the eggs, then fold the raspberries and flour into the batter. Spoon the batter into the paper liners.

Bake in the preheated oven for 20–25 minutes, or until golden brown and springy to the touch. Transfer to a wire rack to cool completely.

To decorate, color the buttercream pale pink, then place in a pastry bag fitted with a large star tip and pipe the buttercream on top of the cakes.

Color the fondant and then mold into different shapes, such as handbags, high-heeled shoes, or rings. Arrange the shapes on the cupcakes, then press silver dragées into the frosting to form the handle of the bag and to decorate the shoes. Use jelly candies to make the gems on the rings.

99 Easy bling cupcakes

To save time, you can decorate the cakes with nonedible cake decorations: Look out for shoes, champagne bottles, or plastic rings and jewelry. Remember to remind people to remove them before eating. These would not be suitable to serve to young children.

100 Gooey chocolate & cream cheese cupcakes

MAKES 12

1¼ cups all-purpose flour	*2 tsp white vinegar*
¼ cup unsweetened cocoa	*½ tsp vanilla extract*
¾ tsp baking soda	*⅔ cup soft cream cheese*
1 cup superfine sugar	*1 egg, lightly beaten*
¼ cup sunflower oil	*heaping ½ cup semisweet chocolate chips*
¾ cup water	

Preheat the oven to 350°F/180°C. Line a 12-hole muffin pan with 12 paper liners. Sift together the flour, cocoa, and baking soda into a large bowl. Stir ¾ cup of the sugar into the flour. Add the oil, water, vinegar, and vanilla extract and stir well together until combined.

Place the remaining sugar, cream cheese, and egg in a large bowl and beat together until well mixed. Stir in the chocolate chips.

Spoon the chocolate mixture into the paper liners and top each with a spoonful of the cream cheese mixture.

Bake in the preheated oven for 25 minutes, or until firm to the touch. Let the cupcakes cool in the pan for 10 minutes, then transfer to a wire rack to cool completely.

101 Lemon cheesecake cupcakes

MAKES 12

4½ tbsp butter
4½ oz/125 g graham crackers, crushed
½ cup superfine sugar
1¼ cups soft cream cheese
2 large eggs
finely grated rind of 1 large lemon
2 tsp lemon juice
½ cup sour cream
4 tbsp all-purpose flour
2 small lemons, sliced, for decorating

Preheat the oven to 325°F/160°C. Line a 12-hole muffin pan with 12 paper liners. Place the butter in a saucepan and heat gently until melted. Remove from the heat, then add the crushed graham crackers and 1 tablespoon of the sugar and mix well. Divide the cracker mixture among the paper liners and press down firmly with the back of a teaspoon. Chill in the refrigerator.

Meanwhile, place the remaining sugar, cream cheese, and eggs in a large bowl and beat together until smooth. Add the lemon rind and juice, and the sour cream and beat together until combined. Add the flour and beat well. Spoon the batter into the paper liners.

Bake in the preheated oven for 30 minutes, or until set but not browned. Let the cupcakes cool for 20 minutes, then transfer to a wire rack to cool completely.

When the cupcakes are cold, chill in the refrigerator for at least 3 hours. Decorate each cupcake with a twisted lemon slice.

102 Orange cheesecake cupcakes

Replace the lemon rind and juice with orange rind and juice, and decorate each cupcake with a twisted orange slice.

103 Easter cupcakes

MAKES 12

8 tbsp butter, softened, or soft margarine
heaping ½ cup superfine sugar
2 eggs, lightly beaten
⅔ cup self-rising flour
¼ cup unsweetened cocoa

TOPPING
6 tbsp butter, softened
1 cup confectioners' sugar
1 tbsp milk
2–3 drops vanilla extract
9 oz/260 g mini sugar-coated chocolate eggs

Preheat the oven to 350°F/180°C. Line a 12-hole muffin pan with 12 paper liners.

Place the butter and sugar in a large bowl and beat together until light and fluffy, then gradually beat in the eggs. Sift in the flour and cocoa and fold into the batter. Spoon the batter into the paper liners.

Bake in the preheated oven for 15–20 minutes, or until well risen and firm to the touch. Transfer to a wire rack to cool.

To make the buttercream topping, place the butter in a bowl and beat until fluffy. Sift in the confectioners' sugar and beat together until well mixed, adding the milk and vanilla extract.

When the cupcakes are cold, place the frosting in a pastry bag, fitted with a large star tip and pipe a circle around the edge of each cupcake to form a nest. Place chocolate eggs in the center of each nest to decorate.

104 Chocolate curl Easter cupcakes

Lightly sprinkle chocolate curls over the top and gently press into the buttercream topping around the edge of the cakes.

105 Really chocolatey Easter cupcakes

Add ½ cup chocolate chips to the cake batter. Top the cupcakes with chocolate buttercream (page 10) and press chocolate shavings into the frosting.

106 Christmas cupcakes

MAKES 12

9 tbsp butter, softened
1 cup superfine sugar
4–6 drops almond extract
4 eggs, lightly beaten
1 heaping cup self-rising flour
½ cup ground almonds

TOPPING
1 lb/450 g white ready-to-roll fondant
2 oz/55 g green ready-to-roll colored fondant
1 oz/25 g red ready-to-roll colored fondant
confectioners' sugar, for dusting

Preheat the oven to 350°F/180°C. Line a 12-hole muffin pan with 12 paper liners. Place the butter, sugar, and almond extract in a large bowl and beat together until light and fluffy, then gradually beat in the eggs. Sift in the flour and fold into the batter, then fold in the ground almonds. Spoon the batter into the paper liners.

Bake in the preheated oven for 20 minutes, or until well risen, golden brown, and firm to the touch. Transfer to a wire rack to cool completely.

When the cupcakes are cold, knead the white fondant until pliable, then roll out on a surface lightly dusted with confectioners' sugar. Cut out 12 circles with a 2¾-inch/7-cm plain round cutter, rerolling the fondant as necessary. Place a circle on top of each cupcake.

Roll out the green fondant on a surface lightly dusted with confectioners' sugar. Using the palm of your hand, rub confectioners' sugar into the fondant to prevent it from spotting. Cut out 24 leaves with a holly leaf-shaped cutter, rerolling the fondant as necessary. Brush each leaf with a little cooled boiled water and place 2 leaves on top of each cupcake. Roll the red fondant between the palms of your hands to form 36 berries and place 3 in the center of the leaves on each cake to decorate.

107 Spicy Christmas cupcakes

Add 1 teaspoon of pumpkin pie spice to the cake batter. To decorate, cover the cakes with the white ready-to-roll fondant. Use green fondant to cut out Christmas tree shapes and use yellow fondant to make a star for the top of the trees.

108 Marzipan & fruit cupcakes

Add heaping ⅓ cup mixed dried fruit to the cake batter. To decorate, roll out some marzipan and cut out star shapes. Brush the tops of the cakes with a little warmed apricot jam and arrange marzipan stars on top.

109 Halloween cupcakes

MAKES 12

8 tbsp butter, softened, or soft margarine
heaping ½ cup superfine sugar
2 eggs
heaping ¾ cup self-rising flour

TOPPING
7 oz/200 g orange ready-to-roll colored fondant
confectioners' sugar, for dusting
2 oz/55 g black ready-to-roll colored fondant
tube of black decorating icing
tube of white decorating icing

Preheat the oven to 350°F/180°C. Line a 12-hole muffin pan with 12 paper liners. Place the butter, sugar, eggs, and flour in a large bowl and beat together until smooth. Spoon the batter into the paper liners.

Bake in the preheated oven for 15–20 minutes, or until well risen, golden, and firm to the touch. Transfer to a wire rack to cool.

When the cupcakes are cold, knead the orange fondant until pliable, then roll out on a surface dusted with confectioners' sugar. Rub confectioners' sugar into the fondant to prevent it from spotting. Cut out 12 circles with a 2¼-inch/5.5-cm round cutter, rerolling the fondant as necessary. Place a circle on top of each cake. Roll out the black fondant on a surface dusted with confectioners' sugar. Rub confectioners' sugar into the fondant to prevent it from spotting. Cut out 12 circles with a 1¼-inch/3-cm round cutter and place them in the center of the cakes. Using black decorating icing, pipe 8 legs onto each spider and draw eyes and a mouth with white decorating icing.

110 Pumpkin-decorated cupcakes

Cover the cakes with white fondant. Use orange fondant to cut out and make pumpkin shapes. Pipe on the stems of the pumpkins with green decorating icing and pipe a jagged mouth and eyes on the pumpkin with black decorating icing.

111 Spiderweb cupcakes

Melt 2 oz/55 g semisweet chocolate and spoon into a pastry bag fitted with a writing tip. Cover the cakes with basic icing (page 10). Pipe circles of chocolate onto the cakes and, using a skewer, quickly drag the frosting from the center to the outside of the cakes several times to feather the chocolate into a spiderweb design.

112 Valentine heart cupcakes

MAKES 6

6 tbsp butter, softened, or soft margarine
½ cup superfine sugar
½ tsp vanilla extract
2 eggs, lightly beaten
½ cup all-purpose flour
1 tbsp unsweetened cocoa
1 tsp baking powder

MARZIPAN HEARTS
confectioners' sugar, for dusting
1¼ oz/35 g marzipan
red food coloring (liquid or paste)

TOPPING
4 tbsp butter, softened
1 cup confectioners' sugar
1 oz/25 g semisweet chocolate, melted
6 chocolate flower decorations

To make the hearts, line a baking sheet with parchment paper and lightly dust with confectioners' sugar. Knead the marzipan until pliable, then add a few drops of red coloring and knead until evenly colored. Roll out the marzipan to a thickness of ¼ inch/5 mm on a surface dusted with confectioners' sugar. Cut out 6 hearts with a small heart-shaped cutter and place on the sheet. Leave for 3–4 hours.

To make the cupcakes, preheat the oven to 350°F/180°C. Line a 12-hole muffin pan with 6 paper liners. Place the butter, sugar, and vanilla extract in a large bowl and beat together until light and fluffy, then gradually beat in the eggs. Sift in the flour, cocoa, and baking powder and fold into the batter. Spoon the batter into the paper liners. Bake in the preheated oven for 20–25 minutes, or until well risen and firm to the touch. Transfer to a wire rack to cool completely.

To make the topping, place the butter in a bowl and beat until fluffy. Sift in the confectioners' sugar and beat until smooth. Add the melted chocolate and beat until mixed. Spread the frosting on top of each cake and decorate with a chocolate flower and a heart.

113 Cherry & vanilla heart cupcakes

Increase the vanilla extract to 1 teaspoon and the flour to ⅔ cup. Omit the cocoa and add ¼ cup quartered candied cherries. Decorate with vanilla buttercream instead of chocolate buttercream.

114 Gold & silver anniversary cupcakes

Makes 24

1 cup butter, softened
heaping 1 cup superfine sugar
1 tsp vanilla extract
4 large eggs, lightly beaten
1⅔ cups self-rising flour
5 tbsp milk

TOPPING
¾ cup butter
3 cups confectioners' sugar
silver or gold dragées

Preheat the oven to 350°F/180°C. Line two 12-hole muffin pans with 24 silver or gold foil cake liners. Place the butter, sugar, and vanilla extract in a large bowl and beat together until light and fluffy, then gradually beat in the eggs. Sift in the flour and fold into the mixture with the milk. Spoon the batter into the foil liners.

Bake in the preheated oven for 15–20 minutes, or until well risen and firm to the touch. Transfer to a wire rack to cool completely.

To make the topping, place the butter in a large bowl and beat until fluffy. Sift in the confectioners' sugar and beat together until well mixed. Place the topping in a pastry bag fitted with a medium star-shaped tip.

When the cupcakes are cold, pipe circles of frosting on top of each cake to cover the tops and sprinkle over the silver or gold dragées.

115 Ruby wedding cupcakes

Add 2 oz/55 g quartered candied cherries to the cake batter and decorate as before using red dragées.

116 Rocky mountain cupcakes

Makes 10

heaping ¾ cup butter, softened, or soft margarine
¾ cup superfine sugar
1 tsp vanilla extract
3 eggs, lightly beaten
heaping 1 cup self-rising flour
½ cup unsweetened cocoa

TOPPING
1 quantity chocolate buttercream (page 10)
3 oz/85 g mini marshmallows
½ cup walnuts, coarsely chopped
2 oz/55 g milk chocolate or semisweet chocolate, broken into pieces

Preheat the oven to 350°F/180°C. Line a 12-hole muffin pan with 10 paper liners. Place the butter and sugar in a large bowl and beat together until light and fluffy, then beat in the vanilla extract. Gradually beat in the eggs. Sift the flour and cocoa together and fold into the mixture. Spoon the batter into the paper liners.

Bake in the preheated oven for 20–25 minutes, or until golden and springy to the touch. Transfer to a wire rack to cool completely.

To decorate, pipe the buttercream on top of each cake to form a peak in the center. Mix the marshmallows and walnuts together and divide among the cakes, then press down lightly. Place the chocolate in a heatproof bowl, set the bowl over a pan of gently simmering water, and heat until melted. Drizzle over the tops of the cakes and let set.

117 Baby shower cupcakes with sugared almonds

MAKES 24

1¾ cups butter, softened
2 cups superfine sugar
finely grated rind of 2 lemons
8 eggs, lightly beaten
3 cups self-rising flour

TOPPING
3 cups confectioners' sugar
6–8 tsp hot water
red or blue food coloring (liquid or paste)
24 sugared almonds

Preheat the oven to 350°F/180°C. Line two 12-hole muffin pans with 24 paper liners. Place the butter, sugar, and lemon rind in a large bowl and beat together until light and fluffy, then gradually beat in the eggs. Sift in the flour and fold into the mixture. Spoon the batter into the paper liners.

Bake in the preheated oven for 20–25 minutes, or until well risen, golden brown, and firm to the touch. Transfer to a wire rack to cool.

When the cakes are cold, make the topping. Sift the confectoners' sugar into a bowl, add the hot water, and stir until smooth and thick enough to coat the back of a wooden spoon. Dip a skewer into the red or blue food coloring and stir it into the frosting until it is evenly colored pink or pale blue. Spoon the frosting on top of each cake. Top each with a sugared almond and let set for about 30 minutes.

118 Scented baby shower cupcakes

Omit the lemon rind and add 1 tablespoon of chopped lavender or rosemary to the cake batter after beating in the eggs. Decorate as before or with confetti-type sugar sprinkles.

119 Chocolate brownie cupcakes

MAKES 12

8 oz/225 g semisweet chocolate, broken into pieces
6 tbsp butter
2 large eggs
1 cup dark brown sugar
1 tsp vanilla extract
1 cup all-purpose flour
¾ cup walnuts, chopped into small pieces

Preheat the oven to 350°F/180°C. Line a 12-hole muffin pan with 12 paper liners. Place the chocolate and butter in a saucepan and heat gently, stirring constantly, until melted. Remove from the heat and stir until smooth. Let cool slightly.

Place the eggs and sugar in a large bowl and whisk together, then add the vanilla extract. Stir in the flour until mixed together, then stir the melted chocolate into the mixture until combined. Stir in the chopped walnuts. Spoon the batter into the paper liners.

Bake in the preheated oven for 30 minutes, or until firm to the touch but still slightly moist in the center. Let the cupcakes cool for 10 minutes, then transfer to a wire rack to cool completely.

120 *Naughty but nice cupcakes*

MAKES 9

2½ oz/70 g semisweet chocolate, broken into pieces, plus extra for decorating
heaping ¾ cup butter
¾ cup superfine sugar
2 large eggs, lightly beaten
2 tbsp brandy
1¼ cups self-rising flour

TOPPING
heaping ¾ cup heavy cream
1 tbsp confectioners' sugar
1 tbsp brandy
9 large ripe strawberries

Preheat the oven to 350°F/180°C. Line a 12-hole muffin pan with 9 paper liners. Place the chocolate in a heatproof bowl, set the bowl over a saucepan of gently simmering water, and heat until melted. Remove from the heat and let cool. Place the butter and sugar in a large bowl and beat together until light and fluffy, then gradually beat in the eggs. Stir in the brandy, followed by the melted chocolate, then carefully fold in the flour. Spoon the batter into the paper liners.

Bake in the preheated oven for 20–25 minutes, or until golden and springy to the touch. Transfer to a wire rack to cool completely.

To decorate, place the cream, sugar, and brandy in a bowl and whip together until just stiff. Spoon the cream into a pastry bag fitted with a star tip and pipe a generous swirl of cream on top of each cake, then place a strawberry on top.

121 *Nice & naughty*

Add 1 cup raspberries to the cake batter and decorate with extra raspberries instead of the strawberries.

122 *Warm spiced apple pie cupcakes*

MAKES 12

3½ tbsp butter, softened
⅓ cup raw brown sugar
1 egg, lightly beaten
heaping 1 cup all-purpose flour
1½ tsp baking powder
½ tsp apple pie spice
1 large baking apple, peeled, cored, and finely chopped
1 tbsp orange juice

TOPPING
5 tbsp all-purpose flour
½ tsp apple pie spice
2 tbsp butter
¼ cup superfine sugar

Preheat the oven to 350°F/180°C. Line a 12-hole muffin pan with 12 paper liners.

To make the topping, place the flour, apple pie spice, butter, and sugar in a large bowl and rub in with your fingertips until the mixture resembles fine breadcrumbs. Set aside.

To make the cupcakes, place the butter and sugar in a large bowl and beat together until light and fluffy, then gradually beat in the egg. Sift in the flour, baking powder, and apple pie spice and fold into the mixture, then fold in the chopped apple and orange juice. Spoon the batter into the paper liners. Add the topping to cover the top of each cupcake and press down gently.

Bake in the preheated oven for 30 minutes, or until golden brown. Let the cupcakes cool in the pan for 2–3 minutes and serve warm, or let cool for 10 minutes and then transfer to a wire rack to cool completely.

123 Chocolate zucchini cupcakes

MAKES 12

1 small zucchini
3 oz/85 g semisweet chocolate, broken into pieces
2 large eggs
¼ cup light brown sugar
⅓ cup sunflower oil
heaping ¾ cup all-purpose flour
½ tsp baking powder
¼ tsp baking soda
1 tbsp pecans, finely chopped
confectioners' sugar, for dusting

Preheat the oven to 350°F/180°C. Line a 12-hole muffin pan with 12 paper liners. Peel and grate the zucchini, discarding any liquid. Set aside.

Place the chocolate in a heatproof bowl, set the bowl over a saucepan of gently simmering water, and heat until melted. Remove from the heat and stir until smooth. Let cool slightly.

Place the eggs, sugar, and oil in a large bowl and whisk together. Sift in the flour, baking powder, and baking soda and stir together until mixed. Stir in the zucchini, pecans, and melted chocolate until combined. Spoon the batter into the paper liners.

Bake in the preheated oven for 25 minutes, or until firm to the touch. Let the cupcakes cool in the pan for 10 minutes, then transfer to a wire rack to cool completely. When the cupcakes are cold, dust with sifted confectioners' sugar.

124 Marbled chocolate cupcakes

MAKES 21

¾ cup soft margarine
1 cup superfine sugar
3 eggs
1¼ cups self-rising flour
2 tbsp milk
2 oz/55 g semisweet chocolate, melted

Preheat the oven to 350°F/180°C. Line two 12-hole muffin pans with 21 paper liners. Place the margarine, sugar, eggs, flour, and milk in a large bowl and beat together until just smooth. Divide the batter among 2 bowls. Add the melted chocolate to one and stir until mixed. Using a teaspoon, and alternating the chocolate batter with the plain, put 4 half-teaspoons into each case.

Bake in the preheated oven for 20 minutes, or until well risen. Transfer to a wire rack to cool.

125 Chocolate orange marbled cupcakes

Add the grated rind and juice of ½ small orange and a few drops of orange food coloring to the plain cake batter.

126 Iced marbled cupcakes

Make the cakes as usual. Sift 2¼ cups confectioners' sugar into a bowl and stir in 2–3 tablespoons of water until smooth. Divide the icing in half and add 1 tablespoon of cocoa to one portion, adding a little extra water if required. Spoon small amounts of each icing on top of the cakes and marble together to cover the cakes with the tip of a knife.

127 Lemon & raspberry cupcakes

MAKES 12

8 tbsp butter, softened
heaping ½ cup superfine sugar
2 eggs, lightly beaten
heaping ¾ cup self-rising flour
finely grated rind of 1 lemon
1 tbsp lemon curd
heaping ¾ cup fresh raspberries

TOPPING
2 tbsp butter
1 tbsp light brown sugar
1 tbsp ground almonds
1 tbsp all-purpose flour

Preheat the oven to 400°F/200°C. Line a 12-hole muffin pan with 12 paper liners. To make the topping, place the butter in a saucepan and heat gently until melted. Pour into a bowl and add the sugar, ground almonds, and flour and stir together until combined.

To make the cupcakes, place the butter and sugar in a large bowl and beat together until light and fluffy, then gradually add the eggs. Sift in the flour and fold into the mixture. Fold in the lemon rind, lemon curd, and raspberries. Spoon the batter into the paper liners. Add the topping to cover the top of each cupcake and press down gently.

Bake in the preheated oven for 15–20 minutes, or until golden brown and firm to the touch. Let the cupcakes cool for 10 minutes, then transfer to a wire rack to cool completely.

128 Chocolate fruit & nut crispy cakes

MAKES 18

10½ oz/300 g semisweet chocolate, broken into pieces
heaping ⅔ cup butter, cut into cubes
¾ cup dark corn syrup
⅔ cup Brazil nuts, coarsely chopped
⅔ cup plumped dried raisins
7 cups cornflakes
18 candied cherries, for decorating

Place 18 paper liners on a baking sheet. Place the chocolate, butter, and dark corn syrup into a large saucepan and heat gently until the butter has melted and the ingredients are runny but not hot. Remove from the heat and stir until well mixed.

Add the chopped nuts and raisins to the pan and stir together until the fruit and nuts are covered in chocolate. Add the cornflakes and stir until combined.

Spoon the mixture evenly into the paper liners and top each with a candied cherry. Let set in a cool place for 2–4 hours before serving.

129 *Devil's food cake with chocolate frosting*

Makes 18

3½ tbsp butter, softened, or soft margarine
heaping ½ cup dark brown sugar
2 large eggs
heaping ¾ cup all-purpose flour
½ tsp baking soda
¼ cup unsweetened cocoa
½ cup sour cream

FROSTING
4½ oz/125 g semisweet chocolate, broken into pieces
2 tbsp superfine sugar
⅔ cup sour cream

CHOCOLATE STICKS (optional)
3½ oz/100 g semisweet chocolate

Preheat the oven to 350°F/180°C. Line two 12-hole muffin pans with 18 paper liners. Place the butter, sugar, eggs, flour, baking soda, and cocoa in a large bowl and beat together until just smooth. Fold in the sour cream. Spoon the batter into the paper liners.

Bake in the preheated oven for 20 minutes, or until well risen and firm to the touch. Transfer to a wire rack to cool completely.

To make the frosting, place the chocolate in a heatproof bowl, set the bowl over a saucepan of gently simmering water, and heat until melted. Let cool slightly, then whisk in the sugar and sour cream until combined. Spread the frosting over the tops of the cakes and chill in the refrigerator before serving.

Decorate with chocolate sticks made by shaving semisweet chocolate with a vegetable peeler, if liked.

130 *Strawberry shortcakes*

Makes 6

6 tbsp butter, plus extra for greasing
1⅔ cups self-rising flour, plus extra for dusting
½ tsp baking powder
½ cup superfine sugar
1 egg, lightly beaten
2–3 tbsp milk, plus extra for brushing

FILLING
1 tsp vanilla extract
heaping 1 cup mascarpone cheese
3 tbsp confectioners' sugar, plus extra for dusting
2¾ cups strawberries

Preheat the oven to 350°F/180°C. Lightly grease a large baking sheet. Sift the flour, baking powder, and sugar into a bowl. Add the butter and rub it in with your fingertips until the mixture resembles breadcrumbs.

Place the egg and 2 tablespoons of the milk in a bowl and beat together, then stir in the dry ingredients with a fork to form a soft, but not sticky, dough, adding more milk if necessary. Turn the dough out onto a lightly floured work surface and roll out to about ¾ inch/2 cm thick. Cut out rounds with a 2¾-inch/7-cm cookie cutter. Press the trimmings together and cut out more rounds until you have 6 rounds. Place the rounds on the baking sheet and brush with milk.

Bake in the preheated oven for 12–15 minutes, until firm and golden brown. Transfer to a wire rack to cool.

To make the filling, stir the vanilla extract into the mascarpone cheese with 2 tablespoons of the confectioners' sugar. Set aside a few whole strawberries, then slice the rest. Sprinkle with the remaining tablespoon of confectioners' sugar. Split the shortcakes in half horizontally.

Spoon half the mascarpone mixture onto the bases and top with sliced strawberries. Spoon over the remaining mascarpone mixture and cover with the tops. Dust with confectioners' sugar and top with the strawberries.

131 *Raspberry shortcakes*

Replace the strawberries with whole raspberries and sandwich with the mascarpone filling.

132 *Sticky toffee squares*

Makes 9

6 tbsp butter, plus extra for greasing
1 cup pitted dates, chopped
¾ cup boiling water
½ tsp baking soda
¾ cup superfine sugar
1 large egg, lightly beaten
½ tsp vanilla extract
1¼ cups self-rising flour

TOFFEE SAUCE
½ cup light brown sugar
3 tbsp butter
2 tbsp light cream or milk

Preheat the oven to 350°F/180°C. Grease and line an 8-inch/20-cm square cake pan.

Place the dates in a small saucepan with the boiling water and baking soda. Heat gently for 5 minutes, without boiling, until the dates are soft.

Place the butter and sugar in a large bowl and beat together until light and fluffy. Beat in the egg, vanilla extract and date mixture. Sift in the flour and fold into the mixture. Pour the batter into the cake pan.

Bake in the preheated oven for 40–45 minutes, or until firm to the touch and starting to shrink away from the sides of the pan.

To make the toffee sauce, place the brown sugar, butter, and cream in a saucepan and heat gently until dissolved, then simmer gently, stirring continuously, for 2 minutes.

Prick all over the surface of the cake with a skewer or fork and pour the hot toffee sauce evenly over the top. Let cool in the pan, then cut into squares.

133 *Sticky toffee & walnut squares*

Reduce the amount of dates to heaping ¾ cup and add ⅓ cup chopped walnuts to the cake batter with the cooked dates. An additional 1 tablespoon of finely chopped walnuts can also be added to the toffee sauce.

134 *Sticky toffee apple squares*

Reduce the amount of dates to heaping ¾ cup and add 1 peeled, cored, and chopped apple to the cake batter with the cooked dates.

135 *Sticky toffee & banana squares*

Add 1 ripe mashed banana to the cake batter after adding the dates.

136 Toffee apple cakes

Makes 12

4 tbsp butter, plus extra for greasing
2 apples
1 tbsp lemon juice
1¾ cups all-purpose flour
2 tsp baking powder
1½ tsp ground cinnamon
⅓ cup light brown sugar
heaping ⅓ cup milk
heaping ⅓ cup apple juice
1 egg, lightly beaten

TOFFEE TOPPING
2 tbsp light cream
¼ cup light brown sugar
1 tbsp butter

Preheat the oven to 400°F/200°C. Grease a 12-hole muffin pan. Core and coarsely grate one of the apples and set aside. Slice the remaining apple into ¼ inch/5 mm thick wedges and toss in the lemon juice. Sift together the flour, baking powder, and cinnamon, then stir in the sugar and grated apple.

Place the butter in a saucepan and heat gently until melted, then mix with the milk, apple juice, and egg. Stir the liquid mixture into the dry ingredients, mixing lightly until just combined.

Spoon the batter into the muffin pan and arrange 2 apple slices on top of each. Bake in the preheated oven for 20–25 minutes, or until risen, firm, and golden brown. Run a knife around the edge of each cake to loosen, then transfer to a wire rack to cool completely.

For the topping, place all the ingredients in a small pan and heat, stirring, until the sugar is dissolved. Increase the heat and boil for 2 minutes, or until syrupy. Cool slightly, then drizzle over the cakes and let set.

137 Toffee pear cakes

Replace the apples with pears and the cinnamon with allspice.

138 Cinnamon rolls

Makes 8

7 tbsp butter, melted, plus extra for greasing
2½ cups self-rising flour, plus extra for dusting
pinch of salt
2 tbsp superfine sugar
1 tsp ground cinnamon
2 egg yolks
generous ¾ cup milk, plus extra for glazing

FILLING
1 tsp ground cinnamon
¼ cup light brown sugar
2 tbsp superfine sugar
1 tbsp butter, melted

ICING
heaping 1 cup confectioners' sugar
2 tbsp cream cheese, softened
1 tbsp butter, softened
about 2 tbsp boiling water
1 tsp vanilla extract

Preheat the oven to 350°F/180°C. Grease an 8-inch/20-cm round cake pan and line the bottom with parchment paper. Place the flour, salt, sugar, and cinnamon in a large bowl and mix together. Place the butter, egg yolks, and milk in a separate bowl and whisk together, then combine with the dry ingredients to form a soft dough. Turn out onto a large piece of parchment paper lightly sprinkled with flour and roll out to a rectangle measuring 12 x 10 inches/30 x 25 cm.

To make the filling, mix the ingredients together, then spread over the dough and roll up like a jelly roll to form a log. Cut the dough into 8 even-size slices with a sharp knife and pack into the pan. Brush gently with extra milk. Bake in the preheated oven for 30–35 minutes, or until golden brown. Let cool for 5 minutes before removing from the pan.

Sift the confectioners' sugar into a large bowl and make a well in the center. Place the cream cheese and butter in the center, pour over the water, and stir to mix. Add extra boiling water, a few drops at a time, until the icing coats the back of a spoon. Stir in the vanilla extract and drizzle over the rolls. Serve warm or cold.

139 Golden raisin & walnut rolls

Sprinkle ¼ cup golden raisins and 1 tablespoon of chopped walnuts over the filling before rolling up.

140 Scones

MAKES ABOUT 10

4 tbsp butter, cut into pieces, plus extra for greasing
3¼ cups all-purpose flour, plus extra for dusting
½ tsp salt
2 tsp baking powder
2 tbsp superfine sugar
generous 1 cup milk, plus extra for brushing
strawberry jam and whipped cream, for serving

Preheat the oven to 425°F/220°C. Grease a baking sheet. Sift the flour, salt, and baking powder into a large bowl. Add the butter and rub it in with your fingertips until the mixture resembles breadcrumbs. Stir in the sugar. Stir in enough of the milk to bring the mixture together into a soft dough.

Gently roll the dough out on a lightly floured work surface until it is about ½ inch/1 cm thick. Cut out the scones with a 2½-inch/6-cm cookie cutter and place on the baking sheet. Brush with a little milk.

Bake in the preheated oven for 10–12 minutes, or until golden and well risen. Cool on a wire rack and serve with strawberry jam and whipped cream.

141 Fruit scones

Stir ⅓ cup golden raisins into the scone mixture with the sugar and serve with butter.

142 Citrus scones

Stir ½ cup candied peel into the scone mixture with the sugar and serve with marmalade and cream.

143 Lemon scones

Stir the grated rind of 1 lemon into the scone mixture with the sugar and serve with lemon curd.

144 Sweet walnut scones

Add ⅓ cup chopped walnuts and use light brown sugar instead of superfine sugar. Serve with butter.

145 Chocolate scones

MAKES 9

5 tbsp butter, cut into pieces, plus extra for greasing
2 cups self-rising flour
1 tbsp superfine sugar
⅓ cup chocolate chips
⅔ cup milk, plus extra for brushing
all-purpose flour, for dusting

Preheat the oven to 425°F/220°C. Lightly grease a baking sheet. Sift the flour into a large bowl. Add the butter and rub it in with your fingertips until the mixture resembles fine breadcrumbs. Stir in the sugar and chocolate chips, then stir in enough of the milk to bring the mixture together into a soft dough.

Roll the dough out on a lightly floured work surface to form a 4 x 6-inch/10 x 15-cm rectangle, about 1 inch/2.5 cm thick. Cut the dough into 9 rectangles and place the scones, spaced well apart, on the baking sheet. Brush the tops with a little milk.

Bake in the preheated oven for 10–12 minutes, or until risen and golden. Transfer to a wire rack to cool.

146 Chocolate & peanut scones

Replace 2 tablespoons of flour with cocoa and replace the chocolate chips with peanut-flavored chips.

147 London cakes

MAKES 10

oil, for greasing
heaping 3½ cups white bread flour
6 tbsp butter, cut into pieces
¼ cup superfine sugar
½ tsp salt
1 tsp active dry yeast
1 tsp caraway seeds (optional)
2 eggs, lightly beaten
about ⅔ cup tepid milk
⅔ cup golden raisins
½ cup candied peel
beaten egg, for glazing
nibbed sugar or crushed sugar cubes, for decorating

Lightly grease a large bowl and 2 baking sheets. Place the flour in a large bowl, add the butter, and rub it in until the mixture resembles breadcrumbs. Stir in the sugar, salt, yeast, and caraway seeds, if using. Add the eggs and enough milk to mix to form a soft pliable dough. Knead well for 10 minutes, then place in the lightly oiled bowl and cover loosely. Leave in a warm place to rise for about 1 hour.

Tip the dough out onto a lightly floured work surface and knead in the golden raisins and candied peel. Divide the dough into 10 pieces. Shape each piece into a ball and place on the baking sheets. Cover loosely and leave in a warm place to rise for about 45 minutes.

Preheat the oven to 400°F/200°C. Brush the bread with the egg and sprinkle a little nibbed sugar on top. Bake in the preheated oven for 12–15 minutes, or until the cakes sound hollow when tapped on the bottom. Transfer to a wire rack to cool.

148 Australian lamingtons

Makes 16

4 tbsp butter, plus extra for greasing
6 eggs
¾ cup superfine sugar
1¼ cups all-purpose flour
2¾ cups dry unsweetened coconut

FROSTING
heaping 3½ cups confectioners' sugar
½ cup unsweetened cocoa
⅓ cup boiling water
5½ tbsp butter, melted

Preheat the oven to 350°F/180°C. Grease an 8-inch/20-cm square cake pan and line the bottom with parchment paper. Place the butter in a saucepan and heat gently until melted, then let cool slightly.

Place the eggs and sugar in a heatproof bowl, set the bowl over a pan of gently simmering water, and whisk until pale and thick enough to leave a trail when the whisk is lifted. Remove from the heat, sift in the flour, and fold in. Fold in the melted butter. Pour into the pan.

Bake in the preheated oven for 35–40 minutes, or until risen, golden, and springy to the touch. Leave in the pan for 2–3 minutes, then turn out onto a wire rack to cool. When cold, cut the cake into 16 squares.

For the frosting, sift together the confectioners' sugar and cocoa into a bowl and stir in the water and butter until smooth. Spread out the coconut on a plate. Dip each piece of cake into the frosting, then place in the coconut and turn to coat. Leave on parchement paper to set.

149 Raspberry lamingtons

Replace the chocolate covering with raspberry jam. Gently heat ½ cup raspberry jam in a small saucepan until runny. Brush the jam over the squares then dip in the dry unsweetened coconut to coat evenly.

150 Cinnamon squares

Makes 16

1 cup butter, softened, plus extra for greasing
heaping 1 cup superfine sugar
3 eggs, lightly beaten
heaping 1 cup self-rising flour
½ tsp baking soda
1 tbsp ground cinnamon
⅔ cup sour cream
¼ cup sunflower seeds

Preheat the oven to 350°F/180°C. Grease a 9-inch/23-cm square cake pan and line the bottom with parchment paper.

Place the butter and sugar in a large bowl and beat together until light and fluffy, then beat in the eggs.

Sift together the flour, baking soda, and cinnamon into the mixture and fold in. Spoon in the sour cream and sunflower seeds and mix gently until well combined. Spoon the batter into the pan and smooth the surface gently with the back of a spoon or a knife.

Bake in the preheated oven for 45 minutes, or until the batter is firm to the touch. Loosen the edges with a round-bladed knife, then transfer to a wire rack to cool completely. Slice into squares before serving.

151 Apple & cinnamon squares

Add 1 apple, peeled, cored, and chopped, to the mixture after beating in the eggs.

152 Seedy ginger squares

Replace the cinnamon with ground ginger and add 1½ oz/40 g chopped preserved ginger after beating in the eggs.

153 Madeleines

Makes 30

generous 8 tbsp butter, plus extra for greasing	*1 tsp vanilla extract*
3 eggs	*¾ cup superfine sugar*
1 egg yolk	*1 cup all-purpose flour*
	1 tsp baking powder

Preheat the oven to 375°F/190°C. Lightly grease 30 holes in 3 standard-size madeleine pans. Place the butter in a saucepan and heat until melted, then let cool.

Place the eggs, egg yolk, vanilla extract, and sugar in a large bowl and whisk until very pale and thick. Sift in the flour and baking powder and fold in, then fold in the melted butter. Spoon the batter into the pans.

Bake in the preheated oven for 8–10 minutes, or until risen and golden brown. Remove the cakes carefully from the pans and let cool on a wire rack. They are best served the day they are made.

154 Almond madeleines

Replace the vanilla extract with almond extract. Reduce the flour to heaping ¾ cup and fold in ¼ cup ground almonds with the flour.

155 Chocolate-dipped madeleines

Place 8 oz/225 g semisweet or milk chocolate in a heatproof bowl, set the bowl over a saucepan of gently simmering water, and heat until melted. Remove from the heat. Line a couple of baking sheets with parchment paper. Dip the plain or almond madeleines in the chocolate to half cover, letting the excess chocolate drip back into the bowl, and place on the parchment paper to set.

156 Lucia saffron buns

MAKES 10

- oil, for greasing
- generous ¾ cup milk
- 1 tsp saffron threads
- heaping 3½ cups white bread flour
- 4 tbsp butter, cut into pieces
- ½ cup confectioners' sugar
- ½ tsp salt
- 1 tsp active dry yeast
- 1 egg
- 40 raisins
- beaten egg, for glazing

Lightly oil a bowl and 2 baking sheets. Heat the milk in a small saucepan until almost boiling. Add the saffron and stir, then remove from the heat and leave for 20 minutes.

Place the flour in a large bowl. Add the butter and rub it in until the mixture resembles breadcrumbs, then stir in the sugar, salt, and yeast.

Add the saffron milk and egg and mix to form a soft pliable dough. Knead well for 10 minutes, then place in the lightly oiled bowl and loosely cover. Leave in a warm place to rise for about 1 hour.

Knead the dough on a lightly floured work surface. Divide the dough into 10 pieces. Shape each piece into a smooth ball, then roll into a rope about 10 inches/ 25 cm long. Pinch the ends of each rope together, then twist into a figure eight and place on the baking sheet so that the ends are in the center and underneath. Press a couple of raisins onto each loop of the dough. Cover and leave in a warm place to rise for 45 minutes.

Preheat the oven to 400°F/ 200°C. Brush the bread with an egg glaze and bake in the preheated oven for 12–15 minutes, or until the bread sounds hollow when tapped on the bottom. Transfer to a wire rack to cool completely.

157 Saffron loaf

After letting it rise, punch down the dough and lightly knead. Form into a sausage shape and place in an oiled 9 x 5 x 3-inch/23 x 13 x 8-cm loaf pan. Cover loosely and let rise until doubled in size. Bake in the preheated oven for 40–45 minutes, or until golden and the loaf sounds hollow when tapped underneath. While still warm, brush the top of the loaf with a little dark corn syrup, then let cool. Serve sliced with butter.

158 Spanish churros

MAKES 28

- 6 tbsp butter, cut into pieces
- 1 cup water
- 6 tbsp superfine sugar
- heaping 1 cup all-purpose flour
- 3 eggs, lightly beaten
- sunflower oil, for deep-frying

Place the butter in a saucepan with the water and 2 tablespoons of the sugar and heat gently until the butter melts. Increase the heat and bring to a rapid boil, then remove from the heat and add the flour all at the same time. Beat until the mixture forms a ball. Let cool slightly, then gradually beat in the eggs until smooth and glossy.

Spoon the mixture into a pastry bag fitted with a large star tip and pipe 4-inch/10-cm strips on a sheet of parchment paper, then chill for 30 minutes, or until just firm.

Heat the oil in a suitable pan to 350°F/180°C. Cooking in batches, remove the churros from the parchment paper and place in the hot oil. Deep-fry for 3–4 minutes, turning once, until crisp and golden. Remove with a slotted spoon and drain on paper towels. Repeat until all the mixture has been used. Dust with the remaining sugar and let cool.

159 Cinnamon churros

Add 1 teaspoon of ground cinnamon to the sugar before dusting. If liked, 1 teaspoon of ground cinnamon can also be added to the mixture itself.

160 French galettes

MAKES 4

2 tbsp butter, plus extra for greasing
12 oz/350 g puff pastry
all-purpose flour, for dusting
2 apples, peeled, cored, and thinly sliced
1 tbsp raw brown sugar
½ tsp fennel seeds

Preheat the oven to 400°F/200°C. Grease a baking sheet. Place the butter in a saucepan and heat gently until melted, then let cool slightly.

Roll the pastry out on a floured work surface and cut out four 5-inch/13-cm rounds using a small saucer as a guide. Place on the baking sheet. Lightly score a ½-inch/1-cm border in the pastry and prick the center of the pastry all over with a fork. Brush the pastry with the melted butter, then arrange the apple slices in a spiral in the center of the pastry, being careful not to overlap the border. Sprinkle with sugar and fennel and brush with melted butter. Bake in the preheated oven for 25–30 minutes, or until the pastry is crisp and golden.

161 Brandied peach galettes

Prepare the pastry as before. Slice 3 peaches and arrange in a spiral in the center of the pastries. Sprinkle with a little brandy and 2 tablespoons of light brown sugar. Dot with a little butter and bake for 20–25 minutes.

162 Pear galettes

Replace the apples with pears and sprinkle with a few chopped pecans.

163 Lemon & cornmeal berry squares

MAKES 9

¾ cup butter, softened, plus extra for greasing
1 cup superfine sugar
3 large eggs, lightly beaten
heaping 1 cup ground almonds
heaping 1 cup cornmeal
2 tsp baking powder
finely grated rind of 1 lemon
2 tbsp lemon juice
2½ cups frozen small berry fruits, such as cranberries, raspberries, and blueberries
confectioners' sugar, for decorating

Preheat the oven to 350°F/180°C. Grease a 9-inch/23-cm shallow square cake pan and line the bottom with parchment paper. Place the butter and sugar in a large bowl and beat together until light and fluffy, then gradually beat the eggs into the mixture until smooth. Add the ground almonds, cornmeal, baking powder, lemon rind and juice, and stir together until well mixed. Stir in the fruit of your choice. Spoon the batter into the pan and spread out evenly.

Bake in the preheated oven for 45 minutes, or until golden brown and firm to the touch. Transfer to a wire rack to cool completely.

Sift confectioners' sugar lightly over to decorate and cut into squares.

164 Double chocolate swirls

MAKES 24

4¼ cups white bread flour, plus extra for dusting
1 envelope or scant 1 tbsp active dry yeast
heaping ½ cup superfine sugar
½ tsp salt
1 tsp ground cinnamon
6 tbsp butter
2 large eggs
1¼ cups milk
oil, for greasing
1 small egg, for glazing

FILLING
6 tbsp chocolate hazelnut spread
7 oz/200 g milk chocolate, chopped

Place the flour, yeast, sugar, salt, and cinnamon in a large bowl and mix together.

Place the butter in a saucepan and heat gently until melted, then let cool slightly. Whisk in the eggs and milk, then pour into the flour mixture and mix well to form a soft dough.

Knead the dough on a floured work surface for 10 minutes, until smooth, then place in a large floured bowl, cover with plastic wrap, and let rise in a warm place for 1½–2 hours.

When you are ready to make the swirls, preheat the oven to 425°F/220°C. Lightly oil 2 baking sheets. Remove the dough from the bowl and punch down. Divide the dough into 4 pieces and roll each piece into a rectangle about 1 inch/2.5 cm thick. Spread each rectangle with the chocolate hazelnut spread and scatter with the chopped chocolate. Roll up each piece from one of the long edges, then cut into 6 pieces.

Place each swirl, cut-side down, on the baking sheets and brush well with the beaten egg.

Bake in the preheated oven for 12–15 minutes, or until cooked through, and serve warm.

165 Extra nutty chocolate swirls

When the dough is rolled out, spread with 9 tablespoons of chocolate hazelnut spread, then sprinkle with 1 cup chopped toasted hazelnuts.

166 Spanish buñuelos

MAKES 12

3 tbsp sunflower oil, plus extra for deep-frying
2 large eggs
⅓ cup milk
2⅔ cups all-purpose flour, plus extra for dusting
1 tsp baking powder
2 tsp light brown sugar
4 tbsp superfine sugar
1 tsp ground cinnamon

Place the oil, eggs, and milk in a large bowl and whisk together. Place the flour, baking powder, and sugar in a separate bowl and mix well, then pour in the egg mixture and mix well to form a dough. Knead the dough on a lightly floured surface until very smooth.

Divide the dough into 12 and roll into balls. Flatten each into 3–4-inch/8–10-cm rounds and let rest for 20 minutes. Place the superfine sugar and cinnamon in a bowl and mix together. Set aside.

Heat the oil in a suitable saucepan to 375°F/190°C and deep-fry the buñuelos in batches for 2–3 minutes, or until puffed and golden on both sides, turning once. Remove with a slotted spoon and drain on paper towels. Repeat until all the buñuelos are cooked. Sprinkle with the cinnamon sugar and serve warm.

167 Doughnuts

Makes 10

sunflower oil, for greasing and cooking
$3^{1}/_{4}$ cups white bread flour
4 tbsp butter, cut into pieces
2 tbsp superfine sugar, plus extra for dusting
½ tsp salt
1 envelope or scant 1 tbsp active dry yeast
1 egg, lightly beaten
¾ cup lukewarm milk
½ cup seedless raspberry jam

Lightly grease a large bowl and 2 baking sheets. Place the flour in a large bowl, add the butter, and rub it in until the mixture resembles breadcrumbs. Stir in the sugar, salt, and yeast. Make a well in the center and add the egg and milk, then mix to form a soft pliable dough. Knead well for 10 minutes, then place in the greased bowl and cover. Leave in a warm place to rise for about 1 hour.

Knead the dough on a floured work surface, then divide into 10 pieces. Shape each piece into a ball and place on the baking sheets. Cover and leave in a warm place to double in size for 45 minutes.

Heat the oil in a suitable saucepan to 350°F/180°C and deep-fry the doughnuts in 2–3 batches for 2–3 minutes on each side. Drain and dust with sugar.

Place the jam in a pastry bag fitted with a plain tip. Insert a sharp knife into each doughnut and twist to make a hole. Push the point of the tip into the hole and pipe in some jam.

168 Ring doughnuts

After the first rise, punch down the dough and knead again. Roll out until it is ½ inch/1 cm thick. Cut $3^{1}/_{4}$-inch/8-cm circles with a round cookie cutter, then use a 1-inch/2.5-cm cutter to cut out the center. Place on baking sheets to rise. Re-roll the dough trimmings as necessary. Deep-fry as before and dust with superfine sugar mixed with ground cinnamon, or spread the tops with a little basic icing (page 10) and sprinkle with colored sugar strands.

169 Sweet cream doughnuts

Fill with sweetened cream and flavor the cream with a little melted chocolate, if liked.

170 Gingerbread

Makes 9

¾ cup butter, plus extra for greasing
¾ cup dark brown sugar
½ cup dark corn syrup
finely grated rind and juice of 1 small orange
2 large eggs, lightly beaten
1⅔ cups self-rising flour
1⅔ cups whole wheat flour
2 tsp ground ginger
1½ oz/40 g chopped candied ginger or preserved ginger
pieces of candied ginger or preserved ginger, for decorating

Preheat the oven to 350°F/180°C. Grease a deep 9-inch/23-cm square cake pan and line the bottom with parchment paper. Place the butter, sugar, and dark corn syrup in a saucepan and heat gently, stirring until melted.

Remove from the heat. Beat in the orange rind and juice, eggs, flours, and ground ginger, then beat thoroughly to mix evenly. Stir in the candied ginger. Spoon the batter into the pan.

Bake in the preheated oven for 40–45 minutes, or until risen and firm to the touch. Let cool in the pan for 10 minutes, then turn out and let cool completely on a wire rack. Cut into squares and decorate with candied ginger.

171 Nutty gingerbread

Replace the ginger pieces with heaping ½ cup chopped walnuts or pecans.

172 Apple gingerbread

Makes 12

heaping ⅔ cup butter, plus extra for greasing
1 cup brown sugar
2 tbsp blackstrap molasses
1⅔ cups all-purpose flour
1 tsp baking powder
2 tsp baking soda
2 tsp ground ginger
⅔ cup milk
1 egg, lightly beaten
2 apples, peeled, chopped, and coated with 1 tbsp lemon juice

Preheat the oven to 325°F/160°C. Grease a 9-inch/23-cm square cake pan and line with parchment paper. Place the butter, sugar, and blackstrap molasses in a saucepan and heat gently until the butter is melted, then let cool.

Sift the all-purpose flour, baking powder, baking soda, and ground ginger into a large bowl. Stir in the milk, egg, and cooled buttery liquid, followed by the chopped apples coated with the lemon juice, and mix together gently. Pour the batter into the pan and smooth the surface.

Bake in the preheated oven for 30–35 minutes, or until the cake has risen and a fine skewer inserted into the center comes out clean. Let the cake cool in the pan before turning out and cutting into 12 bars.

173 Pear gingerbread

Replace the apples with pears. Add 1 oz/25 g chopped preserved ginger to the batter with the ground ginger for an extra ginger flavor.

174 Lemon drizzle squares

MAKES 12

heaping ⅔ cup butter, softened, or soft margarine, plus extra for greasing
1 cup superfine sugar
2 eggs
finely grated rind of 1 lemon
1¼ cups self-rising flour
½ cup milk
confectioners' sugar, for dusting

SYRUP
1¼ cups confectioners' sugar
¼ cup fresh lemon juice

Preheat the oven to 350°F/180°C. Grease a 7-inch/18-cm square cake pan and line with parchment paper.

Place the butter, sugar, and eggs in a large bowl and beat together until light and fluffy. Stir in the lemon rind, then sift in the flour and fold into the mixture. Stir in the milk. Spoon the batter into the cake pan, smoothing the top.

Bake in the preheated oven for 45–50 minutes, or until golden brown and firm to the touch. Leave the pan on a wire rack.

To make the syrup, place the confectioners' sugar and lemon juice in a small saucepan and heat gently, stirring, until the sugar dissolves. Do not boil. Prick the warm cake all over with a fork, and spoon the hot syrup evenly over the top, allowing it to be absorbed.

Let cool completely in the pan, then turn out the cake, cut into 12 pieces, and dust with sifted confectioners' sugar.

175 Citrus drizzle slices

Replace the lemon rind with the grated rind of ½ orange and 1 lime in the cake batter. For the syrup, squeeze the lime and add enough orange juice to make up to ¼ cup, and add the grated rind of ½ orange.

176 Rock cakes

MAKES ABOUT 8

8 tbsp butter, plus extra for greasing
1⅔ cups all-purpose flour
2 tsp baking powder
½ cup light brown sugar
heaping ½ cup mixed dried fruit
finely grated rind of 1 lemon
1 egg
1–2 tbsp milk
2 tsp raw brown sugar

Preheat the oven to 400°F/200°C. Lightly grease 2 baking sheets. Sift the flour and baking powder into a large bowl. Add the butter and rub it in with your fingertips until the mixture resembles breadcrumbs. Stir in the brown sugar, mixed dried fruit, and lemon rind.

Place the egg and a tablespoon of the milk in a bowl and beat lightly, then stir into the flour mixture, adding a little more milk if necessary, until it starts to bind together to form a moist but firm dough. Spoon small heaps of the dough onto the baking sheets. Sprinkle with the raw brown sugar.

Bake in the preheated oven for 15–20 minutes, or until golden brown and firm. Use a spatula to transfer the cakes to a wire rack to cool.

177 Citrus rock cakes

Replace the dried fruit with chopped candied peel and add orange juice instead of the milk.

178 *Walnut & Romano scones*

MAKES ABOUT 16

6 tbsp butter, diced, plus extra for greasing
3 ¼ cups self-rising flour, plus extra for dusting
pinch of salt
¼ cup superfine sugar
1¾ oz/50 g grated Romano cheese
1 cup walnut pieces
about 1¼ cups milk

Preheat the oven to 400°F/200°C. Grease a baking sheet. Sift the flour and salt into a large bowl. Add the butter and rub it in with your fingertips until the mixture resembles fine breadcrumbs. Stir in the sugar, cheese, and walnuts. Stir in enough of the milk to bring the mixture together into a soft dough.

Gently roll the dough out on a lightly floured work surface until it is about 1–1¼ inch/2.5–3 cm thick. Cut out rounds with a 2½-inch/6-cm round cookie cutter (make the scones smaller or larger if you prefer). Place the rounds on a baking sheet.

Bake in the preheated oven for 15 minutes, or until golden brown and firm to the touch. Transfer to a wire rack to cool.

179 *Olive & walnut scones*

Replace the Romano with ⅓ cup pitted green olives, chopped.

180 *Sun-dried tomato & Romano scones*

Replace the walnuts with 4 pieces of sun-dried tomato in oil, chopped.

181 English muffins

Makes about 12

vegetable oil, for greasing and cooking
3 ¼ cups white bread flour,
plus extra for dusting
½ tsp salt
1 tsp superfine sugar
1½ tsp active dry yeast
generous 1 cup lukewarm water
½ cup plain yogurt
¼ cup semolina

Grease a bowl and dust a baking sheet with flour. Sift the flour and salt together into a bowl and stir in the sugar and yeast. Make a well in the center and add the water and yogurt. Stir until the dough begins to come together, then knead until it comes away from the side of the bowl. Knead the dough on a floured surface for 5–10 minutes, or until smooth and elastic.

Shape the dough into a ball, place it in the greased bowl, and cover with a damp dish towel. Let rise in a warm place for 30–40 minutes.

Knead the dough on a floured surface, then roll out until it is about ¾ inch/2 cm thick. Cut out 10–12 rounds with a 3-inch/7.5-cm cookie cutter and sprinkle each round with semolina. Transfer the rounds to the baking sheet, cover, and leave in a warm place for 30 minutes.

Heat a griddle or large skillet over medium–high heat and brush with oil. Add half the muffins and cook for 7–8 minutes on each side, until golden brown. Cook the remaining muffins in the same way.

182 Cheese muffins

Stir in 1 cup finely grated cheddar cheese with the sugar and yeast.

183 Black pepper muffins

Stir in 1 teaspoon of coarsely ground black pepper with the sugar and yeast.

184 Cheese & mustard scones

MAKES 8

3½ tbsp butter, cut into pieces, plus extra for greasing
1⅔ cups self-rising flour, plus extra for dusting
1 tsp baking powder
pinch of salt
heaping 1 cup grated sharp cheddar cheese
1 tsp mustard powder
⅔ cup milk, plus extra for brushing
pepper

Preheat the oven to 425°F/220°C. Lightly grease a baking sheet. Sift the flour, baking powder, and salt into a large bowl. Add the butter and rub it in with your fingertips until the mixture resembles breadcrumbs. Stir in the cheese, mustard and enough milk to form a soft dough.

Knead the dough very lightly on a floured work surface, then flatten it out into a round with the palm of your hand to a thickness of about 1 inch/2.5 cm.

Cut the dough into 8 wedges with a knife. Brush each one with a little milk and sprinkle with pepper to taste.

Bake in the preheated oven for 10–15 minutes, or until golden brown. Transfer to a wire rack to cool slightly before serving.

185 Cheese & herb scones

Replace the mustard with 1 tablespoon of chopped fresh herbs, such as chives, parsley, sage, rosemary, or thyme.

186 Cheddar & caraway scones

Replace the mustard with 1½ teaspoons of caraway seeds.

187 Cornbread squares

MAKES 16

vegetable oil, for greasing
1¼ cups all-purpose flour
1 tsp salt
4 tsp baking powder
1 tsp superfine sugar
2 cups cornmeal
8 tbsp butter, softened, cut into pieces
4 eggs
1 cup milk
3 tbsp heavy cream

Preheat the oven to 400°F/200°C. Oil an 8-inch/20-cm square cake pan. Sift together the flour, salt, and baking powder into a bowl. Add the sugar and cornmeal and stir to mix. Add the butter and rub it in with your fingertips until the mixture resembles breadcrumbs.

Place the eggs, milk, and cream in a bowl and lightly beat together, then stir into the cornmeal mixture until thoroughly combined. Spoon the mixture into the pan and smooth the surface.

Bake in the preheated oven for 30–35 minutes, or until a skewer inserted into the center of the loaf comes out clean. Let cool for 5–10 minutes, then cut into squares and serve warm.

188 Chile cornbread

Stir in 1–2 teaspoons of dried red chile flakes into the mixture with the sugar and cornmeal.

189 Pepper & corn cornbread

Sauté 1 seeded and chopped red bell pepper in 1 tablespoon of oil until just tender. Let cool, then stir in ¾ cup corn kernels and add to the mixture with the milk and cream.

190 Bagels

MAKES 10

vegetable oil, for greasing
2½ cups white bread flour, plus extra for dusting
2 tsp salt
1 envelope or scant 1 tbsp active dry yeast
1 tbsp lightly beaten egg
generous ¾ cup lukewarm water
1 egg white
2 tsp water
2 tbsp caraway seeds

Grease a bowl and 2 baking sheets. Dust another baking sheet with flour. Sift the flour and salt together into a bowl and stir in the yeast. Make a well in the center, pour in the egg and the water, and mix to form a dough. Knead the dough on a lightly floured work surface for 10 minutes, until smooth.

Shape the dough into a ball, place it in the oiled bowl, and cover with a damp dish towel. Let rise in a warm place for 1 hour.

Turn the dough onto a lightly floured work surface and punch down with your fist. Knead for 2 minutes, then divide into 10 pieces. Shape each piece into a ball and let rest for 5 minutes. Gently flatten each ball with a lightly floured hand and make a hole in the center with the handle of a wooden spoon. Put the bagels on the floured sheet, cover with a damp dish towel, and let rise in a warm place for 20 minutes.

Preheat the oven to 425°F/220°C and bring a large saucepan of water to a boil. Reduce the heat until the water is barely simmering, then add 2 bagels. Poach for 1 minute, then turn over and poach for an additional 30 seconds. Remove with a slotted spoon and drain on a dish towel. Poach the remaining bagels in the same way. Transfer the bagels to the oiled baking sheets. Place the egg white and water in a bowl and beat together, then brush it over the bagels. Sprinkle with the caraway seeds.

Bake in the preheated oven for 25–30 minutes, or until golden brown. Transfer to a wire rack to cool completely.

191 Cinnamon & raisin bagels

Add 1 teaspoon of ground cinnamon to the flour and make the dough as described. Let rise. After punching down the dough, knead in ⅓ cup raisins then shape and complete as described, omitting the caraway seeds.

Crowd-Pleasing Cookies

192 Chocolate chip cookies

MAKES 20

8 tbsp butter, softened, plus extra for greasing
heaping ½ cup dark brown sugar
1 egg
1¼ cups rolled oats
1 tbsp milk
1 tsp vanilla extract
1 cup all-purpose flour
1 tbsp unsweetened cocoa
½ tsp baking powder
6 oz/175 g semisweet chocolate, broken into pieces
6 oz/175 g milk chocolate, broken into pieces

Preheat the oven to 350°F/180°C. Grease 2 large baking sheets. Place the butter and sugar in a large bowl and beat together until light and fluffy. Beat in the egg, then add the oats, milk, and vanilla extract and beat together until well blended. Sift the flour, cocoa, and baking powder into the mixture and stir. Stir in the chocolate pieces.

Place tablespoonfuls of the mixture on the baking sheets and flatten slightly with a fork. Bake in the preheated oven for 15 minutes, or until slightly risen and firm.

Let cool on the baking sheets for 2 minutes, then transfer the cookies to wire racks to cool completely.

193 White chocolate chip cookies

Replace the semisweet and milk chocolate with 9¾ oz/275 g chopped white chocolate.

194 Almond cookies with a cherry on top

MAKES 25

heaping ¾ cup butter, cut into cubes, plus extra for greasing
½ cup superfine sugar
½ tsp almond extract
2 cups self-rising flour
heaping ¼ cup ground almonds
25 candied cherries (total weight about 4½ oz/125 g)

Preheat the oven to 350°F/180°C. Grease several large baking sheets.

Place the butter in a large saucepan and heat gently until melted. Remove from the heat. Add the sugar and almond extract to the pan and stir together. Add the flour and ground almonds and mix to form a smooth dough.

Roll small pieces of the dough between your hands into smooth balls to make 25 in total. Place on the baking sheets, spaced well apart, and flatten slightly with your hands, then press a cherry gently into the center of each cookie. Bake in the preheated oven for 10–15 minutes, or until golden brown.

Let cool for 2–3 minutes on the baking sheets, then transfer the cookies to a wire rack to cool completely.

195 Cookies & cream sandwiches

Makes about 15

9 tbsp butter, softened
⅔ cup confectioners' sugar
heaping ¾ cup all-purpose flour
½ cup unsweetened cocoa
½ tsp ground cinnamon

FILLING
4½ oz/125 g semisweet chocolate, broken into pieces
¼ cup heavy cream

Preheat the oven to 325°F/160°C. Line 2 large baking sheets with parchment paper. Place the butter and sugar in a large bowl and beat together until light and fluffy. Sift the flour, cocoa, and cinnamon into the mixture and mix to form a dough.

Place the dough between 2 sheets of parchment paper and roll out until the dough is ⅛ inch/3 mm thick. Cut out 2½-inch/6-cm rounds and place on the baking sheets. Bake in the preheated oven for 15 minutes, or until firm to the touch. Let cool for 2 minutes on the parchment paper, then transfer the cookies to wire racks to cool completely.

Meanwhile, make the filling. Place the chocolate and cream in a saucepan and heat gently until the chocolate has melted. Stir until smooth. Let cool, then chill in the refrigerator for 2 hours, or until firm. Sandwich the cookies together in pairs with a spoonful of the chocolate cream and serve.

196 With strawberry filling

Replace the semisweet chocolate with white chocolate, chop ½ cup dried strawberries into small pieces, and fold into the chilled filling.

197 Classic oatmeal cookies

Makes 30

¾ cup butter or margarine, plus extra for greasing
1⅓ cups raw brown sugar
1 egg
4 tbsp water
1 tsp vanilla extract
scant 4½ cups rolled oats
1 cup all-purpose flour
1 tsp salt
½ tsp baking soda

Preheat the oven to 180°C/350°F. Grease 2 large baking sheets. Place the butter and sugar in a large bowl and beat together until light and fluffy. Beat in the egg, water, and vanilla extract until the mixture is smooth. Mix the oats, flour, salt, and baking soda together in a separate bowl, then gradually stir the oat mixture into the creamed mixture until thoroughly combined.

Place tablespoonfuls of the dough onto the baking sheets, spaced well apart. Bake in the preheated oven for 15 minutes, or until golden brown. Transfer to a wire rack to cool completely.

198 Oatmeal & raisin cookies

Add ½ cup chopped raisins to the dough mix.

199 *Peanut sitting pretties*

Makes 18

8 tbsp unsalted butter, softened
¼ cup raw brown sugar
1 large egg, separated
½ tsp vanilla extract
1 cup all-purpose flour
pinch of salt
1 cup chopped mixed nuts
36 chocolate- or sugar-coated peanuts, for decorating

FROSTING
1 quantity buttercream (page 10)

Place the butter and sugar in a large bowl and beat together until light and fluffy. Stir in the egg yolk and vanilla extract and beat together, then add the flour and salt and beat to combine. Wrap the dough in plastic wrap and chill in the refrigerator for 3 hours.

Preheat the oven to 350°F/180°C. Line a large baking sheet with parchment paper.

Lightly whisk the egg white in a clean bowl and spread the chopped nuts out on a plate. Roll walnut-size pieces of the dough into balls. Dip each ball in the egg white, then roll in the nuts to coat and place on the baking sheet. Bake in the preheated oven for 5 minutes, then remove and make an indentation with your thumb in the middle of each cookie. Bake for an additional 5 minutes, then let the cookies cool completely on the baking sheet.

To make the buttercream, place the butter in a large bowl and beat until soft. Sift in the confectioners' sugar and beat together until smooth. Spoon a little buttercream into the indentation of each cookie and top each one with 2 chocolate- or sugar-coated peanuts.

200 *With hazelnut & chocolate topping*

Replace the buttercream with 5 oz/140 g hazelnut chocolate spread.

201 *Fluttering butterfly cookies*

Makes 25

¾ cup unsalted butter, softened, plus extra for greasing
1 cup superfine sugar
1 large egg, lightly beaten
1 tsp vanilla extract or almond extract
2¼ cups all-purpose flour, plus extra for dusting
pinch of salt

FOR DECORATING
1⅓ cups confectioners' sugar
about 1 tbsp cold water
yellow, pink, and blue food coloring
silver dragées
tubes of colored decorating icing

Place the butter and sugar in a large bowl and beat together until light and fluffy. Whisk the egg and vanilla together in a separate bowl, then beat into the butter mixture. Sift in the flour and salt and mix to form a dough. Wrap in plastic wrap and chill for 30 minutes.

Preheat the oven to 350°F/180°C. Grease a large baking sheet. Roll the dough out on a floured work surface to ¼ inch/5 mm thick. Cut out shapes with a flour-dipped, butterfly-shaped cookie cutter and place on the baking sheet. Bake in the preheated oven for 12–15 minutes, or until they are golden brown. Let cool on wire racks.

To make the frosting, sift the confectioners' sugar into a bowl, add the water, and mix until smooth. Divide the frosting into portions and tint to pastel shades with food coloring. Spread the frosting over the cookies and decorate with silver dragées. Let set, then finish decorating with decorating icing.

202 *Smiley faces*

MAKES 20

¾ cup unsalted butter, softened
½ cup light brown sugar
1 large egg, lightly beaten
1 tbsp honey
2 cups all-purpose flour, plus extra for dusting
½ tsp ground cinnamon

FOR DECORATING
1 cup confectioners' sugar
about ½ tsp cold water
3 tbsp chocolate sprinkles
20 gum drops
tubes of colored decorating icing

Place the butter and sugar in a large bowl and beat together until light and fluffy. Add the egg and honey and stir to combine. Sift in the flour and cinnamon and mix to form a soft dough. Wrap the dough in plastic wrap and chill in the refrigerator for 30 minutes.

Preheat the oven to 375°F/190°C. Line a large baking sheet with parchment paper. Cut the dough in half and roll in the remaining flour, then roll out each piece between 2 sheets of plastic wrap. Using a 2¾-inch/7-cm cookie cutter, cut out 10 disks from each piece and place on the baking sheet. Bake in the preheated oven for 10–12 minutes, or until golden brown. Let cool for 5 minutes, then transfer the cookies to a wire rack to cool completely.

Sift the confectioners' sugar into a bowl, add the water, and mix until smooth. Spread the cookies with a thin layer of frosting, then use the chocolate sprinkles for hair and a gum drop for the nose. Let set, then draw in the eyes and mouth with the decorating icing.

203 *Fairy faces*

For fairy faces, frost the cookies according to the recipe but use 3 tablespoons of pink sprinkles for the hair and use pink decorating icing for the face.

204 *Buttery fork cookies*

MAKES 25

9 tbsp unsalted butter, softened
⅔ cup superfine sugar
1 large egg yolk
¾ cup all-purpose flour
1 tsp ground cinnamon

Preheat the oven to 400°F/200°C. Line a large baking sheet with parchment paper.

Place the butter and 2 tablespoons of the sugar in a large bowl and beat together until light and fluffy. Add the egg yolk and mix together, then sift in the flour and mix to form a soft dough.

Mix the remaining sugar with the cinnamon. Take a teaspoon of dough and roll it in the sugar mixture. Place on the baking sheet and use a fork to press down until the cookie is ½ inch/1 cm thick. Repeat until all the dough is used up. Bake in the preheated oven for 10 minutes, or until golden brown. Let cool on a wire rack.

205 *Coconut buttery fork cookies*

Add 3½ oz/100 g shredded coconut to the dough and roll the cookies in the remaining superfine sugar, but omit the cinnamon.

206 Marshmallow daisies

Makes 30

1 cup butter, softened
¾ cup superfine sugar
1 egg yolk, lightly beaten
2 tsp vanilla extract
1⅔ cups all-purpose flour
½ cup unsweetened cocoa
pinch of salt
about 90 white mini marshmallows, halved horizontally
4 tbsp peach jam
4 tbsp yellow sugar sprinkles

Place the butter and sugar in a large bowl and beat together until light and fluffy, then beat in the egg yolk and vanilla extract.

Sift together the flour, cocoa, and salt into the mixture and stir until thoroughly combined. Halve the dough, roll each piece into a ball, wrap in plastic wrap, and chill in the refrigerator for 30–60 minutes.

Preheat the oven to 375°F/190°C. Line 2 large baking sheets with parchment paper.

Unwrap the dough and roll out between 2 sheets of parchment paper to about ½ inch/1 cm thick. Cut out 30 cookies with a 2-inch/5-cm flower cookie cutter and put them on the baking sheets, making sure they are spaced well apart.

Bake in the preheated oven for 10–12 minutes, or until firm. Remove from the oven but do not turn off the heat. Arrange the marshmallow pieces over the petals of the flowers, cutting them to fit if necessary. Return to the oven for 30–60 seconds, or until the marshmallows have softened.

Let cool on the baking sheets for 5–10 minutes, then transfer the cookies to wire racks to cool completely. Meanwhile, heat the jam in a small saucepan, strain into a bowl, and let cool. Pipe a small circle of jam in the center of each flower and top with the sugar sprinkles.

207 Chocolate daisies

Omit the cocoa from the dough mixture and use small chocolate disks instead of the marshmallows.

208 Chocolate florentines

Makes 20

3½ tbsp unsalted butter
4 tbsp superfine sugar
1 tbsp dark corn syrup
heaping ⅓ cup all-purpose flour
scant ¼ cup candied cherries, chopped
½ cup slivered almonds
heaping ¼ cup candied peel, chopped
6 oz/175 g semisweet chocolate, chopped

Preheat the oven to 350°F/180°C. Line 2 large baking sheets with parchment paper. Heat the butter, sugar, and corn syrup together in a saucepan over low heat until the butter is melted and the sugar is dissolved. Stir in the flour, cherries, almonds, and candied peel.

Make the florentines in batches. Place heaped teaspoons of the mixture on the baking sheets, spaced well apart, and flatten slightly with the back of a spoon. Bake in the preheated oven for 8–10 minutes, or until golden brown. Let cool on the baking sheets for 2–3 minutes, then transfer to a wire rack and leave until cold. Repeat until you have 20 florentines.

Place the chocolate in a heatproof bowl, set the bowl over a saucepan of gently simmering water, and heat until melted. Using a pastry brush, spread the chocolate over the bottom of each florentine and place chocolate-side up on a wire rack to cool and set.

209 Ginger florentines

Replace the candied cherries and candied peel with 3 oz/85 g chopped crystallized ginger.

210 Whirly pinwheel cookies

Makes 20

7 tbsp unsalted butter, softened
¼ cup superfine sugar
heaping ⅓ cup cornstarch
¾ cup all-purpose flour, plus 1 tbsp for dusting
1 large egg yolk
1 tbsp milk
2 tbsp unsweetened cocoa

Place the butter and sugar in a large bowl and beat together until light and fluffy. Sift in the cornstarch and the flour and mix well to combine, then add the egg yolk and a little milk to form a stiff dough.

Divide the dough mixture in half, add the cocoa to one half, and mix well together. Wrap both doughs in plastic wrap and chill in the refrigerator for 30 minutes.

Roll each piece of dough into a rectangle ⅛ inch/3 mm thick. Lay the chocolate dough on top of the white dough, then press together and trim the edges. Roll up lengthwise, wrap tightly in plastic wrap, and chill in the refrigerator for 30 minutes.

Preheat the oven to 350°F/180°C. Unwrap the dough and cut across the roll into 20 slices, then place the cookies on a nonstick baking sheet. Bake in the preheated oven for 15–20 minutes. Let cool on a wire rack.

211 Hazelnut whirly pinwheel cookies

Add 3 tablespoons of finely chopped hazelnuts to the chocolate dough and knead in before chilling the dough.

212 Good-for-you wholemeal cookies

Makes 36

2¼ cups whole wheat flour, plus extra for dusting
2 tbsp wheat germ
¼ tsp baking soda
½ tsp salt
¼ cup superfine sugar
9 tbsp unsalted butter, cubed
1 large egg, lightly beaten
1 tsp vanilla extract

Preheat the oven to 325°F/170°C. Place the flour, wheat germ, baking soda, salt, and sugar in a large bowl and stir together until combined. Add the butter and rub it in until the mixture resembles breadcrumbs.

Whisk the egg and vanilla extract in a separate bowl and add to the mixture, adding a little cold water if needed to bring the dough together. Roll the dough out on a floured board. Use a 2¾-inch/7-cm floured cookie cutter to cut out the cookies and place them on nonstick baking sheets, re-rolling the dough when necessary.

Bake in batches in the preheated oven for 20–25 minutes, or until dry but not brown. Let cool on a wire rack.

213 Fruit wholemeal cookies

Knead 2 tablespoons of chopped raisins or chopped candied peel and ½ teaspoon of apple pie spice into the dough before rolling out.

214 German lebkuchen

MAKES 60

3 eggs
1 cup superfine sugar
heaping ⅓ cup all-purpose flour
2 tsp unsweetened cocoa
1 tsp ground cinnamon
½ tsp ground cardamom
¼ tsp ground cloves
¼ tsp ground nutmeg
2 cups ground almonds
⅓ cup candied peel, finely chopped

FOR DECORATING
4 oz/115 g semisweet chocolate
4 oz/115 g white chocolate
sugar crystals

Preheat the oven to 350°F/180°C. Line several large baking sheets with parchment paper. Place the eggs and sugar in a heatproof bowl set over a saucepan of gently simmering water and whisk until thick and foamy. Remove the bowl from the pan and continue to whisk for 2 minutes.

Sift the flour, cocoa, cinnamon, cardamom, cloves, and nutmeg into the bowl and stir in with the ground almonds and candied peel. Drop heaping teaspoonfuls of the mixture onto the baking sheets, spreading them gently into smooth mounds.

Bake in the preheated oven for 15–20 minutes, or until light brown and slightly soft to the touch. Let cool on the baking sheets for 10 minutes, then transfer the cookies to wire racks to cool completely.

Place the semisweet and white chocolates in 2 separate heatproof bowls, set the bowls over 2 pans of gently simmering water, and heat until melted. Dip half the cookies in the melted semisweet chocolate and half in the white chocolate. Sprinkle with sugar crystals and let set.

215 With violets & ginger topping

Omit the sugar crystals and top each cookie with either a crystallized violet or a piece of crystallized ginger.

216 Pistachio & almond tuiles

MAKES 12

1 egg white
¼ cup superfine sugar
2 tbsp all-purpose flour
1 tbsp pistachios, finely chopped
heaping ¼ cup ground almonds
½ tsp almond extract
3 tbsp butter, melted and cooled

Preheat the oven to 325°F/160°C. Line 2 large baking sheets with parchment paper. Place the egg white and sugar in a large bowl and whisk together lightly, then stir in the flour, pistachios, ground almonds, almond extract, and butter to form a soft paste.

Place walnut-size spoonfuls of the mixture on the baking sheets and use the back of the spoon to spread as thinly as possible. Bake in the preheated oven for 10–15 minutes, or until pale golden.

Quickly lift each cookie with a spatula and place over the side of a rolling pin to shape into a curve. When set, transfer to a wire rack to cool completely.

217 Hazelnut & almond tuiles

Replace the pistachios with 1 tablespoon of finely chopped toasted hazelnuts.

218 Spanish almond cookies

MAKES 15

5½ tbsp unsalted butter, softened, plus extra for greasing
scant ½ cup blanched almonds
scant ½ cup superfine sugar
¼ tsp almond extract
scant ½ cup all-purpose flour
2 large egg whites

Preheat the oven to 350°F/180°C. Grease several large baking sheets with butter.

Finely chop the almonds. Place the butter and sugar in a large bowl and beat together until light and fluffy. Add the almond extract, flour, and chopped almonds and stir together until incorporated.

Place the egg whites in a large bowl and whisk until soft peaks form and they hold their shape but are not dry. Fold the egg whites into the almond mixture, then place 15 teaspoonfuls of the mixture onto the baking sheets, spaced well apart.

Bake in the preheated oven for 15–20 minutes, or until lightly golden brown around the edges. Let cool slightly on the baking sheets for 2–3 minutes, then transfer the cookies to a wire rack to cool completely.

219 Dutch macaroons

MAKES 12

2 large egg whites
pinch of salt
heaping 1 cup superfine sugar
2 cups ground almonds
8 oz/225 g semisweet chocolate, chopped

Preheat the oven to 350°F/180°C. Line 2 large baking sheets with rice paper. Whisk the egg whites in a large bowl until soft peaks form.

Add the salt and half the sugar and whisk again until stiff and glossy, then fold in the remaining sugar and the almonds.

Spoon the mixture into a pastry bag fitted with a ½-inch/1-cm tip and pipe six 3-inch/7.5-cm long fingers of the mixture onto each baking sheet. Bake in the preheated oven for 15–20 minutes, until golden. Cool on a wire rack, then tear off excess rice paper around the cookies.

Line a baking sheet with parchment paper. Place the chocolate in a heatproof bowl, set the bowl over a saucepan of gently simmering water, and heat until melted. Dip the bottom of each cookie into the chocolate, then place upside down on the baking sheet to set.

220 With white chocolate coating

Replace the semisweet chocolate with 8 oz/225 g white chocolate.

221 Tangy lemon jumbles

MAKES 40

1 tsp peanut oil, for greasing
7 tbsp unsalted butter, softened
scant ¾ cup superfine sugar
juice and finely grated rind of 1 lemon
1 large egg, lightly beaten
2½ cups all-purpose flour, plus extra for dusting
1 tsp baking powder
1 tbsp milk
¼ cup confectioners' sugar, for dusting

Preheat the oven to 375°F/170°C. Grease 2 large baking sheets with the oil. Place the butter, sugar, and lemon rind in a large bowl and beat together until light and fluffy. Alternately add the egg and 4 tablespoons of lemon juice to the mixture, beating well between each addition. Sift in the flour and baking powder and mix well, then add the milk to form a smooth dough.

Turn the dough onto a floured work surface and divide into 40 pieces. Roll each piece into a sausage, then form into an S-shape and place on the baking sheets. Bake in the preheated oven for 15–20 minutes. Let cool on a wire rack, then dust with sifted confectioners' sugar.

222 Orange jumbles

Replace the lemon juice and rind with orange juice and rind.

223 Jewish oznei haman

MAKES 20

8 tbsp unsalted butter, softened
½ cup superfine sugar
½ tsp vanilla extract
3 large egg yolks
2¼ cups all-purpose flour, plus extra for dusting
1 large egg, lightly beaten, for brushing

FILLING
1½ tsp poppy seeds
1 tbsp honey
2 tbsp superfine sugar
finely grated rind of 1 lemon
1 tbsp lemon juice
4 tbsp water
scant ½ cup ground almonds
1 large egg, lightly beaten
¼ cup raisins

Place the butter and sugar in a large bowl and beat together until light and fluffy. Whisk the vanilla extract and egg yolks together in a separate bowl, then add to the butter mixture and mix well.

Sift in the flour and mix to a smooth dough. Wrap in plastic wrap and chill in the refrigerator for 30 minutes.

For the filling, place the poppy seeds, honey, sugar, lemon rind and juice, and the water in a saucepan and stir over medium heat until just boiling. Remove from the heat and beat in the almonds, egg, and raisins. Let cool.

Preheat the oven to 350°F/180°C. Line 2 large baking sheets with parchment paper. Roll the dough out on a floured work surface to ¼ inch/5 mm thick. Using a 3¼-inch/8-cm floured cookie cutter, cut out 20 cookies. Re-roll any trimmings. Spoon the filling into the middle of each dough piece and brush the edges with the egg. Bring them to the center to form a tricorn shape, then press the edges together. Place 10 cookies on each baking sheet, spaced well apart and brush with more egg. Bake in the preheated oven for 25–30 minutes, or until golden. Let cool on a wire rack.

224 With fruit filling

Replace the poppy seed filling with ½ cup fruit jam or applesauce.

225 Hearts & diamonds

MAKES ABOUT 30

1 cup butter, softened
¾ cup superfine sugar
1 egg yolk, lightly beaten
2 tsp vanilla extract
2 cups all-purpose flour
pinch of salt
heaping ⅓ cup white chocolate chips

FILLING
5–6 tbsp cranberry jam
½ tsp lemon juice
heaping ⅓ cup curd cheese
2 tbsp heavy cream
2 tsp confectioners' sugar
few drops of vanilla extract

Place the butter and sugar in a bowl and beat together until light and fluffy, then beat in the egg yolk and vanilla extract.

Sift together the flour and salt into the mixture, add the chocolate chips, and stir until combined. Halve the dough, shape into balls, wrap in plastic wrap, and chill for 30–60 minutes.

Preheat the oven to 375°F/190°C. Line 2 large baking sheets with parchment paper. Unwrap the dough and roll out between 2 sheets of parchment paper. Cut out cookies with a 2½-inch/6-cm square, fluted cutter and place half of them on a baking sheet, spaced well apart.

Using small heart- and diamond-shaped cutters, cut out the centers of the remaining cookies and remove them. Place the cookies on the other baking sheet, spaced well apart. Bake in the preheated oven for 10–15 minutes. Let cool for 5–10 minutes, then transfer the cookies to wire racks to cool completely.

To make the jam filling, place the jelly and lemon juice into a small saucepan and heat gently until the mixture is runny, then bring to a boil and boil for 3 minutes. Let cool.

Beat the curd cheese, cream, sifted confectioners' sugar, and vanilla extract together in a bowl until combined. Spread the cream mixture over the whole cookies, add a little of the jam, and top with the cut-out cookies.

226 Lemon hearts & diamonds

Replace the jam in the filling with 1 teaspoon of finely grated lemon rind and ½ teaspoon of lemon oil.

227 Clubs & spades

MAKES ABOUT 15

1 cup butter, softened
¾ cup superfine sugar
1 egg yolk, lightly beaten
2 tsp vanilla extract
2 cups all-purpose flour
pinch of salt
heaping ½ cup semisweet chocolate chips

FILLING
4 tbsp butter, softened
1 tsp dark corn syrup
¾ cup confectioners' sugar
1 tbsp unsweetened cocoa

Place the butter and sugar in a large bowl and beat together until light and fluffy, then beat in the egg yolk and vanilla extract. Sift together the flour and salt into the mixture, add the chocolate chips, and stir until thoroughly combined. Halve the dough, shape into balls, wrap in plastic wrap, and chill in the refrigerator for 30–60 minutes.

Preheat the oven to 375°F/190°C. Line 2 large baking sheets with parchment paper. Unwrap the dough and roll out between 2 sheets of parchment paper. Cut out cookies with a 2½-inch/6-cm square, fluted cutter and put half of them on a baking sheet, spaced well apart. Using small club- and spade-shaped cutters, cut out the centers of the remaining cookies and remove them. Place the cookies on the other baking sheet, spaced well apart.

Bake in the preheated oven for 10–15 minutes, or until light golden brown. Let cool on the baking sheets for 5–10 minutes, then transfer the cookies to wire racks to cool completely.

For the filling, place the butter and syrup in a bowl and sift in the confectioners' sugar and cocoa. Beat until smooth. Spread the chocolate cream over the whole cookies and top with the cut-out cookies.

228 With jam filling

Replace the filling with ½ cup seedless raspberry jam.

229 Dutch speculaas

MAKES 20

9 tbsp unsalted butter, softened
2/3 cup light brown sugar
1 large egg, lightly beaten
pinch of salt
1 3/4 cups all-purpose flour, plus extra for dusting
1 tsp ground cinnamon
1/2 tsp ground nutmeg
1/4 tsp ground cloves
1/4 tsp ground cardamom
1/4 tsp ground ginger
1 tsp baking powder
1 cup slivered almonds

Place the butter and sugar in a large bowl and beat together until light and fluffy, then add the egg and salt and mix to combine. Sift in the flour, spices, and baking powder and mix to form a dough. Wrap the dough in plastic wrap and chill for 6 hours, or overnight.

Preheat the oven to 325°F/160°C. Remove the dough from the refrigerator and let it reach room temperature, then roll out on a floured work surface. Use a floured cookie cutter to cut out the speculaas (or use a speculaas mold), then scatter over the almonds and press into the cookies. Place on 2 large nonstick baking sheets.

Bake in the preheated oven for 18–20 minutes, or until golden brown. Let cool on the baking sheet.

230 Iced speculaas

Bake the cookies without the slivered almonds and, when cool, spread the cookies with icing made by sifting 1 1/3 cups confectioners' sugar and 1 teaspoon of apple pie spice into a bowl, then adding 1 tablespoon of warm water and mixing until smooth. Let set.

231 Melting moments

MAKES 32

1 1/2 cups unsalted butter, softened
3/4 cup confectioners' sugar
1/2 tsp vanilla extract
2 1/4 cups all-purpose flour
heaping 1/3 cup cornstarch

Preheat the oven to 350°F/180°C. Line 2 large baking sheets with parchment paper. Place the butter and sugar in a large bowl and beat together until light and fluffy, then beat in the vanilla extract. Sift over the flour and cornstarch and mix thoroughly.

Spoon the mixture into a pastry bag fitted with a large star tip and pipe 32 cookies onto each baking sheet, spaced well apart.

Bake in the preheated oven for 15–20 minutes, or until golden brown. Let cool on the baking sheet.

232 With mascarpone cheese filling

Make a double quantity of cookies and use scant 1 cup of mascarpone cheese beaten with 2 tablespoons of confectioners' sugar to sandwich the cookies together. Makes 32.

233 Bourbon balls

MAKES 60

8 oz/225 g vanilla wafers
1 cup pecans, chopped
¼ cup unsweetened cocoa
1⅓ cups confectioners' sugar
¼ cup light corn (or use dark corn) syrup
¼ cup bourbon

Place the vanilla wafers in a food processor and pulse to form rough crumbs, then add the nuts and pulse again until they are finely chopped. Tip into a large bowl and sift in half the cocoa and scant 1 cup confectioners' sugar, then stir together. Gradually add the corn syrup and bourbon and mix together thoroughly.

Sift the remaining sugar and cocoa onto a large plate. Shape the mixture into ¾-inch/2-cm balls and roll in the sugar and cocoa mixture to coat. Place the balls in layers between parchment paper in a sealed container and chill in the refrigerator for up to 3 days before serving.

234 Chocolate liqueur balls

Replace the bourbon with chocolate cream liqueur.

235 Thumbprint cookies

MAKES 36

8 tbsp unsalted butter, softened
⅔ cup superfine sugar
1 large egg, separated
1 tsp vanilla extract
1¼ cups all-purpose flour
pinch of salt
heaping ¼ cup ground almonds
heaping ¼ cup seedless raspberry jam

Preheat the oven to 350°F/180°C. Line 2 large baking sheets with parchment paper. Place the butter and ½ cup of the sugar in a large bowl and beat together until light and fluffy. Add the egg yolk and vanilla extract and beat well to combine. Sift in the flour and salt and mix well.

Mix the remaining sugar and the ground almonds together and spread out on a plate. Lightly whisk the egg white in a separate bowl. Roll walnut-size pieces of dough into balls, then dip each ball into the egg white and roll in the almond sugar. Place the balls on the baking sheets and make a deep indentation in each cookie.

Bake in the preheated oven for 10 minutes. Remove from the oven, press down again on each indentation, and fill it with jam. Bake for an additional 10–12 minutes, or until the cookies are golden brown, turning the baking sheets once. Let cool on a wire rack.

236 With lemon curd filling

Replace the raspberry jam with lemon curd.

237 Chocolate buttons

Makes about 30

2 envelopes instant chocolate or fudge chocolate drink
1 tbsp hot water
1 cup butter, softened
¾ cup superfine sugar, plus extra for sprinkling
1 egg yolk, lightly beaten
2 cups all-purpose flour
pinch of salt

Empty the chocolate drink envelopes into a bowl and stir in the hot water to make a paste. Place the butter and sugar in a large bowl and beat together until light and fluffy, then beat in the egg yolk and chocolate paste. Sift the flour and salt into the mixture and stir until thoroughly combined. Halve the dough, shape into rounds, wrap in plastic wrap, and chill in the refrigerator for 30–60 minutes.

Preheat the oven to 375°F/190°C. Line 2 large baking sheets with parchment paper. Unwrap the dough and roll out between 2 sheets of parchment paper to ⅛ inch/3 mm thick. Cut out rounds with a plain 2-inch/5-cm cutter. Using a 1¼-inch/3-cm cap from a soda or mineral water bottle, make an indentation in the center of each button. Using a wooden toothpick, make 4 holes in the center of each button, then put them on the baking sheets, spaced well apart, and sprinkle with superfine sugar. Bake in the preheated oven for 10–15 minutes, or until firm. Let cool on the baking sheets for 5–10 minutes, then transfer to wire racks to cool completely.

238 Spanish panellets

Makes 32

1 small potato, peeled
2½ cups granulated sugar
1 cup water
¼ tsp lemon juice
finely grated rind of 1 lemon
5 cups ground almonds
1 tsp peanut oil, for greasing
1⅓ cups pine nuts
heaping 1¼ cup candied fruit, chopped

Cut the potato in half. Place in a saucepan of boiling water and cook until tender. Drain and mash well with a fork, then cool.

Place the sugar and water in a medium pan and heat gently, stirring until the sugar has dissolved. Increase the heat and bring to a boil, then add the lemon juice and simmer until thick. Remove the pan from the heat and beat in the potato, lemon rind, and ground almonds until the mixture is thick. Let cool, then cover with plastic wrap and chill in the refrigerator overnight.

Preheat the oven to 375°F/190°C/. Grease 2 large baking sheets with the oil. Roll teaspoons of dough into balls, then roll two thirds of the balls in the pine nuts and top the remaining ones with candied fruit pieces. Bake in the preheated oven for 4 minutes, or until just golden brown. Let cool on a wire rack.

239 Cocoa, coffee & coconut panellets

Omit the pine nuts and candied fruit pieces. Divide the dough into 3 portions: Knead in 1 teaspoon of cocoa to one portion and form into balls, use 1 teaspoon of espresso powder for a coffee flavor, and roll the last portion in dry unsweetened coconut before baking.

240 Italian ricciaretti

MAKES 12

heaping ¾ cup blanched almonds
2 tbsp candied orange peel
1½ tbsp all-purpose flour
⅓ cup superfine sugar
4½ tsp water
scant 1 cup confectioners' sugar, plus extra for dusting
heaping ⅓ cup cornstarch
1 large egg white
¾ tsp baking powder

Place the almonds, candied orange peel, and flour in a food processor and pulse to form a paste.

Place the superfine sugar and water in a saucepan and bring to a boil, then reduce the heat and simmer for 2–3 minutes, or until reduced to a thick syrup. Remove from the heat, add the almond paste, and mix together. Transfer to a bowl and let cool for about 1 hour.

Preheat the oven to 275°F/140°C. Line a large baking sheet with rice paper. Set aside 1 teaspoon of the confectioners' sugar and sift the remaining confectioners' sugar and cornstarch onto a work surface.

Place the egg white and reserved confectioners' sugar in a large bowl and whisk until stiff. Add the baking powder to the almond paste, then fold in the whisked egg white until combined. Turn the mixture onto the work surface and roll into a log shape about 2½ inches/6 cm thick, then flatten until it is 1½ inches/4 cm thick. Cut into ½-inch/1-cm slices, place on the baking sheet, and form into a diamond shape.

Bake in the preheated oven for about 30 minutes, or until risen but still soft in the center. Let cool on the baking sheet for 2–3 minutes, then transfer to a wire rack and let cool completely. Serve dusted with sifted confectioners' sugar.

241 Langues de chat

MAKES 28

4 tbsp butter, plus extra for greasing
¼ cup superfine sugar
1 egg, lightly beaten
heaping ⅓ cup self-rising flour

Preheat the oven to 425°F/220°C/. Lightly grease 2 large baking sheets.

Place the butter and sugar in a large bowl and beat together until light and fluffy. Gradually beat in the egg, then fold in the flour.

Spoon the cookie batter into a pastry bag fitted with an ½-inch/1-cm plain tip. Pipe 2-inch/5-cm cookies on the baking sheet, spacing them well apart. Bake for 5 minutes, or until just golden around the edges.

Let stand for 1 minute to firm slightly, then transfer to a wire rack to cool completely.

242 Mocha-filled langues de chat

Make a double quantity of cookies. Beat together 4 tablespoons of butter and ½ cup confectioner's sugar until pale and fluffy, then beat in 1 tablespoon of strong black coffee to make a coffee cream. Use to sandwich the cookies together. Melt 3 oz/85 g chocolate in bowl over a pan of gently simmering water, then let cool slightly. Dip half of each cookie sandwich in the chocolate to coat. Place on baking sheets lined with parchment paper and let set.

243 Chocolate orange langues de chat

Add the grated rind of 1 orange to the cookie batter. Line 2 large baking sheets with parchment paper. Melt 4 oz/115 g semisweet chocolate in a bowl over a pan of gently simmering water, then let cool slightly. Dip each cookie into the chocolate so that half the cookie is covered, letting the excess run back into the bowl. Place on the baking sheets and let set.

244 Chocolate-tipped finger rolls

MAKES 35

2¼ cups confectioners' sugar
scant 1 cup all-purpose flour
pinch of salt
6 large egg whites
1 tbsp heavy cream
1 tsp vanilla extract
9 tbsp unsalted butter, melted and cooled
4½ oz/125 g semisweet chocolate, chopped

Sift the confectioners' sugar, flour, and salt into a large bowl, then stir and make a well in the middle. Lightly whisk the egg whites in a separate bowl, add the cream, vanilla extract, and butter and mix, then pour into the flour and mix until smooth. Cover and chill overnight.

Preheat the oven to 400°F/200°C. Have a wooden spoon and wire rack ready. Spoon 4 tablespoons of the batter onto a large, nonstick baking sheet. Using the back of a spoon, spread thinly into ovals 5 inches/13 cm long, spaced well apart. Bake in the preheated oven for 5–6 minutes, or until just browning at the edges. Prepare the second baking sheet while the first batch is cooking.

Using a spatula, take a cookie and roll around the handle of the wooden spoon to make a cigarette shape. Transfer to the wire rack to cool and repeat with the remaining cookies. Repeat baking and rolling the cookies until all the batter is used.

When the finger rolls are cold, place the chocolate in a heatproof bowl, set the bowl over a saucepan of gently simmering water, and heat until melted. Dip one end of each roll into the chocolate, then place on a wire rack to set, leaving the chocolate section standing off the edge.

245 With white chocolate coating

Once the semisweet chocolate is set, put 4½ oz/125 g white chocolate in a heatproof bowl, set the bowl over a pan of simmering water, and heat until melted. Dip the other end of the cookies in the white chocolate and let set.

246 Chinese fortune cookies

MAKES 12

1–2 tbsp peanut oil, for greasing
2 large egg whites
½ tsp vanilla extract
3 tbsp vegetable oil
¾ cup all-purpose flour
1½ tsp cornstarch
pinch of salt
¾ cup superfine sugar
3 tsp water

Write fortune messages on thin strips of paper. Preheat the oven to 350°F/180°C and grease 2 large baking sheets with a little peanut oil (do not preheat). Place the egg whites, vanilla extract, and vegetable oil in a large bowl then, using an electric mixer, beat together for 1 minute until frothy but not stiff.

Sift the flour, cornstarch, salt, and sugar into a large bowl, stir in the water, and mix. Add the egg white mixture and whisk until smooth. Make the cookies in batches of two by spooning 1 scant tablespoon of batter onto each half of the baking sheet and tilting the baking sheet until the batter circles measure 3 inches/8 cm. Bake for 7–8 minutes, until the edges are beginning to brown.

Work quickly to shape the cookies while still hot. Remove a cookie from the baking sheet with a spatula and fold the cookie in half to form a semicircle. Pinch together at the top and fold the cookie over the rim of a cup. Then insert an index finger into each open end. Bring your thumbs together to press into the middle to form the shape of the fortune cookie. Thread through the strip of paper and place on paper towels to cool. Repeat the process until all the batter is used.

247 Neapolitan cookies

MAKES ABOUT 20

1 cup butter, softened
¾ cup superfine sugar
1 egg yolk, lightly beaten
1 tsp vanilla extract
2¼ cups all-purpose flour
1 tbsp unsweetened cocoa
½ tsp almond extract
few drops of green food coloring
1 egg white, lightly beaten
salt

Place the butter and sugar in a large bowl and beat together until light and fluffy, then beat in the egg yolk. Divide the mixture among 3 bowls.

Beat the vanilla extract into the first bowl. Sift together ¾ cup of the flour and a pinch of salt into the mixture and stir until combined. Shape into a ball, wrap in plastic wrap, and chill in the refrigerator for 30–60 minutes. Sift together ¾ cup of the flour, the cocoa, and a pinch of salt into the second bowl and stir until combined. Shape into a ball, wrap in plastic wrap, and chill in the refrigerator.

Beat the almond extract into the third bowl. Sift together the remaining flour and a pinch of salt into the bowl and stir until combined. Mix in a few drops of green food coloring, then form into a ball, wrap in plastic wrap, and chill in the refrigerator.

Preheat the oven to 375°F/190°C. Line 2 large baking sheets with parchment paper. Roll out each piece of dough between 2 sheets of parchment paper to rectangles. Brush the top of the vanilla dough with a little beaten egg white and place the chocolate rectangle on top. Brush this with a little beaten egg white and place the almond rectangle on top. Using a sharp knife, cut into ¼-inch/5-mm thick slices, then cut each slice in half. Place on the baking sheets and bake in the preheated oven for 10–12 minutes. Let cool for 5–10 minutes, then transfer the cookies to wire racks to cool completely.

248 Chocolate-coated Neapolitan cookies

Put 5½ oz/150 g semisweet chocolate in a heatproof bowl, set the bowl over a saucepan of gently simmering water, and heat until melted. Dip each end of the cooled cookies in the chocolate and let set on parchment paper.

249 White chocolate cookies

MAKES 24

8 tbsp butter, softened, plus extra for greasing
heaping ½ cup light brown sugar
1 egg, lightly beaten
heaping 1¾ cups self-rising flour
pinch of salt
4½ oz/125 g white chocolate, chopped
⅓ cup chopped Brazil nuts

Preheat the oven to 375°F/190°C. Lightly grease several large baking sheets. Place the butter and sugar in a large bowl and beat together until light and fluffy. Gradually add the egg, beating well after each addition. Sift the flour and salt into the creamed mixture and blend well. Stir in the chocolate chunks and chopped nuts.

Place heaping teaspoonfuls of the batter on the baking sheets, putting no more than 6 on each sheet because the cookies will spread during cooking. Bake in the preheated oven for 10–12 minutes, or until just golden brown. Transfer the cookies to wire racks to cool completely.

250 Cardamom & white chocolate cookies

Omit the nuts and add 1 teaspoon of ground cardamom to the cookie batter.

251 Midnight cookies

Makes 25

9 tbsp butter, softened
1 cup superfine sugar
1 egg, lightly beaten
½ tsp vanilla extract
1 cup all-purpose flour
⅓ cup unsweetened cocoa
½ tsp baking soda

Preheat the oven to 350°F/180°C. Line several large baking sheets with parchment paper.

Place the butter and sugar in a large bowl and beat together until light and fluffy. Add the egg and vanilla extract and mix until smooth. Sift in the flour, cocoa, and baking soda and beat until well mixed.

With dampened hands, roll walnut-size pieces of the dough into smooth balls. Place on the baking sheets, spaced well apart.

Bake in the preheated oven for 10–12 minutes, or until set. Let cool on the baking sheets for 5 minutes, then transfer the cookies to wire racks to cool completely before serving.

252 With chocolate topping

As the cookies cool, place 2¾ oz/75 g semisweet chocolate in a heatproof bowl, set the bowl over a saucepan of gently simmering water, and heat until melted. Remove from the heat and stir until smooth. Spoon the chocolate into a pastry bag fitted with a writing tip and drizzle the chocolate over the cookies in a decorative zigzag pattern, then let set.

253 Sugar-coated midnight cookies

Sprinkle ¼ cup granulated sugar on a large plate. Roll each ball of dough in the sugar to coat before placing on the baking sheets.

254 Refrigerator cookies

Makes About 55

3½ cups all-purpose flour, plus extra for dusting
2 tsp baking powder
1 cup butter, cut into cubes, plus extra for greasing
1¼ cups superfine sugar
2 large eggs, lightly beaten
2 tsp vanilla extract

Sift the flour and baking powder into a large bowl. Add the butter and rub it in with your fingertips until the mixture resembles fine breadcrumbs. Stir the sugar into the mixture, add the eggs and vanilla extract, and mix together to form a soft dough.

Turn the mixture onto a lightly floured work surface and divide the dough in half. Shape each piece of dough into a log shape about 2½ inches/6 cm thick. Wrap each log in parchment paper and then in foil and chill in the refrigerator for at least 8 hours, or until required.

Preheat the oven to 375°F/190°C. Grease several large baking sheets. Slice the dough into as many ⅜-inch/8-mm slices as required and place on the baking sheets, spaced well apart. Return any remaining dough to the refrigerator for up to 1 week, or to the freezer until required. Bake in the preheated oven for 10–15 minutes, or until golden brown. Leave on the baking sheet to cool slightly for 2–3 minutes, then transfer the cookies to a wire rack to cool completely.

255 Cherry refrigerator cookies

Finely chop ⅔ cup candied cherries and add to the mixture with the superfine sugar.

256 Chocolate refrigerator cookies

Finely grate 3½ oz/100 g semisweet chocolate and add to the mixture with the superfine sugar.

257 Coconut refrigerator cookies

Add heaping 1 cup dry unsweetened coconut with the superfine sugar.

258 Dried fruit refrigerator cookies

Finely chop heaping ½ cup golden raisins, raisins, or cranberries and add to the mixture with the superfine sugar.

259 Ginger refrigerator cookies

Omit the vanilla extract and sift 3 teaspoons of ground ginger into the mixture with the flour.

260 Lemon refrigerator cookies

Omit the vanilla extract and finely grate the rind of 2 lemons into the mixture with the superfine sugar.

261 Orange refrigerator cookies

Omit the vanilla extract and finely grate the rind of 2 oranges into the mixture with the superfine sugar.

262 Spicy refrigerator cookies

Omit the vanilla extract and sift 4 teaspoons of apple pie spice into the mixture with the flour.

263 Walnut refrigerator cookies

Chop 1 cup walnut halves and add to the mixture with the superfine sugar.

264 Double chocolate cookies

MAKES ABOUT 30

1 cup butter, softened
¾ cup superfine sugar
1 egg yolk, lightly beaten
2 tsp vanilla extract
1¾ cups all-purpose flour
¼ cup unsweetened cocoa
pinch of salt
12 oz/350 g semisweet chocolate, chopped
⅓ cup dried cherries

Preheat the oven to 375°F/190°C. Line 2 large baking sheets with parchment paper. Place the butter and sugar in a large bowl and beat together until light and fluffy, then beat in the egg yolk and vanilla extract. Sift together the flour, cocoa, and salt into the mixture, add the chopped chocolate and dried cherries, and stir until combined.

Scoop up tablespoons of the dough and shape into balls. Place them on the baking sheets, spaced well apart, and flatten slightly.

Bake in the preheated oven for 12–15 minutes. Let cool on the baking sheets for 5–10 minutes, then transfer the cookies to wire racks to cool completely.

265 Triple chocolate cookies

Replace the dried cherries with scant ½ cup white chocolate chips.

266 Simple cookies

MAKES 25

1¼ cups all-purpose flour, plus extra for dusting
¼ tsp ground nutmeg
8 tbsp unsalted butter, softened
¼ cup superfine sugar

Preheat the oven to 350°F/180°C. Sift the flour and nutmeg into a large bowl. Add the butter and rub it into the mixture until it resembles breadcrumbs. Add the sugar and knead together to form a stiff dough. Roll the dough out on a lightly floured work surface to about ¼ inch/5 mm thick. Using a 2¾-inch/7-cm round cookie cutter dipped in flour, cut out 25 cookies. Re-roll any trimmings. Place the cookies on 2 large nonstick baking sheets.

Bake in the preheated oven for 8–10 minutes, or until pale golden. Transfer to a wire rack and let cool completely.

267 Spiced cookies

Add ¼ teaspoon of ground cinnamon, ¼ teaspoon of apple pie spice, and ¼ teaspoon of ground cardamom to the flour and nutmeg.

268 Chocolate fudge squares

MAKES ABOUT 30

1 cup butter, softened
¾ cup superfine sugar
1 egg yolk, lightly beaten
2 tsp vanilla extract
1⅔ cups all-purpose flour
½ cup unsweetened cocoa
pinch of salt

TOPPING
8 chocolate-coated fudge fingers, broken into pieces
4 tbsp heavy cream

Place the butter and sugar in a large bowl and beat together until light and fluffy, then beat in the egg yolk and vanilla.

Sift the flour, cocoa, and salt into the mixture and stir until combined. Halve the dough, shape into balls, wrap in plastic wrap, and chill in the refrigerator for 30–60 minutes.

Preheat the oven to 375°F/190°C. Line 2 large baking sheets with parchment paper.

Unwrap the dough and roll out between 2 sheets of parchment paper to about ⅛ inch/3 mm thick. Cut out cookies with a 2½-inch/6-cm square cutter and place them on the baking sheets, spaced well apart. Bake in the preheated oven for 10–15 minutes or until golden brown. Let cool on the baking sheets for 5–10 minutes, then transfer them to wire racks to cool completely.

To make the chocolate fudge topping, place the fudge fingers into a heatproof bowl, set the bowl over a saucepan of gently simmering water, and heat until melted. Remove the bowl from the heat and gradually whisk in the cream. Let cool, then chill until spreadable. Spread the cold fudge topping over the cookies before serving.

269 Fudge fingers

Cut the dough into long fingers rather than squares and spread with the fudge topping.

270 Apple spice cookies

MAKES ABOUT 15

1 cup butter, softened
¾ cup superfine sugar
1 egg yolk, lightly beaten
2 tsp apple juice
2 cups all-purpose flour
½ tsp ground cinnamon
½ tsp apple pie spice
pinch of salt
heaping ⅓ cup plumped dried apple, finely chopped

FILLING
1 tbsp superfine sugar
1 tbsp vanilla instant pudding mix
½ cup milk
5 tbsp applesauce

Place the butter and sugar in a large bowl and beat together until light and fluffy, then beat in the egg yolk and apple juice. Sift together the flour, cinnamon, apple pie spice, and salt into the mixture, add the apple, and stir until combined. Halve the dough, shape into balls, wrap in plastic wrap, and chill for 30–60 minutes.

Preheat the oven to 375°F/190°C. Line 2 large baking sheets with parchment paper. Unwrap the dough and roll out between 2 sheets of parchment paper. Cut out cookies with a 2-inch/5-cm square cutter and place them on the baking sheets, spaced well apart. Bake in the preheated oven for 10–15 minutes, or until light golden brown. Let cool for 5–10 minutes, then transfer to wire racks to cool completely.

To make the apple filling, mix the sugar, pudding mix, and milk together in a saucepan. Bring to a boil, stirring continuously and cook until thickened. Remove the pan from the heat and stir in the applesauce. Cover the surface with plastic wrap and let cool.

Spread the filling over half the cookies and top with the remainder.

271 Chocolate-dipped apple spice cookies

Omit the apple filling and place 5½ oz/150 g white chocolate in a heatproof bowl, set the bowl over a saucepan of gently simmering water, and heat until melted. Dip half of each cookie and let set on parchment paper. Makes about 30.

272 Blueberry & cranberry cinnamon cookies

MAKES ABOUT 30

1 cup butter, softened
¾ cup superfine sugar
1 egg yolk, lightly beaten
2 tsp vanilla extract
2 cups all-purpose flour
1 tsp ground cinnamon
pinch of salt
½ cup dried blueberries
½ cup dried cranberries
½ cup pine nuts, chopped

Preheat the oven to 375°F/190°C. Line 2 large baking sheets with parchment paper. Place the butter and sugar in a large bowl and beat together until light and fluffy, then beat in the egg yolk and vanilla extract. Sift together the flour, cinnamon, and salt into the mixture. Add the blueberries and cranberries and stir until thoroughly combined.

Spread out the pine nuts in a shallow dish. Scoop up tablespoons of the mixture and roll them into balls. Roll the balls in the pine nuts to coat, then place on the baking sheets, spaced well apart, and flatten slightly. Bake in the preheated oven for 10–15 minutes.

Let cool on the baking sheets for 5–10 minutes, then transfer the cookies to wire racks to cool completely.

273 Macadamia nut cinnamon cookies

Replace the pine nuts with heaping ½ cup chopped macadamia nuts.

274 Blueberry orange cookies

MAKES ABOUT 30

1 cup butter, softened
¾ cup superfine sugar
1 egg yolk, lightly beaten
1 tsp orange extract
2 cups all-purpose flour
pinch of salt
1 cup dried blueberries

TOPPING
scant ½ cup cream cheese
grated rind of 1 orange
¼ cup macadamia nuts, finely chopped

Place the butter and sugar in a large bowl and beat together until light and fluffy, then beat in the egg yolk and orange extract. Sift together the flour and salt into the mixture, add the blueberries, and stir until thoroughly combined. Shape the dough into a log, wrap in plastic wrap, and chill in the refrigerator for 30–60 minutes.

Preheat the oven to 375°F/190°C. Line 2 large baking sheets with parchment paper. Unwrap the log, then cut into ¼-inch/5-mm slices with a sharp serrated knife and place them on the baking sheets, spaced well apart. Bake in the preheated oven for 10–15 minutes, or until golden brown. Let cool on the baking sheets for 5–10 minutes, then transfer the cookies to wire racks to cool completely.

Just before serving, beat the cream cheese in a bowl and stir in the orange rind. Spread the mixture over the cookies and sprinkle with the nuts.

275 Caribbean cookies

MAKES ABOUT 30

1 cup butter, softened	*2 cups all-purpose flour*
¾ cup superfine sugar	*pinch of salt*
1 egg yolk, lightly beaten	*heaping 1 cup dry unsweetened coconut*
2 tsp rum or rum flavoring	*4 tbsp lime marmalade*

Preheat the oven to 375°F/190°C. Line 2 large baking sheets with parchment paper. Place the butter and sugar in a large bowl and beat together until light and fluffy, then beat in the egg yolk and rum. Sift together the flour and salt into the mixture, add the coconut, and stir until combined.

Scoop up tablespoons of the dough and place them on the baking sheets, spaced well apart. Make a hollow in the center of each with the dampened handle of a spoon and fill the hollows with the marmalade.

Bake in the preheated oven for 10–15 minutes, or until light golden brown. Let cool on the baking sheets for 5–10 minutes, then transfer the cookies to wire racks to cool completely.

276 Rainbow cookies

Use a variety of fillings for the cookies—try lime, lemon, or passion fruit curd, and seedless strawberry jam.

277 Chewy candied fruit cookies

MAKES ABOUT 30

1 cup butter, softened	*TOPPING*
¾ cup superfine sugar	*4 tbsp maple syrup*
1 egg yolk, lightly beaten	*4 tbsp butter*
2 tsp vanilla extract	*¼ cup superfine sugar*
2 cups all-purpose flour	*scant ½ cup plumped dried peaches, chopped*
pinch of salt	*⅓ cup candied cherries, chopped*
	½ cup chopped mixed peel
	½ cup macadamia nuts, chopped
	2 tbsp all-purpose flour

Place the butter and sugar in a large bowl and beat together until light and fluffy, then beat in the egg yolk and vanilla extract. Sift together the flour and salt into the mixture and stir until thoroughly combined. Halve the dough, shape into balls, wrap in plastic wrap, and chill in the refrigerator for 30–60 minutes.

Preheat the oven to 375°F/190°C. Line 2 large baking sheets with parchment paper. Unwrap the dough and roll out between 2 sheets of parchment paper. Cut out rounds with a 2½-inch/6-cm plain round cutter and place them on the baking sheets, spaced well apart.

To make the topping, place the maple syrup, butter, and sugar into a saucepan and melt over low heat, stirring occasionally. Meanwhile, place the fruit, mixed peel, nuts, and flour into a bowl and mix well. When the syrup mixture is combined, stir it into the fruit mixture and divide the topping among the cookies, gently spreading it out to the edges.

Bake in the preheated oven for 10–15 minutes, until firm. Let cool for 5–10 minutes, then transfer to wire racks to cool completely.

278 With hazelnut topping

Replace the macadamia nuts in the topping with hazelnuts.

279 Coconut & cranberry cookies

MAKES ABOUT 30

1 cup butter, softened
¾ cup superfine sugar
1 egg yolk, lightly beaten
2 tsp vanilla extract
2 cups all-purpose flour
pinch of salt
scant ½ cup dry unsweetened coconut
½ cup dried cranberries

Preheat the oven to 375°F/190°C. Line 2 large baking sheets with parchment paper. Place the butter and sugar in a large bowl and beat together until light and fluffy, then beat in the egg yolk and vanilla extract. Sift together the flour and salt into the mixture, add the coconut and cranberries, and stir until combined. Scoop up tablespoons of the dough and place in mounds on the baking sheets, spaced well apart.

Bake in the preheated oven for 12–15 minutes, or until golden brown. Let cool on the baking sheets for 5–10 minutes, then transfer the cookies to wire racks to cool completely.

280 Coconut & papaya cookies

Replace the cranberries with chopped dried papaya.

281 Chocolate, date & pecan pinwheels

MAKES ABOUT 30

1 cup butter, softened
1 cup superfine sugar
1 egg yolk, lightly beaten
1⅔ cups all-purpose flour
½ cup unsweetened cocoa
pinch of salt
⅔ cup pecans, finely ground
1⅔ cups dried dates, coarsely chopped
finely grated rind of 1 orange
¾ cup orange flower water

Place the butter and ¾ cup of the sugar in a large bowl and beat together until light and fluffy, then beat in the egg yolk. Sift together the flour, cocoa, and salt into the mixture, add the nuts, and stir until combined. Halve the dough, shape into balls, wrap in plastic wrap, and chill in the refrigerator for 30–60 minutes.

Meanwhile, place the dates, orange rind, orange flower water, and remaining sugar into a saucepan and cook over low heat, stirring, until the sugar has dissolved. Bring to a boil, then reduce the heat and simmer, for 5 minutes. Pour the mixture into a bowl, cool, then chill.

Unwrap the dough and roll out between 2 pieces of parchment paper to rectangles ¼ inch/5 mm thick. Spread the filling over the rectangles and roll up like a jelly roll. Wrap in the paper and chill in a refrigerator for 30 minutes.

Preheat the oven to 375°F/190°C. Line 2 large baking sheets with parchment paper. Unwrap the rolls, cut into ½-inch/1-cm slices and place them on the baking sheets.

Bake in the preheated oven for 15–20 minutes, or until golden brown. Let cool on the baking sheets for 5–10 minutes, then transfer the cookies to wire racks to cool completely.

282 Fig & walnut pinwheels

Replace the dates and nuts with 1 cup chopped dried figs and ⅔ cup chopped walnuts. Replace the orange flower water and orange rind with 2 tablespoons of brandy and 1 teaspoon of vanilla extract.

283 Date & lemon spirals

MAKES ABOUT 30

1 cup butter, softened
1 cup superfine sugar
1 egg yolk, lightly beaten
1 tsp lemon extract
2 cups all-purpose flour
pinch of salt
1⅔ cups dried dates, pitted and finely chopped
2 tbsp lemon blossom honey
5 tbsp lemon juice
1 tbsp finely grated lemon rind
½ cup water
1 tsp ground cinnamon

Place the butter and ¾ cup of the sugar in a large bowl and beat together until light and fluffy, then beat in the egg yolk and lemon extract. Sift together the flour and salt into the mixture and stir until combined. Shape the dough into a ball, wrap in plastic wrap, and chill in the refrigerator for 30–60 minutes.

Meanwhile, place the dates, honey, lemon juice, and lemon rind in a saucepan and stir in the water. Bring to a boil, stirring continuously, then reduce the heat and simmer gently for 5 minutes. Let cool, then chill in the refrigerator for 15 minutes. Mix the cinnamon and remaining sugar together in a small bowl.

Unwrap the dough and roll out between 2 sheets of parchment paper into a 12-inch/30-cm square. Sprinkle the cinnamon and sugar mixture over the dough and roll lightly with the rolling pin.

Spread the date mixture over the dough, then roll up like a jelly roll. Wrap in plastic wrap and chill for 30 minutes in the refrigerator.

Preheat the oven to 375°F/190°C. Line 2 large baking sheets with parchment paper. Unwrap the roll and cut into thin slices with a sharp serrated knife. Put them on the baking sheets spaced well apart. Bake in the preheated oven for 12–15 minutes, or until golden brown. Let cool for 5–10 minutes, then carefully transfer to wire racks to cool completely.

284 Fig & rose water spirals

Replace the dates and lemon extract, juice, and rind with 1 cup dried chopped figs and add 1 teaspoon of rose water to the fig mixture.

285 Chocolate & hazelnut drops

MAKES ABOUT 30

1 cup butter, softened
¾ cup superfine sugar
1 egg yolk, lightly beaten
2 tsp vanilla extract
1⅔ cups all-purpose flour
½ cup unsweetened cocoa
pinch of salt
⅔ cup ground hazelnuts
⅓ cup semisweet chocolate chips
4 tbsp chocolate and hazelnut spread

Preheat the oven to 375°F/190°C. Line 2 baking sheets with parchment paper. Place the butter and sugar in a large bowl and beat together until light and fluffy, then beat in the egg yolk and vanilla extract. Sift together the flour, cocoa, and salt into the mixture, add the ground hazelnuts and chocolate chips, and stir until combined.

Scoop out tablespoons of the batter and shape into balls, then place them on the baking sheets, spaced well apart. Use the dampened handle of a wooden spoon to make a hollow in the center of each cookie. Bake in the preheated oven for 12–15 minutes.

Let cool on the baking sheets for 5–10 minutes, then transfer the cookies to wire racks to cool completely. When cold, fill the hollows with the chocolate and hazelnut spread.

286 Grapefruit & apple mint cookies

Makes About 30

1 cup butter, softened
¾ cup superfine sugar, plus extra for sprinkling
1 egg yolk, lightly beaten
2 tsp grapefruit juice
2 cups all-purpose flour
pinch of salt
grated rind of 1 grapefruit
2 tsp finely chopped fresh apple mint

Place the butter and sugar in a large bowl and beat together until light and fluffy, then beat in the egg yolk and grapefruit juice. Sift together the flour and salt into the mixture, add the grapefruit rind and mint, and stir until thoroughly combined. Halve the dough, shape into balls, wrap in plastic wrap, and chill in the refrigerator for 30–60 minutes.

Preheat the oven to 375°F/190°C. Line 2 large baking sheets with parchment paper. Unwrap the dough and roll out between 2 sheets of parchment paper to ⅛ inch/3 mm thick. Cut out cookies with a 2-inch/5-cm flower cutter and place them on the baking sheets, spaced well apart. Sprinkle with superfine sugar.

Bake in the preheated oven for 10–15 minutes, or until golden brown. Let cool on the baking sheets for 5–10 minutes, then transfer the cookies to wire racks to cool completely.

287 Lemon & thyme cookies

Replace the grapefruit juice with lemon juice and replace the mint with 1 teaspoon of chopped fresh thyme leaves.

288 Chocolate mint cookie sandwiches

Makes About 15

1 cup butter, softened
¾ cup superfine sugar
1 egg yolk, lightly beaten
2 tsp vanilla extract
heaping 1¾ cups all-purpose flour
¼ cup unsweetened cocoa
pinch of salt
scant ⅓ cup candied cherries, finely chopped
15 after-dinner mint thins
4 oz/115 g semisweet chocolate, broken into pieces
2 oz/55 g white chocolate, broken into pieces

Place the butter and sugar in a large bowl and beat together until light and fluffy, then beat in the egg yolk and vanilla extract. Sift together the flour, cocoa, and salt into the mixture, add the cherries, and stir until thoroughly combined. Halve the dough, shape into balls, wrap in plastic wrap, and chill in the refrigerator for 30–60 minutes.

Preheat the oven to 375°F/190°C. Line 2 large baking sheets with parchment paper. Unwrap the dough and roll out between 2 sheets of parchment paper. Cut out cookies with a 2½-inch/6-cm plain square cutter and place them on the baking sheets, spaced well apart.

Bake in the preheated oven for 10–15 minutes, or until firm. Remove from the oven and place an after-dinner mint on top of half of the cookies, then cover with the remaining cookies. Press down gently and let cool on the baking sheets.

Place the semisweet chocolate in a heatproof bowl, set the bowl over a saucepan of gently simmering water, and heat until melted. Let cool. Place the cookies on a wire rack over a sheet of parchment paper. Spoon the semisweet chocolate over them, then tap the rack to level the surface and let set.

Place the white chocolate in a heatproof bowl, set the bowl over a pan of gently simmering water, and heat until melted. Let cool, then pipe or drizzle it over the cookies and let set.

289 *Jam rings*

MAKES ABOUT 15

1 cup butter, softened
¾ cup superfine sugar, plus extra for sprinkling
1 egg yolk, lightly beaten
2 tsp vanilla extract
2 cups all-purpose flour
pinch of salt
1 egg white, lightly beaten

FILLING
4 tbsp butter, softened
1 cup confectioners' sugar
5 tbsp strawberry or raspberry jam, warmed

Place the butter and sugar in a large bowl and beat together until light and fluffy, then beat in the egg yolk and vanilla extract. Sift together the flour and salt into the mixture and stir until combined. Halve the dough, shape into balls, wrap in plastic wrap, and chill in the refrigerator for 30–60 minutes.

Preheat the oven to 375°F/190°C. Line 2 large baking sheets with parchment paper. Unwrap the dough and roll out between 2 sheets of parchment paper. Cut out cookies with a 2¾-inch/7-cm fluted round cutter and place half of them on a baking sheet, spaced well apart. Using a 1½-inch/4-cm plain round cutter, cut out the centers of the remaining cookies and remove, then place the rings on the other baking sheet, spaced well apart.

Bake in the preheated oven for 7 minutes, then brush the cookie rings with beaten egg white and sprinkle with superfine sugar. Bake for an additional 5–8 minutes, or until light golden brown. Let cool on the baking sheets for 5–10 minutes, then transfer the cookies to wire racks to cool completely.

To make the jam filling, place the butter and confectioners' sugar in a large bowl and beat together until smooth and combined. Spread the filling over the whole cookies and top with a little jam. Place the rings on top and press gently together.

290 *Lemon rings*

Add finely grated lemon rind to the butter filling and replace the jam with lemon curd.

291 *Jam sandwich cookies*

MAKES 24

1 cup unsalted butter, softened
½ cup superfine sugar
scant 1½ cups all-purpose flour, plus extra for dusting
pinch of salt
heaping 1 cup ground almonds
2 tbsp seedless raspberry jam
2 tbsp apricot jam
2 tbsp confectioners' sugar

Place the butter and sugar in a large bowl and beat together until light and fluffy. Add the flour, salt, and ground almonds and bring together to form a soft dough. Wrap the dough in plastic wrap and chill in the refrigerator for 2 hours.

Preheat the oven to 300°F/150°C. Roll the dough out on a floured work surface to about ¼ inch/5 mm thick. Using a 2¾-inch/7-cm cookie cutter dipped in flour, cut out 48 shapes. Re-roll any trimmings and cut out more cookies. Use a small round cookie cutter to cut out the center from 24 of the shapes and place the cookies on 2 large, nonstick baking sheets. Bake in the preheated oven for 25–30 minutes, or until golden. Let cool completely on a wire rack.

Spoon the raspberry jam onto 12 of the complete cookies. Spoon the apricot jam onto the remaining 12. Sift the confectioners' sugar over the cut-out cookies and use these to cover the jam-topped halves, pressing down gently.

292 *Chocolate sandwich cookies*

Divide the dough in half, add 2 teaspoons of cocoa to one piece of dough, and knead in before chilling. Make the cookies, cutting out the centers from the chocolate dough. Sandwich together with 4½ oz/125 g chocolate spread.

293 *Ultimate iced sugar cutouts*

Makes 25

6 tbsp unsalted butter, softened
cup superfine sugar
2 large eggs
½ tsp vanilla extract
scant 1½ cups all-purpose flour, plus extra for dusting
1 tsp baking powder
pinch of salt

ICING
1⅓ cups confectioners' sugar
about 1 tbsp cold water
few drops of food coloring

Place the butter and sugar in a large bowl and beat together until light and fluffy. Whisk the eggs and vanilla extract in another bowl, then add to the butter and sugar mixture. Sift in the flour, baking powder, and salt and beat together to form a dough. Wrap in plastic wrap and chill in the refrigerator for 1 hour.

Preheat the oven to 350°F/180°C. Line 2 large baking sheets with parchment paper. Roll the dough out on a floured work surface to about ¼ inch/5 mm thick. Cut out cookies with a variety of cookie cutter shapes dipped in flour and place them on the baking sheets. Bake in the preheated oven for 10–12 minutes, or until golden brown. Let cool on wire racks.

When the cookies are cold, sift the confectioners' sugar into a bowl and mix with the water until smooth. Color the frosting as desired and spread over the cookies, then let set.

294 *Xmas alphabet cutouts*

Use alphabet cookie cutters to cut out letters, ice as before with red tinted icing and decorate with silver dragées.

295 *Chocolate orange cookies*

Makes 30

7 tbsp butter, softened
⅓ cup superfine sugar
1 egg
1 tbsp milk
2 cups all-purpose flour, plus extra for dusting
2 tbsp unsweetened cocoa

FROSTING
1½ cups confectioners' sugar
3 tbsp orange juice
a little semisweet chocolate, broken into pieces

Preheat the oven to 350°F/180°C. Line 2 large baking sheets with sheets of wax paper. Place the butter and sugar in a large bowl and beat together until light and fluffy. Beat in the egg and milk until thoroughly combined. Sift the flour and cocoa into the bowl and gradually mix together to form a soft dough.

Roll out the dough on a lightly floured work surface until it is about ¼ inch/5 mm thick. Cut out rounds with a 2-inch/5-cm fluted round cookie cutter and place them on the baking sheets. Bake in the preheated oven for 10–12 minutes, or until golden. Let cool on the baking sheet for a few minutes, then transfer the cookies to a wire rack to cool completely and become crisp.

To make the frosting, sift the confectioners' sugar in a bowl and stir in enough orange juice to form a thin frosting that will coat the back of the spoon. Place a spoonful of frosting in the center of each cookie and let set.

Place the semisweet chocolate in a heatproof bowl, set the bowl over a saucepan of gently simmering water, and heat until melted. Drizzle thin lines of melted chocolate over the cookies and let set before serving.

296 *With coffee frosting*

Replace the orange juice in the frosting with 2–3 tablespoons of cold, strong espresso coffee.

297 Lemon & lime cookies

MAKES ABOUT 30

5 oz/140 g semisweet chocolate, broken into pieces, for decorating
30 thinly pared strips of lime rind, for decorating
1 cup butter, softened
¾ cup superfine sugar
1 egg yolk, lightly beaten
2 tsp lime juice
2 cups all-purpose flour
pinch of salt
finely grated rind of 1 lemon

FROSTING
1 tbsp lightly beaten egg white
1 tbsp lime juice
1 cup confectioners' sugar

To make the decoration, place the chocolate in a heatproof bowl, set the bowl over a saucepan of gently simmering water, and heat until melted. Let cool slightly. Line a baking sheet with parchment paper. Dip the strips of lime rind into the chocolate until coated, then put on the baking sheet to set.

Place the butter and sugar in a large bowl and beat together until light and fluffy, then beat in the egg yolk and lime juice. Sift together the flour and salt into the mixture, add the lemon rind, and stir until combined. Halve the dough, shape into balls, wrap in plastic wrap, and chill in the refrigerator for 30–60 minutes.

Preheat the oven to 375°F/190°C. Line 2 large baking sheets with parchment paper. Unwrap the dough and roll out between 2 sheets of parchment paper to about ⅛ inch/3 mm thick. Cut out rounds with a 2½-inch/6-cm plain cutter and place them on the baking sheets. Bake in the preheated oven for 10–15 minutes, or until golden brown. Let cool on the baking sheets for 5–10 minutes, then transfer to wire racks to cool completely.

To make the frosting, place the egg white and lime juice in a bowl and mix together, then gradually beat in the confectioners' sugar until smooth. Frost the cookies and top with the chocolate-coated lime rind. Let set.

298 With semisweet chocolate topping

Omit the lime rind and simply drizzle the melted semisweet chocolate over the icing and let set.

299 Lemon & sesame seed cookies

MAKES ABOUT 30

2 tbsp sesame seeds
1 cup butter, softened
¾ cup superfine sugar
1 tbsp finely grated lemon rind
1 egg yolk, lightly beaten
2 cups all-purpose flour
pinch of salt

ICING
1 cup confectioners' sugar
few drops of lemon extract
1 tbsp hot water

Dry-roast the sesame seeds in a heavy-bottom skillet over low heat, stirring frequently, for 2–3 minutes, or until they give off their aroma. Let cool.

Place the butter, sugar, lemon rind, and toasted seeds in a large bowl and beat together until light and fluffy, then beat in the egg yolk. Sift together the flour and salt into the mixture and stir until combined. Halve the dough, form it into balls, wrap in plastic wrap, and chill in the refrigerator for 30–60 minutes.

Preheat the oven to 375°F/190°C. Line 2 large baking sheets with parchment paper. Unwrap the dough and roll out between 2 sheets of parchment paper. Cut out rounds with a 2½-inch/6-cm cutter and place them on the baking sheets, spaced well apart. Bake in the preheated oven for 10–12 minutes, or until light golden brown. Let cool on the baking sheets for 5–10 minutes, then transfer the cookies to wire racks to cool completely.

To make the icing, sift the confectioners' sugar into a bowl, add the lemon extract, and gradually stir in the hot water until the icing is smooth and has the consistency of thick cream. Leave the cooled cookies on the racks and spread the icing over them. Let set.

300 Lime & sesame seed cookies

Omit the lemon in this recipe and replace with lime, then top the icing with finely grated lime rind.

301 Mango, coconut & ginger cookies

MAKES ABOUT 30

1 cup butter, softened
¾ cup superfine sugar
1 egg yolk, lightly beaten
2 oz/55 g preserved ginger, chopped, plus 2 tsp syrup from the jar
2 cups all-purpose flour
pinch of salt
2 oz/55 g plumped dried mango, chopped
heaping 1 cup dry unsweetened coconut

Place the butter and sugar in a large bowl and beat together until light and fluffy, then beat in the egg yolk and ginger syrup. Sift together the flour and salt into the mixture, add the preserved ginger and mango, and stir until combined.

Spread out the coconut in a shallow dish. Shape the dough into a log and roll it in the coconut to coat. Wrap in plastic wrap and chill in the refrigerator for 30–60 minutes.

Preheat the oven to 375°F/190°C. Line 2 large baking sheets with parchment paper. Unwrap the log, cut it into ¼-inch/5-mm slices with a sharp serrated knife, and place them on the baking sheets, spaced well apart.

Bake in the preheated oven for 12–15 minutes, or until light golden brown. Let cool on the baking sheets for 5–10 minutes, then transfer the cookies to wire racks to cool completely.

302 Pineapple, coconut & ginger cookies

Replace the mango with chopped dried pineapple and make an icing by sifting 1 cup confectioners' sugar into a bowl then add 1½ tablespoons of pineapple juice. Beat until smooth and use to ice the cooled cookies.

303 Pineapple & ginger creams

MAKES ABOUT 15

1 cup butter, softened
¾ cup superfine sugar
1 egg yolk, lightly beaten
2 tsp vanilla extract
2 cups all-purpose flour
pinch of salt
3½ oz/100 g plumped dried pineapple, finely chopped
unsweetened cocoa, for dusting
confectioners' sugar, for dusting

GINGER CREAM
⅔ cup strained, whole-milk plain yogurt
1 tbsp dark corn syrup
1 tbsp ground ginger

Place the butter and sugar in a large bowl and beat together until light and fluffy, then beat in the egg yolk and vanilla extract. Sift together the flour and salt into the mixture, add the pineapple, and stir until thoroughly combined. Halve the dough, shape into balls, wrap in plastic wrap, and chill for 30–60 minutes.

Preheat the oven to 375°F/190°C. Line 2 large baking sheets with parchment paper.

Unwrap the dough and roll out between 2 sheets of parchment paper. Cut out cookies with a 2½-inch/6-cm fluted round cutter and place them on the baking sheets, spaced well apart. Bake in the preheated oven for 10–15 minutes, or until light golden brown. Let cool on the baking sheets for 5–10 minutes, then transfer the cookies to wire racks to cool completely.

To make the ginger cream, place the yogurt, dark corn syrup, and ground ginger in a bowl and beat together until thoroughly combined. Sandwich the cookies together with the ginger cream. Cover half of each cookie with a piece of paper and dust the exposed half with sifted cocoa. Cover the cocoa-dusted half of each cookie with a piece of paper and dust the exposed half with sifted confectioners' sugar.

304 With pineapple icing

Instead of dusting the cookies with cocoa and sugar, make a pineapple icing by mixing 1 cup sifted confectioners' sugar and 1 tablespoon of pineapple juice together, then spread over the cookies and let set.

305 Cherry & chocolate diamonds

MAKES ABOUT 30

1 cup butter, softened
¾ cup superfine sugar
1 egg yolk, lightly beaten
2 tsp vanilla extract
2 cups all-purpose flour
pinch of salt
scant ⅓ cup candied cherries, finely chopped
⅓ cup milk chocolate chips

Place the butter and sugar in a large bowl and beat together until light and fluffy, then beat in the egg yolk and vanilla extract. Sift together the flour and salt into the mixture, add the candied cherries and chocolate chips, and stir until thoroughly combined. Halve the dough, shape into balls, wrap in plastic wrap, and chill for 30–60 minutes.

Preheat the oven to 375°F/190°C. Line 2 large baking sheets with parchment paper. Unwrap the dough and roll out between 2 sheets of parchment paper to about ⅛ inch/3 mm thick. Cut out cookies with a diamond-shaped cutter and place them on the baking sheets.

Bake in the preheated oven for 10–15 minutes, or until light golden brown. Let cool on the baking sheets for 5–10 minutes, then transfer the cookies to wire racks to cool completely.

306 Ginger & chocolate diamonds

Replace the cherries and milk chocolate chips with crystallized ginger and white chocolate chips.

307 Tropical fruit cookie sandwiches

MAKES ABOUT 15

1 cup butter, softened
¾ cup superfine sugar
1 egg yolk, lightly beaten
2 tsp passion fruit pulp
2 cups all-purpose flour
pinch of salt
¼ cup plumped dried mango, chopped
¼ cup plumped dried papaya, chopped
heaping 2 tbsp dried dates, pitted and chopped
3–4 tbsp shredded coconut, toasted

MASCARPONE CREAM
⅓ cup mascarpone cheese
3 tbsp strained, whole-milk plain yogurt
scant ½ cup ready-made vanilla pudding
½ tsp ground ginger

Place the butter and sugar in a large bowl and beat together until light and fluffy, then beat in the egg yolk and passion fruit pulp. Sift together the flour and salt into the mixture, add the mango, papaya, and dates, and stir until combined. Shape the dough into a log, wrap in plastic wrap, and chill for 30–60 minutes.

Meanwhile, to make the mascarpone cream, place all the ingredients in a bowl and beat until smooth. Cover and chill in the refrigerator.

Preheat the oven to 375°F/190°C. Line 2 large baking sheets with parchment paper. Unwrap the dough, cut into slices with a sharp serrated knife, and place them on the baking sheets, spaced well apart.

Bake in the preheated oven for 10–15 minutes, or until light golden brown. Let cool on the baking sheets for 5–10 minutes, then transfer the cookies to wire racks to cool completely.

When the cookies are cold, spread the chilled mascarpone cream over half of them, sprinkle with the toasted coconut, and top with the remaining cookies.

308 With coconut cream filling

Omit the mascarpone cream and fill the cookies with 6 tablespoons of butter beaten with 3 tablespoons of creamed coconut, 1 cup confectioners' sugar, and 3 tablespoons of dry unsweetened coconut.

309 Apricot & pecan cookies

Makes About 30

1 cup butter, softened
¾ cup superfine sugar
1 egg yolk, lightly beaten
2 tsp vanilla extract
2 cups all-purpose flour
pinch of salt
finely grated rind of 1 orange
⅓ cup plumped dried apricots, chopped
⅔ cup pecans, finely chopped

Place the butter and sugar in a large bowl and beat together until light and fluffy, then beat in the egg yolk and vanilla extract. Sift together the flour and salt into the mixture, add the orange rind and apricots, and stir until combined. Shape the dough into a log. Spread out the pecans in a shallow dish. Roll the log in the nuts until well coated, then wrap in plastic wrap and chill in the refrigerator for 30–60 minutes.

Preheat the oven to 375°F/190°C. Line 2 large baking sheets with parchment paper. Unwrap the dough, cut into ¼-inch/5-mm slices with a sharp serrated knife, and place the slices on the baking sheets, spaced well apart.

Bake in the preheated oven for 10–12 minutes, or until golden brown. Let cool on the baking sheets for 5–10 minutes, then transfer the cookies to wire racks to cool completely.

310 Cherry or cranberry & pecan cookies

Replace the apricots with scant ½ cup dried cherries or dried cranberries.

311 Chocolate & apricot cookies

Makes About 30

1 cup butter, softened
¾ cup superfine sugar
1 egg yolk, lightly beaten
2 tsp amaretto liqueur
2 cups all-purpose flour
pinch of salt
⅓ cup semisweet chocolate chips
⅓ cup plumped dried apricots, chopped
⅔ cup blanched almonds, chopped

Place the butter and sugar in a large bowl and beat together until light and fluffy, then beat in the egg yolk and amaretto liqueur. Sift together the flour and salt into the mixture, add the chocolate chips and apricots, and stir until thoroughly combined. Shape the mixture into a log. Spread out the almonds in a shallow dish and roll the log in them to coat. Wrap in plastic wrap and chill for 30–60 minutes.

Preheat the oven to 375°F/190°C. Line 2 large baking sheets with parchment paper. Unwrap the dough, cut into ¼-inch/5-mm slices with a sharp serrated knife, and place them on the baking sheets, spaced well apart.

Bake in the preheated oven for 12–15 minutes, or until golden brown. Let cool for 5–10 minutes, then transfer the cookies to wire racks to cool completely.

312 *Margarita cookies*

Makes About 30

1 cup butter, softened
¾ cup superfine sugar
finely grated rind of 1 lime
1 egg yolk, lightly beaten
2 tsp orange liqueur or 1 tsp orange extract
2 cups all-purpose flour
pinch of salt

ICING
1¼ cups confectioners' sugar
2 tbsp white tequila

Preheat the oven to 375°F/190°C. Line 2 large baking sheets with parchment paper. Place the butter, sugar, and lime rind in a large bowl and beat together until light and fluffy, then beat in the egg yolk and orange liqueur. Sift together the flour and salt into the mixture and stir until combined. Scoop up tablespoons of the dough, place them on the baking sheets, and flatten gently.

Bake in the preheated oven for 10–15 minutes, or until light golden brown. Let cool on the baking sheets for 5–10 minutes, then carefully transfer the cookies to wire racks to cool completely.

Sift the confectioners' sugar into a bowl and stir in enough tequila to give the mixture the consistency of thick cream. Leave the cookies on the wire racks and drizzle the icing over them with a teaspoon. Let set.

313 *With lime icing*

Replace the tequila in the icing with 2 tablespoons of fresh lime juice and scatter over finely grated lime zest.

314 *Mixed fruit cookies*

Makes About 30

1 cup butter, softened
¾ cup superfine sugar
1 egg yolk, lightly beaten
2 cups all-purpose flour
½ tsp apple pie spice
pinch of salt
heaping 2 tbsp plumped dried apple, chopped
heaping 2 tbsp plumped dried pears, chopped
2 tbsp plumped prunes, chopped
finely grated rind of 1 orange

Place the butter and sugar in a large bowl and beat together until light and fluffy, then beat in the egg yolk. Sift together the flour, apple pie spice, and salt into the mixture, then add the apple, pear, prunes, and orange rind and stir until combined. Shape the dough into a log, wrap in plastic wrap, and chill for 30–60 minutes.

Preheat the oven to 375°F/190°C. Line 2 large baking sheets with parchment paper.

Unwrap the log, cut it into ¼-inch/5-mm thick slices with a sharp serrated knife, and place the slices on the baking sheets, spaced well apart. Bake in the preheated oven for 10–15 minutes, or until golden brown. Let cool on the baking sheets for 5–10 minutes, then transfer the cookies to wire racks to cool completely.

315 *Tropical fruit cookies*

Replace the apples, pears, and prunes with chopped dried mango, pineapple, and papaya.

316 Oaty raisin & hazelnut cookies

Makes About 30

1/3 cup raisins, chopped
1/2 cup orange juice
1 cup butter, softened
3/4 cup superfine sugar
1 egg yolk, lightly beaten
2 tsp vanilla extract
1 2/3 cups all-purpose flour
pinch of salt
2/3 cup rolled oats
1/3 cup hazelnuts, chopped
about 30 whole hazelnuts

Preheat the oven to 375°F/190°C. Line 2 large baking sheets with parchment paper. Place the raisins in a bowl, add the orange juice, and let soak for 10 minutes.

Place the butter and sugar in a large bowl and beat together until light and fluffy, then beat in the egg yolk and vanilla extract. Sift together the flour and salt into the mixture and add the oats and hazelnuts. Drain the raisins, add them to the mixture, and stir until combined. Scoop up tablespoons of the mixture and place them in mounds on the baking sheets, spaced well apart. Flatten slightly and place a whole hazelnut in the center of each cookie.

Bake in the preheated oven for 12–15 minutes, or until golden brown. Let cool on the baking sheets for 5–10 minutes, then transfer to wire racks to cool completely.

317 Oaty golden raisin & walnut cookies

Replace the raisins and hazelnuts with 1/3 cup chopped golden raisins and 2/3 cup chopped walnuts.

318 Lemon cornmeal cookies

Makes 12

7 tbsp butter, softened
1/3 cup superfine sugar
2 large eggs, lightly beaten
finely grated rind of 1 lemon
1 tbsp lemon juice
1 cup all-purpose flour
1/2 cup cornmeal
12 whole blanched almonds

Preheat the oven to 375°F/190°C. Line several large baking sheets with parchment paper. Place the butter and sugar in a large bowl and whisk until pale and creamy. Whisk the beaten eggs, lemon rind, and juice into the mixture until smooth, then add the flour and cornmeal and beat together until mixed.

Place the mixture in a pastry bag fitted with a plain 3/4-inch/2-cm tip. Pipe swirls, measuring about 2 1/2 inches/6 cm in diameter, onto the baking sheets, spaced well apart, and top each cookie with a blanched almond.

Bake in the preheated oven for 10–15 minutes, or until lightly golden brown. Let cool on the baking sheets for 5 minutes, then transfer the cookies to a wire rack to cool completely.

319 *Orange & chocolate fingers*

MAKES ABOUT 35

1 cup butter, softened
¾ cup superfine sugar
finely grated rind of 1 orange
1 egg yolk, lightly beaten
2 tsp orange juice
2 cups all-purpose flour
1 tsp ground ginger
pinch of salt
4 oz/115 g semisweet chocolate, broken into pieces

Place the butter, sugar, and orange rind in a large bowl and beat together until light and fluffy, then beat in the egg yolk and orange juice. Sift together the flour, ginger, and salt into the mixture and stir until combined. Shape the dough into a ball, wrap in plastic wrap, and chill in the refrigerator for 30–60 minutes.

Preheat the oven to 375°F/190°C. Line 2 large baking sheets with parchment paper. Unwrap the dough and roll out between 2 sheets of parchment paper to a rectangle. Using a sharp knife, cut it into 4 x ¾-inch/10 x 2-cm strips and place them on the baking sheets, spaced well apart.

Bake in the preheated oven for 10–12 minutes, or until light golden brown. Let cool for 5–10 minutes, then transfer to wire racks to cool completely.

Place the chocolate in a heatproof bowl, set the bowl over a saucepan of gently simmering water, and heat until melted, then let cool. When the chocolate is cool but not set, dip the cookies diagonally into it to coat halfway, then place on the wire racks to set. You may find it easier to do this with tongs.

320 *Lemon & white chocolate fingers*

Replace the orange rind and juice with lemon rind and juice and use melted white chocolate to coat the cookies halfway.

321 *Orange & lemon cookies*

MAKES ABOUT 30

1 cup butter, softened
¾ cup superfine sugar
1 egg yolk, lightly beaten
2 cups all-purpose flour
pinch of salt
finely grated rind of 1 orange
finely grated rind of 1 lemon

FOR DECORATING
1 tbsp lightly beaten egg white
1 tbsp lemon juice
1 cup confectioners' sugar
few drops of yellow food coloring
few drops of orange food coloring
about 15 lemon gummy slices
about 15 orange gummy slices

Place the butter and sugar in a large bowl and beat together until light and fluffy, then beat in the egg yolk. Sift together the flour and salt into the mixture and stir until combined. Halve the dough and knead the orange rind into one half and the lemon rind into the other. Shape into balls, wrap, and chill for 30–60 minutes.

Preheat the oven to 375°F/190°C. Line 2 large baking sheets with parchment paper. Unwrap the orange-flavored dough and roll out between 2 sheets of parchment paper. Cut out rounds with a 2½-inch/6-cm plain cutter and place them on a baking sheet, spaced well apart. Repeat with the lemon-flavored dough and cut out crescents. Place them on the other baking sheet, spaced well apart.

Bake in the preheated oven for 10–15 minutes, or until golden brown. Let cool for 5–10 minutes, then transfer to wire racks to cool completely.

To decorate, mix the egg white and lemon juice together. Gradually beat in the confectioners' sugar until smooth. Spoon half the frosting into another bowl. Stir yellow food coloring into one bowl and orange into the other. Leave the cookies on the racks. Spread the frosting over the cookies and decorate with gummy slices. Let set.

322 *Raspberry cookies*

Omit the citrus rind from the dough and replace the orange and yellow food coloring with red food coloring. Top the cookies with raspberry gummy slices.

323 *Chocolate chip & cinnamon cookies*

MAKES ABOUT 30

1 cup butter, softened
¾ cup superfine sugar
1 egg yolk, lightly beaten
2 tsp orange extract
2 cups all-purpose flour
pinch of salt
heaping ½ cup semisweet chocolate chips

CINNAMON COATING
1½ tbsp superfine sugar
1½ tbsp ground cinnamon

Preheat the oven to 375°F/190°C. Line 2 large baking sheets with parchment paper. Place the butter and sugar in a large bowl and beat together until light and fluffy, then beat in the egg yolk and orange extract. Sift together the flour and salt into the mixture, add the chocolate chips, and stir until thoroughly combined.

To make the cinnamon coating, mix the sugar and cinnamon together in a shallow dish. Scoop out tablespoons of the cookie dough, roll them into balls, then roll them in the cinnamon mixture to coat. Place them on the baking sheets, spaced well apart.

Bake in the preheated oven for 12–15 minutes, or until golden brown. Let cool on the baking sheets for 5–10 minutes, then transfer the cookies to wire racks to cool completely.

324 *White chocolate & spice cookies*

Replace the semisweet chocolate chips with heaping ½ cup white chocolate chips and replace the cinnamon with 1 tablespoon of apple pie spice and ½ teaspoon of ground nutmeg.

325 *Papaya & cashew nut cookies*

MAKES ABOUT 30

1 cup butter, softened
¾ cup superfine sugar
1 egg yolk, lightly beaten
2 tsp lime juice
2 cups all-purpose flour
pinch of salt
½ cup plumped dried papaya, chopped
⅔ cup cashew nuts, finely chopped

Place the butter and sugar in a large bowl and beat together until light and fluffy, then beat in the egg yolk and lime juice.

Sift together the flour and salt into the mixture, add the papaya, and stir until thoroughly combined.

Spread out the cashew nuts in a shallow dish. Shape the dough into a log and roll in the nuts to coat. Wrap the dough in plastic wrap, and chill in the refrigerator for 30–60 minutes.

Preheat the oven to 375°F/190°C. Line 2 large baking sheets with parchment paper.

Unwrap the dough, cut into slices with a sharp serrated knife and place them on the baking sheets, spaced well apart.

Bake in the preheated oven for 12–15 minutes, or until light golden. Let cool on the baking sheets for 5–10 minutes, then transfer the cookies to wire racks to cool completely.

326 *With cashew frosting*

Beat 6 tablespoons of butter, 1 cup confectioners' sugar, and heaping ⅓ cup cashew nut butter together until smooth and spread over the cooled cookies.

327 Peach daiquiri cookies

MAKES ABOUT 30

1 cup butter, softened
¾ cup superfine sugar
finely grated rind of 1 lime
1 egg yolk, lightly beaten
2 tsp white rum
2 cups all-purpose flour
pinch of salt
½ cup plumped dried peaches, chopped

ICING
1¼ cups confectioners' sugar
2 tbsp white rum

Preheat the oven to 375°F/190°C. Line 2 baking sheets with parchment paper.

Place the butter, sugar, and lime rind in a large bowl and beat together until light and fluffy, then beat in the egg yolk and rum. Sift together the flour and salt into the mixture, add the peaches, and stir until thoroughly combined. Scoop up tablespoons of the dough and place them on the baking sheets, then flatten gently. Bake in the preheated oven for 10–15 minutes, or until light golden brown. Let cool on the baking sheets for 5–10 minutes, then transfer the cookies to wire racks to cool completely.

Sift the confectioners' sugar into a bowl and stir in enough rum until the mixture is the consistency of thick cream. Leave the cookies on the wire racks and drizzle the icing over them with a teaspoon. Let set.

328 With peach icing

Omit the dried peaches from the cookie dough and instead stir them into a double quantity of icing. Spoon the icing onto the cooled cookies, then spread to cover and let set.

329 Peach, pear & plum cookies

MAKES ABOUT 30

1 cup butter, softened
¾ cup superfine sugar
1 egg yolk, lightly beaten
2 tsp almond extract
2 cups all-purpose flour
pinch of salt
⅓ cup plumped dried peaches, finely chopped
⅓ cup plumped dried pears, finely chopped
4 tbsp plum jam

Preheat the oven to 375°F/190°C. Line 2 large baking sheets with parchment paper. Place the butter and sugar in a large bowl and beat together until light and fluffy, then beat in the egg yolk and almond extract. Sift together the flour and salt into the mixture, add the dried fruit, and stir until thoroughly combined.

Scoop up tablespoons of the mixture, roll them into balls, and place on the baking sheets, spaced well apart. Make a hollow in the center of each with the dampened handle of a wooden spoon and fill the hollows with the jam. Bake in the preheated oven for 12–15 minutes, or until light golden brown.

Leave to cool on the baking sheets for 5–10 minutes, then transfer the cookies to wire racks to cool completely.

330 Extra peachy cookies

Replace the plum jam with peach preserve and serve topped with chopped fresh peach.

331 Pear & mint cookies

MAKES ABOUT 30

1 cup butter, softened
¾ cup superfine sugar
1 egg yolk, lightly beaten
2 tsp vanilla extract
2 cups all-purpose flour
pinch of salt
½ cup plumped dried pears, finely chopped

ICING
1 cup confectioners' sugar
few drops of peppermint extract
1 tbsp hot water

Place the butter and sugar in a large bowl and beat together until light and fluffy, then beat in the egg yolk and vanilla extract. Sift together the flour and salt into the mixture, add the pears, and stir until thoroughly combined. Shape the dough into a log, wrap in plastic wrap, and chill in the refrigerator for 30–60 minutes.

Preheat the oven to 375°F/190°C. Line 2 large baking sheets with parchment paper.

Unwrap the log, cut it into ¼-inch/5-mm slices with a sharp serrated knife, and place them on the baking sheets, spaced well apart. Bake in the preheated oven for 10–15 minutes, or until golden brown. Let cool on the baking sheets for 5–10 minutes, then transfer the cookies to wire racks to cool completely.

To decorate, sift the confectioners' sugar into a bowl and stir in the peppermint extract. Gradually stir in the hot water until the icing has the consistency of heavy cream. Leave the cooled cookies on the wire racks and drizzle lines of icing over them with a teaspoon. Let set.

332 With pear liqueur icing

Replace the peppermint extract in the icing with a few drops of Poire William eau de vie.

333 Pear & pistachio cookies

MAKES ABOUT 30

1 cup butter, softened
¾ cup superfine sugar
1 egg yolk, lightly beaten
2 tsp vanilla extract
2 cups all-purpose flour
pinch of salt
2 oz/55 g plumped dried pears, finely chopped
⅓ cup pistachios, chopped
whole pistachios, for decorating

Preheat the oven to 375°F/190°C. Line 2 large baking sheets with parchment paper. Place the butter and sugar in a large bowl and beat together until light and fluffy, then beat in the egg yolk and vanilla extract. Sift together the flour and salt into the mixture, add the pears and pistachios, and stir until thoroughly combined.

Scoop up tablespoons of the mixture and roll into balls. Place them on the baking sheets, spaced well apart, and flatten slightly. Gently press a whole pistachio into the center of each cookie.

Bake in the preheated oven for 10–15 minutes, or until golden brown. Let cool on the baking sheets for 5–10 minutes, then transfer the cookies to wire racks to cool completely.

334 Mango & macadamia nut cookies

Replace the dried pears and pistachios with ⅓ cup chopped dried mangoes and ½ cup chopped macadamia nuts.

335 Chocolate wholemeals

Makes 20

5½ tbsp butter, plus extra for greasing
scant ⅔ cup raw brown sugar
1 egg
1 tbsp wheat germ
1 cup whole wheat self-rising flour
½ cup self-rising flour
4½ oz/125 g semisweet chocolate, broken into pieces

Preheat the oven to 350°F/180°C. Lightly grease 2 large baking sheets. Place the butter and sugar in a large bowl and beat together until light and fluffy. Add the egg and beat well. Stir in the wheat germ and flours, then bring the mixture together with your hands. Roll rounded teaspoonfuls of the dough into balls and place them on the baking sheets, spaced well apart, then flatten slightly with the tines of a fork.

Bake in the preheated oven for 15–20 minutes, or until golden brown. Let cool for a few minutes, then transfer the cookies to a wire rack to cool completely.

Place the chocolate in a heatproof bowl, set the bowl over a saucepan of gently simmering water, and heat until melted. Dip each cookie in the chocolate to cover the flat side and a little way around the edges. Let the excess drip back into the bowl. Place the cookies on a sheet of parchment paper in a cool place and let set before serving.

336 Nutty chocolate wholemeals

Add heaping ½ cup chopped almonds to the mixture before rolling into balls.

337 Iced cherry rings

Makes About 18

8 tbsp butter, plus extra for greasing
scant ½ cup superfine sugar
1 egg yolk
finely grated rind of ½ lemon
1½ cups all-purpose flour, plus extra for dusting
2 oz/55 g candied cherries, chopped

ICING
¾ cup confectioners' sugar
1½ tbsp lemon juice

Preheat the oven to 400°F/200°C. Lightly grease 2 large baking sheets. Place the butter and sugar in a large bowl and beat together until light and fluffy. Beat in the egg yolk and lemon rind. Sift in the flour, stir, then add the candied cherries and mix to form a soft dough.

Roll the dough out on a lightly floured work surface to ¼ inch/5 mm thick. Cut out 3¼-inch/8-cm rounds with a cookie cutter, then cut out the center of each with a 1-inch/2.5-cm cutter. Place the rings on the baking sheets. Re-roll any trimmings and cut out more cookies.

Bake in the preheated oven for 12–15 minutes, or until golden. Let cool for 2 minutes, then transfer to a wire rack to cool completely.

To make the frosting, mix the confectioners' sugar and lemon juice together until smooth. Drizzle the frosting over the cookies and let set.

338 Fruity rings

Replace the candied cherries with chopped candied peel. Tint the frosting with a little yellow food coloring.

339 *Plum & white chocolate cookies*

MAKES 15

1 cup butter, softened
¾ cup superfine sugar
1 egg yolk, lightly beaten
2 tsp vanilla extract
1⅔ cups all-purpose flour
½ cup unsweetened cocoa
pinch of salt
3½ oz/100 g white chocolate, chopped

TOPPING
2 oz/55 g white chocolate, broken into pieces
15 plumped dried plums, halved

Place the butter and sugar in a large bowl and beat together until light and fluffy, then beat in the egg yolk and vanilla extract. Sift together the flour, cocoa, and salt into the mixture and stir until combined. Halve the dough, shape into balls, wrap in plastic wrap, and chill for 30–60 minutes.

Preheat the oven to 375°F/190°C. Line 2 large baking sheets with parchment paper.

Unwrap a ball of dough and roll out between 2 sheets of parchment paper to about ⅛ inch/3 mm thick. Cut out 15 rounds with a plain 2-inch/5-cm cutter and place them on the baking sheets, spaced well apart. Divide the chopped chocolate among the cookies.

Roll out the remaining dough between 2 sheets of parchment paper and cut out rounds with a 2½–2¾-inch/6–7-cm cutter. Place them on top of the first cookies and press the edges together to seal. Bake in the preheated oven for 10–15 minutes, or until firm. Let cool for 5–10 minutes, then transfer the cookies to wire racks to cool completely.

To decorate, place the chocolate in a heatproof bowl, set the bowl over a saucepan of gently simmering water, and heat until melted. Let cool slightly. Dip the cut sides of the plums into the melted chocolate and stick them in the middle of the cookies. Spoon the remaining chocolate over them and let set.

340 *Walnut & apricot cookies*

Replace the dried plums with 15 walnut halves and 15 plumped dried apricots.

341 *Plum & sweet cream cookies*

MAKES ABOUT 15

1 cup butter, softened
¾ cup superfine sugar
1 egg yolk, lightly beaten
2 tsp vanilla extract
1¼ cups all-purpose flour
4 oz/115 g vanilla instant pudding mix
pinch of salt
3½ oz/100 g plumped dried plums, finely chopped

SWEET CREAM
2 tbsp butter
2 cups confectioners' sugar
2 tbsp milk
few drops of vanilla extract

Place the butter and sugar in a large bowl and beat together until light and fluffy, then beat in the egg yolk and vanilla extract. Sift together the flour, pudding mix, and salt into the mixture, add the plums, and stir until combined. Halve the dough, shape into balls, wrap in plastic wrap, and chill for 30–60 minutes.

Preheat the oven to 375°F/190°C. Line 2 large baking sheets with parchment paper. Unwrap the dough and roll out between 2 sheets of parchment paper. Cut out cookies with a 2½-inch/6-cm fluted round cutter and place them on the baking sheets, spaced well apart. Using a small diamond-shaped cutter, stamp out the centers of half the cookies and remove.

Bake in the preheated oven for 10–15 minutes, or until light golden. Let cool on the baking sheets for 5–10 minutes, then transfer the cookies to wire racks to cool completely.

To make the sweet cream, place the butter in a small saucepan and heat gently until melted, then remove from the heat. Sift the confectioners' sugar into the pan, add the milk and vanilla, and beat until smooth and thoroughly combined. Spread the sweet cream over the whole cookies and top with the cutout cookies.

342 *Banana & sweet cream cookies*

Replace the plums with finely chopped, soft dried bananas.

343 Cranberry & pastry cream cookies

MAKES ABOUT 15

1 cup butter, softened
¾ cup superfine sugar
1 egg yolk, lightly beaten
2 tsp vanilla extract
2 cups all-purpose flour
pinch of salt

PASTRY CREAM
2 egg yolks, lightly beaten
4 tbsp superfine sugar
1 tbsp cornstarch
1 heaping tbsp all-purpose flour
1¼ cups milk
few drops of vanilla extract
1 egg white

FOR DECORATING
15 small cranberries
1 egg white, lightly beaten
2–3 tbsp superfine sugar
2 cups confectioners' sugar, sifted
¼ tsp lemon extract
2 tbsp warm water

Place the butter and sugar in a large bowl and beat together, then beat in the egg yolk and vanilla extract. Sift in the flour and salt and stir until thoroughly combined. Halve the dough, wrap in plastic wrap, and chill in the refrigerator for 45 minutes.

Preheat the oven to 375°F/190°C. Line 2 large baking sheets with parchment paper. Roll out the dough between sheets of parchment paper. Cut out rounds with a 2½-inch/6-cm cookie cutter and place them on the baking sheets. Bake in the preheated oven for 12 minutes, or until golden brown. Let cool for 5 minutes, then transfer to wire racks to cool.

To make the pastry cream, beat the egg yolks and sugar together. Sift in the cornstarch and flour and beat well. Stir in 3 tablespoons of the milk and the vanilla extract. Bring the remaining milk to a boil, then whisk it into the mixture. Return to the pan and bring to a boil, stirring, then beat until cool.

Whisk the egg white until stiff. Spoon a little pastry cream into a bowl, fold in the egg white, then fold into the rest of the cream. Heat for 2 minutes, then let cool. Sandwich the cookies together with the pastry cream.

Dip the cranberries into the beaten egg white and roll in superfine sugar. Mix the confectioners' sugar, lemon, and water until smooth. Spread the icing over the cookies and decorate with the cranberries.

344 Blueberry and pastry cream cookies

Replace the cranberries with blueberries.

345 Strawberry pinks

MAKES ABOUT 30

1 cup butter, softened
¾ cup superfine sugar
1 egg yolk, lightly beaten
1 tsp strawberry flavoring
2 cups all-purpose flour
pinch of salt
1 cup dry unsweetened coconut
4 tbsp strawberry jam

Preheat the oven to 375°F/190°C. Line 2 large baking sheets with parchment paper. Place the butter and sugar in a large bowl and beat together until light and fluffy, then beat in the egg yolk and strawberry flavoring. Sift together the flour and salt into the mixture, add the coconut, and stir until thoroughly combined.

Scoop up tablespoons of the dough and roll them into balls, then place them on the baking sheets, spaced well apart. Use the dampened handle of a wooden spoon to make a hollow in the center of each and fill the hollows with strawberry jam.

Bake in the preheated oven for 12–15 minutes, or until golden brown. Let cool on the baking sheets for 5–10 minutes, then transfer the cookies to wire racks to cool completely.

346 With marmalade filling

Replace the coconut with ⅓ cup chopped candied fruit and ½ teaspoon of finely grated orange rind. Fill the hollows with marmalade.

347 *Banana & caramel cookies*

Makes About 30

1 cup butter, softened
¾ cup superfine sugar
1 egg yolk, lightly beaten
1 oz/25 g preserved ginger, finely chopped, plus 2 tsp syrup from the jar
2 cups all-purpose flour
pinch of salt
3 oz/85 g dried bananas, finely chopped
15 chocolate caramels

Place the butter and sugar in a large bowl and beat together until light and fluffy, then beat in the egg yolk, ginger, and ginger syrup. Sift together the flour and salt into the mixture, add the bananas, and stir until thoroughly combined. Halve the dough, shape into balls, wrap in plastic wrap, and chill in the refrigerator for 30–60 minutes.

Preheat the oven to 375°F/190°C. Line 2 large baking sheets with parchment paper. Unwrap the dough and roll it out between 2 sheets of parchment paper. Cut out cookies with a 2½-inch/6-cm fluted round cutter and place half of them on the baking sheets, spaced well apart. Place a chocolate caramel in the center of each cookie, then top with the remaining cookies and pinch the edges of the rounds together.

Bake in the preheated oven for 10–15 minutes, or until light golden. Cool for 5–10 minutes, then transfer to wire racks to cool completely.

348 *Banana & raisin cookies*

Makes About 30

2 tbsp raisins
½ cup orange juice or rum
1 cup butter, softened
¾ cup superfine sugar
1 egg yolk, lightly beaten
2 cups all-purpose flour
pinch of salt
¾ cup dried bananas, finely chopped

Place the raisins in a bowl, pour in the orange juice or rum, and let soak for 30 minutes. Drain the raisins, reserving any remaining liquid.

Preheat the oven to 375°F/190°C. Line 2 large baking sheets with parchment paper. Place the butter and sugar in a large bowl and beat together until light and fluffy, then beat in the egg yolk and 2 teaspoons of the reserved orange juice. Sift together the flour and salt into the mixture, add the raisins and dried bananas, and stir until combined.

Place tablespoons of the mixture into heaps on the baking sheets, spaced well apart, then flatten them gently.

Bake in the preheated oven for 12–15 minutes, or until golden. Let cool on the baking sheets for 5–10 minutes, then transfer the cookies to wire racks to cool completely.

349 *Banana & coconut cookies*

Replace the raisins with ½ cup dry unsweetened coconut.

350 *Chocolate & orange cookie sandwiches*

MAKES ABOUT 15

1 cup butter, softened
¾ cup superfine sugar
2 tsp finely grated orange rind
1 egg yolk, lightly beaten
2 tsp vanilla extract
1¾ cups all-purpose flour
¼ cup unsweetened cocoa
pinch of salt
3½ oz/100 g semisweet chocolate, finely chopped

CHOCOLATE FILLING
½ cup heavy cream
7 oz/200 g white chocolate, broken into pieces
1 tsp orange extract

Preheat the oven to 375°F/190°C. Line 2 large baking sheets with parchment paper.

Place the butter, sugar, and orange rind in a large bowl and beat together until light and fluffy. Beat in the egg yolk and vanilla. Sift together the flour, cocoa, and salt into the mixture, then add the chocolate and stir well. Scoop up tablespoons of the dough, roll into balls, and place on the baking sheets, spaced well apart. Gently flatten and smooth the tops with the back of a spoon.

Bake in the preheated oven for 10–15 minutes, or until light golden. Let cool on the baking sheets for 5–10 minutes, then transfer to wire racks to cool completely.

To make the filling, bring the cream to a boil in a small saucepan, then remove the pan from the heat. Stir in the chocolate until the mixture is smooth, then stir in the orange extract. When the mixture is completely cool, sandwich the cookies together in pairs.

351 *With semisweet chocolate*

For the chocolate filling, replace the white chocolate with semisweet chocolate and sift over cocoa to finish.

352 *With semisweet & white chocolate*

Replace half the white chocolate with melted semisweet chocolate to make 2 fillings. Fill half the sandwiches with white filling and sift over confectioners' sugar. Fill the remaining cookies with semisweet chocolate filling and sift over cocoa.

353 *Apple suns & pear stars*

MAKES ABOUT 30

1 cup butter, softened
¾ cup superfine sugar
1 egg yolk, lightly beaten
2 cups all-purpose flour
pinch of salt
½ tsp apple pie spice
⅓ cup plumped dried apple, finely chopped
½ tsp ground ginger
⅓ cup plumped dried pears, finely chopped
¼ cup slivered almonds
1 egg white, lightly beaten
raw brown sugar, for sprinkling

Place the butter and sugar in a large bowl and beat together until light and fluffy, then beat in the egg yolk. Sift together the flour and salt into the mixture and stir until combined. Transfer half the dough to another bowl. Add the apple pie spice and dried apple to one bowl and mix well. Shape into a ball, wrap in plastic wrap, and chill for 30–60 minutes.

Add the ginger and dried pear to the other bowl and mix well. Shape into a ball, wrap in plastic wrap, and chill for 30–60 minutes.

Preheat the oven to 375°F/190°C. Line 2 large baking sheets with parchment paper.

Unwrap the apple-flavored dough and roll out between 2 sheets of parchment paper to about ⅛ inch/3 mm thick. Cut out cookies with a sun-shaped cutter and place them on the baking sheet.

Repeat with the pear-flavored dough. Cut out cookies with a star-shaped cutter and place them on the other baking sheet.

Bake in the preheated oven for 5 minutes, then remove the star-shaped cookies from the oven and sprinkle with the slivered almonds. Bake for an additional 5–10 minutes. Remove the cookies from the oven but do not turn off the heat. Brush the apple suns with a little egg white and sprinkle with raw brown sugar, then bake for an additional 2–3 minutes. Let all the cookies cool for 5–10 minutes, then transfer them onto wire racks to cool completely.

354 *With apple icing*

Replace the slivered almonds, egg white, and sugar topping with an apple-flavored basic icing made by sifting 1 cup confectioners' sugar into a bowl and beating in 1½ tablespoons of apple juice with a drop of green food coloring. Spread onto the cooled cookies.

355 *Orangines*

MAKES ABOUT 15

2 tbsp butter, softened, plus extra for greasing
2 tbsp candied orange peel
2 tbsp superfine sugar
2 tbsp all-purpose flour
¼ cup ground almonds
finely grated rind of 1 small orange
1 tsp orange juice

Preheat the oven to 350°F/180°C. Grease several large baking sheets. Very finely chop the candied orange peel.

Place the butter and sugar in a large bowl and whisk together until pale and creamy. Add the flour, ground almonds, grated orange rind, and juice and mix well together.

Place teaspoonfuls of the mixture onto the baking sheets, spacing them well apart. Bake in the preheated oven for 7–8 minutes, or until lightly golden brown around the edges. Leave on the baking sheets for 2–3 minutes, then transfer the cookies to wire racks to cool completely.

356 Citrus crescents

MAKES ABOUT 25

7 tbsp butter, softened, plus extra for greasing
heaping 1/3 cup superfine sugar
1 egg, separated
scant 1½ cups all-purpose flour, plus extra for dusting
finely grated rind of 1 orange
finely grated rind of 1 lemon
finely grated rind of 1 lime
2–3 tbsp orange juice

Preheat the oven to 400°F/200°C. Lightly grease 2 large baking sheets. Place the butter and sugar in a large bowl and beat together until light and fluffy, then gradually beat in the egg yolk. Sift the flour into the creamed mixture and mix until thoroughly combined. Add the orange, lemon, and lime rinds with enough of the orange juice to form a soft dough.

Roll the dough out on a lightly floured work surface and cut out rounds with a 3-inch/7.5-cm cookie cutter. Make crescent shapes by cutting away a quarter of each round. Re-roll the trimmings to make about 25 crescents. Place the crescents on the baking sheets and prick the surface of each crescent with a fork. Lightly whisk the egg white in a small bowl and brush it over the cookies.

Bake in the preheated oven for 12–15 minutes, or until golden brown. Let the cookies cool on a wire rack before serving.

357 With lemon cream

Make a double quantity of the cookies. Prepare the lemon cream by beating 9 tablespoons of softened butter with 1½ cups confectioners' sugar and 1 teaspoon of finely grated lemon rind, 1 tablespoon of lemon juice, and ½ teaspoon of lemon oil, then use to sandwich the cookies together.

358 Chocolate temptations

MAKES 24

5½ tbsp butter, plus extra for greasing
12½ oz/365 g semisweet chocolate
1 tsp strong coffee
2 eggs
¾ cup light brown sugar
1⅓ cups all-purpose flour
¼ tsp baking powder
pinch of salt
2 tsp almond extract
heaping ½ cup Brazil nuts, chopped
heaping ½ cup hazelnuts, chopped
1½ oz/40 g white chocolate

Preheat the oven to 350°F/180°C. Grease 2 large baking sheets. Place 8 oz/225 g of the semisweet chocolate with the butter and coffee into a heatproof bowl, set the bowl over a saucepan of simmering water, and heat until the chocolate is almost melted. Remove and stir until smooth.

Beat the eggs in a bowl until fluffy, then gradually whisk in the sugar until thick. Add the chocolate to the egg mixture and stir to combine. Sift the flour, baking powder, and salt into a separate bowl and stir into the chocolate. Chop 3 oz/85 g of the semisweet chocolate into pieces and stir into the mixture. Stir in the almond extract and nuts. Place 24 tablespoonfuls of the dough onto the baking sheets. Bake in the preheated oven for 16 minutes. Transfer the cookies to a wire rack to cool. To decorate, melt the remaining semisweet chocolate and white chocolate, in turn, then spoon into pastry bags and pipe lines on the cookies. Let set.

359 Marshmallow s'mores

MAKES ABOUT 15

1 cup butter, softened
¾ cup superfine sugar
2 tsp finely grated orange rind
1 egg yolk, lightly beaten
1¾ cups all-purpose flour
¼ cup unsweetened cocoa
½ tsp ground cinnamon
pinch of salt
30 yellow marshmallows, halved horizontally
10½ oz/300 g semisweet chocolate, broken into pieces
4 tbsp orange marmalade
15 walnut halves, for decorating

Place the butter, sugar, and orange rind in a large bowl and beat together until light and fluffy, then beat in the egg yolk. Sift together the flour, cocoa, cinnamon, and salt into the mixture and stir until combined. Halve the dough, shape into balls, wrap in plastic wrap, and chill for 30–60 minutes.

Preheat the oven to 375°F/190°C. Line 2 large baking sheets with parchment paper. Unwrap the dough and roll out between 2 sheets of parchment paper. Cut out cookies with a 2½-inch/6-cm fluted round cutter and place them on the baking sheets, spaced well apart. Bake in the preheated oven for 10–15 minutes. Let cool for 5 minutes. Turn half the cookies upside down and put 4 marshmallow halves on each. Bake for an additional 1–2 minutes. Let the cookies stand on wire racks for 30 minutes.

Place the chocolate in a heatproof bowl, set the bowl over a saucepan of gently simmering water, and heat until melted. Let cool.

Line a baking sheet with parchment paper. Spread the marmalade over the undersides of the uncovered cookies and place them on top of the marshmallow-covered cookies. Dip the cookies in the melted chocolate to coat, letting the excess drip back into the bowl, then place them on the baking sheet. Place a walnut half in the center of each cookie and let set.

360 White s'mores

Replace the semisweet chocolate with white chocolate. Scatter over ⅔ cup shelled, chopped pistachios to replace the walnuts.

361 Thanksgiving cookies

MAKES ABOUT 30

1 cup butter, softened
¾ cup superfine sugar
1 egg yolk, lightly beaten
2 tsp orange juice
2 cups all-purpose flour
pinch of salt
heaping ⅓ cup fresh or dried blueberries
heaping ½ cup fresh or dried cranberries
⅓ cup white chocolate chips

Preheat the oven to 375°F/190°C. Line 2 large baking sheets with parchment paper. Place the butter and sugar in a large bowl and beat together until light and fluffy, then beat in the egg yolk and orange juice. Sift together the flour and salt into the mixture, then add the blueberries, cranberries, and chocolate chips and stir until combined.

Scoop up tablespoons of the dough and place them on the baking sheets, spaced well apart. Bake in the preheated oven for 10–15 minutes, or until light golden brown.

Let cool on the baking sheets for 5–10 minutes, then transfer the cookies to wire racks to cool completely.

362 Cherry Thanksgiving cookies

Replace the blueberries and cranberries with heaping ½ cup chopped, dried cherries. Replace the white chocolate chips with semisweet chocolate chips.

363 Dinosaur cookies

MAKES 30

1 cup unsalted butter, softened
1 cup smooth peanut butter
1 cup granulated sugar
1 cup light brown sugar
2 tsp baking powder
¼ tsp salt
2 large eggs
1 tsp vanilla extract
2 cups all-purpose flour, plus extra for dusting
silver dragées and tube of green decorating icing, for decorating

Place the butter and peanut butter in a large bowl and beat together until smooth. Add the sugars, baking powder, and salt and beat well to combine. Whisk the eggs and vanilla extract together in a separate bowl, then add to the mixture and mix well. Sift in the flour and mix to form a smooth dough. Wrap in plastic wrap and chill for 30 minutes.

Preheat the oven to 350°F/180°C. Roll the dough out on a floured work surface and cut out shapes with dinosaur cookie cutters dipped in flour. Re-roll any trimmings and cut out more cookies. Press silver dragées into the dough for eyes and place on 2 large nonstick baking sheets. Bake in the preheated oven for 10–12 minutes.

Let cool for 2 minutes, then transfer to a wire rack to cool completely. Decorate the dinosaurs with green decorating icing.

364 Chocolate dinosaur cookies

Add 3 teaspoons of cocoa to the dough and knead in before chilling.

365 Bedtime bears

MAKES 25

8 tbsp unsalted butter, softened
½ cup superfine sugar
1 tsp baking powder
pinch of salt
1 large egg, lightly beaten
1 tsp milk
1 tsp vanilla extract
¼ cup unsweetened cocoa, plus extra for dusting
1 cup all-purpose flour
25 cookie bears, 2¾-inch/7-cm tall
3 tbsp smooth peanut butter

Place the butter and sugar in a large bowl and beat together until light and fluffy. Add the baking powder, salt, egg, milk, and vanilla extract and beat well. Sift in the cocoa and flour and mix to form a smooth dough. Wrap in plastic wrap and chill in the refrigerator for 3 hours.

Preheat the oven to 350°F/180°C. Roll the dough out on a work surface dusted with cocoa, then cut into twenty-five 2-inch/5-cm squares. Place a cookie bear diagonally on the square and secure with peanut butter. Fold up the bottom and sides of the dough to form a blanket around the bear, leaving the top third of the bear exposed. Press to secure and place on a large nonstick baking sheet. Bake in the preheated oven for 10 minutes. Cool on a wire rack.

366 With colored blankets

Omit the cocoa and divide the dough into portions. Tint each portion with a few drops of different food coloring. Roll out and cut as usual, and wrap the cookie bears in the colored dough blankets.

367 Farmyard friends

Makes 25

heaping 1 cup unsalted butter, softened
1⅓ cups superfine sugar
2 large eggs, lightly beaten
3¼ cups all-purpose flour, plus extra for dusting
2 tsp baking powder
pinch of salt
few drops of food coloring
tube of decorating icing

Place the butter and sugar in a large bowl and beat together until light and fluffy. Gradually add the eggs and beat to combine, then sift in the flour, baking powder, and salt and mix to form a dough. Wrap the dough in plastic wrap and chill in the refrigerator for 2 hours.

Preheat the oven to 325°F/160°C. Line 2 large baking sheets with parchment paper.

Set aside one third of the dough and leave uncolored. Divide the remaining dough into portions and knead in different food colorings. Shape the dough into animal shapes (see right) and place the cookies on the baking sheets. Bake for 20–25 minutes. Let cool on a wire rack. Add eyes and other features with the decorating icing.

Cow cookie: Shape an oval piece of colored dough to 2½ inches/6 cm across for the body. Roll another piece of dough into a log 2½ inches/6 cm long and ½ inch/1 cm wide, then cut into 3 equal pieces—use 2 for the legs and 1 for the head. Roll uncolored dough into small circles and use as the udder, nose, and markings. Make a thin tail. Press the pieces well together.

Pig cookie: Shape an oval piece of colored dough to 2½ inches/6 cm across for the body; flatten. Shape a smaller oval piece to 1¼ inches/3 cm for the head; flatten. Use uncolored dough for the snout, ears, and tail.

Fluffy sheep cookie: For the body, roll small balls of uncolored dough and lay them on the baking sheet, touching each other in an oval shape. Use colored dough to shape the head and feet.

368 Party cookies

MAKES 15

7 tbsp butter
½ cup light brown sugar
1 tbsp dark corn syrup
heaping 1 cup self-rising flour
3 oz/85 g sugar-coated chocolates

Preheat the oven to 350°F/180°C. Line several large baking sheets with parchment paper. Place the butter and sugar in a large bowl and whisk together until pale and creamy, then whisk the dark corn syrup into the mixture until smooth. Add ½ cup flour and whisk together until mixed. Stir in the sugar-coated chocolates and remaining flour then, with your hands, knead the mixture until smooth.

Roll small pieces of the dough between your hands into smooth balls to make 15 cookies in total and place them on the baking sheets, spacing them well apart. Bake in the preheated oven for 10–15 minutes, or until golden brown.

Leave on the baking sheets for 2–3 minutes, then transfer the cookies to a wire rack and let cool completely.

369 Chocolate-covered raisin cookies

Replace the sugar-coated chocolates with chocolate-covered raisins.

370 Choco mint stars

MAKES ABOUT 30

1 cup butter, softened
¾ cup superfine sugar
1 egg yolk, lightly beaten
1 tsp peppermint extract
2 cups all-purpose flour
pinch of salt
heaping 1 cup dry unsweetened coconut

FOR DECORATING
3½ oz/100 g white chocolate, broken into pieces
3½ oz/100 g milk chocolate, broken into pieces

Place the butter and sugar in a large bowl and beat together until light and fluffy, then beat in the egg yolk and peppermint extract. Sift together the flour and salt into the mixture, add the coconut, and stir until combined. Divide the mixture in half, shape into balls, wrap in plastic wrap, and chill for 30–60 minutes.

Preheat the oven to 375°F/190°C. Line 2 large baking sheets with parchment paper. Unwrap the dough and roll out between 2 sheets of parchment paper to about ⅛ inch/3 mm thick.

Cut out stars with a 2½–2¾-inch/6–7-cm cutter and place them on the baking sheets, spaced well apart.

Bake in the preheated oven for 10–12 minutes, or until light golden. Let cool on the baking sheets for 5–10 minutes, then transfer the cookies to wire racks to cool completely.

Place the white chocolate and the milk chocolate in separate heatproof bowls, set the bowls over 2 saucepans of gently simmering water, and heat until melted. Leave the cooled cookies on the racks and drizzle first with melted white chocolate and then with melted milk chocolate, using a teaspoon. Let set.

371 White mint stars

Omit the milk chocolate and melt 7 oz/200 g white chocolate in a heatproof bowl set over a pan of gently simmering water. Spread to cover each cookie and sprinkle over chocolate sprinkles.

372 Snickerdoodles

MAKES ABOUT 40

1 cup butter, softened
¾ cup superfine sugar
2 large eggs, lightly beaten
1 tsp vanilla extract
3 cups all-purpose flour
1 tsp baking soda
½ tsp freshly grated nutmeg
pinch of salt
⅓ cup pecans, finely chopped

CINNAMON COATING
1 tbsp superfine sugar
2 tbsp ground cinnamon

Place the butter and sugar in a large bowl and beat together until light and fluffy, then beat in the eggs and vanilla extract. Sift together the flour, baking soda, nutmeg, and salt into the mixture, add the pecans, and stir until thoroughly combined. Shape the dough into a ball, wrap in plastic wrap, and chill in the refrigerator for 30–60 minutes.

Preheat the oven to 375°F/190°C. Line 2 large baking sheets with parchment paper.

For the coating, mix the sugar and cinnamon in a shallow dish. Scoop up tablespoons of the dough and roll into balls. Roll each ball in the cinnamon mixture and place on the baking sheets, spaced well apart. Bake in the preheated oven for 10–12 minutes, or until golden brown. Cool for 5–10 minutes, then transfer to wire racks to cool completely.

373 Chocodoodles

Add 2 tablespoons of cocoa to the dough and roll the cookies in 2 tablespoons of superfine sugar mixed with 1 tablespoon of cocoa before baking.

374 Melt-in-the-middles

MAKES ABOUT 30

3 oz/85 g semisweet chocolate, broken into pieces
8 tbsp butter, softened
¾ cup superfine sugar
1 egg yolk, lightly beaten
2 tsp vanilla extract
2 cups all-purpose flour
1 tbsp unsweetened cocoa
pinch of salt

FILLING
1 egg white
¼ cup superfine sugar
1 cup dry unsweetened coconut
1 tsp all-purpose flour
2 tbsp plumped dried papaya, finely chopped

Preheat the oven to 375°F/190°C. Line 2 large baking sheets with parchment paper.

To make the middle filling, whisk the egg white in a large bowl until soft peaks form, then gradually whisk in the sugar. Gently fold in the coconut, flour, and papaya and set aside.

Place the chocolate in a heatproof bowl, set the bowl over a saucepan of gently simmering water, and heat until melted, then remove from the heat. Place the butter and sugar in a large bowl and beat together until light and fluffy, then beat in the egg yolk and vanilla extract. Sift together the flour, cocoa, and salt into the mixture and stir until thoroughly combined. Stir in the melted chocolate and knead lightly.

Roll out the dough between 2 sheets of parchment paper to ¼–⅜ inch/5–8 mm thick. Cut out rounds with a 2¾-inch/7-cm fluted round cutter and place them on the baking sheets. Using a 1¼-inch/3-cm plain round cutter, cut out the centers and remove them. Bake for 8 minutes, then remove from the oven and lower the temperature to 325°F/160°C. Spoon the filling mixture into the center of the cookies. Place a sheet of foil over each baking sheet, crumpled so that it doesn't touch the cookies, to stop the filling mixture from browning.

Bake for an additional 15–20 minutes, or until the middles are firm. Let cool on the baking sheets for 5–10 minutes, then transfer the cookies to wire racks to cool completely.

375 Crunchy muesli cookies

Makes 24

8 tbsp unsalted butter, softened, plus extra for greasing
½ cup raw brown sugar
1 tbsp honey
heaping ¾ cup self-rising flour
pinch of salt
⅓ cup plumped dried apricots, chopped
heaping ¼ cup dried figs, chopped
1⅓ cups rolled oats
1 tsp milk (optional)
¼ cup golden raisins or cranberries
scant ½ cup walnut halves, chopped

Preheat the oven to 325°F/160°C. Grease 2 large baking sheets. Place the butter, sugar, and honey in a saucepan and heat over low heat until melted. Mix to combine. Sift together the flour and salt into a large bowl and stir in the apricots, figs, and oats. Pour in the butter and sugar mixture and mix to form a dough. If it is too stiff, add a little milk.

Divide the dough into 24 pieces and roll each piece into a ball. Place 12 balls on each baking sheet and press flat to a diameter of 2½ inches/6 cm. Mix the golden raisins and walnuts together and press into the cookies. Bake in the preheated oven for 15 minutes, swapping the sheets halfway through. Let cool on the baking sheets.

376 With nutty topping

Chop ⅔ cup mixed nuts and use to top the cookies before baking.

377 Really large coconut macaroons

Makes 8

2 large egg whites
heaping ½ cup superfine sugar
1⅔ cups dry unsweetened coconut
8 candied cherries

Preheat the oven to 350°F/180°C. Line 2–3 large baking sheets with rice paper.

Place the egg whites in a large bowl and whisk until soft peaks form and they hold their shape but are not dry. Add the sugar to the egg whites and, using a large metal spoon, fold in until incorporated. Add the coconut and fold into the mixture. Place 8 heaping tablespoons of the mixture onto the baking sheets and place a cherry on top of each macaroon.

Bake in the preheated oven for 15–20 minutes, or until lightly golden brown around the edges. Leave on the baking sheets for 2–3 minutes, then transfer the macaroons to a wire rack to cool completely.

378 Nutty macaroons

Finely chop ⅓ cup almonds, hazelnuts, macadamia nuts, pecans, or walnuts and add to the mixture with the coconut.

379 *Cherry garlands*

Makes 30

heaping ⅔ cup unsalted butter, softened
½ cup confectioners' sugar
½ tsp vanilla extract
heaping 1 cup all-purpose flour
pinch of salt
⅓ cup candied cherries, chopped

Preheat the oven to 375°F/190°C. Place the butter and sugar in a large bowl and beat together until light and fluffy. Add the vanilla extract and beat until combined. Sift in the flour and salt in batches, mixing well between each addition. Add the cherries and mix well.

Spoon the mixture into a pastry bag fitted with a 1-inch/2.5-cm star tip and pipe rings onto 2 large nonstick baking sheets. Bake in the preheated oven for 8–10 minutes, or until light golden. Let cool on a wire rack.

380 *With cherry frosting*

Make a butter frosting with 6 tablespoons of butter beaten with 1⅓ cups confectioners' sugar and adding ¼ cup chopped candied cherries. Pipe the frosting onto the cookies and decorate with pieces of angelica.

381 *Pistachio & almond cookies*

Makes About 30

1 cup butter, softened
¾ cup superfine sugar
1 egg yolk, lightly beaten
2 tsp almond extract
1⅔ cups all-purpose flour
pinch of salt
heaping ½ cup ground almonds
⅓ cup pistachios, finely chopped

Place the butter and sugar in a large bowl and beat together until light and fluffy, then beat in the egg yolk and almond extract. Sift together the flour and salt into the mixture, add the ground almonds, and stir until thoroughly combined. Halve the dough, shape into balls, wrap in plastic wrap, and chill in the refrigerator for 30–60 minutes.

Preheat the oven to 375°F/190°C. Line 2 large baking sheets with parchment paper. Unwrap the dough and roll out between 2 sheets of parchment paper to about ⅛ inch/3 mm thick. Sprinkle half the pistachios over each piece of dough and roll lightly with the rolling pin. Cut out cookies with a heart-shaped cutter and place them on the baking sheets, spaced well apart.

Bake in the preheated oven for 10–12 minutes. Let cool for 5–10 minutes, then transfer the cookies to wire racks to cool completely.

382 *With pistachio cream*

Whisk scant 1 cup heavy cream to soft peaks with 2 tablespoons of confectioners' sugar and ½ teaspoon of green food coloring. Fold in ½ cup chopped pistachios and spoon into a bowl, then use as a dip for the cookies.

383 Giant chocolate chunk cookies

MAKES 12

8 tbsp butter, softened
scant ⅔ cup superfine sugar
scant ⅔ cup light brown sugar
2 large eggs, lightly beaten
1 tsp vanilla extract
2 cups all-purpose flour
1 tsp baking soda
10½ oz/300 g chocolate chunks

Preheat the oven to 350°F/180°C. Line several large baking sheets with parchment paper.

Place the butter and sugars in a large bowl and whisk together until pale and creamy. Whisk the eggs and vanilla extract into the mixture until smooth. Sift in the flour and baking soda and beat together until well mixed. Stir in the chocolate chunks.

Drop 12 large spoonfuls of the batter onto the baking sheets, spacing them well apart.

Bake in the preheated oven for 15–20 minutes, or until set and golden brown. Let cool on the baking sheets for 2–3 minutes, then transfer the cookies to a wire rack and let cool completely.

384 Giant chocolate chip cookies

Replace the chocolate chunks with chocolate chips. These can be semisweet, milk, or white chocolate, or use some of each.

385 Indulgent chocolate chunk cookies

Scatter 3½ oz/100 g chocolate chunks over the top of the cookies before baking in the oven.

386 Crunchy nut & honey sandwiches

MAKES ABOUT 30

1¼ cups butter, softened
¾ cup superfine sugar
1 egg yolk, lightly beaten
2 tsp vanilla extract
2 cups all-purpose flour
pinch of salt
¼ cup macadamia nuts, cashew nuts or pine nuts, chopped
¾ cup confectioners' sugar
¼ cup clover or other set honey

Preheat the oven to 375°F/190°C. Line 2 large baking sheets with parchment paper. Place 1 cup of the butter and the superfine sugar in a large bowl and beat together until light and fluffy, then beat in the egg yolk and vanilla. Sift together the flour and salt into the mixture and stir until combined. Scoop up tablespoons of the dough and roll into balls. Place half of them on a baking sheet, spaced well apart, and flatten gently. Spread out the nuts in a shallow dish and dip one side of the remaining dough balls into them, then place on the other baking sheet, nut-side up, and flatten gently.

Bake in the preheated oven for 10–15 minutes, or until light golden brown. Let cool on the baking sheets for 5–10 minutes, then transfer the cookies to wire racks to cool completely.

Place the remaining butter, the confectioners' sugar, and honey in a bowl and beat together until creamy. Spread the honey mixture over the plain cookies and top with the nut-coated cookies.

387 Nut & maple syrup sandwiches

Replace the macadamia nuts with chopped pecans in the dough and replace the honey with maple syrup.

388 Golden hazelnut cookies

MAKES ABOUT 30

1 cup butter, softened
¾ cup superfine sugar
1 egg yolk, lightly beaten
1⅔ cups all-purpose flour
pinch of salt
heaping ½ cup ground hazelnuts

TOPPING
8 oz/225 g semisweet chocolate, broken into pieces
about 30 hazelnuts

Place the butter and sugar in a large bowl and beat together until light and fluffy, then beat in the egg yolk. Sift together the flour and salt into the mixture, add the ground hazelnuts, and stir until thoroughly combined. Halve the dough, form into balls, wrap in plastic wrap, and chill in the refrigerator for 30–60 minutes.

Preheat the oven to 375°F/190°C. Line 2 large baking sheets with parchment paper.

Unwrap the dough and roll out between 2 sheets of parchment paper. Cut out rounds with a plain 2½-inch/6-cm cutter and place them on the baking sheet, spaced well apart. Bake in the preheated oven for 10–12 minutes, or until golden brown. Let cool for 5–10 minutes, then transfer the cookies to wire racks to cool.

When the cookies are cool, place the wire racks over a sheet of parchment paper. Place the chocolate in a heatproof bowl, set the bowl over a saucepan of gently simmering water, and heat until melted. Let cool, then spoon the chocolate over the cookies. Gently tap the wire racks to level the surface and let set for a few minutes. Add a hazelnut to the center of each cookie and let set.

389 With white chocolate coating

Replace the semisweet chocolate with white chocolate and chop the hazelnuts before scattering over the chocolate.

390 *Mega chip cookies*

Makes 12

1 cup butter, softened
¾ cup superfine sugar
1 egg yolk, lightly beaten
2 tsp vanilla extract
1⅔ cups all-purpose flour
½ cup unsweetened cocoa
pinch of salt
½ cup milk chocolate chips
½ cup white chocolate chips
4 oz/115 g semisweet chocolate, coarsely chopped

Preheat the oven to 375°F/190°C. Line 2–3 baking sheets with parchment paper. Place the butter and sugar in a large bowl and beat together until light and fluffy, then beat in the egg yolk and vanilla extract. Sift together the flour, cocoa, and salt into the mixture, add both kinds of chocolate chips, and stir until thoroughly combined.

Make 12 balls of the dough, place them on the baking sheets, spaced well apart, and flatten slightly. Press the pieces of semisweet chocolate into the cookies.

Bake in the preheated oven for 12–15 minutes. Let cool on the baking sheets for 5–10 minutes, then transfer the cookies to wire racks to cool completely.

391 *Caramel chip cookies*

Replace the chocolate chips with 10 oz/280 g chopped caramel chocolate.

392 *Peanut partners*

Makes About 30

1 cup butter, softened
¾ cup superfine sugar
1 egg yolk, lightly beaten
2 cups all-purpose flour
1 tsp ground ginger
pinch of salt
2 tsp finely grated lemon rind

TOPPING
3 tbsp smooth peanut butter
3 tbsp confectioners' sugar
whole or chopped roasted peanuts, for decorating

Place the butter and sugar in a large bowl and beat together until light and fluffy, then beat in the egg yolk. Sift together the flour, ginger, and salt into the mixture, add the lemon rind, and stir until thoroughly combined. Halve the dough, shape into balls, wrap in plastic wrap, and chill in the refrigerator for 30–60 minutes.

Preheat the oven to 375°F/190°C. Line 2 large baking sheets with parchment paper. Unwrap the dough and roll out between 2 sheets of parchment paper to ⅛ inch/3 mm thick. Cut out rounds with a 2½-inch/6-cm fluted cutter and place them on the baking sheets, spaced well apart. Bake in the preheated oven for 10–15 minutes, until golden. Cool for 5–10 minutes, then transfer to wire racks to cool completely. To make the topping, beat the peanut butter and confectioners' sugar together in a bowl, adding a little water if necessary. Spread the cookies with the mixture and decorate with peanuts.

393 *With peanut brittle topping*

For an alternative topping, spread the cookies with unsweetened smooth peanut butter and scatter over 5½ oz/150 g crushed peanut brittle.

394 *Rich peanut & cream cookies sandwiches*

MAKES ABOUT 15

6 tbsp salted peanuts
1 cup butter, softened
¾ cup superfine sugar
1 egg yolk, lightly beaten
2 cups all-purpose flour
½ tsp allspice
pinch of salt
3 tbsp heavy cream
⅓ cup cream cheese
¾ cup crystallized pineapple, chopped

Set aside half the peanuts and finely chop the remainder. Place the butter and sugar in a large bowl and beat together until light and fluffy, then beat in the egg yolk. Sift together the flour, allspice, and salt into the mixture and stir until combined. Halve the dough, shape into balls, wrap in plastic wrap, and chill in the refrigerator for 30–60 minutes.

Preheat the oven to 375°F/190°C. Line 2 large baking sheets with parchment paper. Unwrap the dough and roll out between 2 sheets of parchment paper. Sprinkle evenly with the reserved peanuts and lightly roll with the rolling pin. Cut out cookies with a 2–2½-inch/5–6-cm fluted round cutter and place them on the baking sheets, spaced well apart.

Bake in the preheated oven for 10–15 minutes, or until light golden. Let cool on the baking sheets for 5–10 minutes, then transfer the cookies to wire racks to cool completely.

Place the cream and cream cheese in a bowl and beat together until thick and smooth. Fold in the crystallized pineapple. Spread the mixture over the undersides of half the cookies and top with the remaining cookies, peanut-side uppermost.

395 *With coconut peanut cream*

For the filling, sift ½ cup confectioners' sugar into a bowl and beat with 1 tablespoon of coconut rum and ⅓ cup crunchy peanut butter, then use this to sandwich the cookies together.

396 *Pistachio cookies*

MAKES ABOUT 30

1⅔ cups blanched pistachios
9 tbsp unsalted butter
finely grated rind of 1 lemon
½ cup light brown sugar
1 egg
heaping 1 cup self-rising flour
good pinch of salt

Place the pistachios in a clean dish towel and rub vigorously to remove any papery skin. Place the butter, lemon rind, and sugar in a large bowl and beat together until smooth. Add the egg and beat well. Sift together the flour and salt into the mixture. Crush the nuts and stir into the batter until combined. Pour the batter onto a large sheet of plastic wrap and roll it up into a sausage shape. Twist the 2 ends of the plastic wrap and chill in the refrigerator for 20 minutes.

Preheat the oven to 350°F/180°C. Line 2 large baking sheets with parchment paper.

Unwrap the plastic wrap, cut the cookies into ¼-inch/5-mm thick rounds, and place them on the baking sheets, evenly spaced apart. Bake in the preheated oven for 10–15 minutes, or until golden brown. Let cool on a wire rack.

397 Walnut & fig pinwheels

MAKES ABOUT 30

1 cup butter, softened
1 cup superfine sugar
1 egg yolk, lightly beaten
1⅔ cups all-purpose flour
pinch of salt
heaping ⅓ cup ground walnuts
½ cup water
1½ cups dried figs, finely chopped
5 tbsp freshly brewed mint tea
2 tsp finely chopped fresh mint

Place the butter and ¾ cup of the sugar in a large bowl and beat together until light and fluffy, then beat in the egg yolk. Sift together the flour and salt into the mixture, add the walnuts, and stir until combined. Shape the dough into a ball, wrap in plastic wrap, and chill for 30–60 minutes.

Meanwhile, place the remaining sugar in a saucepan and stir in the water, then add the figs, mint tea, and chopped mint. Bring to a boil, stirring continuously, until the sugar has dissolved, then reduce the heat and simmer gently, stirring occasionally, for 5 minutes. Let cool.

Unwrap the dough and roll out between 2 sheets of parchment paper into a 12-inch/30-cm square. Spread the fig filling evenly over the dough, then roll up from a short side like a jelly roll. Wrap in plastic wrap and chill for 30 minutes.

Preheat the oven to 375°F/190°C. Line 2 large baking sheets with parchment paper. Unwrap the roll and cut into thin slices with a sharp serrated knife. Place the slices on the baking sheets, making sure they are spaced well apart.

Bake in the preheated oven for 10–15 minutes, or until golden brown. Let cool on the baking sheets for 5–10 minutes, then transfer to wire racks to cool completely.

398 Date & pecan pinwheels

Replace the walnuts and figs with finely chopped pecans and finely chopped, pitted dried dates.

399 Almond cookies with green tea cream

MAKES ABOUT 15

1 cup butter, softened
¾ cup superfine sugar, plus extra for sprinkling
1 egg yolk, lightly beaten
2 tsp vanilla extract
2 cups all-purpose flour
pinch of salt
¼ cup slivered almonds
1 egg white, lightly beaten

GREEN TEA CREAM
½ cup milk
2 green tea tea bags or 2 tsp green tea leaves
1 tbsp superfine sugar
1 tbsp vanilla instant pudding mix
½ cup cream cheese

Place the butter and sugar in a large bowl and beat together until light and fluffy, then beat in the egg yolk and vanilla. Sift in the flour and salt and stir well. Halve the dough, wrap in plastic wrap, and chill for 30–60 minutes.

Preheat the oven to 375°F/190°C. Line 2 large baking sheets with parchment paper.

Roll out a dough ball between 2 sheets of parchment paper. Cut out cookies with a 2½-inch/6-cm cutter and place on a baking sheet. Roll out the other dough ball until it is ½ inch/1 cm thick. Sprinkle with the almonds, cover with parchment paper, and roll out to ¼ inch/5 mm thick. Cut out 2½-inch/6-cm rounds and place on the other baking sheet. Brush with egg white and sprinkle with sugar. Bake in the preheated oven for 10–15 minutes, or until golden. Cool for 5–10 minutes, then transfer to wire racks.

Bring the milk to a boil, then remove from the heat. Add the tea, cover with plastic wrap, and steep for 15 minutes. Strain into a clean pan. Stir in the sugar and pudding mix and bring to a boil, stirring until thick. Cover and cool.

Beat the cream cheese until smooth. Beat in the green tea cream. Spread the cream over the plain cookies and top with the almond cookies.

400 With almond cream

Replace the green tea cream with almond cream, made by beating 1 tablespoon of confectioners' sugar and 1 teaspoon of almond extract into ½ cup cream cheese.

401 Almond crunchies

MAKES ABOUT 50

1 cup butter, softened
¾ cup superfine sugar
1 egg yolk, lightly beaten
½ tsp almond extract
1⅔ cups all-purpose flour
pinch of salt
1½ cups blanched almonds, chopped

Place the butter and sugar in a large bowl and beat together until light and fluffy, then beat in the egg yolk and almond extract. Sift together the flour and salt into the mixture, add the almonds, and stir until thoroughly combined. Halve the dough, shape it into balls, wrap in plastic wrap, and chill in the refrigerator for 30–60 minutes.

Preheat the oven to 375°F/190°C. Line 2–3 baking sheets with parchment paper.

Shape the dough into about 50 small balls, flatten them slightly between the palms of your hands, and place them on the baking sheets, spaced well apart. Bake in the preheated oven for 15–20 minutes, or until golden brown. Let cool on the baking sheets for 5–10 minutes, then transfer to wire racks to cool completely.

402 With marzipan filling

Cut 3½ oz/100 g marzipan into small cubes and press one piece into the middle of each cookie. Form the dough around the marzipan to completely enclose and bake as before.

403 Almond & raspberry jam drops

MAKES ABOUT 25

1 cup butter, softened
¾ cup superfine sugar
1 egg yolk, lightly beaten
2 tsp almond extract
2 cups all-purpose flour
pinch of salt
heaping ⅓ cup almonds, toasted and chopped
½ cup chopped candied peel
4 tbsp raspberry jam

Preheat the oven to 375°F/190°C. Line 2 baking sheets with parchment paper. Place the butter and sugar in a large bowl and beat together until light and fluffy, then beat in the egg yolk and almond extract. Sift together the flour and salt into the mixture, add the almonds and candied peel, and stir until thoroughly combined.

Scoop out tablespoons of the dough and shape into balls with your hands, then place them on the baking sheets, spaced well apart. Use the dampened handle of a wooden spoon to make a hollow in the center of each cookie and fill with raspberry jam. Bake in the preheated oven for 12–15 minutes, or until golden brown. Let cool for 5–10 minutes, then transfer to wire racks to cool completely.

404 Almond & strawberry jam drops

Replace the candied peel with ⅓ cup chopped dried strawberries and replace the raspberry jam with strawberry jam.

405 *Nutty drizzles*

MAKES 24

heaping ¾ cup butter, plus extra for greasing
scant 1½ cups raw brown sugar
1 egg
1 cup all-purpose flour
1 tsp baking powder
1 tsp baking soda
1½ cups rolled oats
1 tbsp bran
1 tbsp wheat germ
¾ cup mixed nuts, toasted and coarsely chopped
scant 1¼ cups semisweet chocolate chips
¾ cup mixed raisins and golden raisins
6 oz/175 g semisweet chocolate, coarsely chopped

Preheat the oven to 350°F/180°C. Grease 2 large baking sheets. Place the butter, sugar, and egg in a large bowl and beat together until light and fluffy. Sift in the flour, baking powder, and baking soda. Add the oats, bran, and wheat germ and mix together until well combined. Stir in the nuts, chocolate chips, and raisins. Place 24 rounded tablespoons of the dough on the baking sheets.

Bake in the preheated oven for 12 minutes, or until golden brown. Let cool on wire racks.

Meanwhile, place the chocolate pieces in a heatproof bowl, set the bowl over a saucepan of gently simmering water, and heat until melted. Stir the chocolate, then let cool slightly. Use a spoon to drizzle the chocolate in waves over the cookies, or spoon it into a pastry bag and pipe zigzag lines over the cookies.

406 **With nut chocolate topping**

Add ¾ cup chopped mixed nuts to the melted chocolate and spread over the cookies.

407 *Cashew & poppy seed cookies*

MAKES ABOUT 20

1 cup butter, softened
¾ cup superfine sugar
1 egg yolk, lightly beaten
2 cups all-purpose flour
1 tsp ground cinnamon
pinch of salt
¾ cup cashew nuts, chopped
2–3 tbsp poppy seeds

Place the butter and sugar in a large bowl and beat together until light and fluffy, then beat in the egg yolk. Sift together the flour, cinnamon, and salt into the mixture, add the nuts, and stir until combined. Shape the dough into a log. Spread out the poppy seeds in a dish and roll the log in them until coated. Wrap in plastic wrap and chill in the refrigerator for 30–60 minutes.

Preheat the oven to 375°F/190°C. Line 2 large baking sheets with parchment paper.

Unwrap the dough, cut into ½-inch/1-cm slices with a sharp serrated knife, and place them on the baking sheets. Bake in the preheated oven for 12 minutes, or until golden brown. Let cool on the baking sheets for 5–10 minutes, then transfer to wire racks to cool completely.

408 **Cashew nut cookies**

Omit the poppy seeds and roll the dough in 1½ cups finely chopped cashew nuts.

409 Chocolate & coffee whole wheat cookies

MAKES 24

scant ¾ cup butter, plus extra for greasing
1 cup light brown sugar
1 egg
½ cup all-purpose flour, plus extra for dusting (optional)
1 tsp baking soda
pinch of salt
½ cup whole wheat flour
1 tbsp bran
heaping 1¼ cups semisweet chocolate chips
scant 2¼ cups rolled oats
1 tbsp strong coffee
⅔ cup hazelnuts, toasted and coarsely chopped

Preheat the oven to 375°F/190°C. Grease 2 large baking sheets. Place the butter and sugar in a large bowl and beat together until light and fluffy. Add the egg and beat well. Sift together the all-purpose flour, baking soda, and salt into another bowl, then add in the whole wheat flour and bran. Mix in the egg mixture, then stir in the chocolate chips, oats, coffee, and hazelnuts and mix well.

Place 24 rounded tablespoons of the dough on the baking sheets, spaced well apart. Alternatively, with lightly floured hands, break off pieces of the dough and roll into 24 balls, place on the baking sheets, and flatten.

Bake in the preheated oven for 16–18 minutes, or until golden brown. Let cool for 5 minutes, then transfer to a wire rack to cool completely.

410 With ice cream filling

Remove a tub of semisweet chocolate ice cream from the freezer and let soften at room temperature. Tip into a bowl and add 2 tablespoons of Kahlúa coffee liqueur and beat together. Use to sandwich the baked cookies together, then freeze the cookies for 10 minutes until firm. Makes 12.

411 Jumbo oat & raisin chippers

MAKES 15

1 cup rolled oats
¾ cup all-purpose flour
½ tsp baking soda
pinch of salt
4½ tbsp unsalted butter, softened
½ cup light brown sugar
¼ cup granulated sugar
1 large egg
½ tsp vanilla extract
1 cup raisins

Preheat the oven to 375°F/190°C. Place the oats in a food processor and pulse briefly, then tip into a bowl and sift in the flour, baking soda, and salt and stir together.

Place the butter and sugars in a large bowl and beat together until light and fluffy. Place the egg and vanilla extract in a separate bowl and whisk together, then add to the butter and mix well. Add the flour mixture, mix together, then add the raisins and mix thoroughly.

Divide the dough into 15 balls and place on 2 large nonstick baking sheets, spaced well apart. Press the cookies into rough rounds. Bake in the preheated oven for 12 minutes, or until golden brown. Let cool for 5 minutes, then transfer to a wire rack to cool completely.

412 Jumbo oat, apricot & prune chippers

Replace the raisins with heaping ½ cup chopped dried apricots and heaping ½ cup chopped pitted prunes.

413 Mocha walnut cookies

MAKES ABOUT 16

8 tbsp butter, softened, plus extra for greasing
heaping ½ cup dark brown sugar
scant ½ cup superfine sugar
1 tsp vanilla extract
1 tbsp instant coffee granules, dissolved in 1 tbsp hot water
1 egg
1¼ cups all-purpose flour
½ tsp baking powder
¼ tsp baking soda
⅓ cup milk chocolate chips
½ cup walnut halves, coarsely chopped

Preheat the oven to 350°F/180°C. Grease 2 large baking sheets. Place the butter and sugars in a large bowl and beat together until light and fluffy. Place the vanilla, coffee, and egg in a separate bowl and whisk together. Gradually add the coffee mixture to the butter and sugar, beating until fluffy. Sift the flour, baking powder, and baking soda into the mixture and fold in carefully. Fold in the chocolate chips and walnuts.

Spoon heaping teaspoons of the dough onto the baking sheets, spaced well apart. Bake in the preheated oven for 10–15 minutes, or until crisp on the outside but soft inside. Let cool on the baking sheets for 2 minutes, then transfer to wire racks to cool completely.

414 With mocha icing

Sift 1 cup confectioners' sugar into a bowl. Stir ½ teaspoon of instant espresso powder, ½ teaspoon of cocoa, and 1 tablespoon of boiling water together until smooth. Add to the confectioners' sugar and mix to a smooth icing, spread over the cookies, and let set on a wire rack.

415 Almond tuilles

MAKES 24

1 tsp peanut oil, for greasing
6 tbsp unsalted butter, softened
heaping ⅓ cup superfine sugar
heaping ⅓ cup all-purpose flour
pinch of salt
¾ cup slivered almonds

Preheat the oven to 400°F/200°C and oil 2 large baking sheets with the oil. Place the butter and sugar in a large bowl and beat together until light and fluffy. Sift together the flour and salt and fold into the mixture, then add the almonds and mix together.

Drop 12 teaspoons of batter on each baking sheet, spaced well apart, and spread into flat ovals with the back of a spoon.

Bake in the preheated oven for 5 minutes, or until golden. While the cookies are still warm, lift each one in turn and drape over a wooden rolling pin to make a curved shape. Leave for 1 minute to harden, then transfer to a wire rack to cool completely.

416 With chocolate coating

Place 5½ oz/150 g semisweet chocolate in a heatproof bowl, set the bowl over a saucepan of gently simmering water, and heat until melted. Dip each tuile into the melted chocolate and let set on parchment paper.

417 Camomile cookies

MAKES ABOUT 30

1 cup butter, softened
¾ cup superfine sugar, plus extra for coating
1 tbsp (3–4 tea bags) camomile or camomile and lime flower infusion tea
1 egg yolk, lightly beaten
1 tsp vanilla extract
2 cups all-purpose flour
pinch of salt

Place the butter and sugar in a large bowl and beat together until light and fluffy. If using tea bags, remove the tea leaves from the bags. Stir the tea into the butter mixture, then beat in the egg yolk and vanilla extract. Sift together the flour and salt into the mixture and stir until thoroughly combined. Shape the dough into a log. Spread out the extra sugar in a shallow dish and roll the log in the sugar to coat. Wrap in plastic wrap and chill in the refrigerator for 30–60 minutes.

Preheat the oven to 375°F/190°C. Line 2 large baking sheets with parchment paper.

Unwrap the log, cut into ¼-inch/5-mm slices with a sharp serrated knife and place them on the baking sheets, spaced well apart. Bake in the preheated oven for 10 minutes, or until golden. Let cool on the baking sheets for 5–10 minutes, then transfer the cookies to wire racks to cool completely.

418 Lemon verbena cookies

Replace the camomile tea with lemon verbena tea and add ½ teaspoon of finely grated lemon rind to the dough.

419 Nutty pecan cookies

MAKES 20

⅔ cup unsalted butter, softened
¾ cup superfine sugar
1⅔ cups self-rising flour
1–2 tbsp milk
½ tsp vanilla extract
2 cups pecans

Preheat the oven to 375°F/190°C. Line 2 large baking sheets with parchment paper. Place the butter and sugar in a large bowl and beat together until light and fluffy. Sift in the flour and beat to combine. Add 1 tablespoon of milk and the vanilla extract and mix to form a dough, adding more milk if the dough is too stiff.

Set aside 20 pecan halves. Chop the remaining pecans and knead in to the dough. Divide the dough into 20 and roll each piece into a ball. Place 10 balls on each baking sheet, spaced well apart. Press down to a thickness of ½ inch/1 cm, then press a pecan half into the center of each cookie. Bake in the preheated oven for 10–15 minutes. Let the cookies cool on the baking sheets.

420 Cappuccino cookies

MAKES ABOUT 30

2 envelopes instant cappuccino
1 tbsp hot water
1 cup butter, softened
¾ cup superfine sugar
1 egg yolk, lightly beaten
2 cups all-purpose flour
pinch of salt

TOPPING
6 oz/175 g white chocolate, broken into pieces
unsweetened cocoa, for dusting

Empty the cappuccino envelopes into a small bowl and stir in the hot, but not boiling, water to make a paste. Place the butter and sugar in a large bowl and beat together until light and fluffy, then beat in the egg yolk and cappuccino paste. Sift together the flour and salt into the mixture and stir until combined. Halve the dough, shape into balls, wrap in plastic wrap, and chill for 30–60 minutes.

Preheat the oven to 375°F/190°C. Line 2 large baking sheets with parchment paper. Unwrap the dough and roll out between 2 sheets of parchment paper. Cut out cookies with a 2½-inch/6-cm round cutter and place them on the baking sheets, spaced well apart. Bake in the preheated oven for 10–12 minutes, or until golden brown. Let cool for 5–10 minutes, then transfer to wire racks to cool completely.

Place the wire racks over a sheet of parchment paper. Place the chocolate into a heatproof bowl, set the bowl over a saucepan of gently simmering water, and heat until melted. Let cool, then spoon the chocolate over the cookies. Let set, then dust lightly with cocoa.

421 With coffee bean topping

Replace the cocoa with 3½ oz/100 g crushed chocolate-covered coffee beans, scatter them over the melted white chocolate topping, and let set.

422 Cinnamon & caramel cookies

MAKES ABOUT 25

1 cup butter, softened
¾ cup superfine sugar
1 egg yolk, lightly beaten
1 tsp vanilla extract
2 cups all-purpose flour
1 tsp ground cinnamon
½ tsp allspice
pinch of salt
25–30 caramels

Preheat the oven to 375°F/190°C. Line 2 large baking sheets with parchment paper. Place the butter and sugar in a large bowl and beat together until light and fluffy, then beat in the egg yolk and vanilla extract. Sift together the flour, cinnamon, allspice, and salt into the mixture and stir until thoroughly combined.

Scoop up tablespoons of the dough, shape into balls, and place on the baking sheets, spaced well apart. Bake in the preheated oven for 8 minutes. Place a caramel on top of each cookie and bake for an additional 6–7 minutes. Let cool on the baking sheets for 5–10 minutes, then transfer to wire racks to cool completely.

423 Lemon & candy cookies

Replace the cinnamon and allspice with 1 teaspoon of finely grated lemon rind. Replace the caramels with 25 lemon-flavored hard candies.

424 Fennel & angelica cookies

MAKES ABOUT 20

1 cup butter, softened
¾ cup superfine sugar
1 egg yolk, lightly beaten
1 tbsp finely chopped angelica
2 cups all-purpose flour
pinch of salt
1 tbsp fennel seeds

Place the butter and sugar in a large bowl and beat together until light and fluffy, then beat in the egg yolk and angelica. Sift together the flour and salt into the mixture, add the fennel seeds, and stir until thoroughly combined. Shape the dough into a log, wrap in plastic wrap, and chill in the refrigerator for 30–60 minutes.

Preheat the oven to 375°F/190°C. Line 2 large baking sheets with parchment paper. Unwrap the dough, cut into ½-inch/1-cm slices with a sharp serrated knife, and place them on the baking sheets, spaced well apart. Bake in the preheated oven for 12–15 minutes, or until golden.

Let cool on the baking sheets for 5–10 minutes, then transfer the cookies to wire racks to cool completely.

425 Fennel, lemon & angelica cookies

Add 1 teaspoon of finely grated lemon rind and ½ teaspoon of lemon oil to the dough.

426 Sticky ginger cookies

MAKES ABOUT 20

1 cup butter, softened
¾ cup superfine sugar
1 egg yolk, lightly beaten
2 oz/55 g preserved ginger, coarsely chopped, plus 1 tbsp syrup from the jar
2 cups all-purpose flour
pinch of salt
⅓ cup semisweet chocolate chips

Place the butter and sugar in a large bowl and beat together until light and fluffy, then beat in the egg yolk and ginger syrup. Sift together the flour and salt into the mixture, add the preserved ginger and chocolate chips, and stir until thoroughly combined. Shape the mixture into a log, wrap in plastic wrap, and chill in the refrigerator for 30–60 minutes.

Preheat the oven to 375°F/190°C. Line 2 large baking sheets with parchment paper.

Unwrap the log, cut it into ¼-inch/5-mm slices with a sharp serrated knife, and place them on the baking sheets, spaced well apart. Bake in the preheated oven for 12–15 minutes, or until golden brown.

Let cool on the baking sheets for 5–10 minutes, then transfer the cookies to wire racks to cool completely.

427 Sticky citrus cookies

Replace the chocolate chips with chopped candied peel.

428 Blackstrap molasses & spice drizzles

MAKES ABOUT 25

scant 1 cup butter, softened
2 tbsp blackstrap molasses
¾ cup superfine sugar
1 egg yolk, lightly beaten
2 cups all-purpose flour
1 tsp ground cinnamon
½ tsp grated nutmeg
½ tsp ground cloves
pinch of salt
2 tbsp chopped walnuts

FROSTING
1 cup confectioners' sugar
1 tbsp hot water
few drops of yellow food coloring
few drops of pink food coloring

Place the butter, blackstrap molasses, and sugar in a large bowl and beat together until fluffy, then beat in the egg yolk.

Sift together the flour, cinnamon, nutmeg, cloves, and salt into the mixture, add the walnuts, and stir until thoroughly combined. Halve the dough, shape into balls, wrap in plastic wrap, and chill for 30–60 minutes.

Preheat the oven to 375°F/190°C. Line 2 baking sheets with parchment paper. Unwrap the dough and roll out between 2 sheets of parchment paper to about ¼ inch/5 mm thick. Cut out rounds with a 2½-inch/6-cm fluted cutter and place them on the baking sheets.

Bake in the preheated oven for 10–15 minutes, or until firm. Let cool on the baking sheets for 5–10 minutes, then transfer the cookies to wire racks to cool completely.

To make the frosting, sift the confectioners' sugar into a bowl, then gradually stir in the hot water until it has the consistency of thick cream. Spoon half the icing into another bowl and stir a few drops of yellow food coloring into one bowl and a few drops of pink food coloring into the other. Leave the cookies on the racks and, using teaspoons, drizzle the yellow frosting over them in one direction and the pink frosting over them at right angles. Let set.

429 Syrup drizzles

Replace the blackstrap molasses with dark corn syrup and decorate the cookies with the frosting, leaving out the food coloring.

430 Cinnamon & orange crisps

MAKES ABOUT 30

1 cup butter, softened
1 cup superfine sugar
finely grated rind of 1 orange
1 egg yolk, lightly beaten
4 tsp orange juice
2 cups all-purpose flour
pinch of salt
2 tsp ground cinnamon

Place the butter, ¾ cup of the sugar, and the orange rind in a large bowl and beat together until light and fluffy, then beat in the egg yolk and 2 teaspoons of the orange juice. Sift together the flour and salt into the mixture and stir until thoroughly combined. Shape the dough into a ball, wrap in plastic wrap, and chill for 30–60 minutes.

Unwrap the dough and roll out between 2 sheets of parchment paper into a 12-inch/30-cm square. Brush with the remaining orange juice and sprinkle with cinnamon. Lightly roll with the rolling pin. Roll up the dough like a jelly roll. Wrap in plastic wrap and chill for 30 minutes.

Preheat the oven to 375°F/190°C. Line 2 large baking sheets with parchment paper.

Unwrap the dough and cut into thin slices, then place on the baking sheets, spaced well apart. Bake in the preheated oven for 10–12 minutes. Let cool for 5–10 minutes, then transfer to wire racks to cool completely.

431 With white chocolate coating

Place 5½ oz/150 g white chocolate in a heatproof bowl, set the bowl over a saucepan of gently simmering water, and heat until melted. Dip the cooled cookies to coat half of each one and let set on a wire rack.

432 *Classic saffron cookies*

MAKES ABOUT 30

⅔ cup raisins
½ cup sweet white wine
1 cup butter, softened
¾ cup superfine sugar
1 egg yolk, lightly beaten
2 cups all-purpose flour
½ tsp powdered saffron
pinch of salt

Place the raisins in a bowl, pour in the wine, and let soak for 1 hour. Drain the raisins and set aside any remaining wine.

Preheat the oven to 375°F/190°C. Line 2 large baking sheets with parchment paper. Place the butter and sugar in a large bowl and beat together until light and fluffy, then beat in the egg yolk and 2 teaspoons of the reserved wine. Sift together the flour, saffron, and salt into the mixture and stir until thoroughly combined.

Scoop up tablespoons of the dough and place them on the baking sheets, spaced well apart. Flatten gently and smooth the tops with the back of the spoon.

Bake in the preheated oven for 10–15 minutes, or until light golden brown. Let cool on the baking sheets for 5–10 minutes, then transfer the cookies to wire racks to cool completely.

433 *With sweet wine frosting*

Omit the raisins from the dough and drizzle the cookies with frosting made from sifting 1 cup confectioners' sugar into a bowl and mixing with 1 tablespoon of sweet white wine until smooth. Let set.

434 *Mint cookies with white chocolate ganache*

MAKES ABOUT 15

1 cup butter, softened
¾ cup superfine sugar
1 egg yolk, lightly beaten
2 tsp vanilla extract
2 cups all-purpose flour
pinch of salt
3½ oz/100 g chocolate mint sticks, finely chopped
confectioners' sugar, for dusting

WHITE CHOCOLATE GANACHE
2 tbsp heavy cream
3½ oz/100 g white chocolate, broken into pieces

Place the butter and sugar in a large bowl and beat together until light and fluffy, then beat in the egg yolk and vanilla extract. Sift together the flour and salt into the mixture, add the chocolate sticks, and stir until combined. Halve the dough, shape into balls, wrap, and chill for 30–60 minutes.

Preheat the oven to 375°F/190°C. Line 2 large baking sheets with parchment paper. Unwrap the dough and roll out between 2 sheets of parchment paper. Cut out cookies with a 2½-inch/6-cm fluted round cutter and place them on the baking sheets, spaced well apart. Bake in the preheated oven for 10–15 minutes, or until light golden brown.

Let the cookies cool on the baking sheets for 5–10 minutes, then transfer to wire racks to cool completely.

Pour the cream into a saucepan, add the chocolate, and melt over low heat, stirring occasionally, until smooth. Let cool, then chill in the refrigerator until the mixture has a spreadable consistency. Spread the ganache over half the cookies and top with the remaining cookies, then dust with sifted confectioners' sugar.

435 *With mint ganache*

Replace the white chocolate in the ganache with chopped semisweet mint chocolate.

436 *Flower gems*

MAKES ABOUT 30

1 cup butter, softened
¾ cup superfine sugar
1 egg yolk, lightly beaten
1 tsp lemon juice
2 cups all-purpose flour
pinch of salt
2 tbsp jasmine tea leaves

FOR DECORATING
1 tbsp lemon juice
1 tbsp water
1¾ cups confectioners' sugar
orange, pink, blue, and yellow food coloring
orange, pink, blue, and yellow sugar flowers

Place the butter and sugar in a large bowl and beat together until light and fluffy, then beat in the egg yolk and lemon juice. Sift together the flour and salt into the mixture, add the tea leaves, and stir until thoroughly combined. Halve the dough, shape it into balls, wrap in plastic wrap, and chill for 30–60 minutes.

Preheat the oven to 375°F/190°C. Line 2 large baking sheets with parchment paper. Roll out the dough between 2 sheets of parchment paper to about ⅛ inch/3 mm thick. Cut out flowers with a 2-inch/5-cm flower cutter and place them on the baking sheets, spaced well apart.

Bake in the preheated oven for 10–12 minutes, or until golden brown. Let cool on the baking sheets for 5–10 minutes, then transfer the cookies to wire racks to cool completely.

To decorate, mix the lemon juice and water together in a bowl, then gradually stir in enough confectioners' sugar until it is the consistency of thick cream. Divide the frosting among 4 separate bowls and add a drop of different food coloring to each.

Leave the cookies on the racks. Spread orange frosting on one quarter of the cookies, pink on another quarter, and so on. When the frosting is beginning to set, add a matching flower to the center of each. Let cool.

437 *Petal gems*

Roll out the dough as before but cut out the dough with a 1-inch/2.5-cm round cutter and press 6 disks together for each cookie as petals to form a flower, then use the sugar flowers as the centers. Makes about 20.

438 *Lavender cookies*

MAKES ABOUT 40

1 cup butter, softened
1 cup superfine sugar
1 large egg, lightly beaten
1¾ cups all-purpose flour
2 tsp baking powder
1 tbsp dried lavender, chopped

Preheat the oven to 375°F/190°C. Line 2–3 large baking sheets with parchment paper. Place the butter and sugar in a bowl and beat together until light and fluffy, then beat in the egg. Sift together the flour and baking powder into the mixture, add the lavender, and stir well.

Place tablespoons of the mixture on the baking sheets, spaced well apart. Bake in the preheated oven for 15 minutes, or until golden brown. Let cool on the baking sheets for 5–10 minutes, then transfer the cookies to wire racks to cool completely.

439 *Rosemary cookies*

Replace the lavender with 1½ teaspoons of chopped dried rosemary.

440 Rose flower cookies

MAKES ABOUT 60

1 cup butter, softened
heaping 1 cup superfine sugar
1 large egg, lightly beaten
1 tbsp rose water
2 cups all-purpose flour
1 tsp baking powder
pinch of salt

FROSTING
1 egg white
scant 2¼ cups confectioners' sugar
2 tsp all-purpose flour
2 tsp rose water
few drops of pink food coloring

Place the butter and sugar in a large bowl and beat together until light and fluffy, then beat in the egg and rose water. Sift together the flour, baking powder, and salt into the mixture and stir until combined. Shape the dough into a log, wrap in plastic wrap, and chill in the refrigerator for 1–2 hours.

Preheat the oven to 375°F/190°C. Line 2–3 baking sheets with parchment paper.

Unwrap the dough, cut into thin slices with a sharp serrated knife and place on the baking sheets, spaced well apart.

Bake in the preheated oven for 10–12 minutes, or until light golden brown. Let cool on the baking sheets for 10 minutes, then transfer the cookies to wire racks to cool completely.

To make the frosting, use a fork to lightly beat the egg white in a bowl. Sift in half the confectioners' sugar and stir well, then sift in the remaining confectioners' sugar and flour and mix in enough rose water to make a smooth, easy-to-spread frosting. Stir in a few drops of pink food coloring.

Leave the cookies on the racks. Gently spread the frosting over them and let set.

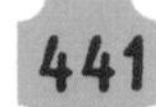

441 Violet flower cookies

Omit the rose water and pink food coloring. Tint the frosting with a little lavender or violet food coloring, then spread the frosting on the cookies and scatter over 3 oz/85 g chopped crystallized violets.

442 Zebra cookies

MAKES ABOUT 20

2 oz/55 g semisweet chocolate, broken into pieces
1 cup all-purpose flour
1 tsp baking powder
1 egg
¾ cup superfine sugar
¼ cup sunflower oil, plus extra for greasing
½ tsp vanilla extract
2 tbsp confectioners' sugar
1 small package milk chocolate disks
1 small package white chocolate disks

Place the chocolate in a heatproof bowl, set the bowl over a saucepan of gently simmering water, and heat until melted. Let cool. Sift the flour and baking powder together. Meanwhile, place the egg, sugar, oil, and vanilla extract in a large bowl and whisk together. Whisk in the cooled, melted chocolate until well blended, then gradually stir in the sifted flour. Cover the bowl and chill in the refrigerator for at least 3 hours.

Preheat the oven to 375°F/190°C. Oil 1–2 large baking sheets with the oil.

Using your hands, shape tablespoonfuls of the dough into log shapes, each measuring about 2 inches/5 cm. Roll the logs generously in the confectioners' sugar, then place on the baking sheets, spaced well apart. Bake in the preheated oven for 15 minutes, or until firm. As soon as the cookies are done, place 3 chocolate disks down the center of each, alternating the colors. Transfer to a wire rack and let cool.

443 With zebra frosting

Sift 1 cup confectioners' sugar into a bowl, add 1 tablespoon of water, and mix until smooth. Set aside one quarter and tint with black food coloring. Use the white frosting to frost the cookies then add stripes with the black frosting and let set.

444 Rum & raisin cookies with orange filling

MAKES ABOUT 30

½ cup raisins
⅔ cup rum
1 cup butter, softened
¾ cup superfine sugar
1 egg yolk, lightly beaten
2 cups all-purpose flour
pinch of salt

ORANGE FILLING
1½ cups confectioners' sugar
6 tbsp butter, softened
2 tsp finely grated orange rind
1 tsp rum
few drops of yellow food coloring (optional)

Place the raisins in a bowl, pour in the rum, and let soak for 15 minutes, then drain, reserving the remaining rum.

Preheat the oven to 375°F/190°C. Line 2 large baking sheets with parchment paper.

Place the butter and sugar in a large bowl and beat together until light and fluffy, then beat in the egg yolk and 2 teaspoons of the reserved rum. Sift together the flour and salt into the mixture, add the raisins, and stir until thoroughly combined.

Scoop up tablespoons of the dough and place them on the baking sheets, spaced well apart. Flatten gently and smooth the tops with the back of a spoon.

Bake in the preheated oven for 10–15 minutes, or until light golden brown. Let cool on the baking sheets for 5–10 minutes, then transfer the cookies to wire racks to cool completely.

To make the orange filling, sift the confectioners' sugar into a bowl, add the butter, orange rind, rum, and food coloring, if using, and beat well until smooth. Spread the filling over half the cookies and top with the remaining cookies.

445 With semisweet chocolate filling

Replace the orange filling with a chocolate filling made by heating ½ cup heavy cream to boiling point and pouring over 4½ oz/125 g chopped semisweet chocolate, then mixing until smooth. Cool and chill until thick, then use to sandwich the cookies together.

446 Gingersnaps

MAKES 30

2½ cups self-rising flour
pinch of salt
1 cup superfine sugar
1 tbsp ground ginger
1 tsp baking soda
9 tbsp butter, plus extra for greasing
¼ cup dark corn syrup
1 egg, lightly beaten
1 tsp grated orange rind

Preheat the oven to 325°F/160°C. Lightly grease several large baking sheets.

Sift together the flour, salt, sugar, ginger, and baking soda into a large bowl. Heat the butter and dark corn syrup together in a saucepan over very low heat until the butter has melted. Let cool slightly, then pour it onto the dry ingredients. Add the egg and orange rind and mix thoroughly to form a dough. Using your hands, carefully shape the dough into 30 even-size balls.

Place the balls on the baking sheets, spaced well apart, then flatten them slightly with your fingers.

Bake in the preheated oven for 15–20 minutes, then carefully transfer the cookies to a wire rack to cool.

447 Extra ginger gingersnaps

Drain 3 balls of preserved ginger in syrup, chop finely, and add to the dough before baking.

448 Checkerboard cookies

MAKES ABOUT 20

1 cup butter, softened
¾ cup superfine sugar
1 egg yolk, lightly beaten
2 tsp vanilla extract
2 cups all-purpose flour
pinch of salt
1 tsp ground ginger
1 tbsp finely grated orange rind
1 tbsp unsweetened cocoa
1 egg white, lightly beaten

Place the butter and sugar in a large bowl and beat together until light and fluffy, then beat in the egg yolk and vanilla. Sift together the flour and salt into the mixture and stir until combined.

Divide the dough in half. Add the ginger and orange rind to one half and mix well. Shape the dough into a log 6 inches/15 cm long. Flatten the sides and top to square off the log to 2 inches/5 cm high. Wrap in plastic wrap and chill for 30–60 minutes.

Sift the cocoa into the other half of the dough and mix well. Shape into a flattened log exactly the same size as the first one, wrap in plastic wrap, and chill in the refrigerator for 30–60 minutes.

Unwrap the dough and cut each log lengthwise into 3 slices. Cut each slice lengthwise into 3 strips. Brush the strips with egg white and stack them in threes, alternating the colors, so they are the same shape as the original logs. Wrap in plastic wrap and chill for 30–60 minutes.

Preheat the oven to 375°F/190°C. Line 2 large baking sheets with parchment paper.

Unwrap the logs and cut into slices with a sharp serrated knife, then place the cookies on the baking sheets, spaced well apart. Bake in the preheated oven for 12–15 minutes, or until firm. Let cool for 5–10 minutes, then transfer the cookies to wire racks to cool completely.

449 Battenberg cookies

Omit the orange rind and ginger. Use pink food coloring to tint one half of the dough and add cocoa to the other. Shape each dough portion into 2 logs and after chilling, cut each into 2 strips. Brush with egg white and stack a pink log on top of a chocolate one. Repeat and press the 4 pieces together into a rectangle. Wrap and chill. Cut into slices, then bake as before.

450 Crunchy peanut cookies

MAKES 20

9 tbsp butter, softened, plus extra for greasing
heaping ½ cup chunky peanut butter
heaping 1 cup granulated sugar
1 egg, lightly beaten
heaping 1 cup all-purpose flour
½ tsp baking powder
pinch of salt
½ cup unsalted natural peanuts, chopped

Lightly grease 2 large baking sheets. Place the butter and peanut butter in a large bowl and beat together. Gradually add the sugar and beat together well. Add the egg, a little at a time, until it is combined. Sift the flour, baking powder, and salt into the peanut butter mixture. Add the peanuts and bring all of the ingredients together to form a soft dough. Wrap the dough in plastic wrap and chill for 30 minutes.

Preheat the oven to 375°F/190°C. Form the dough into 20 balls and place them on the baking sheets, about 2 inches/5 cm apart. Flatten them slightly with your hand.

Bake in the preheated oven for 15 minutes, or until golden brown. Let cool on wire racks.

451 "I love you" vanilla hearts

MAKES 12

1⅔ cups all-purpose flour, plus extra for dusting
heaping ⅔ cup butter, cut into small pieces, plus extra for greasing
scant ⅔ cup superfine sugar, plus extra for dusting
1 tsp vanilla extract

Preheat the oven to 350°F/180°C. Grease a large baking sheet. Sift the flour into a large bowl, add the butter, and rub it in with your fingertips until the mixture resembles fine breadcrumbs. Stir in the sugar and vanilla extract and mix together to form a firm dough.

Roll out the dough on a lightly floured work surface until it is ½ inch/1 cm thick. Cut out 12 hearts with a heart-shaped cookie cutter measuring about 2 inches/5 cm across and arrange the hearts on the baking sheet.

Bake in the preheated oven for 15–20 minutes, or until just colored. Transfer to a wire rack and let cool completely. Dust with a little superfine sugar just before serving.

452 With vanilla topping

Beat 7 tablespoons of unsalted butter with the seeds from a vanilla bean, sift in 1⅓ cups confectioners' sugar, and beat until smooth. Spread over the hearts.

453 Sugared hearts

MAKES ABOUT 30

1 cup butter, softened
1½ cups superfine sugar
1 egg yolk, lightly beaten
2 tsp vanilla extract
heaping 1¾ cups all-purpose flour
¼ cup unsweetened cocoa
pinch of salt
3–4 food coloring pastes
3½ oz/100 g semisweet chocolate, broken into pieces

Place the butter and half the sugar in a large bowl and beat together until light and fluffy, then beat in the egg yolk and vanilla extract. Sift together the flour, cocoa, and salt into the mixture and stir until combined. Halve the dough, shape into balls, wrap in plastic wrap, and chill for 30–60 minutes.

Preheat the oven to 375°F/190°C. Line 2 large baking sheets with parchment paper. Unwrap the dough and roll out between 2 sheets of parchment paper. Cut out cookies with a heart-shaped cutter and place them on the baking sheets, spaced well apart. Bake in the preheated oven for 10–15 minutes, or until firm. Let cool on the baking sheets for 5–10 minutes, then transfer to wire racks to cool completely.

Meanwhile, divide the remaining sugar among 4 small plastic bags or bowls. Add a little food coloring paste to each and rub in until well mixed. Wear a plastic glove if mixing in bowls to prevent your hands from getting stained. Place the chocolate in a heatproof bowl, set the bowl over a saucepan of gently simmering water, and heat until melted. Let cool slightly.

Leave the cookies on the racks. Spread the melted chocolate over them and sprinkle with the colored sugar. Let set.

454 White sugar hearts

Replace the semisweet chocolate with white chocolate and sprinkle with dry unsweetened coconut instead of the colored sugar.

455 Traditional Easter cookies

MAKES ABOUT 30

1 cup butter, softened
¾ cup superfine sugar, plus extra for sprinkling
1 egg yolk, lightly beaten
2 cups all-purpose flour
1 tsp apple pie spice
pinch of salt
1 tbsp candied peel
⅓ cup raisins
1 egg white, lightly beaten

Place the butter and sugar in a large bowl and beat together until light and fluffy, then beat in the egg yolk. Sift together the flour, apple pie spice, and salt into the mixture, add the candied peel and raisins, and stir until thoroughly combined. Halve the dough, shape into balls, wrap in plastic wrap, and chill in the refrigerator for 30–60 minutes.

Preheat the oven to 375°F/190°C. Line 2 large baking sheets with parchment paper.

Unwrap the dough and roll out between 2 sheets of parchment paper. Cut out cookies with a 2½-inch/6-cm fluted round cutter and place them on the baking sheets, spaced well apart. Bake in the preheated oven for 7 minutes, then brush with the egg white and sprinkle with the sugar. Bake for an additional 5–8 minutes, or until light golden brown. Let cool on the baking sheets for 5–10 minutes, then transfer to wire racks to cool completely.

456 Easter bunny cookies

MAKES 15

1 cup butter, softened
¾ cup superfine sugar, plus extra for sprinkling
1 egg yolk, lightly beaten
2 tsp vanilla extract
heaping 1¾ cups all-purpose flour
¼ cup unsweetened cocoa
pinch of salt
2 tbsp finely chopped preserved ginger
1 egg white, lightly beaten
15 white mini marshmallows

ICING
1¼ cups confectioners' sugar
few drops of pink food coloring

Place the butter and sugar in a large bowl and beat together until light and fluffy, then beat in the egg yolk and vanilla. Sift together the flour, cocoa, and salt into the mixture, add the ginger, and stir until combined. Halve the dough, shape into balls, wrap in plastic wrap, and chill for 30–60 minutes.

Preheat the oven to 375°F/190°C. Line 2 large baking sheets with parchment paper. Unwrap the dough and roll out between 2 sheets of parchment paper. Cut out 15 rounds with a 2-inch/5-cm plain cutter (bodies), 15 rounds with a 1¼-inch/3-cm plain cutter (heads), 30 rounds with a ¾-inch/2-cm plain cutter (ears), and 15 rounds with a ½-inch/1-cm plain cutter (tails). Make up the bunnies on the baking sheets, spaced well apart.

Bake in the preheated oven for 7 minutes, then brush the bunnies with egg white and sprinkle with superfine sugar. Bake for an additional 5–8 minutes, then remove from the oven and put a mini marshmallow in the center of each tail. Return to the oven for 1 minute. Let cool for 5–10 minutes, then transfer to wire racks to cool completely.

Sift the confectioners' sugar into a bowl and stir in enough water until it is the consistency of thick cream. Add a few drops of food coloring. Pipe a collar where the heads and bodies join and add initials if desired. Let set.

457 Easter egg cookies

Use half the dough to make Easter bunnies and use the remaining dough to cut out Easter egg shapes. Use tubes of colored decorating icing, dragées, and mini marshmallows to decorate.

458 Easter nest cookies

MAKES ABOUT 25

1 cup butter, softened, plus extra for greasing
¾ cup superfine sugar
1 egg yolk, lightly beaten
2 tsp lemon juice
2 cups all-purpose flour
pinch of salt
1 tbsp chopped candied peel
scant ⅓ cup candied cherries, finely chopped

FOR DECORATING
1¾ cups confectioners' sugar
few drops of yellow food coloring
mini sugar-coated Easter eggs
yellow sugar sprinkles

Place the butter and sugar in a large bowl and beat together until light and fluffy, then beat in the egg yolk and lemon juice. Sift together the flour and salt into the mixture, add the candied peel and candied cherries, and stir until combined. Halve the dough, shape into balls, wrap in plastic wrap, and chill for 30–60 minutes.

Preheat the oven to 375°F/190°C. Generously grease several muffin pans with butter.

Unwrap the dough and roll out between 2 sheets of parchment paper. Cut out cookies with a 2¾–3¼-inch/7–8-cm sun-shaped cutter and place them in the prepared pans.

Bake in the preheated oven for 10–15 minutes, or until light golden brown. Cool in the pans.

Sift the confectioners' sugar into a bowl, add the food coloring, and stir in just enough water to until it is the consistency of thick cream. Place the cookies on wire racks and gently spread the frosting on them. When it is just beginning to set, gently press 3–4 eggs into it and sprinkle the sugar sprinkles around them. Let set.

459 Chocolate nests

Add 2 teaspoons of cocoa to the dough to make chocolate nests and replace the sugar-coated eggs with a mixture of chocolate-covered peanuts and yogurt-coated raisins.

460 Halloween spiderweb cookies

MAKES ABOUT 30

1 cup butter, softened
¾ cup superfine sugar
1 egg yolk, lightly beaten
1 tsp peppermint extract
heaping 1¾ cups all-purpose flour
¼ cup unsweetened cocoa
pinch of salt

FROSTING
1½ cups confectioners' sugar
few drops of vanilla extract
1–1½ tbsp hot water
few drops of black food coloring

Place the butter and sugar in a large bowl, and beat together until light and fluffy, then beat in the egg yolk and peppermint extract. Sift together the flour, cocoa, and salt into the mixture and stir until thoroughly combined. Halve the dough, shape into balls, wrap in plastic wrap, and chill in the refrigerator for 30–60 minutes.

Preheat the oven to 375°F/190°C. Line 2 large baking sheets with parchment paper. Unwrap the dough and roll out between 2 sheets of parchment paper. Cut out cookies with a 2½-inch/6-cm plain round cutter and place them on the baking sheets, spaced well apart. Bake in a preheated oven for 10–15 minutes, or until light golden brown. Let cool for 5–10 minutes, then transfer to wire racks to cool completely.

Sift the confectioners' sugar into a bowl, add the vanilla, and stir in the hot water until it is smooth and has the consistency of thick cream. Leave the cookies on the racks and spread the white frosting over them, reserving 2 tablespoons.

Add a few drops of black food coloring to the remaining frosting and spoon it into a pastry bag fitted with a fine tip. Starting from the middle of the cookie, pipe a series of concentric circles. Carefully draw a toothpick through the frosting from the middle to the outside edge to divide the cookie first into quarters and then into eighths. Let set.

461 Halloween spook cookies

Use half the dough to make spiderwebs and cut the remaining dough out with novelty cookie cutters to make bat, pumpkin, and cauldron shapes. Decorate with orange, green, and black decorating icing.

462 Christmas angels

Makes About 25

1 cup butter, softened
¾ cup superfine sugar
1 egg yolk, lightly beaten
2 tsp passion fruit pulp
2 cups all-purpose flour
pinch of salt
½ cup dry unsweetened coconut

FOR DECORATING
1½ cups confectioners' sugar
1–1½ tbsp passion fruit pulp
edible silver glitter

Place the butter and sugar in a large bowl and beat together until light and fluffy then beat in the egg yolk and passion fruit pulp. Sift together the flour and salt into the mixture, add the coconut, and stir until thoroughly combined. Halve the dough, shape into balls, wrap in plastic wrap, and chill for 30–60 minutes.

Preheat the oven to 375°F/190°C. Line 2 baking sheets with parchment paper.

Unwrap the dough and roll out between 2 sheets of parchment paper. Cut out cookies with a 2¾-inch/7-cm angel-shaped cutter and place them on the baking sheets, spaced well apart.

Bake in the preheated oven for 10–15 minutes, or until light golden brown. Let cool for 5–10 minutes, then transfer to wire racks to cool completely.

Sift the confectioners' sugar into a bowl and stir in the passion fruit pulp until it is the consistency of thick cream. Leave the cookies on the racks and spread the frosting over them. Sprinkle with the edible glitter and let set.

463 Angel ornaments

Before baking, make a hole with a metal skewer or straw in the top of each cookie. Check the holes are big enough when the cookies come out of the oven and pierce again if necessary. Cool and decorate as before. Using thin white ribbon, string chains of the angels together to hang on the Christmas tree.

464 Christmas bells

Makes About 30

1 cup butter, softened
¾ cup superfine sugar
finely grated rind of 1 lemon
1 egg yolk, lightly beaten
2 cups all-purpose flour
½ tsp ground cinnamon
pinch of salt
heaping ½ cup semisweet chocolate chips

FOR DECORATING
2 tbsp lightly beaten egg white
2 tbsp lemon juice
2 cups confectioners' sugar
30 silver dragées
food coloring pens

Place the butter, sugar, and lemon rind in a large bowl and beat together until light and fluffy, then beat in the egg yolk. Sift together the flour, cinnamon, and salt into the mixture, add the chocolate chips, and stir until thoroughly combined. Halve the dough, shape into balls, wrap in plastic wrap, and chill in the refrigerator for 30–60 minutes.

Preheat the oven to 375°F/190°C. Line 2 large baking sheets with parchment paper. Unwrap the dough and roll out between 2 sheets of parchment paper. Cut out cookies with a 2-inch/5-cm bell-shaped cutter and place them on the baking sheets, spaced well apart.

Bake in a preheated oven for 10–15 minutes, or until light golden brown. Let the cookies cool for 5–10 minutes, then transfer to wire racks to cool completely.

Mix the egg white and lemon juice together in a bowl, then gradually beat in the confectioners' sugar until smooth. Leave the cookies on the racks and spread the frosting over them. Place a silver dragée on the clapper shape at the bottom of the cookie and let set. When dry, use food coloring pens to draw patterns on the cookies.

465 Colored bells

Divide the frosting into 3 portions. Leave one white, color one portion with red food coloring, and the third with green and use to decorate the bells. Let set, then tie 3 cookies together in a stack, one of each color, using ribbon.

466 Christmas tree decorations

MAKES ABOUT 25

1 cup butter, softened
¾ cup superfine sugar
1 egg yolk, lightly beaten
2 tsp vanilla extract
2 cups all-purpose flour
pinch of salt
1 egg white, lightly beaten
2 tbsp colored sprinkles
14 oz/400 g fruit-flavored hard candies in different colors
25 lengths of ribbon, to hang

Place the butter and sugar into a bowl and beat together until light and fluffy, then beat in the egg yolk and vanilla extract. Sift together the flour and salt into the mixture and stir until combined. Halve the dough, shape into balls, wrap in plastic wrap, and chill in the refrigerator for 30–60 minutes.

Preheat the oven to 375°F/190°C. Line 2 large baking sheets with parchment paper. Unwrap the dough and roll out between 2 sheets of parchment paper. Cut out cookies with Christmas-themed cutters and place them on the baking sheets, spaced well apart.

Using the end of a large plain piping tip, cut out rounds from each shape and remove them. Make a small hole in the top of each cookie with a skewer so that they can be threaded with ribbon. Brush with egg white and sprinkle with colored sprinkles. Bake in the preheated oven for 7 minutes. Meanwhile, lightly crush the candies by tapping them with a rolling pin. Unwrap and sort into separate bowls by color. Remove the cookies from the oven and fill the holes with the crushed candies. Return to the oven and bake for an additional 5–8 minutes, or until they are light golden brown and the candies have melted and filled the holes. Let cool on the baking sheets and then transfer to wire racks. Thread thin ribbon through the holes in the top and hang.

467 Star-shaped cookies

MAKES 36

½ cup all-purpose flour, plus extra for dusting
1 tsp ground cinnamon
1 tsp ground ginger
6½ tbsp butter, cut into cubes
scant ½ cup light brown sugar
finely grated rind of 1 orange
1 egg, lightly beaten

FOR DECORATING
1¾ cups confectioners' sugar
3–4 tsp cold water
edible silver cake sparkles
silver dragées

Preheat the oven to 350°F/180°C. Line several large baking sheets with parchment paper.

Sift the flour, cinnamon, and ginger into a large bowl. Add the butter and rub it in with your fingertips until the mixture resembles fine breadcrumbs. Stir the sugar and orange rind into the mixture, add the egg, and mix together to form a soft dough.

Roll the dough out thinly to about ¼ inch/5 mm thick on a lightly floured work surface. Cut out shapes with a 2½-inch/6.5-cm snowflake- or star-shaped cutters and place on the baking sheets.

Bake in the preheated oven for 10–15 minutes, or until golden brown. Let cool on the baking sheets for 2–3 minutes, then transfer the cookies to a wire rack and let cool completely.

To make the frosting, sift the confectioners' sugar into a large bowl and add enough water to make a smooth frosting. Spread a little on each cookie, then sprinkle with sparkles and dragées.

468 Easter animal cookies

Use a rabbit-shaped cutter instead of a snowflake and add a raisin for the eyes. Alternatively, use a chick-shaped cutter and add a few drops of yellow food coloring to the frosting.

469 Double heart cookies

MAKES ABOUT 30

- *1 envelope instant latte*
- *1½ tsp hot water*
- *1 cup butter, softened*
- *¾ cup superfine sugar*
- *1 egg yolk, lightly beaten*
- *heaping 1¾ cups all-purpose flour*
- *1 tsp vanilla extract*
- *3 tbsp unsweetened cocoa*
- *pinch of salt*

Place the instant latte into a small bowl and stir in the hot, but not boiling, water to make a paste.

Place the butter and sugar in a large bowl and beat together until light and fluffy, then beat in the egg yolk. Divide the mixture in half. Beat the latte paste into one half. Sift 1 cup of the flour with the salt into the mixture and stir until combined. Shape the dough into a ball, wrap in plastic wrap, and chill in the refrigerator for 30–60 minutes. Beat the vanilla extract into the other bowl, then sift together the remaining flour, the cocoa, and salt into the mixture. Stir until thoroughly combined. Shape the dough into a ball, wrap in plastic wrap, and chill for 30–60 minutes.

Preheat the oven to 375°F/190°C. Line 2 large baking sheets with parchment paper.

Unwrap both flavors of dough and roll out each between 2 sheets of parchment paper. Cut out cookies with a 2¾-inch/7-cm heart-shaped cutter and place them on the baking sheets, spaced well apart. Using a 1½–2-inch/4–5-cm/ heart-shaped cutter, cut out the centers of each larger heart and remove from the baking sheets. Place a small chocolate-flavored heart in the center of each large coffee-flavored heart and vice versa.

Bake in the preheated oven for 10–15 minutes. Let cool for 5–10 minutes, then transfer to wire racks to cool completely.

470 Pink hearts

Divide the dough into 3 portions and add pink food coloring to one portion, then make the cookies as before, contrasting the 3 different colored doughs.

471 Chocolate-dipped Viennese fingers

MAKES ABOUT 16

- *7 tbsp butter, plus extra for greasing*
- *2 tbsp superfine sugar*
- *½ tsp vanilla extract*
- *¾ cup self-rising flour*
- *3½ oz/100 g semisweet chocolate*

Preheat the oven to 325°F/160°C. Grease 2 large baking sheets. Place the butter, sugar, and vanilla extract in a large bowl and beat together until light and fluffy. Stir in the flour, mixing evenly to make a fairly stiff dough.

Place the mixture in a pastry bag fitted with a large star tip and pipe about 16 fingers, each 2½ inches/6 cm long, onto the baking sheets. Bake in the preheated oven for 10–15 minutes, or until pale golden. Let cool on the baking sheets for 2–3 minutes, then transfer to a wire rack to cool completely.

Place the chocolate in a small heatproof bowl, set over a saucepan of gently simmering water, and heat until melted. Remove from the heat. Dip the ends of each cookie into the chocolate to coat, then place on a sheet of parchment paper and let set.

472 Viennese pinks

Omit the chocolate and dip each end of the fingers into pink frosting made by beating 1 cup sifted confectioners' sugar with 1 tablespoon of water and a drop of pink food coloring. Before the frosting is dry, dip the tips into pink sprinkles, then let set.

473 Alphabet cookies

MAKES ABOUT 30

1 cup butter, softened
¾ cup superfine sugar
1 egg yolk, lightly beaten
2 tsp grenadine
2 cups all-purpose flour
pinch of salt
5–6 tbsp unsalted dried pomegranate seeds or roasted melon seeds

Place the butter and sugar in a large bowl and beat together until light and fluffy, then beat in the egg yolk and grenadine. Sift together the flour and salt into the mixture and stir until combined. Halve the dough, shape into balls, wrap in plastic wrap, and chill in the refrigerator for 30–60 minutes.

Preheat the oven to 375°F/190°C. Line 2 large baking sheets with parchment paper.

Unwrap the dough and roll out between 2 sheets of parchment paper to about ⅛ inch/3 mm thick. Sprinkle half the seeds over each piece of dough and lightly roll the rolling pin over them. Cut out letters with alphabet cutters and place them on the baking sheets, spaced well apart.

Bake in the preheated oven for 10–12 minutes, or until golden brown. Let cool on the baking sheets for 5–10 minutes, then transfer the cookies to wire racks to cool completely.

474 Tutti frutti cookies

Replace the seeds with 1 oz/25 g each of chopped candied fruit, candied cherries, and angelica and add to the cookie dough.

475 Iced stars

MAKES ABOUT 30

1 cup butter, softened
¾ cup superfine sugar
1 egg yolk, lightly beaten
½ tsp vanilla extract
2 cups all-purpose flour
pinch of salt

FOR DECORATING
1¾ cups confectioners' sugar
1–2 tbsp warm water
food colorings
silver and gold dragées
colored sprinkles
dry unsweetened coconut
sugar sprinkles
sugar stars, hearts, and flowers

Place the butter and sugar in a large bowl and beat together until light and fluffy, then beat in the egg yolk and vanilla extract. Sift together the flour and salt into the mixture and stir until thoroughly combined. Halve the dough, shape into balls, wrap in plastic wrap, and chill for 30–60 minutes.

Preheat the oven to 375°F/190°C. Line 2 large baking sheets with parchment paper.

Unwrap the dough and roll out between 2 sheets of parchment paper to about ⅛ inch/3 mm thick. Cut out cookies with a star-shaped cutter and place them on the baking sheets, spaced well apart. Bake in the preheated oven for 10–15 minutes, or until light golden brown. Let cool on the baking sheets for 5–10 minutes, then transfer to wire racks to cool completely.

To decorate, sift the confectioners' sugar into a bowl and stir in enough warm water until it is the consistency of thick cream. Divide the frosting among 3–4 bowls and add a few drops of your chosen food colorings to each. Leave the cookies on the racks and spread the different colored frostings over them to the edges. Arrange silver and gold dragées on top and/or sprinkle with colored sprinkles and sugar shapes. If you like, color dry unsweetened coconut with food coloring in a contrasting color and sprinkle on top. Let the cookies set.

476 Marzipan stars

Omit the frosting and thinly roll 5½ oz/150 g white marzipan out on a work surface dusted with confectioners' sugar. Cut out 30 stars with the star-shaped cutter and use a little beaten egg white to secure the marzipan to the cookies, then use a kitchen blow torch to toast the edges of the marzipan.

477 *Name cookies*

MAKES ABOUT 30

1 cup butter, softened
¾ cup superfine sugar
1 egg yolk, lightly beaten
2 tsp orange juice or orange liqueur
finely grated rind of 1 orange
2 cups all-purpose flour
pinch of salt

FOR DECORATING
1 egg white
2 cups confectioners' sugar
few drops each of 2 food colorings
green balls or crystallized flowers

Place the butter and sugar in a large bowl and beat together until light and fluffy, then beat in the egg yolk, orange juice, and grated rind. Sift together the flour and salt into the mixture and stir until combined. Halve the dough, shape into balls, wrap in plastic wrap, and chill in the refrigerator for 30–60 minutes.

Preheat the oven to 375°F/190°C. Line 2 large baking sheets with parchment paper. Unwrap the dough and roll out to ⅛ inch/3 mm thick. Depending on the occasion and age group, cut out appropriate shapes with cookie cutters and place them on the baking sheets, spaced well apart. Bake in the preheated oven for 10–15 minutes, or until light golden brown.

Let cool on the baking sheets for 5–10 minutes, then transfer the cookies to wire racks to cool completely.

Leave the cookies on the racks. Place the egg white and confectioners' sugar in a bowl and beat until smooth, adding a little water if necessary. Transfer half the frosting to another bowl and color each bowl with a different color. Place both frostings in pastry bags with fine tips and use to decorate the cookies and write initials. Finish with green balls or flowers and let set.

478 *Number crunchers*

MAKES ABOUT 35

1 cup butter, softened
¾ cup superfine sugar
1 egg yolk, lightly beaten
2 tsp vanilla extract
2 cups all-purpose flour

1 tsp ground ginger
¼ tsp ground cinnamon
¼ tsp ground cloves
pinch of salt
4–5 tbsp chopped macadamia nuts

Place the butter and sugar in a large bowl and beat together until light and fluffy, then beat in the egg yolk and vanilla extract. Sift together the flour, ginger, cinnamon, cloves, and salt into the mixture and stir until thoroughly combined. Halve the dough, shape into balls, wrap in plastic wrap, and chill in the refrigerator for 30–60 minutes.

Preheat the oven to 375°F/190°C. Line 2 large baking sheets with parchment paper. Unwrap the dough and roll out between 2 sheets of parchment paper to ⅛ inch/3 mm thick. Sprinkle half the nuts over each piece of dough and roll the rolling pin over them. Cut out numbers with number-shaped cutters and place them on the baking sheets, spaced well apart. Bake in the preheated oven for 10–12 minutes, or until golden brown. Let cool for 5–10 minutes, then transfer to wire racks to cool completely.

479 *Peanut number crunchers*

Omit the spices and macadamia nuts. Chop ¾ cup salted peanuts and sprinkle over the rolled dough.

480 S'mores

MAKES 12

24 graham crackers
24 squares milk or semisweet chocolate
12 marshmallows

Prepare a barbecue or preheat the oven to 350°F/180°C. If baking in the oven, line a baking sheet with parchment paper.

Place 12 graham crackers on the baking sheet, then place 2 squares of chocolate on each, and top with a marshmallow.

Bake in the preheated oven for 4–6 minutes, or until the chocolate is melting and the marshmallow soft and spreading. Remove from the oven and top each with a second graham cracker, then serve immediately.

Alternatively, carefully place the loaded cookies onto the barbecue. When the chocolate and marshmallow are starting to melt, lift off and top with the second cookie. Press down and serve immediately.

481 S'mores with banana

MAKES 4

8 marshmallows
8 chocolate cookies
1 banana, thinly sliced
4 squares semisweet chocolate

Place 2 marshmallows at a time onto the end of a skewer and toast over a hot barbecue for a few minutes until they start to soften.

Place the marshmallows onto one of the cookies, top with a few slices of banana, then a square of chocolate, then sandwich together with the remaining cookies.

Squeeze together well and repeat with the remaining cookies and marshmallows.

482 Painted butterflies

MAKES ABOUT 20

2 envelopes instant malted food drink
1 tbsp hot water
1 cup butter, softened
¾ cup superfine sugar
1 egg yolk, lightly beaten
2 cups all-purpose flour
pinch of salt
egg yolk and food coloring, for decorating

Place the malted drink in a bowl and stir in the hot, but not boiling water to make a paste.

Place the butter and sugar in a large bowl and beat together until light and fluffy, then beat in the egg yolk and malted drink paste. Sift together the flour and salt into the mixture and stir until thoroughly combined. Halve the dough, shape into balls, wrap in plastic wrap, and chill in the refrigerator for 30–60 minutes.

Preheat the oven to 375°F/190°C. Line 2 large baking sheets with parchment paper. Unwrap the dough and roll out between 2 sheets of parchment paper. Cut out cookies with a butterfly-shaped cutter and place them on the baking sheets.

Whisk an egg yolk and put a little of it in an egg cup. Add a few drops of food coloring and mix well. Using a fine paintbrush, paint a pattern on the butterflies' wings. Mix other colors with the beaten egg yolk in egg cups and add to the pattern.

Bake in the preheated oven for 10–15 minutes, or until firm. Let cool on the baking sheets for 5–10 minutes, then transfer the cookies to wire racks to cool completely.

483 Traffic lights

MAKES ABOUT 40

1 cup butter, softened
¾ cup superfine sugar
1 egg yolk, lightly beaten
2 tsp vanilla extract
2 cups all-purpose flour, plus extra for dusting
pinch of salt
heaping 1 cup dry unsweetened coconut

FOR DECORATING
1½ tbsp lightly beaten egg white
1½ tbsp lemon juice
1½ cups confectioners' sugar
red, yellow, and green candied cherries
red and green gummy bears

Place the butter and sugar in a large bowl and beat together until light and fluffy, then beat in the egg yolk and vanilla extract. Sift together the flour and salt into the mixture, add the coconut, and stir until thoroughly combined. Halve the dough, roll each piece into a ball, wrap in plastic wrap, and chill for 30–60 minutes.

Preheat the oven to 375°F/190°C. Line 2 large baking sheets with parchment paper.

Roll out each piece of dough between 2 sheets of parchment paper to a rectangle about ¼ inch/5 mm thick. Using a sharp knife, cut the dough into bars about 4 x ¾ inches/10 x 2 cm in size and place them on the baking sheets, spaced well apart. Bake in the preheated oven for 10–12 minutes, or until golden brown. Let cool on the baking sheets for 5–10 minutes, then transfer the to wire racks to cool completely.

To make the frosting, mix the egg white and lemon juice together in a bowl, then gradually beat in the confectioners' sugar until smooth. Leave the cookies on the racks and spoon the frosting over them. Decorate some with a vertical row of red, yellow, and green candied cherries for traffic lights. For pedestrian lights, put a red gummy bear at the top of a cookie and a green one at the bottom. Let set.

484 With jelly bean topping

Instead of the frosting, place 5½ oz/150 g semisweet chocolate in a heatproof bowl, set the bowl over a saucepan of gently simmering water, and heat until melted. Spread the chocolate over the bars and press 3 jelly beans onto each.

485 Stained-glass window cookies

MAKES ABOUT 25

- 2½ cups all-purpose flour, plus extra for dusting
- pinch of salt
- 1 tsp baking soda
- 7 tbsp unsalted butter
- 1 cup superfine sugar
- 1 large egg
- 1 tsp vanilla extract
- 4 tbsp dark corn syrup
- 50 mixed colored hard fruit candies (about 9 oz/250 g), chopped
- 25 lengths of ribbon, to hang

Sift the flour, salt, and baking soda into a large bowl, add the butter, and rub it in until the mixture resembles breadcrumbs. Stir in the sugar. Place the egg, vanilla extract, and corn syrup in a separate bowl and whisk together. Pour the egg into the flour mixture and mix to form a smooth dough. Wrap in plastic wrap and chill in the refrigerator for 30 minutes.

Preheat the oven to 350°F/180°C. Line 2 large baking sheets with parchment paper. Roll the dough out on a floured work surface to ¼ inch/5 mm thick. Use a variety of floured cookie cutters to cut out the cookies. Transfer them to the baking sheets and cut out shapes from the center of the cookies. Fill the holes with candies. Using a skewer, make a hole at the top of each cookie.

Bake in the preheated oven for 10–12 minutes, or until the candies are melted. Make sure the holes are still there, and pierce again if necessary. Let cool on the baking sheets until the centers have hardened. When cold, thread thin ribbon through the holes to hang up the cookies.

486 Mint window cookies

Cut all the cookies out with a round cookie cutter and use chopped, clear mint hard candies to fill the cavities. Hang using lengths of white ribbon.

487 Chocolate dominoes

MAKES ABOUT 28

- 1 cup butter, softened
- ¾ cup superfine sugar
- 1 egg yolk, lightly beaten
- 2 tsp vanilla extract
- heaping 1¾ cups all-purpose flour
- ¼ cup unsweetened cocoa
- pinch of salt
- heaping ¼ cup dry unsweetened coconut
- heaping ¼ cup white chocolate chips

Place the butter and sugar in a large bowl and beat together until light and fluffy, then beat in the egg yolk and vanilla extract. Sift together the flour, cocoa, and salt into the mixture, add the coconut, and stir until combined. Halve the dough, shape into balls, wrap in plastic wrap, and chill in the refrigerator for 30–60 minutes.

Preheat the oven to 375°F/190°C. Line 2 large baking sheets with parchment paper.

Unwrap the dough and roll out between 2 sheets of parchment paper. Cut out cookies with a 3½-inch/9-cm plain square cutter, then cut them in half to make rectangles. Place them on the baking sheets and, using a knife, make a line across the center of each without cutting through. Arrange the chocolate chips on top of the cookies to look like dominoes, pressing them in gently.

Bake in the preheated oven for 10–15 minutes, or until golden brown. Let cool for 5–10 minutes, then transfer to wire racks to cool completely.

488 With black frosting

Sift 1 cup confectioners' sugar into a bowl and beat in 1 tablespoon of water until smooth. Add a few drops of black food coloring and mix until black. Use to frost the cookies, let set, then add the white dots with white decorating icing.

489 Nut lovers' cookie brittle

MAKES ABOUT 35 PIECES

½ tsp peanut oil, for greasing
1 cup unsalted butter, softened
1 cup granulated sugar
1 tsp vanilla extract
2 cups all-purpose flour
pinch of salt
1 cup milk chocolate chips
1 cup pecans, chopped
1 cup almonds, toasted and chopped

Preheat the oven to 375°F/190°C. Grease a 15 x 10-inch/38 x 25-cm/ jelly roll pan with the oil. Place the butter and sugar in a large bowl and beat together until light and fluffy, then stir in the vanilla extract. Sift together the flour and salt into the mixture and beat until combined. Mix in ½ cup of the chocolate chips and the nuts and press the dough into the pan, making sure the dough fills the pan and is evenly spread. Bake in the preheated oven for 20–25 minutes, or until golden. Let cool in the pan.

Place the remaining chocolate chips in a heatproof bowl, set the bowl over a saucepan of gently simmering water, and heat until melted. Drizzle the chocolate over the cookie brittle and let set, then break the brittle into irregular pieces.

490 Lemon almond brittle

Omit the chocolate and nuts, and add the finely grated rind of 2 lemons to the dough before pressing into the pan. Top with 1½ cups slivered almonds and bake as before. Cool and break into pieces.

491 Dark & white chocolate cookies

MAKES ABOUT 24

heaping ¾ cup butter, softened, plus extra for greasing
1 cup superfine sugar
½ tsp vanilla extract
1 large egg
1⅔ cups all-purpose flour
pinch of salt
1 tsp baking soda
⅔ cup white chocolate chips
4 oz/115 g semisweet chocolate chips

Preheat the oven to 350°F/180°C. Grease 2 large baking sheets. Place the butter, sugar, and vanilla extract in a large bowl and beat together. Gradually beat in the egg until the mixture is light and fluffy. Sift the flour, salt, and baking soda over the mixture and fold in. Fold in the chocolate chips.

Drop heaping teaspoonfuls of the batter onto the baking sheets, spaced well apart. Bake in the preheated oven for 10–12 minutes, or until crisp outside but still soft inside.

Let cool on the baking sheets for 2 minutes, then transfer the cookies to wire racks to cool completely.

492 Dark chocolate & hazelnut cookies

Replace the white chocolate chips with chopped toasted hazelnuts.

493 Ice cream cookie sandwiches

MAKES ABOUT 30

1 cup butter, softened
¾ cup superfine sugar
1 egg yolk, lightly beaten
2 tbsp finely chopped preserved ginger, plus 2 tsp syrup from the jar
heaping 1¾ cups all-purpose flour
¼ cup unsweetened cocoa
½ tsp ground cinnamon
pinch of salt
scant 2 cups vanilla, chocolate, or coffee ice cream

Place the butter and sugar in a large bowl and beat together until light and fluffy, then beat in the egg yolk, ginger, and ginger syrup. Sift together the flour, cocoa, cinnamon, and salt into the mixture and stir until combined. Halve the dough, shape into balls, wrap in plastic wrap, and chill for 30–60 minutes.

Preheat the oven to 375°F/190°C. Line 2 large baking sheets with parchment paper. Unwrap the dough and roll out between 2 sheets of parchment paper. Cut out cookies with a 2½-inch/6-cm fluted round cutter and place them on the baking sheets, spaced well apart.

Bake in the preheated oven for 10–15 minutes, or until light golden brown. Let cool for 5–10 minutes, then transfer to wire racks to cool completely.

Remove the ice cream from the freezer about 15 minutes before serving, to allow it to soften. Put a generous scoop of ice cream on half the cookies and top with the remaining cookies. Press together gently so that the filling spreads to the edges. If not serving immediately, wrap the cookies individually in foil and store in the freezer.

494 Chocolate mint sandwiches

Replace the preserved ginger in the cookie dough with 1 teaspoon of peppermint extract, then fill the cookies with chocolate chip ice cream.

495 Coffee cream & walnut cookies

MAKES ABOUT 30

1 cup butter, softened
¾ cup superfine sugar
1 egg yolk, lightly beaten
2 tsp vanilla extract
1⅔ cups all-purpose flour
pinch of salt
½ cup ground walnuts
½ cup walnuts, finely chopped
confectioners' sugar, for dusting (optional)

COFFEE CREAM
6 tbsp butter, softened
1¼ cups confectioners' sugar
1½ tsp strong black coffee

Place the butter and sugar in a large bowl and beat together until light and fluffy, then beat in the egg yolk and vanilla extract. Sift together the flour and salt into the mixture, add the ground walnuts, and stir until combined. Halve the dough, shape into balls, wrap in plastic wrap, and chill in the refrigerator for 30–60 minutes.

Preheat the oven to 375°F/190°C. Line 2 baking sheets with parchment paper. Unwrap the dough and roll out between 2 sheets of parchment paper. Cut out cookies with a 2½-inch/6-cm fluted round cutter and place them on the baking sheets, spaced well apart.

Bake in the preheated oven for 10–15 minutes, or until light golden brown. Let cool on the baking sheets for 5–10 minutes, then transfer the cookies to wire racks to cool completely.

To make the coffee cream, place the butter and confectioners' sugar in a bowl and beat together until smooth and thoroughly combined, then beat in the coffee.

Sandwich the cookies together in pairs with the coffee cream, then press together gently so that the cream oozes out of the sides. Smooth the sides with a dampened finger. Spread out the chopped walnuts in a shallow dish and roll the cookies in them to coat the sides of the coffee cream filling. Dust the tops with sifted confectioners' sugar, if liked.

496 Chocolate cream & walnut cookies

Replace the coffee with 1 teaspoon of cocoa.

497 The gooiest chocolate cookies

MAKES ABOUT 12

8 tbsp unsalted butter, softened
1¼ cups light brown sugar
1 large egg, lightly beaten
2 tsp vanilla extract
2 cups all-purpose flour
1 tbsp unsweetened cocoa
1 tsp baking soda
1 tsp salt
7 oz/200 g semisweet chocolate, chopped
5½ oz/150 g milk chocolate, chopped

Preheat the oven to 350°F/180°C. Line 2 large baking sheets with nonstick parchment paper. Place the butter and sugar in a large bowl and beat together until light and fluffy. Place the egg and vanilla extract in a separate bowl and whisk together, then gradually add to the butter mixture and beat until smooth. Mix in the flour, cocoa, baking soda, and salt until well combined. Add 3½ oz/100 g each of the semisweet and milk chocolates, then mix well.

Spoon 6 heaping tablespoons of the batter onto each baking sheet, spacing them well apart. Divide the remaining chocolate among the cookies and press in lightly.

Bake in the preheated oven for 15–17 minutes. Let cool on the baking sheets for 5 minutes, then transfer to a wire rack to cool.

498 With extra chocolate

Place 5½ oz/150 g milk chocolate in a heatproof bowl, set the bowl over a saucepan of gently simmering water, and heat until melted. Let cool for a few minutes, then spread over the cold cookies and let set.

499 Peanut butter cookies

MAKES ABOUT 26

8 tbsp butter, softened, plus extra for greasing
½ cup crunchy peanut butter
heaping ½ cup superfine sugar
heaping ½ cup dark brown sugar
1 egg, lightly beaten
½ tsp vanilla extract
½ cup all-purpose flour
½ tsp baking soda
½ tsp baking powder
pinch of salt
1⅓ cups rolled oats

Preheat the oven to 350°F/180°C. Grease 3 large baking sheets. Place the butter and peanut butter in a bowl and beat together, then beat in the sugars. Gradually beat in the egg and vanilla extract. Sift the flour, baking soda, baking powder, and salt into the mixture, add the oats, and stir until just combined.

Place spoonfuls of the dough on the baking sheets, spaced well apart, and flatten slightly with a fork. Bake in the preheated oven for 12 minutes, or until lightly browned. Let cool on the baking sheets for 2 minutes, then transfer to wire racks to cool completely.

500 With banana filling

Spread a cookie with smooth peanut butter and top with thin slices of banana tossed in lemon juice, then top with a second cookie and sandwich together. Makes about 13.

501 Carrot cake cookies

MAKES ABOUT 30

8 tbsp butter, softened
scant ½ cup superfine sugar
heaing ⅓ cup light brown sugar
1 large egg
½ tsp vanilla extract
heaping 1 cup all-purpose flour
½ tsp baking soda
½ tsp ground cinnamon
½ cup finely grated carrot
¼ cup walnut halves, chopped
heaping ¼ cup dry unsweetened coconut

Preheat the oven to 375°F/190°C. Line several large baking sheets with parchment paper.

Place the butter and sugars in a large bowl and whisk together until pale and creamy. Whisk the egg and vanilla extract into the mixture until smooth. Sift in the flour, baking soda, and cinnamon, then beat together until well mixed. Add the grated carrot, chopped walnuts, and coconut to the mixture and mix well together.

Drop heaping teaspoonfuls of the batter onto the baking sheets, spaced well apart. Bake in the preheated oven for 8–10 minutes, or until lightly golden brown around the edges.

Let cool on the baking sheets for 2–3 minutes, then transfer to a wire rack to cool completely.

502 Frosted carrot cake cookies

When the cookies are cold, top with a cream cheese frosting. Put scant ¼ cup soft cream cheese, 2 tablespoons of butter, and ½ teaspoon of vanilla extract in a large bowl and beat together until smooth. Sift in 1¾ cups confectioners' sugar and beat together until combined, then spread on top of the cookies.

503 Banana & chocolate cookies

MAKES ABOUT 20

9 tbsp butter
⅔ cup superfine sugar
1 large egg, lightly beaten
1 ripe banana, mashed
1¼ cups self-rising flour
1 tsp apple pie spice
2 tbsp milk
3½ oz/100 g chocolate, cut into chunks
⅓ cup raisins

Preheat the oven to 375°F/190°C. Line 2 large baking sheets with parchment paper. Place the butter and sugar in a large bowl and beat together until light and fluffy. Gradually add the egg, beating well after each addition. Mash the banana and add it to the mixture, beating well until smooth.

Sift together the flour and apple pie spice into the mixture and fold in with a spatula. Add the milk to give a soft consistency, then fold in the chocolate and raisins. Drop tablespoons of the batter onto the baking sheets, spaced well apart. Bake in the center of the preheated oven for 15–20 minutes, or until lightly golden. Let cool slightly, then transfer to a wire rack to cool completely.

504 Chocolate sprinkle cookies

MAKES 30

1 cup butter, softened
¾ cup superfine sugar
1 egg yolk, lightly beaten
2 tsp vanilla extract
1⅔ cups all-purpose flour, plus extra for dusting
½ cup unsweetened cocoa
pinch of salt
7 oz/200 g white chocolate, broken into pieces
chocolate sprinkles, for decorating

Place the butter and sugar in a large bowl and mix well with a wooden spoon, then beat in the egg yolk and vanilla extract.

Sift together the flour, cocoa, and salt into the mixture and stir until thoroughly combined. Halve the dough, roll each piece into a ball, wrap in plastic wrap, and chill in the refrigerator for 30–60 minutes.

Preheat the oven to 375°F/190°C. Line 2 large baking sheets with parchment paper.

Unwrap the dough and roll out between 2 pieces of parchment paper to about ¼ inch/5 mm thick. Cut out 30 cookies with a 2½–2¾-inch/6–7-cm fluted round cutter and place them on the baking sheets, spaced well apart.

Bake in the preheated oven for 10–12 minutes. Let cool on the baking sheets for 5–10 minutes, then transfer the cookies to wire racks to cool completely.

Place the white chocolate in a heatproof bowl, set the bowl over a saucepan of gently simmering water, and heat until melted. Immediately remove from the heat and spread the melted chocolate over the cookies. Let cool slightly, then sprinkle with the chocolate sprinkles. Let cool and set before serving.

505 Marbled cookies

Omit the chocolate sprinkles and use 3½ oz/100 g melted semisweet chocolate to swirl into the white chocolate topping to create a marbled effect.

506 Shortbread

MAKES 8

8 tbsp butter, cut into small pieces, plus extra for greasing
1¼ cups all-purpose flour, plus extra for dusting
pinch of salt
¼ cup superfine sugar, plus extra for sprinkling

Preheat the oven to 300°F/150°C. Grease a loose-bottom, 8-inch/20-cm round fluted tart pan with butter.

Place the flour, salt, and sugar in a large bowl and mix together. Add the butter and rub it into the dry ingredients. Continue to work the mixture until it forms a soft dough. Make sure you do not overwork the shortbread or it will be tough.

Lightly press the dough into the tart pan. If you don't have a fluted pan, roll out the dough on a lightly floured board, place on a baking sheet, and pinch the edges to form a scalloped pattern.

Using a knife, mark the dough into 8 pieces and prick all over with a fork. Bake in the preheated oven for 45–50 minutes, or until the shortbread is firm and just colored. Let cool for a few minutes in the pan, then sprinkle with sugar. Cut into portions and transfer to a wire rack to cool.

507 Lemon & vanilla shortbread

Split a vanilla bean in half lengthwise, carefully scrape out the seeds, and add to the flour along with the finely grated rind of 1 lemon.

508 Greek shortbread

MAKES ABOUT 20

¾ cup butter, softened
scant ½ cup confectioners' sugar, plus extra for dusting
1 small egg yolk
2½ tsp brandy
2¾ cups all-purpose flour
¼ tsp baking powder

Preheat the oven to 350°F/180°C. Line 2–3 large baking sheets with parchment paper.

Place the butter and confectioners' sugar in a large bowl and beat together until light and fluffy. Add the egg yolk and brandy and beat until the mixture is smooth. Sift the flour and baking powder into the mixture and beat until combined, then, using your hands, knead the dough until smooth.

Roll small pieces of the dough into smooth balls, then place them on the baking sheets, spaced well apart, and flatten slightly with your hands. Bake in the preheated oven for 15 minutes, or until firm to the touch and pale golden brown. Meanwhile, sift a layer of confectioners' sugar into a large roasting pan.

Let the shortbread cool for 2–3 minutes on the baking sheets, then place in the roasting pan in a single layer. Sift more confectioners' sugar generously over the top and let cool completely.

509 Greek almond shortbread

Use only 2 teaspoons of brandy and add ½ teaspoon of almond extract. Replace 1 cup of the flour with ground almonds.

510 Greek pistachio shortbread

Add ⅓ cup finely chopped pistachios to the mixture after adding the flour and baking powder.

511 Greek lemon shortbread

Add the finely grated rind of 1 lemon to the mixture with the egg yolk and replace the brandy with 2½ teaspoons of lemon juice.

512 Pistachio biscotti

Makes About 30

1 cup butter, softened
¾ cup superfine sugar
finely grated rind of 1 lemon
1 egg yolk, lightly beaten
2 tsp brandy
2 cups all-purpose flour
½ cup pistachios
pinch of salt
confectioners' sugar, for dusting

Place the butter, sugar, and lemon rind in a large bowl and beat together until light and fluffy, then beat in the egg yolk and brandy. Sift together the flour, pistachios, and salt into the mixture and stir until thoroughly combined. Shape the mixture into a log, flatten slightly, wrap in plastic wrap, and chill in the refrigerator for 30–60 minutes.

Preheat the oven to 375°F/190°C. Line 2 large baking sheets with parchment paper. Unwrap the log, cut it slightly on the diagonal into ¼-inch/5-mm slices with a sharp serrated knife, and place them on the baking sheets.

Bake in the oven for 10 minutes, or until golden brown. Let cool for 5–10 minutes, then transfer to wire racks to cool completely. Dust with sifted confectioners' sugar.

513 Hazelnut biscotti

Replace the pistachios with hazelnuts and replace the lemon rind with the finely grated rind of 1 orange.

514 Zesty lemon biscotti

Makes About 20

butter, for greasing
2 cups all-purpose flour, plus extra for dusting
1 tsp baking powder
¾ cup superfine sugar
½ cup blanched almonds
2 large eggs, lightly beaten
finely grated rind and juice of 1 lemon

Preheat the oven to 350°F/180°C. Grease a large baking sheet. Sift the flour and baking powder into a large bowl. Add the sugar, almonds, beaten eggs, lemon rind, and juice to the flour and mix together to form a soft dough. Turn the dough onto a lightly floured work surface and, with floured hands, knead for 2–3 minutes, or until smooth.

Divide the dough in half and shape each portion into a log shape measuring about 1½ inches/4 cm in diameter. Place the logs on the baking sheet and flatten until each is about 1 inch/2.5 cm thick.

Bake in the preheated oven for 25 minutes, or until lightly golden brown. Remove from the oven. Reduce the oven temperature to 300°F/150°C. Let cool for 15 minutes.

Using a serrated knife, cut the baked dough into ½-inch/1-cm thick slices and place cut-side down on ungreased baking sheets. Bake for an additional 10 minutes. Turn and bake for 10–15 minutes, or until golden brown and crisp. Transfer to a wire rack and let cool and harden.

515 Zesty orange & walnut biscotti

Replace the grated lemon rind and juice with orange rind and juice. Replace the almonds with chopped walnut halves.

516 Almond biscotti

MAKES ABOUT 20

heaping 1¾ cups all-purpose flour, plus extra for dusting
1 tsp baking powder
pinch of salt
¾ cup superfine sugar
2 eggs, lightly beaten
finely grated rind of 1 orange
⅔ cup whole blanched almonds, lightly toasted

Preheat the oven to 350°F/180°C. Lightly dust a large baking sheet with flour. Sift the flour, baking powder, and salt into a bowl. Add the sugar, eggs, and orange rind and mix to form a dough. Knead in the almonds.

Roll the dough into a ball, cut in half, roll out each portion into a log about 1½ inches/4 cm in diameter, and place the logs on the baking sheet. Bake in the preheated oven for 10 minutes. Let cool for 5 minutes.

Using a serrated knife, cut the baked dough into ½-inch/1-cm thick diagonal slices. Arrange the slices on ungreased baking sheets and return to the oven for 15 minutes, or until slightly golden. Transfer to a wire rack to cool and harden.

517 Vanilla & almond biscotti

Omit the grated orange rind and add 2 teaspoons of vanilla extract to the mixture with the eggs. Sprinkle 2 tablespoons of chopped blanched almonds on top of the logs before baking and press lightly into the dough.

518 Rose water biscotti

Omit the orange rind and add 2 teaspoons of rose water to the mixture with the eggs. Before baking, mix 1 egg white with 1 teaspoon of water. Brush over the dough and sprinkle 1 tablespoon of superfine sugar over each log.

519 Chocolate & almond biscotti

Makes 24

butter, for greasing
1 cup blanched almonds
5½ oz/150 g semisweet chocolate, broken into pieces
heaping 1¾ cups all-purpose flour, plus extra for dusting
1 tsp baking powder
¾ cup superfine sugar
2 large eggs, lightly beaten
1 tsp vanilla extract

Preheat the oven to 325°F/160°C. Grease a large baking sheet. Spread the almonds on another baking sheet and bake in the preheated oven for 5–10 minutes, or until lightly toasted. Let cool.

Place the chocolate in a heatproof bowl, set the bowl over a saucepan of gently simmering water, and heat until melted. Remove from the heat and stir until smooth, then let cool.

Sift the flour and baking powder into a large bowl. Add the sugar, cooled almonds, chocolate, eggs, and vanilla extract and mix together to form a soft dough.

Turn the dough onto a lightly floured work surface and, with floured hands, knead for 2–3 minutes, or until smooth. Divide the dough in half and shape each portion into a log shape measuring about 2 inches/5 cm in diameter. Place the logs on the baking sheet and flatten until each is 1 inch/2.5 cm thick.

Bake in the preheated oven for 20–30 minutes, or until firm to the touch. Let cool for 15 minutes.

Reduce the oven temperature to 300°F/150°C. Using a serrated knife, cut the baked dough into ½-inch/1-cm thick slices and place, cut-side down, on ungreased baking sheets.

Bake in the oven for 10 minutes. Turn and bake for an additional 10–15 minutes, or until crisp. Transfer to a wire rack to cool and harden.

520 Double chocolate biscotti

Replace the almonds with heaping ½ cup white chocolate chips, adding them with the sugar.

521 Chocolate & orange biscotti

Omit the almonds and vanilla extract and add the finely grated rind of 1 orange and scant 1 cup chopped candied orange peel with the sugar.

522 Marbled biscotti

MAKES 20

3½ oz/100 g semisweet chocolate, broken into pieces
6 tbsp butter, softened
¾ cup superfine sugar
2 large eggs, lightly beaten
½ tsp vanilla extract
2 cups all-purpose flour, plus extra for dusting
1½ tsp baking powder
½ cup blanched almonds, chopped
finely grated rind of 1 orange

Preheat the oven to 375°F/190°C. Place the chocolate in a heatproof bowl, set the bowl over a saucepan of simmering water, and heat until melted. Remove from the heat, stir until smooth, then cool.

Place the butter and sugar in a large bowl and whisk together until pale and creamy. Whisk in the eggs and vanilla extract. Sift the flour and baking powder into the mixture.

Add the chopped almonds and mix together to form a soft dough. Divide the dough in half and put each half into a bowl. Add the melted chocolate to one half, then mix together. Add the grated orange rind to the other half, then mix together.

Turn the dough halves onto a lightly floured work surface and, with floured hands, knead each separately for 2–3 minutes, or until smooth. Divide each piece of dough in half and roll each portion into a sausage shape measuring about 12 inches/30 cm long.

Place a roll of each color, side by side, on a baking sheet and twist the rolls around each other. Flatten to a thickness of about 1 inch/2.5 cm. Repeat with the remaining dough rolls. Bake in the preheated oven for 25 minutes, or until lightly browned. Remove from the oven and let cool for 15 minutes. Reduce the oven temperature to 325°F/170°C.

Using a serrated knife, cut the dough into ½-inch/1-cm thick slices and place, cut-side down, on ungreased baking sheets. Bake in the oven for 10 minutes. Turn and bake for an additional 10–15 minutes, or until golden brown and crisp. Transfer to a wire rack to cool and harden.

523 Walnut & rosemary biscotti

MAKES ABOUT 16

4 tbsp butter, softened, plus extra for greasing
scant ½ cup superfine sugar
2 large eggs, lightly beaten
1⅔ cups all-purpose flour, plus extra for dusting
1¼ tsp baking powder
scant 1 cup walnut halves, coarsely chopped
1¼ tsp dried rosemary

Preheat the oven to 375°F/190°C. Grease a large baking sheet.

Place the butter and sugar in a large bowl and whisk together until pale and creamy. Whisk in the eggs. Sift in the flour and baking powder. Add the chopped walnuts and dried rosemary and mix together to form a soft dough.

Turn the dough onto a lightly floured work surface and with floured hands, knead for 2–3 minutes, or until smooth. Divide the dough in half and shape each portion into a log shape measuring 1½ inches/4 cm in diameter. Place the logs on the baking sheet and flatten to a thickness of 1 inch/2.5 cm. Bake in the preheated oven for 20–25 minutes, or until lightly browned. Remove from the oven and let cool for 15 minutes. Reduce the oven temperature to 325°F/160°C.

Using a serrated knife, cut the baked dough into ½-inch/1-cm thick slices and place, cut-side down, on ungreased baking sheets. Bake in the oven for 10 minutes. Turn and bake for an additional 10–15 minutes, or until golden brown and crisp. Transfer to a wire rack to cool and harden.

524 Pine nut & lemon biscotti

Replace the walnuts with pine nuts. Replace the rosemary with the finely grated rind of 1 large lemon.

525 Apricot biscotti

MAKES ABOUT 20

butter, for greasing
scant 1 cup plumped dried apricots
2 cups all-purpose flour, plus extra for dusting
1 tsp baking powder
¾ cup superfine sugar
2 large eggs, lightly beaten
¼ tsp almond extract
finely grated rind of 1 lemon

Preheat the oven to 375°F/190°C. Grease a large baking sheet. Using scissors, snip the apricots into small pieces.

Sift the flour and baking powder into a large bowl. Add the snipped apricots and sugar and mix together. Add the eggs, almond extract, and lemon rind and mix together to form a soft dough.

Turn the dough onto a lightly floured work surface and, with floured hands, knead for 2–3 minutes, or until smooth. Divide the dough in half and shape each portion into a log shape measuring about 1½ inches/4 cm in diameter. Place the logs on the baking sheet and flatten until each is about 1 inch/2.5 cm thick.

Bake in the preheated oven for 20–30 minutes, or until lightly browned. Remove from the oven and let cool for 15 minutes. Reduce the oven temperature to 325°F/160°C. Using a serrated knife, cut the baked dough into ½-inch/1-cm thick slices and place, cut-side down, on ungreased baking sheets. Bake in the preheated oven for 10 minutes. Turn and bake for an additional 10 minutes, or until crisp. Transfer to a wire rack to cool and harden.

526 Golden raisin biscotti

Replace the apricots with golden raisins or raisins and replace the almond extract with vanilla extract.

527 Saffron-flecked biscotti

MAKES ABOUT 24

butter, for greasing
⅔ cup blanched almonds
2 cups all-purpose flour, plus extra for dusting
½ tsp baking soda
¾ cup superfine sugar
2 large pinches of saffron strands
2 large eggs, lightly beaten

Preheat the oven to 375°F/190°C. Grease a large baking sheet. Spread the almonds on a baking sheet and bake in the preheated oven for 5–10 minutes, or until lightly toasted. Let cool.

Sift the flour and baking soda into a large bowl. Add the sugar, cooled almonds, and saffron and stir together. Add the eggs and mix together to form a soft dough.

Turn the dough onto a lightly floured work surface and, with floured hands, knead for 2–3 minutes, or until smooth. Divide the dough in half and shape each portion into a log shape measuring about 1½ inches/4 cm/ in diameter. Place the logs on the baking sheet and flatten slightly until each is about 1 inch/2.5 cm thick.

Bake in the preheated oven for 15 minutes, or until lightly golden brown. Remove from the oven and let cool for 15–20 minutes. Reduce the oven temperature to 325°F/160°C. Using a serrated knife, cut the baked dough into ½-inch/1-cm thick slices and place, cut-side down, on ungreased baking sheets. Bake in the oven for 5 minutes. Turn and bake for an additional 5–10 minutes, or until lightly golden brown and crisp. Transfer to a wire rack to cool and harden.

528 Mocha biscotti

MAKES ABOUT 24

3½ tbsp butter, softened, plus extra for greasing
½ cup superfine sugar
2 large eggs, lightly beaten
4 tsp chicory and coffee extract
scant 2¼ cups all-purpose flour, plus extra for dusting
1 tsp baking powder
1 tbsp unsweetened cocoa
¼ cup chopped blanched almonds

Preheat the oven to 375°F/190°C. Grease a large baking sheet. Place the butter and sugar in a large bowl and whisk together until pale and creamy. Whisk the eggs and chicory and coffee extract into the mixture. Sift in the flour, baking powder, and cocoa. Add the almonds and mix together to form a soft dough.

Turn the dough onto a lightly floured work surface and, with floured hands, knead for 2–3 minutes, or until smooth. Divide the dough in half and shape each portion into a log shape measuring about 1½ inches/4 cm in diameter. Place the logs on the baking sheet and flatten until each is about 1 inch/2.5 cm thick.

Bake in the preheated oven for 20–25 minutes, or until firm to the touch. Remove from the oven and let cool for 15 minutes. Reduce the oven temperature to 325°F/160°C. Using a serrated knife, cut the baked dough into ½-inch/1-cm thick slices and place, cut-side down, on ungreased baking sheets. Bake for an additional 10 minutes. Turn and bake for another 10–15 minutes, or until crisp. Transfer to a wire rack to cool and harden.

529 Honey & sesame biscotti

MAKES ABOUT 20

3 tbsp butter, softened, plus extra for greasing
4 tbsp superfine sugar
2 large eggs, lightly beaten
¼ cup honey
scant 2¼ cups all-purpose flour, plus extra for dusting
1 tsp baking powder
5 tbsp sesame seeds

Preheat the oven to 375°F/190°C. Grease a large baking sheet. Place the butter and sugar in a large bowl and whisk together until pale and creamy. Whisk the eggs and honey into the mixture. Sift in the flour and baking powder. Add 3 tablespoons of the sesame seeds and mix together to form a soft dough.

Turn the dough onto a lightly floured work surface and, with floured hands, knead for 2–3 minutes, or until smooth. Divide the dough in half and shape each portion into a log shape measuring about 1½ inches/4 cm in diameter.

Sprinkle the remaining sesame seeds on a sheet of parchment paper and roll the logs in the seeds. Place the logs on the baking sheet and flatten to a thickness of about 1 inch/2.5 cm. Sprinkle any remaining sesame seeds on top of the logs and press into the dough.

Bake in the preheated oven for 15–20 minutes, or until lightly golden brown. Remove from the oven and let cool for 15 minutes. Reduce the oven temperature to 325°F/160°C. Using a serrated knife, cut the baked dough into ½-inch/1-cm thick slices and place, cut-side down, on ungreased baking sheets. Bake the cookies in the oven for 10 minutes. Turn and bake for an additional 5–10 minutes, or until crisp. Transfer to a wire rack and let cool and harden.

530 *Spicy nut biscotti*

Makes About 20

3½ tbsp butter, softened, plus extra for greasing
¼ cup superfine sugar
¼ cup light brown sugar
2 large eggs, lightly beaten
2 cups all-purpose flour, plus extra for dusting
1¼ tsp baking powder
¼ tsp ground cinnamon
¼ tsp grated nutmeg
¼ tsp ground ginger
⅔ cup blanched almonds, chopped

Preheat the oven to 375°F/190°C. Grease a large baking sheet. Place the butter and sugars in a large bowl and whisk together until pale and creamy. Whisk the eggs into the mixture. Sift in the flour, baking powder, cinnamon, nutmeg, and ginger. Add the chopped almonds, reserving 2 tablespoons, and mix together to form a soft dough.

Turn the dough onto a lightly floured work surface and, with floured hands, knead for 2–3 minutes, or until smooth. Divide the dough in half and shape each portion into a log shape measuring about 1½ inches/4 cm in diameter.

Place the logs on the baking sheet and flatten until each is about 1 inch/2.5 cm thick. Sprinkle the reserved almonds on top of the logs and press into the dough.

Bake in the preheated oven for 20–25 minutes, or until lightly golden brown. Remove from the oven and let cool for 15 minutes. Reduce the oven temperature to 325°F/160°C. Using a serrated knife, cut the baked dough into ½-inch/1-cm thick slices and place, cut-side down, on ungreased baking sheets. Bake for an additional 10 minutes. Turn and bake for another 10–15 minutes, or until lightly golden brown and crisp. Transfer to a wire rack to cool and harden.

531 *Cherry & almond biscotti*

Makes About 30

3½ tbsp butter, softened, plus extra for greasing
½ cup superfine sugar
1 large egg, lightly beaten
scant 1½ cups all-purpose flour, plus extra for dusting
1¼ tsp baking powder
3½ oz/100 g candied cherries, halved
¼ cup blanched almonds, coarsely chopped

Preheat the oven to 375°F/190°C. Grease a large baking sheet. Place the butter and sugar in a large bowl and whisk together until pale and creamy. Whisk in the egg. Sift the flour and baking powder into the mixture. Add the cherries and chopped almonds and mix together to form a soft dough. Turn the dough onto a lightly floured work surface and, with floured hands, knead for 2–3 minutes, or until smooth. Divide the dough in half and shape each portion into a log shape measuring about 1½ inches/4 cm in diameter. Place the logs on the baking sheet and flatten until each is about 1 inch/2.5 cm thick.

Bake in the preheated oven for 20–25 minutes, or until lightly golden brown. Remove from the oven and let cool for 15 minutes. Reduce the oven temperature to 325°F/160°C. Using a serrated knife, cut the baked dough into ½-inch/1-cm thick slices and place, cut-side down, on ungreased baking sheets. Bake for an additional 10 minutes. Turn and bake for another 10–15 minutes until crisp. Transfer to a wire rack to cool and harden.

532 *Mixed berry biscotti*

Replace the cherries with ½ cup dried cranberries and ¼ cup dried blueberries.

533 *Mixed cherry biscotti*

Use multicolored candied cherries that include red, green, and yellow ones.

534 *Traditional oatcakes*

MAKES ABOUT 20

2⅔ cups rolled oats, plus extra for dusting
½ tsp baking soda
½ tsp salt
1 tbsp unsalted butter, melted
⅔ cup warm water

Preheat the oven to 350°F/180°C. Place the oats and baking soda into a large bowl and stir in the salt, making a well in the middle. Pour the melted butter and warm water into the oatmeal mixture and mix together to form a soft dough.

Roll the dough out on a work surface lightly dusted with oats. Cut out oatcakes with a cookie cutter. Re-roll any trimmings and cut out more oatcakes. Place the oatcakes on 2 large nonstick baking sheets.

Bake in the preheated oven for 20 minutes, turning them 3 times while cooking. Leave on a wire rack to cool completely.

535 *Cranberry oatcakes*

Add ¼ cup chopped dried cranberries to the dough and knead in before rolling out the dough.

536 *Gingerbread people*

MAKES ABOUT 20

8 tbsp butter, plus extra for greasing
3¼ cups all-purpose flour, plus extra for dusting
2 tsp ground ginger
1 tsp pupkin pie spice
2 tsp baking soda
heaping ¼ cup dark corn syrup
heaping ½ cup dark brown sugar
1 egg, lightly beaten

FOR DECORATING
raisins
candied cherries
¾ cup confectioners' sugar
3–4 tsp water

Preheat the oven to 325°F/160°C. Grease 3 large baking sheets. Sift the flour, ginger, pumpkin pie spice, and baking soda into a large bowl. Place the butter, dark corn syrup, and dark brown sugar in a saucepan over low heat and stir until melted. Pour onto the dry ingredients and add the egg. Mix together to form a dough. The dough will be sticky to start with, but will become firmer as it cools.

Roll out the dough on a lightly floured work surface to about ⅛ inch/3 mm thick and cut out gingerbread people shapes. Place the shapes on the baking sheets. Reknead and reroll the trimmings and cut out more shapes. Decorate with raisins for the eyes and pieces of candied cherry for the mouths.

Bake in the preheated oven for 15–20 minutes, or until firm and lightly browned. Let cool on the baking sheets for a few minutes, then transfer the cookies to wire racks to cool completely.

Place the confectioners' sugar and water in a small bowl and mix together until it is thick. Place the frosting in a small pastry bag fitted with a plain tip and use to pipe buttons and bows onto the cookies.

537 *Gingerbread ark*

Use animal cookie cutters to make gingerbread animals. Make a Noah's Ark gift box with 2 gingerbread people and several animals.

538 Cheese sables

MAKES ABOUT 35

heaping 1 cup all-purpose flour, plus extra for dusting
1⅓ cups grated sharp cheddar cheese
heaping ⅔ cup butter, diced, plus extra for greasing
1 egg yolk
sesame seeds, for sprinkling

Place the flour and cheese in a bowl and mix together. Add the butter and rub it in with your fingertips until combined. Stir in the egg yolk and mix to form a dough. Wrap the dough in plastic wrap and chill in the refrigerator for about 30 minutes.

Preheat the oven to 400°F/200°C. Lightly grease several large baking sheets. Roll out the dough thinly on a lightly floured work surface. Cut out 2½-inch/6-cm rounds with a cookie cutter. Re-roll the trimmings to make about 35 rounds and place them on the baking sheets. Sprinkle the sesame seeds over the top of them.

Bake in the preheated oven for 10 minutes, or until the sables are light golden brown. Transfer the cookies to a wire rack to cool slightly before serving.

539 Gruyère sables

Replace the cheddar cheese with finely grated Gruyère cheese.

540 Cheese straws

MAKES ABOUT 24

heaping ¾ cup all-purpose flour, plus extra for dusting
pinch of salt
1 tsp curry powder
4 tbsp butter, plus extra for greasing
½ cup grated cheddar cheese
1 egg, lightly beaten
poppy and cumin seeds, for sprinkling

Sift the flour, salt, and curry powder into a bowl. Add the butter and rub it in with your fingertips until the mixture resembles breadcrumbs. Add the cheese and half the egg and mix to form a dough. Wrap in plastic wrap and chill in the refrigerator for 30 minutes.

Preheat the oven to 400°F/200°C. Grease several large baking sheets. Roll out the dough on a floured work surface to ¼ inch/5 mm thick, then cut into 3 x ½-inch/7.5 x 1-cm strips. Pinch the strips lightly along the sides and place on the baking sheets.

Brush the strips with the remaining egg and sprinkle half with poppy seeds and half with cumin seeds. Bake in the preheated oven for 10–15 minutes, or until golden. Transfer to wire racks to cool.

541 Celery & cheese straws

Replace the curry powder with 1½ teaspoons of celery salt.

542 *Breadsticks*

MAKES ABOUT 30

2½ cups white bread flour, plus extra for dusting
1½ tsp salt
1½ tsp active dry yeast
heaping ¾ cup lukewarm water
3 tbsp olive oil, plus extra for greasing
sesame seeds, for coating

Sift together the flour and salt into a warmed bowl. Stir in the yeast and make a well in the middle. Add the water and oil to the well and mix to form a soft dough. Turn out the dough onto a floured work surface and knead for 5–10 minutes, or until smooth and elastic. Place the dough in an oiled bowl, cover with a damp dish towel, and let rise in a warm place for 1 hour, or until doubled in size.

Preheat the oven to 400°F/200°C. Lightly grease 2 large baking sheets. Turn out the dough and knead lightly, then roll out into a 9 x 8-inch/23 x 20-cm rectangle. Cut the dough into three 8-inch/20-cm long strips, then cut each strip across into 10 pieces. Roll and stretch each piece into a 12-inch/30-cm long stick and brush with oil.

Spread out the sesame seeds on a large plate. Roll each breadstick in the sesame seeds, then put on the baking sheets, spaced well apart. Brush with oil, cover with a damp dish towel, and leave in a warm place for 15 minutes.

Bake in the preheated oven for 10 minutes. Turn over and bake for an additional 5–10 minutes, until golden. Transfer to a wire rack to cool.

543 *With mixed seed coating*

Crush 1 tablespoon each of cumin and coriander seeds. Mix with 1 tablespoon each of poppy seeds and sesame seeds and use to coat the breadsticks.

544 *Savory oat crackers*

MAKES ABOUT 14

7 tbsp unsalted butter, plus extra for greasing
heaping 1 cup rolled oats
2 tbsp whole wheat flour
½ tsp coarse sea salt
1 tsp dried thyme
scant ½ cup walnut halves, finely chopped
1 egg, lightly beaten
scant ¼ cup sesame seeds

Preheat the oven to 350°F/180°C. Grease 2 large baking sheets. Place the oats and flour in a large bowl. Add the butter and rub it in with your fingertips. Stir in the salt, thyme, and walnuts, then add the egg and mix to form a soft dough. Spread out the sesame seeds on a large plate.

Roll walnut-size pieces of dough into balls, then roll in the sesame seeds to coat and put on the baking sheets, spaced well apart. Roll the rolling pin over them to flatten as much as possible.

Bake in the preheated oven for 12–15 minutes, or until firm and pale golden. Let cool on the baking sheets for 3–4 minutes, then transfer to a wire rack to cool completely.

545 *Spiced oat crackers*

Add ½ teaspoon of ground cumin and ½ teaspoon of crushed coriander seeds to the dough and replace half the sesame seeds with 2 tbsp poppy seeds.

Blissful Brownies and Bars

546 Chocolate brownies

MAKES 15

1 cup butter, diced, plus extra for greasing
5½ oz/150 g semisweet chocolate, chopped
1⅔ cups self-rising flour
scant ⅔ cup dark brown sugar
4 eggs, lightly beaten
scant ½ cup blanched hazelnuts, chopped
⅓ cup golden raisins
heaping ½ cup semisweet chocolate chips
4 oz/115 g white chocolate, melted, for decorating

Preheat the oven to 350°F/180°C. Grease and line a shallow 11 x 7-inch/ 28 x 18-cm rectangular baking pan. Place the butter and chocolate in a saucepan and stir over low heat until melted. Remove the pan from the heat.

Sift the flour into a large bowl, add the sugar, and mix well. Stir the eggs into the chocolate mixture, then beat into the flour mixture. Add the nuts, golden raisins, and chocolate chips and mix well. Spoon evenly into the cake pan and smooth the surface.

Bake in the preheated oven for 30 minutes, or until firm and a skewer inserted into the center comes out clean. Let cool for 15 minutes, then turn out onto a wire rack to cool completely.

To decorate, drizzle the melted white chocolate in fine lines over the cake, then cut into squares. Let set before serving.

547 Sugar-coated chocolates brownies

Use light brown sugar instead of the dark brown sugar. Replace the golden raisins with 5½ oz/150 g sugar-coated chocolates.

548 Chocolate & date brownies

Replace the hazelnuts, golden raisins, and chocolate chips with 1 cup chopped dried dates. Decorate with milk chocolate instead of white chocolate.

549 Chocolate chile brownies

Add ¼ teaspoon of chile flakes to the melted butter and chocolate.

550 *Cappuccino brownies*

MAKES 15

1 cup butter, softened, plus extra for greasing
1⅔ cups self-rising flour
1 tsp baking powder
1 tsp unsweetened cocoa, plus extra for dusting
heaping 1 cup superfine sugar
4 eggs, lightly beaten
3 tbsp instant coffee granules, dissolved in 2 tbsp hot water, cooled

WHITE CHOCOLATE FROSTING
4 oz/115 g white chocolate, broken into pieces
4 tbsp butter, softened
3 tbsp milk
1½ cups confectioners' sugar

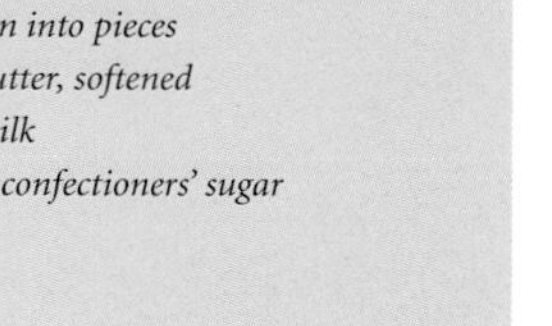

Preheat the oven to 350°F/180°C. Grease and line the bottom of a shallow 11 x 7-inch/28 x 18-cm rectangular baking pan. Sift the flour, baking powder, and cocoa into a bowl and add the butter, sugar, eggs, and coffee. Beat well until smooth, then spoon into the pan and smooth the top.

Bake in the preheated oven for 35–40 minutes, or until risen and firm. Let cool in the pan for 10 minutes, then turn out onto a wire rack and peel off the lining paper. Let cool completely.

To make the frosting, place the chocolate, butter, and milk in a saucepan and stir over low heat until the chocolate has melted. Remove the pan from the heat and sift in the confectioners' sugar. Beat until smooth, then spread over the cake. Dust the top with sifted cocoa and cut into squares.

551 *Coffee-frosted brownies*

Replace the white chocolate frosting with coffee frosting. Melt 4 tablespoons of butter in a small saucepan with 3 tablespoons of milk, then add 4 teaspoons of instant coffee granules and stir until dissolved. Sift 2 cups confectioners' sugar into a bowl and beat in the coffee mixture to form a smooth frosting. Let cool slightly until thickened. Spread over the brownies and let set before cutting into squares.

552 *Black Russian brownies*

MAKES ABOUT 8

8 tbsp butter, plus extra for greasing
4 oz/115 g semisweet chocolate, broken into pieces
½ tsp coarsely ground black peppercorns
4 eggs, lightly beaten
2¼ cups superfine sugar
½ tsp vanilla extract
3 tbsp Kahlúa liqueur
2 tbsp vodka
heaping 1 cup all-purpose flour
¼ tsp baking powder
⅓ cup chopped walnuts, plus extra for decorating
unsweetened cocoa, for dusting

KAHLÚA CREAM TOPPING
2 tbsp Kahlúa liqueur
heaping ¾ cup sour cream

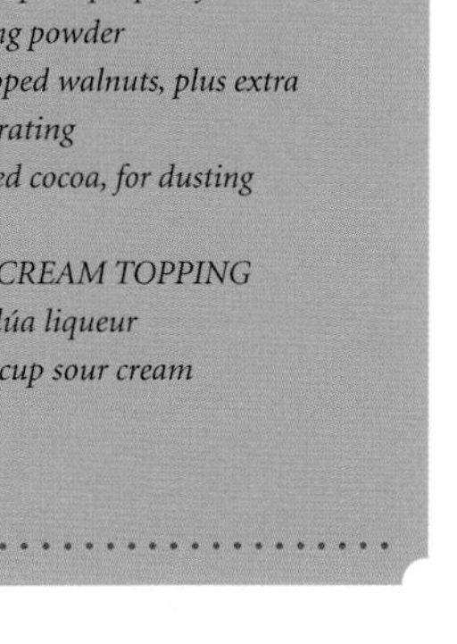

Preheat the oven to 350°F/180°C. Grease and line the bottom of a shallow 12 x 8-inch/30 x 20-cm rectangular baking pan. Place the chocolate, butter, and peppercorns in a small saucepan and heat gently until the chocolate and butter are melted. Let cool slightly.

Place the eggs, sugar, and vanilla extract in a large bowl and beat together, then stir in the chocolate mixture, Kahlúa, and vodka. Sift together the flour and baking powder and stir into the chocolate mixture. Stir in the walnuts and pour into the pan. Bake in the preheated oven for 20–25 minutes, or until just firm to the touch. Let cool for a few minutes, then cut into bars or squares and lift carefully from the pan onto serving plates.

To make the topping, stir the Kahlúa into the sour cream and spoon a generous dollop on each serving of brownie. Sprinkle with a little cocoa, decorate with walnuts, and serve immediately.

553 Black forest brownies

Makes 8

8 tbsp butter, plus extra for greasing
⅔ cup all-purpose flour
½ tsp baking powder
½ cup unsweetened cocoa
2 eggs, lightly beaten
heaping ¾ cup superfine sugar
1 tsp vanilla extract
½ tsp almond extract
⅔ cup pitted dark cherries, quartered
chocolate curls and whole fresh cherries, for decorating

CHERRY CREAM
⅔ cup heavy cream
1 tbsp Kirsch liqueur

Preheat the oven to 350°F/180°C. Grease a shallow 11 x 7-inch/ 28 x 18-cm rectangular baking pan. Sift together the flour and baking powder. Place the butter in a large saucepan over medium heat and stir until melted. Remove from the heat and add the cocoa, stirring until smooth. Beat in the eggs, sugar, vanilla extract, and almond extract. Fold in the flour mixture and cherries and pour into the pan.

Bake in the preheated oven for 25–30 minutes, or until just firm to the touch. Cool slightly, then cut into squares and remove from the pan.

To make the cherry cream, place the cream and Kirsch in a bowl and whip together. Spoon a little onto each brownie, then decorate with chocolate curls and serve with fresh cherries.

554 Chocolate & raspberry brownies

Replace the cherries with raspberries. To serve, whip the cream with 1 tablespoon of framboise and serve with extra raspberries.

555 Chocolate blueberry brownies

Replace the cherries with blueberries and serve with cassis-flavored cream and extra blueberries.

556 Double chocolate brownies

MAKES 9

8 tbsp butter, plus extra for greasing
4 oz/115 g semisweet chocolate, broken into pieces
1½ cups superfine sugar
pinch of salt
1 tsp vanilla extract
2 large eggs
1 cup all-purpose flour
2 tbsp unsweetened cocoa
heaping ½ cup white chocolate chips

FUDGE SAUCE
4 tbsp butter
heaping 1 cup superfine sugar
⅔ cup milk
generous 1 cup heavy cream
⅔ cup dark corn syrup
7 oz/200 g semisweet chocolate, broken into pieces

Preheat the oven to 350°F/180°C. Grease and line the bottom of a 7-inch/18-cm square cake pan. Place the butter and chocolate in a saucepan and stir over low heat until melted. Remove from the heat, then stir until smooth and let cool slightly. Stir in the sugar, salt, and vanilla extract. Add the eggs, one at a time, and stir until blended.

Sift the flour and cocoa into the mixture and beat until smooth. Stir in the chocolate chips, then pour into the pan.

Bake in the preheated oven for 35–40 minutes, until a toothpick inserted into the center comes out almost clean. Let cool slightly.

Place the butter, sugar, milk, cream, and dark corn syrup in a small saucepan and heat gently until the sugar has dissolved. Bring to a boil and stir for 10 minutes, or until the mixture is caramel-colored. Remove from the heat and add the chocolate. Stir until smooth. Cut the brownies into squares and serve with the sauce.

557 Chocolate & butterscotch brownies

Replace the white chocolate chips with butterscotch chips.

558 Cranberry sour cream brownies

MAKES 12

8 tbsp butter, plus extra for greasing
1 cup self-rising flour, plus extra for dusting
4 tbsp unsweetened cocoa
1 cup light brown sugar
2 eggs, lightly beaten
1¼ cups fresh cranberries

TOPPING
⅔ cup sour cream
1 tbsp superfine sugar
1 tbsp self-rising flour
1 egg yolk
½ tsp vanilla extract

Preheat the oven to 350°F/180°C. Grease and lightly flour a shallow 12 x 8-inch/30 x 20-cm rectangular baking pan. Place the butter, cocoa, and sugar in a saucepan and stir over low heat until just melted. Let cool slightly. Quickly stir in the flour and eggs and beat hard until thoroughly mixed to a smooth batter. Stir in the cranberries, then spread the batter into the pan.

To make the topping, place all the ingredients in a bowl and beat together until smooth, then spoon over the chocolate mixture, swirling evenly with a spatula. Bake in the preheated oven for 35–40 minutes, or until risen and firm. Let cool in the pan, then cut into squares.

559 Brownie base cheesecake

SERVES 12

BROWNIE BASE

8 tbsp butter, plus extra for greasing
heaping ¾ cup all-purpose flour, plus extra for dusting
4 oz/115 g semisweet chocolate
1 cup superfine sugar
2 eggs, lightly beaten
¼ cup milk
strawberries dipped in melted chocolate, for serving

TOPPING

1 lb 2 oz/500 g soft cream cheese
scant ⅔ cup superfine sugar
3 eggs
1 tsp vanilla extract
½ cup plain yogurt
melted chocolate, for drizzling

Preheat the oven to 350°F/180°C. Lightly grease and flour a 9-inch/23-cm round cake pan. Place the butter and chocolate in a saucepan and stir over low heat until melted and smooth. Remove from the heat and beat in the sugar. Add the eggs and milk, beating well. Stir in the flour, mixing until just blended. Spoon into the pan, spreading evenly.

Bake in the preheated oven for 25 minutes. Remove from the oven and reduce the oven temperature to 325°F/160°C.

To make the topping, place the cheese, sugar, eggs, and vanilla extract in a bowl and beat together until well blended. Stir in the yogurt, then pour over the brownie base. Bake for an additional 45–55 minutes, or until the center is almost set.

Run a knife around the edge of the cheesecake to loosen it from the pan. Let cool before removing from the pan.

Chill in the refrigerator for 4 hours or overnight before cutting into slices. Drizzle the top with the melted chocolate and serve with chocolate-dipped strawberries.

560 Chocolate peach cheesecake

For the topping, replace the vanilla extract with the finely grated rind of 1 orange and use a peach-flavored yogurt.

561 White chocolate brownie cheesecake

For the topping, omit the yogurt and fold in 4½ oz/125 g melted white chocolate and heaping ⅓ cup heavy cream after the vanilla extract is added.

 562 Chocolate chip brownies

Makes 12

1 cup butter, softened, plus extra for greasing
5½ oz/150 g semisweet chocolate, broken into pieces
2 cups all-purpose flour
½ cup superfine sugar
4 eggs, lightly beaten
½ cup chopped pistachios
3½ oz/100 g white chocolate, coarsely chopped
confectioners' sugar, for dusting (optional)

Preheat the oven to 350°F/180°C. Lightly grease and line a 9-inch/23-cm square baking pan.

Place the butter and semisweet chocolate in a saucepan and stir over low heat until melted. Let cool slightly.

Sift the flour into a separate bowl and stir in the sugar.

Stir the eggs into the melted chocolate mixture, then pour this mixture into the flour and sugar mixture, beating well. Stir in the pistachios and white chocolate, then pour the batter into the pan, spreading it evenly into the corners.

Bake in the preheated oven for 30–35 minutes, or until firm to the touch. Let cool in the pan for 20 minutes, then turn out onto a wire rack and let cool completely. Cut into 12 bars and dust with sifted confectioners' sugar, if using.

563 Peanut butter chip brownies

Replace the pistachios with peanuts and the white chocolate with peanut butter chips.

564 Minted chocolate chip brownies

Replace the chocolate chips and pistachios with 6 oz/175 g mint chocolate, coarsely chopped.

565 Low-fat banana cardamom brownies

MAKES 16

butter, for greasing
heaping ¼ cup all-purpose flour
3 tbsp unsweetened cocoa
2 tbsp dried milk powder
¼ tsp baking powder
¼ tsp salt
2 ripe bananas
¾ cup light brown sugar
2 egg whites
⅔ cup low-fat plain yogurt
seeds from 2 cardamom pods, crushed
shredded coconut, toasted, for decorating

Preheat the oven to 350°F/180°C. Grease a shallow 9-inch/23-cm square baking pan. Sift the flour, cocoa, milk powder, baking powder, and salt into a large bowl and make a well in the center.

Mash the bananas in a separate bowl, add the sugar, egg whites, yogurt, and cardamom seeds, and beat together until combined. Stir into the dry ingredients, mixing evenly, then spoon the batter into the pan.

Bake in the preheated oven for 25–30 minutes, or until just firm. Let cool in the pan, then cut into squares and decorate with toasted shredded coconut.

566 Spiced banana brownies

Make the brownies with whole-milk yogurt or sour cream and add ¼ cup chopped walnuts or pecans. Replace the cardamom pods with ¼ teaspoon of freshly grated nutmeg, if liked.

567 Maple-glazed pistachio brownies

MAKES 16

¾ cup butter, plus extra for greasing
4 oz/115 g semisweet chocolate
1¼ cups superfine sugar
4 eggs, lightly beaten
1 tsp vanilla extract
scant 1½ cups all-purpose flour
½ cup pistachios, skinned and chopped

GLAZE
4 oz/115 g semisweet chocolate
½ cup sour cream
2 tbsp maple syrup

Preheat the oven to 375°F/190°C. Lightly grease a shallow 12 x 8-inch/30 x 20-cm rectangular baking pan. Place the chocolate and butter in a small saucepan over very low heat and stir until melted. Remove the pan from the heat.

Place the sugar, eggs, and vanilla extract in a large bowl and whisk together until pale and creamy. Beat in the melted chocolate mixture. Fold in the flour evenly, then stir in the pistachios. Spoon into the pan and smooth the top. Bake in the preheated oven for 25–30 minutes, or until firm and golden brown. Let cool in the pan.

To make the glaze, place the chocolate in a heatproof bowl, set the bowl over a saucepan of gently simmering water, and heat until melted. Stir in the sour cream and maple syrup and beat until smooth and glossy. Spread the glaze over the brownies evenly, then sprinkle with the remaining pistachios. Let set, then cut into squares to serve.

568 Maple-glazed pecan brownies

Replace the pistachios with pecans and make the glaze with milk or semisweet chocolate.

569 Mocha brownies

MAKES 8

4 tbsp butter, plus extra for greasing
4 oz/115 g semisweet chocolate, broken into pieces
1 cup dark brown sugar
2 eggs
1 tbsp instant coffee granules, dissolved in 1 tbsp hot water, cooled
heaping ½ cup all-purpose flour
½ tsp baking powder
⅓ cup pecans, coarsely chopped

TOPPING
scant 1 cup confectioners' sugar
1–2 tbsp water
chopped pecans

Preheat the oven to 350°F/180°C. Grease and line the bottom of an 8-inch/20-cm square baking pan. Place the butter and chocolate in a saucepan and stir over low heat until melted. Let cool.

Place the sugar and eggs in a large bowl and beat together until light and fluffy. Fold in the chocolate mixture and cooled coffee and mix thoroughly. Sift in the flour and baking powder and lightly fold into the mixture. Carefully fold in the pecans and pour the batter into the pan. Bake in the preheated oven for 25–30 minutes, or until firm and a skewer inserted into the center comes out clean.

Let cool in the pan for a few minutes, then run a knife around the edge of the cake to loosen it. Turn the cake out onto a wire rack, peel off the lining paper, and let cool. When cold, cut into squares.

Place the confectioners' sugar and water in a bowl and mix together until smooth, then trickle around each brownie. Sprinkle the brownie and icing with the pecans.

570 Mochachino brownies with white mocha sauce

MAKES ABOUT 8

8 tbsp butter, plus extra for greasing
4 oz/115 g semisweet chocolate
2 tbsp strong black coffee
1¼ cups superfine sugar
½ tsp ground cinnamon
3 eggs, lightly beaten
heaping ½ cup all-purpose flour
⅓ cup milk chocolate chips
⅓ cup toasted walnuts, skinned and chopped, plus extra for decorating

WHITE MOCHA SAUCE
heaping ⅓ cup heavy cream
3 oz/85 g white chocolate, broken into pieces
1 tbsp strong black coffee

Preheat the oven to 350°F/180°C. Grease and line a 9-inch/23-cm square baking pan.

Place the butter, chocolate, and coffee in a saucepan and stir over low heat until melted. Let cool slightly, then whisk in the sugar, cinnamon, and eggs. Beat in the flour, chocolate chips, and walnuts. Pour into the pan.

Bake in the preheated oven for 30–35 minutes, until just firm but still moist inside. Cool in the pan then cut into squares or bars.

To make the sauce, place all the ingredients in a small pan and stir over low heat until smooth.

Place the brownies on serving plates and spoon the warm sauce on top. Decorate with chopped walnuts and serve.

571 With rich brandy sauce

For the sauce, replace the white chocolate with semisweet chocolate. Heat the heavy cream and chocolate in a small saucepan over low heat and stir until smooth. Remove from the heat and stir in 1 tablespoon of brandy instead of the coffee.

572 *Pecan brownies*

MAKES 20

1 cup butter, plus extra for greasing
2½ oz/70 g semisweet chocolate, broken into pieces
1 cup all-purpose flour
¾ tsp baking soda
¼ tsp baking powder
⅓ cup pecans
½ cup raw brown sugar, plus extra for decorating
½ tsp almond extract
1 egg
1 tsp milk

Preheat the oven to 350°F/180°C. Grease and line a shallow 11 x 7-inch/28 x 18-cm rectangular baking pan.

Place the chocolate in a heatproof bowl, set the bowl over a saucepan of gently simmering water, and heat until melted. Meanwhile, sift together the flour, baking soda, and baking powder in a large bowl.

Finely chop the pecans and set aside. Place the butter and sugar in a separate bowl and beat together until light and fluffy, then mix in the almond extract and egg. Remove the chocolate from the heat and stir into the butter mixture. Add the flour mixture, milk, and chopped nuts to the bowl and stir until well combined. Spoon the batter into the pan and smooth the top.

Bake in the preheated oven for 30 minutes, or until firm to the touch and still a little soft in the center. Let cool completely. Sprinkle with raw brown sugar and cut into 20 squares before serving.

573 *Walnut brownies*

Replace the pecans with walnuts.

574 *Apricot brownies*

Replace the pecans with chopped dried apricots.

575 Upside-down toffee apple brownies

MAKES 9

8 tbsp butter, plus extra for greasing
1 cup light brown sugar
2 eggs, lightly beaten
scant 1½ cups all-purpose flour
1 tsp baking powder
½ tsp baking soda
1½ tsp apple pie spice
2 apples, peeled and coarsely grated
½ cup hazelnuts, chopped

TOFFEE APPLE TOPPING
scant ½ cup light brown sugar
4 tbsp butter
1 apple, cored and thinly sliced

Preheat the oven to 350°F/180°C. Grease a shallow 9-inch/23-cm square baking pan. To make the topping, place the sugar and butter in a small saucepan and heat gently, stirring, until melted. Pour into the pan and arrange the apple slices over the mixture.

To make the brownies, place the butter and sugar in a large bowl and beat together until light and fluffy, then gradually beat in the eggs. Sift together the flour, baking powder, baking soda, and apple pie spice, and fold into the mixture. Stir in the apples and nuts, then pour into the pan.

Bake in the preheated oven for 35–40 minutes, or until firm and golden. Let cool in the pan for 10 minutes, then cut into squares.

576 Upside-down pineapple brownies

For the topping, replace the apple with 4 canned pineapple slices. Replace the apples in the brownie batter with 6 chopped canned pineapple slices.

577 Upside-down toffee pear brownies

For the topping, replace the apple with 1 peeled, cored, and sliced pear. Replace the apples in the brownie batter with pears.

578 Ginger chocolate chip brownies

MAKES 24

4 pieces preserved ginger in syrup
1½ cups all-purpose flour
1½ tsp ground ginger
1 tsp ground cinnamon
¼ tsp ground cloves
¼ tsp grated nutmeg
heaping ½ cup light brown sugar
8 tbsp butter
⅓ cup dark corn syrup
heaping ½ cup semisweet chocolate chips

Preheat the oven to 300°F/150°C. Finely chop the preserved ginger. Sift the flour, ground ginger, cinnamon, cloves, and nutmeg into a large bowl, then stir in the chopped preserved ginger and sugar.

Place the butter and the dark corn syrup in a saucepan and heat gently until melted. Bring to a boil, then pour the mixture into the flour, stirring continuously. Beat until the mixture is cool enough to handle. Add the chocolate chips and press the mixture evenly into a shallow 12 x 8-inch/30 x 20-cm rectangular baking pan.

Bake in the preheated oven for 30 minutes, or until golden brown. Cut into fingers and let cool in the pan.

579 Chocolate chip & cherry brownies

Replace the preserved ginger with 1½ oz/40 g chopped candied cherries. Sift the flour and spices into a bowl, omitting the ground ginger.

580 Carrot streusel brownies

MAKES 15

8 tbsp butter, softened, plus extra for greasing
1¾ cups light brown sugar
2 eggs, lightly beaten
1 tsp vanilla extract
1¼ cups all-purpose flour
½ tsp baking soda
½ tsp baking powder
½ cup golden raisins
scant ¾ cup finely grated carrot
⅓ cup walnuts, chopped

STREUSEL TOPPING
¼ cup finely chopped walnuts
scant ¼ cup dark brown sugar
1½ tbsp all-purpose flour
½ tsp ground cinnamon
1 tbsp butter, melted

Preheat the oven to 350°F/180°C. Grease a shallow 12 x 8-inch/30 x 20-cm rectangular baking pan. Place the sugar and butter in a large bowl and beat together until light and fluffy, then beat in the eggs and vanilla extract. Sift the flour, baking soda, and baking powder into the mixture and fold in evenly. Stir in the golden raisins, carrot, and walnuts, then spread the batter into the pan.

Place all the ingredients for the topping in a bowl and mix together to make a crumbly mixture, then sprinkle evenly over the cake batter.

Bake in the preheated oven for 45–55 minutes, or until golden brown and firm to the touch. Cool in the pan, then cut into bars.

581 Hazelnut streusel brownies

Replace the golden raisins and walnuts with raisins and chopped toasted hazelnuts, and the cinnamon with ground nutmeg.

582 Rich ginger brownies with port cream

MAKES 8

¾ cup butter,
plus extra for greasing
7 oz/200 g semisweet chocolate, broken into pieces
1 cup granulated sugar
4 eggs, lightly beaten
2 tsp vanilla extract
2 oz/55 g preserved ginger in syrup, chopped, plus 1 tbsp preserved ginger syrup
¾ cup all-purpose flour
1 oz/25 g chopped crystallized ginger, for decorating

PORT CREAM

generous ¾ cup ruby port
heaping ¾ cup heavy cream
1 tbsp confectioners' sugar
1 tsp vanilla extract

Preheat the oven to 350°F/180°C. Grease a shallow 8-inch/20-cm round baking pan. Place the chocolate and butter in a saucepan and heat gently, stirring, until melted. Remove from the heat and stir in the sugar.

Beat the eggs, vanilla extract, and ginger syrup into the chocolate mixture, stir in the flour and ginger, and pour into the pan. Bake in the preheated oven for 30–35 minutes, or until just firm to the touch.

Meanwhile, to make the port cream, place the port in a pan and simmer over medium–high heat until reduced to about 4 tablespoons. Let cool. Place the cream in a bowl and whip until beginning to thicken, then beat in the sugar, reduced port, and vanilla extract, continuing to whip until soft peaks form.

Remove the brownies from the oven, cool for 2–3 minutes in the pan, then cut into 8 wedges. Place on serving plates and add a spoonful of port cream. Top with crystallized ginger and serve.

583 Walnut & cherry brownies

Replace the ginger syrup with maple syrup, omit the preserved ginger, and add ⅓ cup chopped walnuts. Decorate with 3 tbsp chopped candied cherries.

584 With brandy cream

For a brandy cream, whip the cream until it starts to thicken, then beat in 2 tablespoons of confectioners' sugar and 3 tablespoons of brandy. Whip to soft peaks.

585 White chocolate brownies

MAKES 9

8 tbsp butter, plus extra for greasing
8 oz/225 g white chocolate
¾ cup walnut pieces
2 eggs
heaping ½ cup light brown sugar
¾ cup self-rising flour

Preheat the oven to 350°F/180°C. Lightly grease a 7-inch/18-cm square baking pan. Coarsely chop 6 oz/175 g of the chocolate and all the walnuts. Place the remaining chocolate and the butter in a heatproof bowl, set the bowl over a saucepan of gently simmering water, and heat until melted. Stir together, then cool slightly.

Place the eggs and sugar in a large bowl and whisk together, then beat in the cooled chocolate mixture until combined. Fold in the flour, chopped chocolate, and walnuts, spoon the batter into the pan, and smooth the surface.

Bake in the preheated oven for about 30 minutes, or until just set and still a little soft in the center. Cool in the pan, then cut into squares.

586 Milk chocolate & pistachio brownies

Replace the white chocolate with milk chocolate and the walnuts with chopped pistachios.

587 Sour cream brownies

MAKES 8

4 tbsp butter, plus extra for greasing
4 oz/115 g semisweet chocolate, broken into pieces
1 cup soft brown sugar
2 eggs
2 tbsp strong coffee, cooled
⅔ cup all-purpose flour
½ tsp baking powder
pinch of salt
⅓ cup walnuts, chopped
mini chocolate balls, for decorating

FROSTING
4 oz/115 g semisweet chocolate, broken into pieces
⅔ cup sour cream

Preheat the oven to 350°F/180°C. Grease and line an 8-inch/20-cm square baking pan. Place the butter and chocolate in a saucepan and stir over low heat until melted. Let cool.

Place the sugar and eggs in a large bowl and whisk together until pale and thick. Fold in the chocolate and coffee and mix well. Sift the flour, baking powder, and salt into the mixture and fold in. Fold in the walnuts and pour into the pan. Bake in the preheated oven for 20–25 minutes, or until set. Let cool in the pan.

To make the frosting, melt the chocolate in a heatproof bowl set over a pan of simmering water. Stir in the sour cream and beat well. Spoon the topping over the brownies and let set. Cut into bars, remove from the pan, and decorate with mini chocolate balls.

588 Yogurt-topped brownies

For the brownies, replace the semisweet chocolate with milk chocolate and the coffee with milk. For the frosting, replace the semisweet chocolate with milk chocolate and sour cream with whole-milk plain yogurt. Add the yogurt after the melted chocolate has been taken off the heat.

589 *Marbled chocolate cheesecake brownies*

MAKES 12

¾ cup butter, plus extra for greasing
3 tbsp unsweetened cocoa
1 cup superfine sugar
2 eggs, lightly beaten
1 cup all-purpose flour

CHEESECAKE MIX
heaping 1 cup ricotta cheese
scant ¼ cup superfine sugar
1 egg

Preheat the oven to 350°F/180°C. Grease an 11 x 7-inch/28 x 18-cm rectangular baking pan. Place the butter in a saucepan and heat gently until melted. Remove from the heat and stir in the cocoa and sugar. Beat in the eggs, add the flour, and stir to mix evenly. Pour into the pan.

For the cheesecake mix, place the ricotta, sugar, and egg in a bowl and beat together, then drop teaspoonfuls of the mixture over the chocolate mixture. Use a spatula to swirl the mixtures together lightly.

Bake in the preheated oven for 40–45 minutes, or until just firm to the touch. Let cool in the pan, then cut into rectangles.

590 *Marbled creamy brownies*

Add ¼ cup chopped walnuts to the brownie mix. Replace the ricotta with cream cheese, and fold ¼ cup chocolate chips into the cheese mix.

591 *Marbled chocolate orange brownies*

Finely grate the rind of 1 orange and juice the orange. Add half the rind and juice to the brownie mix with the eggs, and add the rest to the ricotta mix.

592 Super mocha brownies

MAKES 12

7 tbsp butter, plus extra for greasing
5½ oz/150 g semisweet chocolate
1 tsp strong instant coffee
1 tsp vanilla extract
heaping 1 cup ground almonds
1 cup superfine sugar
4 eggs, separated
confectioners' sugar, for dusting (optional)

Preheat the oven to 350°F/180°C. Grease and line the bottom of an 8-inch/20-cm square baking pan.

Place the butter and chocolate in a saucepan and stir over low heat until melted. Let cool slightly, then stir in the coffee and vanilla extract. Add the ground almonds and superfine sugar and mix until combined.

Place the egg yolks in a separate bowl and beat together lightly, then stir into the chocolate mixture.

Whisk the egg whites in a separate large bowl until stiff peaks form. Gently fold a large spoonful of the egg whites into the chocolate mixture, then fold in the remainder until completely incorporated and spoon the batter into the pan.

Bake in the preheated oven for 35–40 minutes, or until risen and firm on top but still slightly gooey in the center. Let cool in the pan, then turn out, remove the lining paper, and cut into squares. Dust with sifted confectioners' sugar before serving, if using.

593 Mocha & macadamia nut brownies

Replace the ground almonds with all-purpose flour. Fold ¼ cup coarsely chopped macadamia nuts into the chocolate mixture before adding the egg whites.

594 Rocky road brownies

MAKES 16

1 cup butter, melted, plus extra for greasing
¾ cup all-purpose flour, plus extra for dusting
¾ cup superfine sugar
3 tbsp unsweetened cocoa
½ tsp baking powder
2 eggs, lightly beaten
1 tsp vanilla extract
2½ oz/70 g candied cherries, quartered
½ cup blanched almonds, chopped
3½ oz/100 g marshmallows, chopped

FUDGE FROSTING
1¾ cups confectioners' sugar
2 tbsp unsweetened cocoa
3 tbsp evaporated milk
½ tsp vanilla extract

Preheat the oven to 325°F/160°C. Grease and lightly flour a shallow 9-inch/23-cm square baking pan. Sift together the flour, sugar, cocoa, and baking powder into a large bowl and make a well in the center. Stir in the melted butter, eggs, and vanilla extract and beat well. Stir in the cherries and almonds and pour into the pan.

Bake in the preheated oven for 35–40 minutes, or until just firm on top. Let cool in the pan.

To make the frosting, place all the ingredients in a large bowl and beat well until smooth. Spread the cooled brownies with the frosting, and sprinkle with marshmallows. Let set, then cut into squares.

595 Chocolate fudge brownies

MAKES 16

6 tbsp butter, plus extra for greasing
scant 1 cup low-fat soft cheese
½ tsp vanilla extract
1 cup superfine sugar
2 eggs
3 tbsp unsweetened cocoa
¾ cup self-rising flour
⅓ cup pecans, chopped
pecan halves, for decorating (optional)

FUDGE FROSTING
4 tbsp butter
1 tbsp milk
⅔ cup confectioners' sugar
2 tbsp unsweetened cocoa

Preheat the oven to 350°F/180°C. Lightly grease and line a shallow 8-inch/20-cm square cake pan.

Place the cheese, vanilla extract, and 5 teaspoons of the sugar in a large bowl and beat together until smooth.

Place the eggs and remaining sugar in a separate bowl and beat together until light and fluffy. Place the butter and cocoa in a small saucepan and heat gently, stirring until the butter melts and the mixture combines, then stir it into the egg mixture.

Fold in the flour and nuts, pour half of the batter into the pan, and smooth the top. Spread the cheese mixture over, then cover it with the remaining batter. Bake in the preheated oven for 40–45 minutes. Let cool in the pan.

To make the frosting, melt the butter with the milk in a pan. Stir in the confectioners' sugar and cocoa. Spread the frosting over the brownies and decorate with pecans, if using. Let set, then cut into squares or rectangles.

596 Nutty walnut fudge brownies

Replace the pecans in the brownies with heaping ½ cup chopped walnuts and decorate with walnut halves.

597 Blonde brownie hearts with raspberry sauce

MAKES 8

8 tbsp butter, plus extra for greasing
1 cup all-purpose flour, plus extra for dusting
4 oz/115 g white chocolate
2 eggs, lightly beaten
¾ cup superfine sugar
seeds from 1 vanilla bean
8 small squares semisweet chocolate

RASPBERRY SAUCE
2 cups raspberries, fresh or frozen (thawed)
2 tbsp amaretto
1 tbsp confectioners' sugar

Preheat the oven to 350°F/180°C. Grease and lightly flour 8 individual heart-shaped baking pans, each ⅔-cup capacity. Place the white chocolate and butter in a saucepan and stir over low heat until just melted. Remove from the heat.

Place the eggs, sugar, and vanilla seeds in a bowl and whisk together until smooth and thick. Fold in the flour, then stir in the chocolate mixture. Pour the mixture into the pans, adding a square of chocolate to the center of each, without pressing down. Bake in the preheated oven for 20–25 minutes, or until just firm. Leave in the pans for 5 minutes.

To make the raspberry sauce, place half the raspberries, the amaretto, and confectioners' sugar in a food processor and process until smooth. Transfer the mixture to a strainer placed on top of a bowl and rub through to remove the seeds.

Run a knife around the edge of each heart to loosen from the pan and turn out onto serving plates. Spoon the raspberry sauce around, decorate with the remaining raspberries, and serve.

598 With strawberry sauce

For a strawberry sauce, blend 1¼ cups hulled strawberries, 2 tablespoons of orange-flavored liqueur, and 1 tablespoon of confectioners' sugar until smooth, then push through a strainer. Serve the brownies with extra strawberries.

599 Walnut & cinnamon blondies

Makes 9

8 tbsp butter, plus extra for greasing
heaping 1 cup light brown sugar
1 egg
1 egg yolk
1 cup self-rising flour
1 tsp ground cinnamon
heaping ½ cup coarsely chopped walnuts

Preheat the oven to 350°F/180°C. Grease and line the bottom of a shallow 7-inch/18-cm square baking pan. Place the butter and sugar in a saucepan over low heat and stir until the sugar has dissolved. Cook, stirring, for an additional 1 minute. The mixture will bubble slightly, but do not let it boil. Let cool for 10 minutes.

Stir the egg and egg yolk into the mixture. Sift in the flour and cinnamon, add the nuts, and stir until just blended, then pour the batter into the pan and smooth the top.

Bake in the preheated oven for 20–25 minutes, or until springy in the center and a skewer inserted into the middle of the cake comes out clean. Let cool in the pan for a few minutes, then run a knife around the edge of the cake to loosen it. Turn the cake out onto a wire rack and peel off the paper. Let cool completely, then cut into squares.

600 Apple & cinnamon blondies

Replace the walnuts with 1 apple, peeled, cored, and finely diced.

601 Butterfudge blondies

Makes 9

9 tbsp butter, softened, plus extra for greasing
1 cup light brown sugar
2 large eggs, lightly beaten
1 tsp vanilla extract
heaping 1¾ cups all-purpose flour
1 tsp baking powder
4½ oz/125 g soft butter fudge, chopped into small pieces
½ cup macadamia nuts, coarsely chopped
confectioners' sugar, for dusting

Preheat the oven to 350°F/180°C. Grease and line a shallow 8-inch/20-cm square baking pan.

Place the butter and sugar in a large bowl and whisk together until pale and creamy. Gradually whisk in the eggs and vanilla extract. Sift the flour and baking powder into the mixture and beat together until well mixed. Add the fudge pieces and chopped nuts and stir together until combined. Pour the batter into the pan and smooth the surface.

Bake in the preheated oven for 40–45 minutes, or until risen and golden brown. Let cool in the pan, then dust with sifted confectioners' sugar for decorating and cut into squares.

602 Chocolate & creamy cheese blondies

MAKES 9

9 tbsp butter, softened, plus extra for greasing
2/3 cup cream cheese
heaping 1/2 cup semisweet chocolate chips
1 cup light brown sugar
2 large eggs, lightly beaten
1/2 tsp vanilla extract
heaping 1 3/4 cups all-purpose flour
1 tsp baking powder

Preheat the oven to 350°F/180°C. Grease and line a shallow 8-inch/20-cm square baking pan. Place the cream cheese and chocolate chips in a large bowl and beat together until creamy.

Place the butter and sugar in a separate large bowl and whisk together until pale and creamy. Gradually whisk in the eggs and vanilla extract. Sift the flour and baking powder into the mixture and beat together until mixed. Place half of the batter into the pan and smooth the surface.

Place half the cream cheese mixture in spoonfuls, spaced well apart, on top of the batter in the pan. Flatten the spoonfuls slightly. Repeat the layers and then draw a knife through the batter in a spiral. Bake in the oven for 40–45 minutes, or until risen and golden brown. Let cool in the pan, then cut into squares.

603 Chocolate chip & ginger blondies

MAKES 9

9 tbsp butter, softened, plus extra for greasing
1 cup light brown sugar
2 large eggs, lightly beaten
heaping 1 3/4 cups all-purpose flour
1 tsp baking powder
1 tsp ground ginger
4 pieces preserved ginger, finely chopped
heaping 1/2 cup semisweet chocolate chips
confectioners' sugar, for dusting

Preheat the oven to 350°F/180°C. Grease and line a shallow 8-inch/20-cm square baking pan.

Place the butter and sugar in a large bowl and whisk together until pale and creamy. Gradually whisk in the eggs. Sift the flour, baking powder, and ground ginger into the mixture and beat together until mixed. Add the preserved ginger and chocolate chips and stir together until mixed. Spoon the mixture into the pan and smooth the surface.

Bake in the preheated oven for 40–45 minutes, or until risen and golden brown. Let cool in the pan, then dust with sifted confectioners' sugar for decorating and cut into squares.

604 Cherry & coconut blondies

Makes 9

9 tbsp butter, softened, plus extra for greasing
1 cup light brown sugar
2 large eggs, lightly beaten
1 tsp vanilla extract
heaping 1¾ cups all-purpose flour
1 tsp baking powder
⅔ cup candied cherries, cut into quarters
1 cup dry unsweetened coconut

Preheat the oven to 350°F/180°C. Grease and line an 8-inch/20-cm square baking pan. Place the butter and sugar in a large bowl and whisk together until pale and creamy. Gradually whisk in the eggs and vanilla extract. Sift the flour and baking powder into the mixture and beat together until well mixed. Add the chopped cherries and ⅔ cup of the coconut and stir together until combined. Pour the batter into the pan and smooth the surface. Sprinkle the remaining coconut over the top.

Bake in the preheated oven for 40–45 minutes, or until risen and golden brown. Let cool in the pan, then cut into squares.

605 Strawberry & almond blondies

Makes 9

9 tbsp butter, softened, plus extra for greasing
1 cup light brown sugar
2 large eggs, lightly beaten
½ tsp almond extract
heaping 1¾ cups all-purpose flour
1 tsp baking powder
⅓ cup blanched almonds, chopped
¾ cup fresh small strawberries
¼ cup slivered almonds

Preheat the oven to 350°F/180°C. Grease and line a shallow 8-inch/20-cm square baking pan. Place the butter and sugar in a large bowl and whisk together until pale and creamy. Gradually whisk the eggs and almond extract into the mixture. Sift in the flour and baking powder and beat together until mixed. Add the chopped almonds and stir together until combined. Add the strawberries to the mixture and fold in, then spoon the batter into the pan and smooth the surface. Scatter the slivered almonds over the top.

Bake in the preheated oven for 40–45 minutes, or until risen and golden brown. Let cool in the pan, then cut into squares.

606 Rich apricot blondies

MAKES 12

6 tbsp butter, plus extra for greasing
12 oz/350 g white chocolate
1 tsp vanilla extract
3 eggs, lightly beaten
¾ cup light brown sugar
heaping ¾ cup self-rising flour
heaping ½ cup macadamia nuts, coarsely chopped
heaping ½ cup plumped dried apricots, coarsely chopped

Preheat the oven to 375°F/190°C. Grease and line a shallow 11 x 7-inch/28 x 18-cm rectangular baking pan.

Chop half the chocolate into small chunks. Place the remaining chocolate and the butter in a small saucepan and stir over very low heat until melted. Remove from the heat and stir in the vanilla extract.

Place the eggs and sugar in a large bowl and whisk together until pale and creamy. Beat in the melted chocolate mixture. Fold in the flour, then stir in the macadamia nuts, apricots, and chopped chocolate. Spoon into the pan and smooth the top.

Bake in the preheated oven for 25–30 minutes, or until firm and golden brown. Let cool in the pan, then cut into triangles.

607 Prune blondies

Replace the apricots with plumped pitted prunes, coarsely chopped, and the macadamia nuts with chopped hazelnuts.

608 Date blondies

Replace the apricots with plumped pitted dates, coarsely chopped, and the macadamia nuts with chopped walnuts.

609 Fig blondies

Replace the apricots with chopped dried figs and the macadamia nuts with chopped almonds.

610 *Apple & walnut blondies*

MAKES 9

9 tbsp butter, softened, plus extra for greasing
1 cup light brown sugar
2 large eggs, lightly beaten
1 tsp vanilla extract
heaping 1¾ cups all-purpose flour
1 tsp baking powder
1 small baking apple, peeled, cored, and finely chopped.
1 cup walnut halves, coarsely chopped
confectioners' sugar, for dusting

Preheat the oven to 350°F/180°C. Grease and line a shallow 8-inch/20-cm square baking pan. Place the butter and sugar in a large bowl and whisk together until pale and creamy. Gradually whisk in the eggs and vanilla extract. Sift the flour and baking powder into the mixture and beat together until well mixed. Add the chopped apple and walnuts to the batter and stir together until well mixed. Spoon the batter into the pan and smooth the surface.

Bake in the preheated oven for 40–45 minutes, or until risen and golden brown. Let cool in the pan, then dust with sifted confectioners' sugar for decorating and cut into squares.

611 *Bursting cranberry blondies*

MAKES 9

9 tbsp butter, softened, plus extra for greasing
1 cup light brown sugar
2 large eggs, lightly beaten
1 tsp vanilla extract
heaping 1¾ cups all-purpose flour
1 tsp baking powder
heaping ¾ cup dried or frozen cranberries
confectioners' sugar, for dusting

Preheat the oven to 350°F/180°C. Grease and line a shallow 8-inch/20-cm square baking pan.

Place the butter and sugar in a large bowl and whisk together until pale and creamy. Gradually whisk the eggs and vanilla into the mixture.

Sift in the flour and baking powder and beat together until well mixed. Add the cranberries and stir together until combined. Spoon the batter into the pan and smooth the surface. Bake in the preheated oven for 40–45 minutes, or until risen and golden brown.

Let the blondies cool in the pan, then dust them with sifted confectioners' sugar for decorating and cut into squares before serving.

612 *Bursting berry blondies*

Use dried cranberries and reduce the quantity to scant ½ cup, then add scant ½ cup dried blueberries to the batter.

613 *Cranberry & chocolate blondies*

Use dried cranberries and reduce the quantity to ⅔ cup, then add scant ½ cup white chocolate chips to the batter.

614 Nutty granola bars

MAKES 16

8 tbsp butter, plus extra for greasing
2⅔ cups rolled oats
¾ cup chopped hazelnuts
scant ½ cup all-purpose flour
2 tbsp dark corn syrup
scant ½ cup light brown sugar

Preheat the oven to 350°F/180°C. Grease a 9-inch/23-cm square cake pan. Place the oats, hazelnuts, and flour in a large bowl and stir together.

Place the butter, dark corn syrup, and sugar in a saucepan over low heat and stir until melted. Pour onto the dry ingredients and mix well. Spoon the mixture into the pan and smooth the top. Bake in the preheated oven for 20–25 minutes, or until golden and firm to the touch. Cut into 16 pieces and let cool in the pan until cold.

615 Chocolate-dipped nutty bars

Melt 6½ oz/185 g semisweet or milk chocolate, broken into squares, in a heatproof bowl set over a saucepan of gently simmering water. Line a baking sheet with parchment paper. Dip the bars in the chocolate until half covered and place on the lined baking sheet. Let set before serving.

616 Hazelnut chocolate granola bars

MAKES 12

8 tbsp butter, plus extra for greasing
2⅔ cups rolled oats
heaping ⅓ cup hazelnuts, lightly toasted and chopped
heaping ⅓ cup all-purpose flour
scant ½ cup light brown sugar
2 tbsp dark corn syrup
⅓ cup semisweet chocolate chips

Preheat the oven to 350°F/180°C. Grease a shallow 9-inch/23-cm square baking pan. Place the oats, hazelnuts, and flour in a large bowl and mix together.

Place the butter, sugar, and dark corn syrup in a large saucepan and heat gently until the sugar has dissolved. Pour in the dry ingredients and mix well. Stir in the chocolate chips, then spoon the mixture into the pan.

Bake in the preheated oven for 20–25 minutes, or until golden brown and firm to the touch. Mark into 12 triangles and let cool completely in the pan.

617 Apricot granola bars

MAKES 10

sunflower oil, for greasing
¾ cup butter or margarine
scant ½ cup raw brown sugar
scant ¼ cup honey
heaping ¾ cup dried apricots, chopped
2 tsp sesame seeds
2⅔ cups rolled oats

Preheat the oven to 350°F/180°C. Very lightly grease a shallow 10½ x 6½-inch/26 x 17-cm rectangular baking pan. Place the butter, sugar, and honey in a small saucepan over low heat and heat until the ingredients have melted together. Stir in the apricots, sesame seeds, and oats. Spoon the mixture into the pan and lightly smooth the top.

Bake in the preheated oven for 20–25 minutes, or until golden brown. Cut into 10 bars and let cool completely in the pan.

618 Date granola bars

Replace the apricots with chopped pitted dates and omit the sesame seeds.

619 Cranberry granola bars

Replace the apricots with chopped dried cranberries and the sesame seeds with sunflower seeds.

620 Figgy granola bars

Replace the apricots with chopped dried figs and the sesame seeds with scant ¼ cup chopped almonds or walnuts.

621 Fruity granola bars

MAKES 14

sunflower oil, for greasing
1⅔ cups rolled oats
heaping ½ cup raw brown sugar
½ cup raisins
8 tbsp butter, melted

Preheat the oven to 375°F/190°C. Lightly grease a shallow11 x 7-inch/ 28 x 18-cm rectangular baking pan. Place the oats, sugar, raisins, and butter in a large bowl and stir well to combine. Spoon the oat mixture into the pan and press down firmly with the back of the spoon.

Bake in the preheated oven for 15–20 minutes, or until golden brown. Mark into 14 bars. Let cool in the pan for 10 minutes, then transfer the bars to a wire rack to cool completely.

622 Chocolate chip granola bars

MAKES 12

8 tbsp butter, plus extra for greasing
⅓ cup superfine sugar
1 tbsp dark corn syrup
heaping 4 cups rolled oats
½ cup semisweet chocolate chips
½ cup golden raisins

Preheat the oven to 350°F/180°C. Lightly grease a shallow 8-inch/ 20-cm square cake pan. Place the butter, sugar, and dark corn syrup in a saucepan and cook over low heat, stirring continuously, until the butter and sugar melt and the mixture is well combined.

Remove the saucepan from the heat and stir in the rolled oats until they are well coated. Add the chocolate chips and golden raisins and mix well to combine. Spoon into the pan and press down well.

Bake in the preheated oven for 30 minutes. Let cool slightly, then mark into squares. When almost cold, cut into bars and transfer to a wire rack to cool completely.

623 Panforte di siena

MAKES 16

butter, for greasing
2/3 cup blanched almonds
2/3 cup blanched hazelnuts
heaping 1/4 cup plumped dried figs
1/2 cup walnut halves
scant 1 cup chopped mixed candied peel
heaping 1/3 cup all-purpose flour
1/2 cup unsweetened cocoa
1/8 tsp ground white pepper
1/4 tsp ground mace
1/4 tsp ground cloves
1/4 tsp ground coriander
1 tsp ground cinnamon
1/2 cup superfine sugar
generous 1/4 cup honey
confectioners' sugar, for dredging

Preheat the oven to 325°F/160°C. Grease an 8-inch/20-cm loose-bottom cake pan and line the bottom with rice paper. Spread the almonds and hazelnuts on a baking sheet and bake in the preheated oven for 5–10 minutes, until lightly toasted. Let cool.

Using scissors, snip the figs into small pieces and put in a large bowl. Coarsely chop all the nuts, then add to the figs with the candied peel.

Sift the flour, cocoa, pepper, mace, cloves, coriander, and cinnamon into the fruit and nuts and stir together until well mixed.

Place the sugar and honey in a saucepan and heat gently until the sugar has dissolved. Bring to a boil and boil, without stirring, until a little of the mixture, when dropped into a cup of cold water, forms a ball between your fingers. If you have a sugar thermometer, it should reach 241°F/116°C (soft ball stage). Immediately remove the pan from the heat and quickly stir in the dry ingredients until mixed together. Spoon the mixture into the pan, press down with the back of a wet spoon, and smooth the surface.

Bake in the preheated oven for 30–40 minutes, or until firm. Let cool in the pan. When cold, dredge with sifted confectioners' sugar and cut into wedges to serve.

624 Torrone molle

MAKES 16

3/4 cup butter, plus extra for greasing
6 oz/175 g butter cookies
7 oz/200 g semisweet chocolate, broken into pieces
1/3 cup blanched almonds, chopped
1/3 cup blanched hazelnuts, chopped
1/2 cup walnut halves, chopped
1 cup superfine sugar
3 tbsp water
1 large egg, lightly beaten
2 tbsp brandy

Grease and line a shallow 9-inch/23-cm square pan. Place the cookies in a strong plastic bag and, using a wooden rolling pin, coarsely crush into small pieces.

Place the butter and chocolate in a saucepan and stir over low heat until melted. Remove from the heat and stir until smooth. Add the chopped nuts and stir well together.

Place the sugar in a separate saucepan, add the water, and heat gently, stirring all the time, until the sugar dissolves. Bring to a boil and boil until the mixture starts to turn pale golden brown. Immediately pour the syrup into the chocolate mixture and mix together until combined.

Add the egg and brandy to the mixture and mix together, then add the crushed cookies and stir until the ingredients are well mixed and coated in chocolate. Spoon the mixture into the pan, press down with the back of a wet spoon, and smooth the surface. Let cool, then chill in the refrigerator for at least 2 hours, or until set.

When the mixture has set, remove from the pan and, using a hot, sharp knife, cut into 16 slices to serve.

625 Canadian namaimo bars

Makes 16

7 tbsp butter, plus extra for greasing
7 oz/200 g graham crackers
¼ cup superfine sugar
4 tbsp unsweetened cocoa
1 large egg
½ cup macadamia nuts, chopped
1 cup dry unsweetened coconut

TOPPING
6½ tbsp butter
2⅔ cups confectioners' sugar
2 tbsp milk
7 oz/200 g semisweet chocolate, broken into pieces

Grease and line a shallow 9-inch/23-cm square pan. Place the crackers in a strong plastic bag and, using a rolling pin, crush the crackers into small pieces, then place in a large bowl.

Place the butter, sugar, cocoa, and egg in a large heatproof bowl, set the bowl over a saucepan of gently simmering water, and heat, whisking until the mixture thickens slightly. Remove from the heat.

Add the nuts and coconut to the crackers and stir together. Add the chocolate mixture and mix together, then spoon into the pan and press down with the back of a spoon. Chill in the refrigerator for 1 hour.

To make the topping, place 5½ tablespoons of the butter in a large bowl and beat until creamy. Sift in the confectioners' sugar. Add the milk and beat until smooth. Spread the mixture over the bottom of the pan. Place the chocolate and the remaining butter in a heatproof bowl, set the bowl over a saucepan of gently simmering water, and heat gently until the chocolate has melted. Remove from the heat and stir until smooth. Let cool for 5 minutes, then pour into the pan and spread to coat the top. Let set for about 1 hour.

When the chocolate has set, chill in the refrigerator for at least 3 hours. Before serving, remove from the pan and, using a hot, sharp knife, cut into 16 slices.

626 Chocolate pistachio bars

Makes 24

2 tbsp butter, plus extra for greasing
6 oz/175 g semisweet chocolate, broken into pieces
2½ cups self-rising flour, plus extra for dusting
1½ tsp baking powder
scant ½ cup superfine sugar
½ cup cornmeal
finely grated rind of 1 lemon
2 tsp amaretto
1 egg, lightly beaten
¾ cup pistachios, coarsely chopped
2 tbsp confectioners' sugar, for dusting

Preheat the oven to 325°F/160°C. Grease a baking sheet. Place the butter and chocolate in a saucepan and stir over low heat until melted and smooth. Let cool slightly.

Sift the flour and baking powder into a large bowl and mix in the sugar, cornmeal, lemon rind, amaretto, egg, and pistachios. Stir in the chocolate mixture and mix to form a soft dough.

Lightly dust your hands with flour, divide the dough in half, and shape each piece into a 11-inch/28-cm long cylinder. Transfer the cylinders to the baking sheet and flatten with the palm of your hand, to about ¾ inch/2 cm thick.

Bake in the preheated oven for about 20 minutes, or until firm to the touch. Let cool but don't turn the oven off. When cool, place the baked dough on a cutting board and cut into thin diagonal slices. Return them to the baking sheet and bake for an additional 10 minutes, or until crisp. Transfer the bars to a wire rack to cool, then dust lightly with sifted confectioners' sugar.

627 Treasure chest gold bars

MAKES 10

6 tbsp butter, plus extra for greasing
4 oz/115 g semisweet chocolate, broken into pieces
¼ cup superfine sugar
3 large eggs, separated
heaping ⅓ cup self-rising flour
¼ cup ground almonds

FOR DECORATING
1 tbsp butter
4 tbsp milk
3 tbsp unsweetened cocoa
2 cups confectioners' sugar
½ quantity buttercream (page 10)
chocolate coins
gold sugar-coated almonds
gold dragées

Preheat the oven to 350°F/180°C. Lightly grease and line a 7-inch/18-cm square cake pan. Place the chocolate in a heatproof bowl, set the bowl over a saucepan of gently simmering water, and heat until melted. Let cool.

Place the butter and sugar in a large bowl and beat together until light and fluffy, then beat in the melted chocolate. Beat in the egg yolks, 1 at a time.

Place the egg whites in a separate bowl and whisk until stiff peaks form, then fold half the egg whites into the chocolate mixture. Fold in the flour and almonds before folding in the remaining egg white. Pour into the pan.

Bake in the preheated oven for 25 minutes, or until springy to the touch. Let cool in the pan for 5 minutes, then transfer to a wire rack to cool completely. Cut the cake into 10 bars, then return the bars to the wire rack and place over a tray.

To decorate, melt the butter in the milk over low heat, then stir in the cocoa and beat until smooth. Whisk in the confectioners' sugar until smooth. Let cool slightly, then spread the frosting over the chocolate bars and let set.

Pipe a line of buttercream down the center of the bars and decorate with chocolate coins, sugar almonds, and gold dragées. Remember to remove the foil from the coins before eating!

628 Chocolate peppermint bars

MAKES 16

4 tbsp butter, plus extra for greasing
¼ cup superfine sugar
heaping ¾ cup all-purpose flour
1½ cups confectioners' sugar
1–2 tbsp warm water
½ tsp peppermint extract
2 tsp green food coloring (optional)
6 oz/175 g semisweet chocolate, broken into pieces

Preheat the oven to 350°F/180°C. Grease and line a shallow 12 x 8-inch/30 x 20-cm baking pan. Place the butter and sugar in a large bowl and beat together until light and fluffy. Stir in the flour until the mixture binds together.

Knead the mixture to form a smooth dough, then press into the pan and prick the surface all over with a fork. Bake in the preheated oven for 10–15 minutes, or until lightly browned and just firm to the touch. Let cool in the pan.

Sift the confectioners' sugar into a bowl. Gradually add the water, then add the peppermint extract and food coloring, if using. Spread the frosting over the base, then let set.

Place the chocolate in a heatproof bowl, set the bowl over a saucepan of gently simmering water, and heat until melted. Spread the chocolate over the frosting, then let set. Cut into slices to serve.

629 Coconut bars

MAKES 10

9 tbsp butter, plus extra for greasing
heaping 1 cup superfine sugar
2 eggs, lightly beaten
finely grated rind of 1 orange
3 tbsp orange juice
⅔ cup sour cream
1 cup self-rising flour
1 cup dry unsweetened coconut
toasted shredded coconut, for decorating

FROSTING
1 egg white
1¾ cups confectioners' sugar
1 cup dry unsweetened coconut
about 1 tbsp orange juice

Preheat the oven to 350°F/180°C. Grease a 9-inch/23-cm square cake pan and line the bottom with parchment paper. Place the butter and sugar in a large bowl and beat together until light and fluffy, then gradually beat in the eggs. Stir in the orange rind, orange juice, and sour cream. Fold in the flour and dry unsweetened coconut evenly, then spoon the batter into the cake pan and smooth the surface.

Bake in the preheated oven for 35–40 minutes, or until risen and firm to the touch. Let cool in the pan for 10 minutes, then turn out and finish cooling on a wire rack.

To make the frosting, place the egg white in a bowl and beat lightly, just enough to break it up. Stir in the confectioners' sugar and dry unsweetened coconut and add enough orange juice to mix to a thick paste. Spread over the top of the cake, sprinkle with toasted shredded coconut, then let set before slicing into bars.

630 Coconut & cherry bars

Omit the orange rind and replace the orange juice with milk. Add heaping ¼ cup quartered candied cherries to the cake batter with the coconut.

631 Coconut & lime bars

Replace the orange juice and rind with lime juice and rind.

632 Rocky road bars

Makes 8

6 oz/175 g milk or semisweet chocolate
4 tbsp butter
3½ oz/100 g shortcake cookies, broken into pieces
3 oz/85 g mini marshmallows
heaping ½ cup walnuts or peanuts

Line a 7-inch/18-cm cake pan with parchment paper. Break the chocolate into squares and place in a heatproof bowl, then set the bowl over a saucepan of gently simmering water and heat until melted. Add the butter and stir until melted and combined. Let cool slightly. Stir the broken cookies, marshmallows, and nuts into the chocolate mixture.

Pour the chocolate mixture into the prepared pan, pressing down with the back of a spoon. Chill in the refrigerator for at least 2 hours, or until firm. Carefully turn out of the pan and cut into 8 pieces.

633 Nutty granola squares

Makes 16

8 tbsp butter, plus extra for greasing
4 tbsp honey
2 tbsp superfine sugar
3 cups rolled oats
¼ cup dried cranberries
heaping ¼ cup pitted dried dates, chopped
scant ¼ cup hazelnuts, chopped
¾ cup slivered almonds

Preheat the oven to 375°F/190°C. Grease an 8-inch/20-cm square baking pan. Place the butter, honey, and sugar in a saucepan and stir together over low heat until the butter is melted. Add the remaining ingredients and mix thoroughly. Spoon the mixture into the pan and press down.

Bake in the preheated oven for 20–30 minutes, or until golden brown. Let cool in the pan. When cold, cut into 16 squares to serve.

634 *Oaty chocolate caramel squares*

MAKES 16

5½ tbsp butter or margarine, plus extra for greasing
⅓ cup light brown sugar
1 cup all-purpose flour
½ cup rolled oats

CARAMEL FILLING
¾ cup butter
heaping ½ cup light brown sugar
1 cup condensed milk

TOPPING
3½ oz/100 g semisweet chocolate, broken into pieces
1 oz/25 g white chocolate, broken into pieces (optional)

Preheat the oven to 350°F/180°C and grease a shallow 8-inch/20-cm square cake pan. Place the butter and sugar in a bowl and beat together until light and fluffy. Beat in the flour and the oats, then use your fingertips to bring the mixture together, if necessary, and press the mixture into the bottom of the pan.

Bake in the preheated oven for 25 minutes, or until just golden and firm. Let cool in the pan.

To make the caramel filling, place all the ingredients in a saucepan and heat gently, stirring until the sugar has dissolved. Bring slowly to a boil over very low heat and boil very gently for 3–4 minutes, stirring continuously, until thickened. Pour the caramel filling over the oat layer in the pan and let set.

Place the semisweet chocolate in a heatproof bowl, set the bowl over a pan of simmering water and heat until melted, then spread the chocolate over the caramel. If using the white chocolate, melt it in a heatproof bowl set over a pan of gently simmering water, then pipe lines of white chocolate over the semisweet chocolate. Using a toothpick, feather the white chocolate into the semisweet chocolate. Let set, then cut into squares to serve.

635 *Macadamia nut caramel squares*

MAKES 16

8 tbsp butter, plus extra for greasing
¾ cup macadamia nuts
2 cups all-purpose flour
1 cup light brown sugar

TOPPING
8 tbsp butter
½ cup light brown sugar
scant 1¼ cups milk chocolate chips

Preheat the oven to 350°F/180°C. Grease a shallow 12 x 8-inch/30 x 20-cm rectangular baking pan. Coarsely chop the macadamia nuts. To make the base, place the flour, sugar, and butter in a large bowl and rub together until the mixture resembles fine breadcrumbs. Press the mixture into the bottom of the pan and sprinkle over the macadamia nuts.

To make the topping, place the butter and sugar in a saucepan and, stirring continuously, slowly bring the mixture to a boil. Boil for 1 minute, stirring continuously, then carefully pour the mixture over the macadamia nuts.

Bake in the preheated oven for about 20 minutes, or until the caramel topping is bubbling. Remove from the oven and immediately sprinkle the chocolate chips evenly on top. Let cool for 2–3 minutes, or until the chocolate chips start to melt then, using the blade of a knife, swirl the chocolate over the top. Let cool in the pan, then cut into squares to serve.

636 Chocolate peanut butter squares

MAKES 20

1 cup butter, plus extra for greasing
10½ oz/300 g milk chocolate
2½ cups all-purpose flour
1 tsp baking powder
1¾ cups light brown sugar
2 cups rolled oats
½ cup chopped mixed nuts
1 egg, lightly beaten
1¾ cups condensed milk
¼ cup crunchy peanut butter

Preheat the oven to 350°F/180°C. Grease a shallow 12 x 8-inch/30 x 20-cm rectangular baking pan. Finely chop the chocolate. Sift the flour and baking powder into a large bowl, add the butter, and rub it in until the mixture resembles breadcrumbs. Stir in the sugar, oats, and chopped nuts. Place a quarter of the mixture into a bowl and stir in the chopped chocolate. Set aside.

Stir the egg into the remaining mixture, then press into the bottom of the pan. Bake the base in the preheated oven for 15 minutes.

Meanwhile, place the condensed milk and peanut butter in a bowl and mix together. Pour the mixture over the base and spread evenly, then sprinkle the reserved chocolate mixture on top and press down lightly. Return to the oven and bake for an additional 20 minutes, or until golden brown. Let cool in the pan, then cut into squares.

637 Coconut paradise slices

MAKES 16

7 tbsp butter, plus extra for greasing
7 oz/200 g semisweet chocolate, broken into pieces
1 cup superfine sugar
2 large eggs, lightly beaten
2¼ cups dry unsweetened coconut
heaping ½ cup golden raisins
3½ oz/100 g candied cherries

Grease and line a 9-inch/23-cm square baking pan. Place the chocolate in a heatproof bowl, set the bowl over a saucepan of gently simmering water, and heat until melted. Remove from the heat and stir until smooth. Pour into the pan and let set for about 1 hour.

Preheat the oven to 350°F/180°C. Place the butter and sugar in a large bowl and whisk together until pale and creamy. Gradually whisk in the eggs, then add the coconut, golden raisins, and candied cherries and stir together until combined. Spoon the mixture into the pan on top of the chocolate and spread out evenly.

Bake in the preheated oven for 30–35 minutes, or until golden brown. Let cool in the pan, then turn out and cut into 16 slices to serve.

638 Sticky pecan pie slices

Makes 10

8 tbsp butter, plus extra for greasing
1¼ cups all-purpose flour
⅔ cup light brown sugar
2 large eggs
⅓ cup pecans, chopped into small pieces
½ cup dark corn syrup
½ tsp vanilla extract

Preheat the oven to 375°F/190°C. Grease and line a shallow 9-inch/23-cm square baking pan. Grease the paper. Place 2 tablespoons of the butter in a saucepan and heat gently until melted. Let cool slightly.

Place the flour and remaining butter, cut into cubes, in a large bowl and rub the butter in with your fingertips until the mixture resembles fine breadcrumbs. Stir in scant ¼ cup of the sugar, then spoon the mixture into the pan and press down firmly with the back of a spoon. Bake in the preheated oven for 20 minutes.

Meanwhile, place the eggs in a large bowl and beat lightly. Add the remaining sugar, the pecans, melted butter, dark corn syrup, and vanilla extract and stir together until combined. Pour the mixture over the base in the pan and bake in the oven for an additional 15–20 minutes, or until firm to the touch and golden brown. Remove from the pan and let cool. When cold, cut into 10 slices to serve.

639 Chocolate pecan pie slices

Add ¼ cup semisweet chocolate chips to the mixture with the pecans.

640 Almond slices

Makes 8

8 tbsp butter, plus extra for greasing
⅔ cup ground almonds
2 cups dried milk powder
1 cup granulated sugar
½ tsp saffron strands
3 eggs, lightly beaten
1 tbsp slivered almonds

Preheat the oven to 325°F/160°C. Grease a shallow 8-inch/20-cm square baking pan. Place the ground almonds, dried milk powder, sugar, and saffron in a large bowl and stir to mix well.

Place the butter in a small saucepan and melt over low heat. Pour the melted butter over the dry ingredients and mix until thoroughly combined. Add the eggs to the mixture and stir to blend well.

Spread the mixture evenly in the pan and sprinkle with the slivered almonds. Bake in the preheated oven for 45 minutes, or until a skewer inserted into the center comes out clean.

Cut into triangles or slices and serve hot or cold.

641 Hazelnut slices

Replace the ground almonds with ground toasted hazelnuts. Sprinkle the top with finely chopped toasted hazelnuts.

642 Strawberry chocolate slices

Makes 16

1⅔ cups all-purpose flour
1 tsp baking powder
½ cup superfine sugar
scant ½ cup light brown sugar
1 cup butter
1¾ cups rolled oats
⅔ cup strawberry jam
heaping ½ cup semisweet chocolate chips
¼ cup slivered almonds

Preheat the oven to 375°F/190°C. Line a 12 x 8-inch/30 x 20-cm rectangular baking pan. Sift the flour and baking powder into a large bowl, add the sugars, and mix well. Add the butter and rub it in with your fingertips until the mixture resembles breadcrumbs. Stir in the oats, then press three quarters of the mixture into the bottom of the pan. Bake in the preheated oven for 10 minutes.

Spread the jam over the cooked base and sprinkle over the chocolate chips. Place the remaining flour mixture and the almonds in a bowl and mix together, then sprinkle evenly over the chocolate chips and press down gently. Bake for an additional 20–25 minutes, or until golden brown. Let cool in the pan, then cut into slices to serve.

643 Apricot & chocolate slices

Replace the strawberry jam with apricot jam.

644 Raspberry oat slices

Add 1 teaspoon of almond extract with the butter. Replace the strawberry jam with raspberry jam. Omit the chocolate chips and increase the slivered almonds to ½ cup.

645 Chocolate cheesecake slices

MAKES 16

6 tbsp butter, plus extra for greasing
7 oz/200 g chocolate graham crackers
1¾ cups cream cheese
⅔ cup superfine sugar
¾ cup sour cream
3 large eggs
½ tsp vanilla extract
⅓ cup all-purpose flour
2¾ oz/75 g semisweet chocolate, broken into pieces

Preheat the oven to 325°F/160°C. Grease and line a shallow 9-inch/23-cm square baking pan. Place the crackers in a strong plastic bag and, using a rolling pin, crush into small pieces. Place the butter in a saucepan and heat gently until melted. Remove from the heat, add the crushed crackers, and mix together. Spoon the mixture into the pan, press down firmly with the back of a spoon, and let chill in the refrigerator.

Meanwhile, place the cream cheese, sugar, sour cream, eggs, and vanilla extract in a large bowl and whisk together until smooth. Add the flour and whisk together. Pour the mixture over the crackers in the pan.

Bake in the preheated oven for about 40 minutes, or until set but not browned. Cool in the pan, then chill for at least 3 hours.

When ready for decorating, remove the cheesecake from the pan. Place the chocolate in a heatproof bowl, set the bowl over a saucepan of gently simmering water, and heat until melted. Remove from the heat and stir until smooth. Using a teaspoon, drizzle the chocolate over the top of the cheesecake, backward and forward in a zigzag design. Let set for 1 hour. Before serving, use a hot, sharp knife to cut into 16 bars.

646 Chocolate marshmallow fingers

MAKES 18

12 oz/350 g graham crackers
4½ oz/125 g semisweet chocolate, broken into pieces
1 cup butter
2 tbsp superfine sugar
2 tbsp unsweetened cocoa
2 tbsp honey
2 oz/55 g mini marshmallows
heaping ½ cup white chocolate chips

Place the crackers in a plastic bag and, using a rolling pin, crush into small pieces. Place the chocolate, butter, sugar, cocoa, and honey in a saucepan and heat gently until melted. Remove from the heat and let cool slightly.

Stir the crushed crackers into the chocolate mixture until well mixed. Add the marshmallows and mix well, then stir in the chocolate chips. Spoon the mixture into an 8-inch/20-cm square baking pan and lightly smooth the top. Chill in the refrigerator for 2–3 hours, or until set. Cut into fingers before serving.

647 No-bake chocolate fingers

MAKES 14

6 oz/175 g semisweet chocolate, broken into squares	*4 oz/115 g graham crackers, broken into small pieces*
4 tbsp butter	*6 oz/175 g mixed dried fruit*
2 tbsp dark corn syrup	*2 oz/55 g/ candied cherries*

Place the chocolate in a heatproof bowl, set the bowl over a saucepan of gently simmering water, and heat until melted. Add the butter and dark corn syrup and stir until combined. Remove from the heat. Stir the crackers into the chocolate along with the mixed fruit and cherries.

Line a 7-inch/18-cm cake pan with parchment paper and pour in the chocolate mixture, pressing down well with the back of a spoon. Chill for 2 hours, or until firm. Cut into 14 fingers to serve.

648 Chocolate fruit & nut bar

Melt the chocolate, butter, and syrup as before. Stir in the crackers and add ⅔ cup golden raisins and ¾ cup chopped pecans. Chill until set.

649 Chocolate caramel shortbread

MAKES 12

8 tbsp butter, plus extra for greasing
1¼ cups all-purpose flour
¼ cup superfine sugar

FILLING AND TOPPING
¾ cup butter
½ cup superfine sugar
3 tbsp dark corn syrup
14 oz/400 g canned condensed milk
7 oz/200 g semisweet chocolate, broken into pieces

Preheat the oven to 350°F/180°C. Grease and line the bottom of a shallow 9-inch/23-cm square cake pan. Place the butter, flour, and sugar in a food processor and process until it begins to bind together. Press the mixture into the pan and smooth the top. Bake in the preheated oven for 20–25 minutes, or until golden brown.

Meanwhile, to make the filling, place the butter, sugar, dark corn syrup, and condensed milk in a saucepan and heat gently until the sugar has dissolved. Bring to a boil, then reduce the heat and simmer for 6–8 minutes, stirring, until the mixture becomes very thick. Pour over the shortbread base and chill in the refrigerator until firm.

To make the topping, place the chocolate in a heatproof bowl set over a pan of simmering water and heat until melted. Cool, then spread over the caramel. Chill until set, then cut into 12 pieces to serve.

650 No-bake chocolate & raisin cookie cakes

MAKES ABOUT 20

7 tbsp butter
¼ cup unsweetened cocoa
7 oz/200 g graham crackers, crushed
½ cup raisins or dried cranberries
1 egg, lightly beaten
4 oz/125 g milk chocolate, broken into squares

Line a 9½-inch/24-cm square baking pan with foil or parchment paper. Place the butter in a saucepan and heat gently until melted. Stir in the cocoa, then remove from the heat and add the crackers and dried fruit and stir well.

Add the egg and mix again until thoroughly mixed, then tip the mixture into the baking pan and press down with the back of a spoon.

Place the chocolate in a heatproof bowl, set the bowl over a pan of gently simmering water, and heat until melted. Spread the chocolate evenly over the top of the cake and leave in a cool place to set. Cut into squares to serve.

Note: This recipe contains raw egg.

Marvelous Muffins

651 Blueberry muffins

MAKES 12

6 tbsp sunflower oil or 6 tbsp butter, melted and cooled, plus extra for greasing
2 cups all-purpose flour
1 tbsp baking powder
pinch of salt
heaping ½ cup light brown sugar
heaping 1 cup frozen blueberries
2 eggs
generous 1 cup milk
1 tsp vanilla extract
finely grated rind of 1 lemon

Preheat the oven to 400°F/200°C. Grease a 12-hole muffin pan. Sift together the flour, baking powder, and salt into a large bowl. Stir in the sugar and blueberries.

Place the eggs in a large pitcher or bowl and beat lightly, then beat in the milk, oil, vanilla extract, and lemon rind. Make a well in the center of the dry ingredients and pour in the beaten liquid ingredients. Stir until just combined; do not overmix. Spoon the batter into the muffin pan.

Bake in the preheated oven for 20 minutes, or until well risen, golden brown, and firm to the touch. Let cool in the pan for 5 minutes, then serve warm or transfer to a wire rack to cool completely.

652 With white chocolate topping

Rub 3 tablespoons of butter into heaping ⅓ cup all-purpose flour until the mixture resembles breadcrumbs, then stir in 2 tablespoons of superfine sugar, 2 tablespoons of dried blueberries, and 1¾ oz/50 g grated white chocolate and scatter over the muffins before baking.

653 Blackberry & apple muffins

MAKES 12

6 tbsp sunflower oil or 6 tbsp butter, melted and cooled, plus extra for greasing
2 cups all-purpose flour
1 tbsp baking powder
pinch of salt
heaping ½ cup light brown sugar
1 large apple
2 eggs
generous 1 cup buttermilk
1 tsp vanilla extract
1 cup frozen blackberries
scant ¼ cup raw brown sugar

Preheat the oven to 400°F/200°C. Grease a 12-hole muffin pan. Sift together the flour, baking powder, and salt into a large bowl. Stir in the brown sugar. Peel, core, and finely chop the apple. Add to the flour mixture and stir together.

Place the eggs in a large pitcher or bowl and beat lightly, then beat in the buttermilk, oil, and vanilla extract. Make a well in the center of the dry ingredients, pour in the beaten liquid ingredients, and add the blackberries. Stir gently until just combined; do not overmix. Spoon the batter into the muffin pan. Sprinkle the raw brown sugar over the tops of the muffins.

Bake in the preheated oven for 20 minutes, until well risen, golden brown, and firm to the touch. Let cool in the pan for 5 minutes, then serve warm or transfer to a wire rack to cool completely.

654 Mixed berry muffins

Omit the apple and replace the blackberries with 1⅓ cups mixed fresh berries.

655 Apple streusel muffins

MAKES 12

2 cups all-purpose flour
1 tbsp baking powder
½ tsp ground cinnamon
pinch of salt
heaping ½ cup light brown sugar
1 large apple
2 eggs
generous 1 cup milk
6 tbsp sunflower oil or 6 tbsp butter, melted and cooled

STREUSEL TOPPING
scant ½ cup all-purpose flour
¼ tsp ground cinnamon
2½ tbsp butter, cut into small pieces
2 tbsp light brown sugar

Preheat the oven to 400°F/200°C. Line a 12-hole muffin pan with 12 paper liners.

To make the streusel topping, place the flour and cinnamon in a bowl. Add the butter and rub it in with your fingertips until the mixture resembles fine breadcrumbs. Stir in the sugar and set aside.

To make the muffins, sift together the flour, baking powder, cinnamon, and salt into a large bowl. Stir in the sugar. Peel, core, and finely chop the apple. Add to the flour mixture and stir together. Place the eggs in a large pitcher or bowl and beat lightly, then beat in the milk and oil.

Make a well in the center of the dry ingredients and pour in the beaten liquid ingredients. Stir gently until just combined; do not overmix. Spoon the batter into the paper liners. Scatter the streusel topping over each muffin.

Bake in the preheated oven for 20 minutes, or until well risen, golden brown, and firm to the touch. Let cool in the pan for 5 minutes, then serve warm or transfer to a wire rack to cool completely.

656 With apple brandy butter

Beat 1 tablespoon of apple brandy and 2 tablespoons of finely chopped dried apple into 6 tablespoons of softened butter and serve with the muffins.

657 Apricot & banana muffins

MAKES 12

6 tbsp sunflower oil or 6 tbsp butter, melted and cooled, plus extra for greasing
2 cups all-purpose flour
1 tbsp baking powder
pinch of salt
heaping ½ cup superfine sugar
⅓ cup dried apricots, finely chopped
2 bananas
about ⅔ cup milk
2 eggs

Preheat the oven to 400°F/200°C. Grease a 12-hole muffin pan. Sift together the flour, baking powder, and salt into a large bowl. Stir in the sugar and apricots.

Mash the bananas and place in a pitcher, then add enough milk to make up the purée to a heaping 1 cup.

Place the eggs in a large pitcher or bowl and beat lightly, then beat in the banana and milk mixture and the oil. Make a well in the center of the dry ingredients and pour in the beaten liquid ingredients. Stir until just combined; do not overmix. Spoon the batter into the muffin pan.

Bake in the preheated oven for 20 minutes, or until well risen, golden brown, and firm to the touch. Let cool in the pan for 5 minutes, then serve warm or transfer to a wire rack to cool completely.

658 Double banana muffins

Omit the apricots and add heaping 1 cup chopped, soft dried banana.

659 *Apple & cinnamon muffins*

MAKES 12

scant 1½ cups whole wheat flour
½ cup fine oats
2 tsp baking powder
scant ⅔ cup light brown sugar
2 large eggs
1 cup low-fat milk
generous ⅓ cup peanut oil
1 tsp vanilla extract
1 tsp ground cinnamon
1 large baking apple

Preheat the oven to 350°F/180°C. Line a 12-hole muffin pan with paper liners.

Sift the flour, oats, and baking powder together into a large bowl, then add the larger particles left in the strainer. Stir in the sugar. Place the eggs, milk, and oil in a separate bowl and beat together until well combined. Add to the dry ingredients, along with the vanilla extract and cinnamon, and stir until just combined; do not overmix.

Peel, core, and grate the apple and stir into the batter, then spoon the batter into the paper liners.

Bake in the preheated oven for 20–25 minutes, or until risen and golden brown. Let cool in the pan for a few minutes before serving warm or transfer to a wire rack to cool completely.

660 *Buttermilk berry muffins*

MAKES 12

6 tbsp sunflower oil or 6 tbsp butter, melted and cooled, plus extra for greasing
heaping 1 cup frozen mixed berries, such as blueberries, raspberries, blackberries, strawberries
2 cups all-purpose flour
1 tbsp baking powder
pinch of salt
heaping ½ cup superfine sugar
2 eggs
generous 1 cup buttermilk
1 tsp vanilla extract
confectioners' sugar, for dusting

Preheat the oven to 400°F/200°C. Grease a 12-hole muffin pan. Cut any large berries, such as strawberries, into small pieces.

Sift together the flour, baking powder, and salt into a large bowl. Stir in the sugar.

Place the eggs in a large pitcher or bowl and beat lightly, then beat in the buttermilk, oil, and vanilla extract. Make a well in the center of the dry ingredients, pour in the beaten liquid ingredients, and add the berries. Stir until combined; do not overmix. Spoon the batter into the muffin pan.

Bake in the preheated oven for 20 minutes, or until well risen, golden brown, and firm to the touch. Let cool in the pan for 5 minutes, then serve warm or transfer to a wire rack to cool completely. Dust with a little sifted confectioners' sugar before serving.

661 *Buttermilk cranberry muffins*

Replace the frozen berries with 1½ cups frozen cranberries mixed with ½ teaspoon of finely grated orange rind.

662 Frosted chocolate orange muffins

Makes 12

6 tbsp sunflower oil or 6 tbsp butter, melted and cooled, plus extra for greasing
2 oranges
about ½ cup milk
1⅔ cups all-purpose flour
½ cup unsweetened cocoa
1 tbsp baking powder
pinch of salt
heaping ½ cup light brown sugar
scant 1 cup semisweet chocolate chips
2 eggs
strips of orange zest, for decorating

FROSTING
2 oz/55 g semisweet chocolate, broken into pieces
2 tbsp butter
2 tbsp water
1½ cups confectioners' sugar

Preheat the oven to 400°F/200°C. Grease a 12-hole muffin pan. Finely grate the rind from the oranges and squeeze the juice. Add enough milk to make up the juice to a heaping 1 cup, then add the orange rind. Sift together the flour, cocoa, baking powder, and salt into a large bowl. Stir in the brown sugar and chocolate chips.

Place the eggs in a large pitcher or bowl and beat lightly, then beat in the milk and orange mixture and the oil. Make a well in the center of the dry ingredients and pour in the beaten liquid ingredients. Stir gently until just combined; do not overmix. Spoon the batter into the muffin pan.

Bake in the preheated oven for 20 minutes, or until well risen and firm to the touch. Let cool in the pan for 5 minutes, then transfer to a wire rack to cool completely.

To make the frosting, place the chocolate in a heatproof bowl, add the butter and water, then set the bowl over a saucepan of gently simmering water and heat, stirring, until melted. Remove from the heat, sift in the confectioners' sugar, and beat until smooth, then spread the frosting on top of the muffins and decorate with strips of orange zest.

663 With white chocolate frosting

Replace the semisweet chocolate with 2 oz/55 g white chocolate and top the muffins with crushed orange-flavored chocolate.

664 Brandied peach muffins

Makes 12

14 oz/400 g canned peaches in natural juice
2 cups all-purpose flour
1 tbsp baking powder
pinch of salt
heaping ½ cup superfine sugar
2 eggs
¾ cup buttermilk
6 tbsp sunflower oil or 6 tbsp butter, melted and cooled
3 tbsp brandy
finely grated rind of 1 orange

Preheat the oven to 400°F/200°C. Line a 12-hole muffin pan with 12 paper liners. Drain and finely chop the peaches. Sift together the flour, baking powder, and salt into a large bowl. Stir in the sugar.

Place the eggs in a large pitcher or bowl and beat lightly, then beat in the buttermilk, oil, brandy, and orange rind. Make a well in the center of the dry ingredients, pour in the beaten liquid ingredients, and add the chopped peaches. Stir gently until just combined; do not overmix. Spoon the batter into the paper liners.

Bake in the preheated oven for 20 minutes, or until well risen, golden brown, and firm to the touch. Let cool in the pan for 5 minutes, then serve warm or transfer to a wire rack to cool completely.

665 Pear and liqueur muffins

Replace the peaches with 14 oz/400 g canned pears, drained and chopped, and use Poire William liqueur to replace the brandy.

666 Brandy & apricot muffins

MAKES 12

heaping ½ cup dried apricots, coarsely chopped
3 tbsp brandy
2 cups all-purpose flour
1 tbsp baking powder
pinch of salt
heaping ½ cup superfine sugar
2 eggs
¾ cup buttermilk
6 tbsp sunflower oil or 6 tbsp butter, melted and cooled

Put the chopped apricots in a bowl, add the brandy, and let soak for 1 hour. Preheat the oven to 400°F/200°C. Line a 12-hole muffin pan with 12 paper liners. Put the apricots and brandy in a food processor and process to form a coarse purée. Sift together the flour, baking powder, and salt into a large bowl. Stir in the sugar.

Place the eggs in a large pitcher or bowl and beat lightly, then beat in the apricot purée, buttermilk, and oil. Make a well in the center of the dry ingredients and pour in the beaten liquid ingredients. Stir gently until just combined; do not overmix. Spoon the batter into the paper liners. Bake in the preheated oven for 20 minutes, or until well risen, golden brown, and firm to the touch. Let cool in the pan for 5 minutes, then serve warm or transfer to a wire rack to cool completely.

667 With apricot brandy icing

Sift 1 cup confectioners' sugar into a bowl and mix to a smooth icing with 1 tablespoon of apricot brandy. Drizzle over the muffins and let set.

668 Caribbean rum & raisin muffins

MAKES 12

1¼ cups raisins
3 tbsp rum
6 tbsp sunflower oil or 6 tbsp butter, melted and cooled, plus extra for greasing
2 cups all-purpose flour
1 tbsp baking powder
pinch of salt
heaping ½ cup dark brown sugar
2 eggs
generous ¾ cup milk

Put the raisins in a bowl, add the rum, and let soak for 1 hour. Preheat the oven to 400°F/200°C. Grease a 12-hole muffin pan. Sift together the flour, baking powder, and salt into a large bowl. Stir in the sugar.

Place the eggs in a large pitcher or bowl and beat lightly, then beat in the milk and oil. Make a well in the center of the dry ingredients, pour in the beaten liquid ingredients, and add the raisins. Stir gently until just combined; do not overmix. Spoon the batter into the muffin pan.

Bake in the preheated oven for 20 minutes, or until well risen, golden brown, and firm to the touch. Let cool in the pan for 5 minutes, then serve warm or transfer to a wire rack to cool completely.

669 With coconut icing

Sift 1 cup confectioners' sugar into a bowl and mix until smooth with 1–2 tablespoons of coconut cream. Spread over the cooled muffins.

670 Cherry & coconut muffins

MAKES 12

2 cups all-purpose flour
1 tbsp baking powder
pinch of salt
heaping ½ cup superfine sugar
scant ½ cup dry unsweetened coconut
4½ oz/125 g candied cherries, cut into small pieces
2 eggs
generous 1 cup coconut milk
6 tbsp sunflower oil or 6 tbsp butter, melted and cooled
1 tsp vanilla extract
12 whole fresh cherries on their stalks

Preheat the oven to 400°F/200°C. Line a 12-hole muffin pan with 12 paper liners. Sift together the flour, baking powder, and salt into a large bowl. Stir in the sugar, coconut, and chopped candied cherries.

Place the eggs in a large pitcher or bowl and beat lightly, then beat in the coconut milk, oil, and vanilla extract. Make a well in the center of the dry ingredients and pour in the beaten liquid ingredients. Stir gently until just combined; do not overmix. Spoon the batter into the paper liners. Top each muffin with a whole fresh cherry.

Bake in the preheated oven for 20 minutes, or until well risen, golden brown, and firm to the touch. Let cool in the pan for 5 minutes, then serve warm or transfer to a wire rack to cool completely.

671 With coconut topping

Omit the whole cherry on each muffin. Place 1 cup dried coconut, 3 tablespoons of brown sugar, and 3 oz/85 g candied cherries in a food processor and pulse to chop, then sprinkle over the muffins before baking.

672 Citrus fruit muffins

MAKES 12

2 cups all-purpose flour
1 tbsp baking powder
½ tsp baking soda
pinch of salt
heaping ½ cup superfine sugar
2 eggs
heaping 1 cup plain yogurt
6 tbsp sunflower oil or 6 tbsp butter, melted and cooled
finely grated rind of 1 lemon
finely grated rind of 1 lime
finely grated rind of 1 orange
strips of citrus zest, for decorating

FROSTING
2 tbsp butter
scant ½ cup soft cream cheese
1 cup confectioners' sugar
1 tsp fresh lemon, lime, or orange juice

Preheat the oven to 400°F/200°C. Line a 12-hole muffin pan with 12 paper liners. Sift together the flour, baking powder, baking soda, and salt into a large bowl. Stir in the sugar. Place the eggs in a large pitcher or bowl and beat lightly, then beat in the yogurt, oil, and all the citrus rinds. Make a well in the center of the dry ingredients and pour in the beaten liquid ingredients. Stir gently until just combined; do not overmix. Spoon the batter into the paper liners.

Bake in the preheated oven for 20 minutes, or until well risen and golden brown. Let cool in the pan for 5 minutes, then transfer to a wire rack to cool completely.

To make the frosting, place the butter and cream cheese in a large bowl and, using an electric hand-held mixer, beat together until smooth. Sift the confectioners' sugar into the mixture, then beat together until mixed. Gradually beat in the citrus juice, adding enough to form a spreading consistency.

When the muffins are cold, spread the frosting on top of each, then decorate them with strips of citrus zest.

673 Kiwi muffins

Omit the citrus zest and rind and replace with 3 peeled, chopped kiwis.

674 Cranberry & almond muffins

MAKES 12

6 tbsp sunflower oil or 6 tbsp butter, melted and cooled, plus extra for greasing
1⅔ cups all-purpose flour
1 tbsp baking powder
pinch of salt
heaping ½ cup superfine sugar
heaping ½ cup ground almonds
2 eggs
generous 1 cup buttermilk
½ tsp almond extract
heaping ½ cup fresh or frozen cranberries
scant ¼ cup raw brown sugar
scant ½ cup slivered almonds

Preheat the oven to 400°F/200°C. Grease a 12-hole muffin pan. Sift together the flour, baking powder, and salt into a large bowl. Stir in the superfine sugar and ground almonds.

Place the eggs in a large pitcher or bowl and beat lightly, then beat in the buttermilk, oil, and almond extract. Make a well in the center of the dry ingredients, pour in the beaten liquid ingredients, and add the cranberries. Stir gently until just combined; do not overmix. Spoon the batter into the muffin pan. Sprinkle the raw brown sugar and slivered almonds over the tops of the muffins.

Bake in the preheated oven for 20 minutes, or until well risen, golden brown, and firm to the touch. Let cool in the pan for 5 minutes, then serve warm or transfer to a wire rack to cool completely.

675 With almond crunch topping

Chop the slivered almonds and mix with the raw brown sugar and 4 crushed amaretti cookies, then sprinkle the mixture over the top of the muffins before baking.

676 Fresh flower muffins

MAKES 12

2 cups all-purpose flour
1 tbsp baking powder
pinch of salt
heaping ½ cup superfine sugar
2 eggs
generous 1 cup buttermilk
6 tbsp sunflower oil or 6 tbsp butter, melted and cooled
finely grated rind of 1 lemon

TOPPING
6 tbsp butter, softened
1½ cups confectioners' sugar
12 edible flower heads, such as lavender, nasturtiums, violets, primroses, or roses, for decorating

Preheat the oven to 400°F/200°C. Line a 12-hole muffin pan with 12 paper liners. Carefully wash the flower heads and let dry on paper towels.

Sift together the flour, baking powder, and salt into a large bowl. Stir in the sugar. Place the eggs in a large pitcher or bowl and beat lightly, then beat in the buttermilk, oil, and lemon rind. Make a well in the center of the dry ingredients and pour in the beaten liquid ingredients. Stir gently until just combined; do not overmix. Spoon the batter into the paper liners.

Bake in the preheated oven for 20 minutes, or until well risen, golden brown, and firm to the touch. Let cool in the pan for 5 minutes, then transfer to a wire rack to cool completely.

To make the frosting, place the butter in a large bowl and beat until fluffy. Sift in the confectioners' sugar and beat together until smooth, then place in a pastry bag fitted with a large star tip and pipe circles on top of each muffin. Just before serving, place a flower head on top for decorating.

677 Sugared rose petal muffins

Brush 12 fresh rose petals with beaten egg white and dredge in superfine sugar, place on parchment paper to dry, and use for decorating the muffins.

678 Fresh orange muffins

MAKES 12

6 tbsp sunflower oil, plus extra for greasing
5 oranges
1 cup whole wheat flour
1 cup all-purpose flour
1 tbsp baking powder
heaping ½ cup superfine sugar
2 eggs
generous 1 cup fresh orange juice

Preheat the oven to 400°F/200°C. Grease a 12-hole muffin pan. Grate the rind from 2 of the oranges and set aside. Remove the peel from all of the oranges, discarding the white pith. Cut the flesh into segments, reserving 6 segments. Cut the reserved segments in half and set aside. Cut the remaining segments into small pieces.

Sift together both types of flour and the baking powder into a large bowl, adding any bran left in the strainer. Stir in the sugar.

Place the eggs in a large pitcher or bowl and beat lightly, then beat in the orange juice, oil, and reserved orange rind.

Make a well in the center of the dry ingredients, pour in the beaten liquid ingredients, and add the chopped oranges. Stir until combined; do not overmix. Spoon the batter into the muffin pan. Place the halved orange segments on the top.

Bake in the preheated oven for 20 minutes, or until well risen, golden brown, and firm to the touch. Cool for 5 minutes, then serve warm or transfer to a wire rack to cool completely.

679 Fresh peach muffins

Pit and peel 5 fresh peaches and proceed as for the oranges. Replace the orange juice with peach nectar.

680 Fresh strawberry & cream muffins

MAKES 12

6 tbsp sunflower oil or 6 tbsp butter, melted and cooled, plus extra for greasing
1 cup strawberries
2 cups all-purpose flour
1 tbsp baking powder
pinch of salt
heaping ½ cup superfine sugar
2 eggs
generous 1 cup light cream
1 tsp vanilla extract

TOPPING
½ cup heavy cream
12 whole small strawberries, for decorating

Preheat the oven to 400°F/200°C. Grease a 12-hole muffin pan. Chop the strawberries into small pieces. Sift together the flour, baking powder, and salt into a large bowl. Stir in the sugar and chopped strawberries.

Place the eggs in a large pitcher or bowl and lightly beat, then beat in the light cream, oil, and vanilla extract. Make a well in the center of the dry ingredients and pour in the beaten liquid ingredients.

Stir gently until just combined; do not overmix. Spoon the batter into the muffin pan.

Bake in the preheated oven for 20 minutes until well risen, golden brown, and firm to the touch. Let cool in the pan for 5 minutes, then transfer to a wire rack to cool completely.

Place the heavy cream in a bowl and whip until stiff. When the muffins are cold, pipe or spread the cream on top of each muffin, then top with a small strawberry.

681 With sweet wine & strawberry topping

Hull and slice the strawberries, pour over 2 tablespoons of sweet white wine, and let macerate for 10 minutes before spooning a few strawberry slices onto each muffin.

682 Chocolate cream muffins

Makes 12

1⅔ cups all-purpose flour
½ cup unsweetened cocoa
1 tbsp baking powder
pinch of salt
heaping ½ cup light brown sugar
scant 1 cup white chocolate chips
2 eggs
generous 1 cup heavy cream
6 tbsp sunflower oil or 6 tbsp butter, melted and cooled

Preheat the oven to 400°F/200°C. Line a 12-hole muffin pan with 12 paper liners. Sift together the flour, cocoa, baking powder, and salt into a large bowl. Stir in the sugar and white chocolate chips.

Place the eggs in a large pitcher or bowl and beat lightly, then beat in the cream and oil. Make a well in the center of the dry ingredients and pour in the beaten liquid ingredients. Stir gently until just combined; do not overmix. Spoon the batter into the paper liners.

Bake in the preheated oven for 20 minutes, or until well risen and firm to the touch. Let cool in the pan for 5 minutes, then serve warm or transfer to a wire rack to cool completely.

683 Chocolate fudge muffins

Add 2 oz/55 g chopped chocolate fudge to the batter and bake as before.

684 Frosted cream cheese muffins

Makes 12

scant 1 cup soft cream cheese
scant ½ cup confectioners' sugar
2 cups all-purpose flour
1 tbsp baking powder
pinch of salt
heaping ½ cup dark brown sugar
2 eggs
heaping ¾ cup sour cream
6 tbsp sunflower oil or 6 tbsp butter, melted and cooled
finely grated rind of 1 lemon
2 tsp fresh lemon juice

Preheat the oven to 400°F/200°C. Line a 12-hole muffin pan with 12 paper liners. Put scant ½ cup of the cream cheese in a bowl. Sift in scant ¼ cup of the confectioners' sugar and beat together.

Sift together the flour, baking powder, and salt into a large bowl. Stir in the brown sugar.

Place the eggs in a large pitcher or bowl and beat lightly, then beat in the sour cream, oil, and lemon rind. Make a well in the center of the dry ingredients and pour in the beaten liquid ingredients. Stir gently until just combined; do not overmix. Spoon half of the batter into the paper liners. Add a spoonful of the cream cheese mixture to the center of each then spoon in the remaining batter.

Bake in the preheated oven for 20 minutes, or until well risen, golden brown, and firm to the touch. Let cool in the pan for 5 minutes, then transfer to a wire rack to cool completely.

To make the frosting, place the remaining cream cheese in a bowl and sift in the remaining confectioners' sugar. Add the lemon juice and beat well together. Spread the frosting on top of the muffins and chill in the refrigerator until ready to serve.

685 *Coffee & cream muffins*

Makes 12

6 tbsp sunflower oil or 6 tbsp butter, melted and cooled, plus extra for greasing
2 tbsp instant coffee granules
2 tbsp boiling water
2 cups all-purpose flour
1 tbsp baking powder
pinch of salt
heaping ½ cup dark brown sugar
2 eggs
heaping ¾ cup heavy cream

TOPPING
1¼ cups whipping cream
unsweetened cocoa, for dusting
12 chocolate-covered coffee beans, for decorating

Preheat the oven to 400°F/200°C. Grease a 12-hole muffin pan. Put the coffee granules and boiling water in a cup and stir until dissolved. Let cool.

Meanwhile, sift together the flour, baking powder, and salt into a large bowl. Stir in the sugar. Place the eggs in a large pitcher or bowl and beat lightly, then beat in the heavy cream, oil, and dissolved coffee. Make a well in the center of the dry ingredients and pour in the beaten liquid ingredients. Stir gently until just combined; do not overmix. Spoon the batter into the muffin pan.

Bake in the preheated oven for 20 minutes, or until risen, golden, and firm to the touch. Cool in the pan for 5 minutes, then transfer to a wire rack to cool completely.

Just before serving, whip the whipping cream until it holds its shape. Spoon a dollop of the cream on top of each muffin, dust lightly with cocoa, and top with a chocolate-covered coffee bean.

686 *With mocha cream topping*

Mix ½ teaspoon of cocoa, ½ teaspoon of espresso coffee powder, and 1 tablespoon of coffee liqueur together in a bowl until smooth, then whip into the whipping cream before topping the muffins.

687 *Decadent chocolate dessert muffins*

Makes 12

6 tbsp sunflower oil or 6 tbsp butter, melted and cooled, plus extra for greasing
1⅔ cups all-purpose flour
½ cup unsweetened cocoa
1 tbsp baking powder
pinch of salt
heaping ½ cup light brown sugar
2 eggs
generous 1 cup light cream
3 oz/85 g semisweet chocolate, broken into pieces

SAUCE
7 oz/200 g semisweet chocolate
2 tbsp butter
¼ cup light cream

Preheat the oven to 400°F/200°C. Grease a 12-hole muffin pan. Sift together the flour, cocoa, baking powder, and salt into a large bowl. Stir in the sugar.

Place the eggs in a large pitcher or bowl and beat lightly, then beat in the cream and oil. Make a well in the center of the dry ingredients and pour in the beaten liquid ingredients. Stir gently until just combined; do not overmix. Spoon half of the batter into the muffin pan, then place a piece of chocolate into the center of each. Spoon in the remaining batter.

Bake in the preheated oven for 20 minutes, or until well risen and firm to the touch.

Meanwhile, to make the sauce, place the chocolate and butter in a heatproof bowl set over a saucepan of gently simmering water. Stir until blended, then stir in the cream and mix together. Remove from the heat and stir until smooth.

Leave the muffins in the pan for 5 minutes, then remove and place on serving plates. Serve warm with the chocolate sauce poured over the top of each muffin.

688 *With Kirsch cherry topping*

Place 12 pitted black cherries in a small bowl. Pour over 2 tablespoons of Kirsch, stir, and leave for 15 minutes. Top each muffin with a cherry before pouring over the sauce.

689 After-dinner coffee liqueur muffins

MAKES 12

2 tbsp instant coffee granules
2 tbsp boiling water
2 cups all-purpose flour
1 tbsp baking powder
pinch of salt
heaping ½ cup light brown sugar
2 eggs
generous ⅓ cup milk
6 tbsp sunflower oil or 6 tbsp butter, melted and cooled
6 tbsp coffee liqueur
scant ¼ cup raw brown sugar

Preheat the oven to 400°F/200°C. Line a 12-hole muffin pan with 12 paper liners. Put the coffee granules and boiling water in a cup and stir until dissolved. Let cool.

Meanwhile, sift together the flour, baking powder, and salt into a large bowl. Stir in the brown sugar. Place the eggs in a large pitcher or bowl and beat lightly, then beat in the milk, oil, dissolved coffee, and liqueur. Make a well in the center of the dry ingredients and pour in the beaten liquid ingredients. Stir gently until just combined; do not overmix. Spoon the batter into the paper liners. Sprinkle the raw brown sugar over the tops of the muffins.

Bake in the preheated oven for 20 minutes, or until well risen, golden brown, and firm to the touch. Let cool in the pan for 5 minutes, then serve warm or transfer to a wire rack to cool completely.

690 With espresso icing

Sift 1 cup confectioners' sugar into a bowl, mix 1 teaspoon of espresso coffee powder with 1 tablespoon of boiling water, and add to the confectioners' sugar, then mix until smooth and spoon over the muffins.

691 Mocha muffins

MAKES 12

1⅔ cups all-purpose flour
1 tbsp baking powder
2 tbsp unsweetened cocoa
pinch of salt
8 tbsp butter, melted
¾ cup raw brown sugar
1 large egg, lightly beaten
½ cup milk
1 tsp almond extract
2 tbsp strong coffee
1 tbsp instant coffee powder
⅓ cup semisweet chocolate chips
scant ¼ cup raisins

COCOA TOPPING
3 tbsp raw brown sugar
1 tbsp unsweetened cocoa
1 tsp allspice

Preheat the oven to 375°F/190°C. Line a 12-hole muffin pan with 12 muffin paper liners. Sift the flour, baking powder, cocoa, and salt into a large bowl.

Place the butter and raw brown sugar in a separate bowl and beat together until light and fluffy, then stir in the beaten egg. Pour in the milk, almond extract, and coffee, then add the coffee powder, chocolate chips, and raisins and gently mix together.

Add the raisin mixture to the flour mixture and stir together until just combined. Do not overmix. Spoon the batter into the paper liners.

To make the topping, place the raw brown sugar in a bowl, add the cocoa and allspice, and mix together well, then sprinkle the topping over the muffins.

Bake in the preheated oven for 20 minutes, or until well risen and golden brown. Let cool in the pan for 5 minutes, then serve warm or transfer to a wire rack to cool completely.

692 With molten chocolate filling

Omit the raisins from the batter; you will need 3½ oz/100 g semisweet chocolate chips to make the centers. Spoon half the batter into each muffin paper and add a few chocolate chips to the middle, then top with the remaining batter and bake as before.

693 Spiced chocolate muffins

MAKES 12

7 tbsp butter, softened
¾ cup superfine sugar
heaping ½ cup light brown sugar
2 large eggs
⅔ cup sour cream
5 tbsp milk
heaping 1¾ cups all-purpose flour
1 tsp baking soda
2 tbsp unsweetened cocoa
1 tsp allspice
scant 1¼ cups semisweet chocolate chips

Preheat the oven to 375°F/190°C. Line a 12-hole muffin pan with 12 paper liners. Place the butter, superfine sugar, and brown sugar in a large bowl and beat together, then beat in the eggs, sour cream, and milk until thoroughly mixed.

Sift the flour, baking soda, cocoa, and allspice into a separate bowl and stir into the mixture. Add the chocolate chips and mix well. Spoon the batter into the paper liners.

Bake in the preheated oven for 25–30 minutes. Let cool in the pan for 10 minutes, then transfer to a wire rack to cool completely.

694 Rhubarb, ginger & raisin muffins

MAKES 12

9 oz/250 g rhubarb
9 tbsp butter, melted and cooled
generous ⅓ cup milk
2 eggs, lightly beaten
scant ½ cup all-purpose flour
2 tsp baking powder
⅔ cup superfine sugar
3 tbsp raisins
3 pieces preserved ginger, chopped

Preheat the oven to 375°F/190°C. Line a 12-hole muffin pan with 12 paper liners. Chop the rhubarb into lengths of about ½ inch/1 cm. Pour the melted butter and milk into a large bowl and beat in the eggs. Sift the flour and baking powder together and lightly fold into the wet mixture with the sugar. Gently stir in the rhubarb, raisins, and preserved ginger. Spoon the batter into the paper liners.

Bake in the preheated oven for 15–20 minutes, or until the muffins are risen and golden and spring back when gently touched in the center with the tip of an index finger. Let cool in the pan for 5 minutes, then serve warm.

695 With yogurt frosting

Stir 1 tablespoon of ginger syrup into ⅔ cup strained, whole-milk plain yogurt and spread over the warm muffins.

696 Dark chocolate & ginger muffins

MAKES 12

6 tbsp sunflower oil or 6 tbsp butter, melted and cooled, plus extra for greasing
1⅔ cups all-purpose flour
½ cup unsweetened cocoa
1 tbsp baking powder
1 tbsp ground ginger
pinch of salt
heaping ½ cup dark brown sugar
3 pieces preserved ginger in syrup, finely chopped, plus 2 tbsp syrup from the jar
2 eggs
generous ¾ cup milk

Preheat the oven to 400°F/200°C. Grease a 12-hole muffin pan. Sift together the flour, cocoa, baking powder, ground ginger, and salt into a large bowl. Stir in the sugar and finely chopped preserved ginger.

Place the eggs in a large pitcher or bowl and beat lightly, then beat in the milk, oil, and ginger syrup. Make a well in the center of the dry ingredients and pour in the beaten liquid ingredients. Stir gently until just combined; do not overmix. Spoon the batter into the muffin pan.

Bake in the preheated oven for 20 minutes, or until well risen and firm to the touch. Let cool in the pan for 5 minutes, then serve warm or transfer to a wire rack to cool completely.

697 With ginger buttermilk frosting

Beat scant ½ cup cream cheese with 3 tablespoons of buttermilk, 1 cup confectioners' sugar, and ½ teaspoon of ground ginger, then spread the frosting over the cooled muffins and drizzle over a little ginger syrup.

698 Ginger wheat germ muffins

MAKES 12

6 tbsp sunflower oil, plus extra for greasing
1 cup all-purpose flour
1 tbsp baking powder
4 tsp ground ginger
heaping ½ cup dark brown sugar
1¼ cups wheat germ
3 pieces preserved ginger in syrup, finely chopped
2 eggs
generous 1 cup skim milk

Preheat the oven to 400°F/200°C. Grease a 12-hole muffin pan. Sift together the flour, baking powder, and ground ginger into a large bowl. Stir in the sugar, wheat germ, and preserved ginger.

Place the eggs in a large pitcher or bowl and beat lightly, then beat in the milk and oil. Make a well in the center of the dry ingredients and pour in the beaten liquid ingredients. Stir gently until just combined; do not overmix. Spoon the batter into the muffin pan.

Bake in the preheated oven for 20 minutes, or until well risen, golden brown, and firm to the touch. Let cool in the pan for 5 minutes then serve warm or transfer to a wire rack to cool completely.

699 With ginger crunch topping

Crush 7 oz/200 g gingersnap cookies and mix with 2 tablespoons of soft brown sugar, then spoon over the muffins before baking.

700 Low-fat blueberry muffins

MAKES 12

1⅔ cups all-purpose flour
1 tsp baking soda
¼ tsp salt
1 tsp allspice
heaping ½ cup superfine sugar
3 large egg whites
3 tbsp low-fat margarine
⅔ cup thick low-fat plain yogurt or blueberry-flavored yogurt
1 tsp vanilla extract
½ cup fresh blueberries

Preheat the oven to 375°F/190°C. Line a 12-hole muffin pan with 12 paper liners. Sift the flour, baking soda, salt, and half the allspice into a large bowl. Add 6 tablespoons of the sugar and mix well.

Place the egg whites in a separate bowl and whisk together. Add the margarine, yogurt, and vanilla extract and mix well, then stir in the blueberries until thoroughly mixed. Add the fruit mixture to the dry ingredients, then gently stir until just combined; do not overmix. Spoon the batter into the paper liners. Mix the remaining sugar with the remaining allspice, then sprinkle the mixture over the muffins.

Bake in the preheated oven for 25 minutes, or until well risen, golden brown, and firm to the touch. Let cool in the pan for 5 minutes, then serve warm or transfer to a wire rack to cool completely.

701 Low-fat cherry muffins

Replace the blueberries with fresh pitted cherries, cut in half, and use low-fat cherry yogurt.

702 Low-fat muffins

MAKES 12

2 cups all-purpose flour
1 tbsp baking powder
½ tsp baking soda
heaping ½ cup superfine sugar
2 egg whites
heaping 1 cup low-fat plain yogurt
3 tbsp sunflower oil
1 tsp vanilla extract

Preheat the oven to 400°F/200°C. Line a 12-hole muffin pan with 12 paper liners. Sift together the flour, baking powder, and baking soda into a large bowl. Stir in the sugar.

Place the egg whites in a large pitcher or bowl and beat lightly, then beat in the yogurt, oil, and vanilla extract. Make a well in the center of the dry ingredients and pour in the beaten liquid ingredients. Stir gently until just combined; do not overmix. Spoon the batter into the paper liners.

Bake in the preheated oven for 20 minutes, or until well risen, golden brown, and firm to the touch. Let cool in the pan for 5 minutes, then serve warm.

703 High-fiber muffins

MAKES 12

4 cups high-fiber bran cereal
generous 1 cup skim milk
1 cup all-purpose flour
1 tbsp baking powder
1 tsp ground cinnamon
½ tsp freshly grated nutmeg
heaping ½ cup superfine sugar
⅔ cup raisins
2 eggs
6 tbsp sunflower oil

Preheat the oven to 400°F/200°C. Line a 12-hole muffin pan with 12 paper liners. Put the cereal and milk in a bowl and let soak for about 5 minutes, or until the cereal has softened.

Meanwhile, sift together the flour, baking powder, cinnamon, and nutmeg into a large bowl. Stir in the sugar and raisins.

Place the eggs in a large pitcher or bowl and beat lightly, then beat in the oil. Make a well in the center of the dry ingredients and pour in the beaten liquid ingredients and the cereal mixture. Stir gently until just combined; do not overmix. Spoon the batter into the paper liners.

Bake in the preheated oven for 20 minutes, or until well risen, golden brown, and firm to the touch. Let cool in the pan for 5 minutes, then serve warm or transfer to a wire rack to cool completely.

704 High-fiber seed muffins

Add 3 tablespoons of chopped mixed seeds, such as pumpkin, sunflower, and hemp seeds with the raisins.

705 Sunflower seed muffins

MAKES 12

1 cup all-purpose flour
1 tbsp baking powder
heaping ½ cup light brown sugar
1⅔ cups rolled oats
heaping ½ cup golden raisins
½ cup sunflower seeds
2 eggs
generous 1 cup skim milk
6 tbsp sunflower oil
1 tsp vanilla extract

Preheat the oven to 400°F/200°C. Line a 12-hole muffin pan with 12 paper liners. Sift together the flour and baking powder into a large bowl. Stir in the sugar, oats, golden raisins, and scant ½ cup of the sunflower seeds.

Place the eggs in a large pitcher or bowl and beat lightly, then beat in the milk, oil, and vanilla extract. Make a well in the center of the dry ingredients and pour in the beaten liquid ingredients. Stir gently until just combined; do not overmix. Spoon the batter into the paper liners. Sprinkle the remaining sunflower seeds over the tops of the muffins.

Bake in the preheated oven for 20 minutes, or until well risen, golden brown, and firm to the touch. Let cool in the pan for 5 minutes, then serve warm or transfer to a wire rack to cool completely.

706 With cheese topping

Beat ⅔ cup cream cheese, ⅓ cup finely grated cheddar cheese, and ½ teaspoon of Tabasco sauce together and spread over the cooled muffins.

707 Muesli muffins

Makes 12

1 cup all-purpose flour
1 tbsp baking powder
heaping 1¾ cups unsweetened muesli
heaping ½ cup light brown sugar
2 eggs
generous 1 cup buttermilk
6 tbsp sunflower oil

Preheat the oven to 400°F/200°C. Line a 12-hole muffin pan with 12 paper liners. Sift together the flour and baking powder into a large bowl. Stir in the muesli and sugar.

Place the eggs in a large pitcher or bowl and beat lightly, then beat in the buttermilk and oil. Make a well in the center of the dry ingredients and pour in the beaten liquid ingredients. Stir gently until just combined; do not overmix. Spoon the batter into the paper liners.

Bake in the preheated oven for 20 minutes, or until well risen, golden brown, and firm to the touch. Let cool in the pan for 5 minutes, then serve warm or transfer to a wire rack to cool completely.

708 Apple & muesli muffins

Add heaping ¼ cup chopped dried apple to the muffin batter and add a dried apple ring to the top of each muffin before baking.

709 Wheat germ, banana & pumpkin seed muffins

Makes 12

6 tbsp sunflower oil, plus extra for greasing
1 cup all-purpose flour
1 tbsp baking powder
heaping ½ cup superfine sugar
1¼ cups wheat germ
⅓ cup pumpkin seeds
2 bananas
about ⅔ cup skim milk
2 eggs

Preheat the oven to 400°F/200°C. Grease a 12-hole muffin pan. Sift together the flour and baking powder into a large bowl. Stir in the sugar, wheat germ, and ¼ cup of the pumpkin seeds. Mash the bananas and place in a pitcher, then add enough milk to make up the purée to a heaping 1 cup.

Place the eggs in a large pitcher or bowl and beat lightly, then beat in the banana and milk mixture and the oil. Make a well in the center of the dry ingredients and pour in the beaten liquid ingredients. Stir gently until just combined; do not overmix. Spoon the batter into the muffin pan. Sprinkle the remaining pumpkin seeds over the top.

Bake in the preheated oven for 20 minutes, or until well risen, golden brown, and firm to the touch. Let cool in the pan for 5 minutes, then serve warm or transfer to a wire rack to cool completely.

710 With crunchy topping

Chop 2 tablespoons of pumpkin seeds and 3 oz/85 g banana chips and mix with 2 tablespoons of soft brown sugar. Scatter over the muffins before baking.

711 *Whole wheat banana muffins*

Makes 12

⅓ cup raisins
3 tbsp fresh orange juice
1 cup all-purpose flour
1 cup whole wheat flour
1 tbsp baking powder
heaping ½ cup superfine sugar
2 bananas
about ⅓ cup skim milk
2 eggs
6 tbsp sunflower oil
finely grated rind of 1 orange

Put the raisins in a bowl, add the orange juice, and let soak for 1 hour. Preheat the oven to 400°F/200°C. Line a 12-hole muffin pan with 12 paper liners.

Sift together both types of flour and the baking powder into a large bowl, adding any bran left in the strainer. Stir in the sugar.

Mash the bananas and place in a pitcher, then add enough milk to make up the purée to a heaping ¾ cup. Place the eggs in a large pitcher or bowl and beat lightly, then beat in the banana and milk mixture, oil, soaked raisins, and orange rind. Make a well in the center of the dry ingredients and pour in the beaten liquid ingredients. Stir gently until just combined; do not overmix. Spoon the batter into the paper liners.

Bake in the preheated oven for 20 minutes, or until well risen, golden brown, and firm to the touch. Let cool in the pan for 5 minutes, then serve warm or transfer to a wire rack to cool completely.

712 *With banana topping*

Mash 1 ripe banana with ½ teaspoon of lemon juice. Beat ⅔ cup cream cheese with 2 tablespoons of confectioners' sugar and mix in the banana, then spread over the muffins.

713 *Yogurt & spice muffins*

Makes 12

1 cup whole wheat flour
1 cup all-purpose flour
1 tbsp baking powder
½ tsp baking soda
4 tsp apple pie spice
heaping ½ cup superfine sugar
½ cup mixed dried fruit
2 eggs
heaping 1 cup low-fat plain yogurt
6 tbsp sunflower oil

Preheat the oven to 400°F/200°C. Line a 12-hole muffin pan with 12 paper liners. Sift together both types of flour, the baking powder, baking soda, and apple pie spice into a large bowl, adding any bran left in the strainer. Stir in the sugar and dried fruit.

Place the eggs in a large pitcher or bowl and beat lightly, then beat in the yogurt and oil. Make a well in the center of the dry ingredients and pour in the beaten liquid ingredients. Stir gently until just combined; do not overmix. Spoon the batter into the paper liners.

Bake in the preheated oven for 20 minutes, or until well risen, golden brown, and firm to the touch. Let cool in the pan for 5 minutes, then serve warm or transfer to a wire rack to cool completely.

714 *Vanilla & spice muffins*

Omit the dried fruit and use vanilla yogurt and the seeds from a vanilla bean.

715 Three grain muffins

MAKES 12

6 tbsp sunflower oil, plus extra for greasing
½ cup whole wheat flour
½ cup all-purpose flour
1 tbsp baking powder
heaping ½ cup dark brown sugar
scant ½ cup medium cornmeal
scant 1 cup rolled oats
2 eggs
generous 1 cup buttermilk
1 tsp vanilla extract

Preheat the oven to 400°F/200°C. Grease a 12-hole muffin pan. Sift together the flours and the baking powder into a large bowl, adding any bran left in the strainer. Stir in the sugar, cornmeal, and oats.

Place the eggs in a large pitcher or bowl and beat lightly, then beat in the buttermilk, oil, and vanilla extract. Make a well in the center of the dry ingredients and pour in the beaten liquid ingredients. Stir gently until just combined; do not overmix. Spoon the batter into the muffin pan.

Bake in the preheated oven for 20 minutes, or until well risen, golden brown, and firm to the touch. Let cool in the pan for 5 minutes, then serve warm or transfer to a wire rack to cool completely.

716 With goat cheese topping

Chop 3 tablespoons of soft herbs, such as chervil, dill, chive, and parsley, and stir into 7 oz/200 g soft goat cheese. Spread over the muffins to serve.

717 Corn muffins

MAKES 12

6 tbsp sunflower oil or 6 tbsp butter, melted and cooled, plus extra for greasing
1¼ cups all-purpose flour
1 tbsp baking powder
pinch of salt
freshly ground black pepper
heaping 1 cup medium cornmeal
2 eggs
generous 1 cup milk
1 cup frozen corn kernels

Preheat the oven to 400°F/200°C. Grease a 12-hole muffin pan. Sift together the flour, baking powder, salt, and pepper to taste into a large bowl. Stir in the cornmeal.

Place the eggs in a large pitcher or bowl and beat lightly, then beat in the milk and oil. Make a well in the center of the dry ingredients, pour in the beaten liquid ingredients, and add the corn. Stir gently until just combined; do not overmix. Spoon the batter into the muffin pan.

Bake in the preheated oven for 20 minutes, or until well risen, golden brown, and firm to the touch. Let cool in the pan for 5 minutes, then serve warm or transfer to a wire rack to cool completely.

718 Oat & cranberry muffins

Makes 12

6 tbsp sunflower oil, plus extra for greasing
1 cup all-purpose flour
1 tbsp baking powder
heaping ½ cup dark brown sugar
1⅔ cups rolled oats
¾ cup dried cranberries
2 eggs
generous 1 cup buttermilk
1 tsp vanilla extract

Preheat the oven to 400°F/200°C. Grease a 12-hole muffin pan. Sift together the flour and baking powder into a large bowl. Stir in the sugar, oats, and cranberries.

Place the eggs in a large pitcher or bowl and beat lightly, then beat in the buttermilk, oil, and vanilla extract. Make a well in the center of the dry ingredients and pour in the beaten liquid ingredients. Stir gently until just combined; do not overmix. Spoon the batter into the muffin pan.

Bake in the preheated oven for 20 minutes, or until well risen, golden brown, and firm to the touch. Let cool in the pan for 5 minutes, then serve warm or transfer to a wire rack to cool completely.

719 Fresh cranberry oat-topped muffins

Omit the dried cranberries and replace with 1⅓ cups fresh cranberries. Scatter 3 tablespoons of rolled oats over the muffins before baking.

720 Raisin bran muffins

Makes 12

6 tbsp sunflower oil, plus extra for greasing
1 cup all-purpose flour
1 tbsp baking powder
scant 3 cups wheat bran
heaping ½ cup superfine sugar
1 cup raisins
2 eggs
generous 1 cup skim milk
1 tsp vanilla extract

Preheat the oven to 400°F/200°C. Grease a 12-hole muffin pan. Sift together the flour and baking powder into a large bowl. Stir in the bran, sugar, and raisins.

Place the eggs in a large pitcher or bowl and beat lightly, then beat in the milk, oil, and vanilla extract. Make a well in the center of the dry ingredients and pour in the beaten liquid ingredients. Stir gently until just combined; do not overmix. Spoon the batter into the muffin pan.

Bake in the preheated oven for 20 minutes, or until well risen, golden brown, and firm to the touch. Let cool in the pan for 5 minutes, then serve warm or transfer to a wire rack to cool completely.

721 Golden raisin bran muffins

Omit the raisins and replace with 2 tablespoons of chopped golden raisins.

722 *Healthy oat & prune muffins*

MAKES 12

1 cup all-purpose flour
1 tbsp baking powder
heaping ½ cup light brown sugar
1⅔ cups rolled oats
¾ cup pitted prunes, chopped
2 eggs
generous 1 cup buttermilk
6 tbsp sunflower oil
1 tsp vanilla extract

Preheat the oven to 400°F/200°C. Line a 12-hole muffin pan with 12 paper liners. Sift together the flour and baking powder into a large bowl. Stir in the sugar, oats, and prunes.

Place the eggs in a large pitcher or bowl and beat lightly, then beat in the buttermilk, oil, and vanilla extract. Make a well in the center of the dry ingredients and pour in the beaten liquid ingredients. Stir gently until just combined; do not overmix. Spoon the batter into the paper liners.

Bake in the preheated oven for 20 minutes, or until well risen, golden brown, and firm to the touch. Let cool in the pan for 5 minutes, then serve warm or transfer to a wire rack to cool completely.

723 *Apricot & sunflower seed muffins*

Omit the prunes and replace with ¾ cup chopped soft dried apricots and scatter over 3 tablespoons of sunflower seeds before baking the muffins.

724 *Granola muffins*

MAKES 12

6 tbsp sunflower oil, plus extra for greasing
¼ cup whole wheat flour
1 cup all-purpose flour
1 tbsp baking powder
scant ½ cup light brown sugar
2 eggs
generous 1 cup skim milk

GRANOLA
scant 1 cup rolled oats
scant ¼ cup blanched almonds, chopped
scant 2 tbsp sunflower seeds
scant ¼ cup raisins
2 tbsp light brown sugar

To make the granola, place the oats in a large, dry skillet and toast over low heat for 1 minute. Add the almonds, sunflower seeds, and raisins and toast for 6–8 minutes, or until browned. Add the sugar and stir for 1 minute until it melts. Remove from the heat and stir until mixed.

Preheat the oven to 400°F/200°C. Grease a 12-hole muffin pan. Sift together both flours and the baking powder into a large bowl, adding any bran left in the strainer. Stir in the sugar and granola.

Place the eggs in a large pitcher or bowl and beat lightly, then beat in the milk and oil. Make a well in the center of the dry ingredients and pour in the beaten liquid ingredients. Stir gently until just combined; do not overmix. Spoon the batter into the muffin pan.

Bake in the preheated oven for 20 minutes, or until well risen, golden brown, and firm to the touch. Let cool in the pan for 5 minutes, then serve warm or transfer to a wire rack to cool completely.

725 *Apricot & pecan muffins*

Omit the raisins from the granola, add ⅓ cup chopped dried apricots, and replace the almonds with scant ¼ cup chopped pecans.

726 *Malted chocolate muffins*

Makes 12

6 tbsp sunflower oil or 6 tbsp butter, melted and cooled, plus extra for greasing
5½ oz/150 g malted chocolate balls
1⅔ cups all-purpose flour
½ cup unsweetened cocoa
1 tbsp baking powder
pinch of salt
heaping ½ cup light brown sugar
2 eggs
generous 1 cup buttermilk

FROSTING
2 oz/55 g semisweet chocolate, broken into pieces
8 tbsp butter, softened
2 cups confectioners' sugar

Preheat the oven to 400°F/200°C. Grease a 12-hole muffin pan. Coarsely crush the chocolate balls, reserving 12 whole ones for decorating. Sift together the flour, cocoa, baking powder, and salt into a large bowl. Stir in the brown sugar and the crushed chocolate balls.

Place the eggs in a large pitcher or bowl and beat lightly, then beat in the buttermilk and oil. Make a well in the center of the dry ingredients and pour in the beaten liquid ingredients. Stir gently until just combined; do not overmix. Spoon the batter into the muffin pan.

Bake in the preheated oven for 20 minutes, or until well risen and firm to the touch. Let cool in the pan for 5 minutes, then transfer to a wire rack to cool completely.

To make the frosting, place the chocolate in a heatproof bowl, set the bowl over a saucepan of gently simmering water, and heat until melted. Remove from the heat. Place the butter in a large bowl and beat until fluffy. Sift in the confectioners' sugar and beat together until smooth and creamy. Add the melted chocolate and beat together. Spread the frosting on top of the muffins and decorate each with one of the reserved chocolate balls.

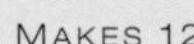

727 *Glazed honey muffins*

Makes 12

6 tbsp sunflower oil, plus extra for greasing
1 cup whole wheat flour
1 cup all-purpose flour
1 tbsp baking powder
½ tsp baking soda
½ tsp pumpkin pie spice
¼ cup light brown sugar
heaping ½ cup golden raisins
2 eggs
heaping ¾ cup low-fat plain yogurt
8 tbsp honey

Preheat the oven to 400°F/200°C. Grease a 12-hole muffin pan. Sift together both flours, the baking powder, baking soda, and pumpkin pie spice into a large bowl, adding any bran left in the strainer. Stir in the sugar and golden raisins.

Place the eggs in a large pitcher or bowl and beat lightly, then beat in the yogurt, oil, and 4 tablespoons of the honey. Make a well in the center of the dry ingredients and pour in the beaten liquid ingredients. Stir until combined; do not overmix. Spoon the batter into the muffin pan.

Bake in the preheated oven for 20 minutes, or until well risen, golden brown, and firm to the touch. Let cool in the pan for 5 minutes, then drizzle 1 teaspoon of the remaining honey on top of each muffin. Serve warm or transfer to a wire rack to cool completely.

728 *With honey ricotta topping*

Beat ⅔ cup ricotta with 2 tablespoons of honey and use to top the muffins.

729 Carrot cake muffins

MAKES 12

6 tbsp sunflower oil, plus extra for greasing
2 cups all-purpose flour
1 tbsp baking powder
1 tsp pumpkin pie spice
pinch of salt
heaping ½ cup dark brown sugar
heaping 1 cup grated carrot
⅓ cup walnuts or pecans, coarsely chopped
⅓ cup golden raisins
2 eggs
¾ cup milk
finely grated rind and juice of 1 orange
strips of orange zest, for decorating

FROSTING
⅓ cup soft cream cheese
3 tbsp butter
⅓ cup confectioners' sugar

Preheat the oven to 400°F/200°C. Grease a 12-hole muffin pan. Sift together the flour, baking powder, pumpkin pie spice, and salt into a large bowl. Stir in the brown sugar, carrot, walnuts, and golden raisins.

Place the eggs in a large pitcher or bowl and beat lightly, then beat in the milk, oil, orange rind, and orange juice. Make a well in the center of the dry ingredients and pour in the beaten liquid ingredients. Stir gently until just combined; do not overmix. Spoon the batter into the muffin pan.

Bake in the preheated oven for 20 minutes, or until well risen, golden brown, and firm to the touch. Let cool in the pan for 5 minutes, then transfer to a wire rack to cool completely.

To make the frosting, place the cream cheese and butter in a bowl and sift in the confectioners' sugar. Beat together until light and fluffy. When the muffins are cold, spread the frosting on top of each, then decorate with strips of orange zest. Chill the muffins in the refrigerator until ready to serve.

730 With carrot decoration

Cut 6 plumped dried apricots in half and roll lengthwise to form a carrot shape, place on each muffin and add green "stalks" with pieces of angelica.

731 Gooey butterscotch cream muffins

MAKES 12

5½ oz/150 g hard butterscotch candies
2 cups all-purpose flour
1 tbsp baking powder
pinch of salt
heaping ½ cup dark brown sugar
2 eggs
generous 1 cup heavy cream
6 tbsp sunflower oil or 6 tbsp butter, melted and cooled

Preheat the oven to 400°F/200°C. Line a 12-hole muffin pan with 12 paper liners. Place the butterscotch candies in a strong plastic bag and hit with a meat mallet or the end of a wooden rolling pin until finely crushed.

Sift together the flour, baking powder, and salt into a large bowl. Stir in the sugar and crushed candies.

Place the eggs in a large pitcher or bowl and beat lightly, then beat in the cream and oil. Make a well in the center of the dry ingredients and pour in the beaten liquid ingredients. Stir gently until just combined; do not overmix. Spoon the batter into the paper liners.

Bake in the preheated oven for 20 minutes, or until well risen, golden brown, and firm to the touch. Let cool in the pan for 5 minutes, then serve warm or transfer to a wire rack to cool completely.

732 With butterscotch topping

Whip ¾ cup heavy cream with ½ teaspoon of vanilla extract, spread over the muffins, and scatter over 3 oz/85 g crushed butterscotch candies.

733 Crunchy peanut butter muffins

MAKES 12

2 cups all-purpose flour
1 tbsp baking powder
pinch of salt
heaping ½ cup dark brown sugar
2 eggs
¾ cup milk
6 tbsp sunflower oil or 6 tbsp butter, melted and cooled
¾ cup crunchy peanut butter

PEANUT TOPPING
⅓ cup unsalted roasted peanuts
scant ¼ cup raw brown sugar

Preheat the oven to 400°F/200°C. Line a 12-hole muffin pan with 12 paper liners. To make the peanut topping, finely chop the peanuts, place in a bowl, add the raw brown sugar, mix together, and set aside.

Sift together the flour, baking powder, and salt into a large bowl. Stir in the brown sugar.

Place the eggs in a large pitcher or bowl and beat lightly, then beat in the milk, oil, and peanut butter. Make a well in the center of the dry ingredients and pour in the beaten liquid ingredients. Stir gently until just combined; do not overmix. Spoon the batter into the paper liners. Sprinkle the peanut topping over the muffins.

Bake in the preheated oven for 20 minutes, or until well risen, golden brown, and firm to the touch. Let cool in the pan for 5 minutes, then serve warm or transfer to a wire rack to cool completely.

734 With peanut frosting

Omit the peanut topping and bake the muffins as before. Beat 1 tablespoon of crunchy peanut butter with scant ½ cup cream cheese and 1 cup confectioners' sugar, then spread over the cooled muffins and sprinkle over ⅔ cup chopped peanuts.

735 Double chocolate muffins

MAKES 12

7 tbsp butter, softened
scant ⅔ cup superfine sugar
½ cup dark brown sugar
2 eggs
⅔ cup sour cream
5 tbsp milk
heaping 1¾ cups all-purpose flour
1 tsp baking soda
2 tbsp unsweetened cocoa
heapng 1 cup semisweet chocolate chips

Preheat the oven to 375°F/190°C. Line a 12-hole muffin pan with 12 paper liners. Place the butter and both sugars into a large bowl and beat well. Beat in the eggs, sour cream, and milk until mixed.

Sift the flour, baking soda, and cocoa into a separate bowl and stir into the mixture. Add the chocolate chips and mix well. Spoon the batter into the paper liners.

Bake in the preheated oven for 25–30 minutes. Let cool in the pan for 10 minutes, then transfer to a wire rack to cool completely.

736 Hazelnut & coffee muffins

MAKES 12

6 tbsp sunflower oil or 6 tbsp butter, melted and cooled, plus extra for greasing
2 tbsp instant coffee granules
2 tbsp boiling water
1 cup hazelnuts
2 cups all-purpose flour
1 tbsp baking powder
pinch of salt
heaping ½ cup light brown sugar
2 eggs
generous ¾ cup buttermilk

Preheat the oven to 400°F/200°C. Grease a 12-hole muffin pan. Put the coffee granules and boiling water in a cup and stir until dissolved. Let cool.

Meanwhile, finely chop ⅔ cup of the hazelnuts and coarsely chop the remaining hazelnuts. Sift together the flour, baking powder, and salt into a large bowl. Stir in the sugar and finely chopped hazelnuts.

Place the eggs in a large pitcher or bowl and beat lightly, then beat in the buttermilk, oil, and dissolved coffee. Make a well in the center of the dry ingredients and pour in the beaten liquid ingredients. Stir gently until just combined; do not overmix. Spoon the batter into the muffin pan. Scatter the reserved chopped hazelnuts over the tops of the muffins.

Bake in the preheated oven for 20 minutes, or until well risen, golden brown, and firm to the touch. Let cool in the pan for 5 minutes, then serve warm or transfer to a wire rack to cool completely.

737 With hazelnut cream topping

Whip heaping ¾ cup heavy cream until thick. Stir in 1 tablespoon of hazelnut liqueur, whip again until stiff, then spoon over the cooled muffins.

738 Chocolate chip muffins

MAKES 12

6 tbsp butter, plus extra for greasing
1 cup superfine sugar
2 large eggs
⅔ cup plain yogurt
5 tbsp milk
2 cups all-purpose flour
1 tsp baking soda
1 cup semisweet chocolate chips

Preheat the oven to 400°F/200°C. Grease a 12-hole muffin pan. Place the butter and sugar in a large bowl and beat together until light and fluffy, then beat in the eggs, yogurt, and milk until thoroughly combined.

Sift the flour and baking soda into the mixture and stir until just blended. Stir in the chocolate chips, then spoon the batter into the muffin pan.

Bake in the preheated oven for 25 minutes, or until a fine skewer inserted into the center of one of the muffins comes out clean. Let cool in the pan for 5 minutes, then transfer to a wire rack to cool completely.

739 White chocolate & raspberry muffins

Replace the semisweet chocolate chips with 4½ oz/125 g white chocolate chips and add heaping ½ cup fresh raspberries.

740 Pecan brownie muffins

MAKES 12

¾ cup pecans
¾ cup all-purpose flour
scant 1 cup superfine sugar
¼ tsp salt
1 tbsp baking powder
1 cup butter
4 oz/115 g semisweet chocolate
4 eggs, lightly beaten
1 tsp vanilla extract

Preheat the oven to 400°F/200°C. Line a 12-hole muffin pan with 12 paper liners. Set aside 12 pecan halves and coarsely chop the rest.

Sift the flour, sugar, salt, and baking powder into a large bowl and make a well in the center. Melt the butter and chocolate in a small saucepan over very low heat, stirring frequently. Add to the flour mixture and stir to mix evenly.

Add the eggs and vanilla extract and mix together just until the ingredients are evenly moistened. Stir in the chopped pecans. Spoon the batter into the paper liners and add a pecan half on top of each.

Bake in the preheated oven for 20–25 minutes, or until well risen and firm to the touch. Let cool in the pan for 5 minutes, then serve warm or transfer to a wire rack to cool completely.

741 With vanilla pecan topping

Omit the pecans from the top of each muffin and set aside. Beat ⅔ cup butter with the seeds from a vanilla bean, add ½ cup brown sugar, and beat until smooth, then spread over the muffins and top each with the pecans.

742 Jam doughnut muffins

MAKES 12

6 tbsp sunflower oil or 6 tbsp butter, melted and cooled, plus extra for greasing
2 cups all-purpose flour
1 tbsp baking powder
pinch of salt
heaping ½ cup superfine sugar
2 eggs
generous ¾ cup milk
1 tsp vanilla extract
4 tbsp strawberry jam or raspberry jam

TOPPING
¾ cup granulated sugar
8 tbsp butter, melted

Preheat the oven to 400°F/200°C. Grease a 12-hole muffin pan. Sift together the flour, baking powder, and salt into a large bowl. Stir in the superfine sugar.

Place the eggs in a large pitcher or bowl and beat lightly, then beat in the milk, oil, and vanilla extract. Make a well in the center of the dry ingredients and pour in the beaten liquid ingredients. Stir gently until just combined; do not overmix.

Spoon half of the batter into the muffin pan. Add a teaspoon of jam to the center of each, then spoon in the remaining batter. Bake in the preheated oven for 20 minutes, or until they are well risen, golden brown, and firm to the touch.

Leave the muffins in the pan to cool for 5 minutes.

To make the topping, spread the sugar in a wide, shallow bowl, then dip the tops of the muffins in the melted butter and roll in the sugar. Serve warm or transfer to a wire rack to cool.

743 Vanilla cream doughnut muffins

Omit the jam and replace with 4–5 tablespoons of ready-made vanilla pudding.

744 Triple chocolate chip muffins

MAKES 12

6 tbsp sunflower oil or 6 tbsp butter, melted and cooled, plus extra for greasing
2 cups all-purpose flour
1 tbsp baking powder
pinch of salt
heaping ½ cup light brown sugar
heaping ¼ cup semisweet chocolate chips
heaping ¼ cup milk chocolate chips
heaping ¼ cup white chocolate chips
2 eggs
heaping 1 cup sour cream
1 tsp vanilla extract

Preheat the oven to 400°F/200°C. Grease a 12-hole muffin pan. Sift together the flour, baking powder, and salt into a large bowl. Stir in the sugar and chocolate chips.

Place the eggs in a large pitcher or bowl and beat lightly, then beat in the sour cream, oil, and vanilla extract. Make a well in the center of the dry ingredients and pour in the beaten liquid ingredients. Stir until combined; do not overmix. Spoon the batter into the muffin pan.

Bake in the preheated oven for 20 minutes, or until well risen, golden brown, and firm to the touch. Let cool in the pan for 5 minutes, then serve warm or transfer to a wire rack to cool completely.

745 Marzipan muffins

MAKES 12

6 oz/175 g marzipan
2 cups all-purpose flour
1 tbsp baking powder
pinch of salt
heaping ½ cup superfine sugar
2 eggs
generous ¾ cup milk
6 tbsp sunflower oil or 6 tbsp butter, melted and cooled
1 tsp almond extract
12 whole blanched almonds

Preheat the oven to 400°F/200°C. Line a 12-hole muffin pan with 12 paper liners. Cut the marzipan into 12 equal pieces.

Roll each piece into a ball, and then flatten with the palm of your hand, making sure that they are no larger than the paper liners.

Sift together the flour, baking powder, and salt into a large bowl. Stir in the sugar. Place the eggs in a large pitcher or bowl and beat lightly, then beat in the milk, oil, and almond extract.

Make a well in the center of the dry ingredients and pour in the beaten liquid ingredients. Stir gently until just combined; do not overmix. Spoon half of the batter into the paper liners.

Place a piece of marzipan in the center of each, then spoon in the remaining batter. Top each muffin with a whole blanched almond. Bake in the preheated oven for 20 minutes, or until well risen, golden brown, and firm to the touch. Let cool in the pan for 5 minutes, then serve warm or transfer to a wire rack to cool completely.

746 Strawberry & amaretto muffins

Add 1 tablespoon of amaretto liqueur and 12 hulled chopped strawberries to the muffin batter and bake as before.

747 Maple pecan muffins

MAKES 12

2 cups all-purpose flour
1 tbsp baking powder
pinch of salt
heaping ½ cup superfine sugar
⅔ cup pecans, coarsely chopped
2 eggs
¾ cup buttermilk
generous ¼ cup maple syrup, plus extra for glazing
6 tbsp sunflower oil or 6 tbsp butter, melted and cooled
12 pecan halves

Preheat the oven to 400°F/200°C. Line a 12-hole muffin pan with 12 paper liners. Sift together the flour, baking powder, and salt into a large bowl. Stir in the sugar and pecans.

Place the eggs in a large pitcher or bowl and beat lightly, then beat in the buttermilk, maple syrup, and oil. Make a well in the center of the dry ingredients and pour in the beaten liquid ingredients. Stir gently until just combined; do not overmix. Spoon the batter into the paper liners and top each muffin with a pecan half.

Bake in the preheated oven for 20 minutes, or until well risen, golden brown, and firm to the touch. Let cool in the pan for 5 minutes, then brush the tops with the maple syrup to glaze. Serve warm or transfer to a wire rack to cool completely.

748 With maple crunch topping

Omit the pecans from the top. Chop 1 cup pecans and mix with 3 tablespoons of brown sugar and 2 tablespoons of maple syrup, then spoon over the muffins before baking.

749 Lemon cornmeal muffins

MAKES 12

6 tbsp sunflower oil, plus extra for greasing
4 lemons
about 3 tbsp low-fat plain yogurt
1¼ cups all-purpose flour
1 tbsp baking powder
½ tsp baking soda
heaping 1¾ cups medium cornmeal
heaping ½ cup superfine sugar
2 eggs

Preheat the oven to 400°F/200°C. Grease a 12-hole muffin pan. Finely grate the rind from the lemons and squeeze the juice. Add enough yogurt to make the juice up to a heaping 1 cup, then stir in the lemon rind.

Sift the flour, baking powder, and baking soda into a large bowl. Stir in the cornmeal and sugar. Place the eggs in a large pitcher or bowl and beat lightly, then beat in the oil. Make a well in the center of the dry ingredients and pour in the beaten liquid ingredients with the lemon and yogurt mixture. Stir gently until just combined; do not overmix. Spoon the batter into the muffin pan.

Bake in the preheated oven for 20 minutes, or until well risen, golden brown, and firm to the touch. Let cool in the pan for 5 minutes, then serve warm or transfer to a wire rack to cool completely.

750 With Limoncello frosting

Beat ⅔ cup mascarpone cheese, scant ½ cup confectioners' sugar, and 1 tablespoon of Limoncello liqueur together and spread over the cooled muffins. Scatter over chopped candied lemon peel.

751 Mini orange & cardamom muffins

MAKES 48

2 oranges
about 1⅓ cup milk
2 cups all-purpose flour
1 tbsp baking powder
pinch of salt
heaping ½ cup superfine sugar
6 cardamom pods, seeds removed and crushed
2 eggs
6 tbsp sunflower oil or 6 tbsp butter, melted and cooled

Preheat the oven to 400°F/200°C. Line two 24-hole mini muffin pans with 48 mini paper liners. Finely grate the rind from the oranges and squeeze the juice. Add enough milk to make the juice up to a generous 1 cup, then stir in the orange rind.

Sift together the flour, baking powder, and salt into a large bowl. Stir in the sugar and crushed cardamom seeds. Place the eggs in a pitcher and beat lightly, then beat in the orange and milk mixture and the oil. Make a well in the center of the dry ingredients and pour in the beaten liquid ingredients. Stir gently until just combined; do not overmix. Spoon the batter into the paper liners. Bake in the preheated oven for 15 minutes, or until well risen, golden brown, and firm to the touch. Let cool in the pans for 5 minutes, then serve warm or transfer to a wire rack to cool completely.

752 With white chocolate icing

Place 5½ oz/150 g white chocolate in a heatproof bowl, set the bowl over a saucepan of simmering water, and heat until melted. Stir in ½ teaspoon of orange flower water and drizzle over the muffins.

753 Mint chocolate chip muffins

MAKES 12

2 cups all-purpose flour
1 tbsp baking powder
pinch of salt
heaping ½ cup superfine sugar
scant 1 cup semisweet chocolate chips
2 eggs
generous 1 cup milk
6 tbsp sunflower oil or 6 tbsp butter, melted and cooled
1 tsp peppermint extract
1–2 drops of green food coloring (optional)
confectioners' sugar, for dusting

Preheat the oven to 400°F/200°C. Line a 12-hole muffin pan with 12 paper liners.

Sift together the flour, baking powder, and salt into a large bowl, then stir in the superfine sugar and chocolate chips. Place the eggs in a large pitcher or bowl and beat lightly, then beat in the milk, oil, and peppermint extract. Add 1–2 drops of food coloring, if using.

Make a well in the center of the dry ingredients and pour in the beaten liquid ingredients. Stir gently until just combined; do not overmix. Spoon the batter into the paper liners.

Bake in the preheated oven for 20 minutes, or until well risen and firm to the touch. Let cool in the pan for 5 minutes, then serve warm or transfer to a wire rack to cool completely. Dust with a little sifted confectioners' sugar before serving.

754 With chocolate ganache

Heat ¾ cup heavy cream in a saucepan until simmering, then pour over 6 oz/175 g chopped semisweet chocolate and stir until smooth. Cool and chill until thick, then spread over the muffins.

755 Moist gingerbread muffins

MAKES 12

6 tbsp sunflower oil or 6 tbsp butter, melted and cooled, plus extra for greasing
2 cups all-purpose flour
1 tbsp baking powder
4 tsp ground ginger
1½ tsp ground cinnamon
pinch of salt
heaping ½ cup light brown sugar
3 pieces preserved ginger in syrup, finely chopped
2 eggs
¾ cup milk
4 tbsp dark corn syrup

Preheat the oven to 400°F/200°C. Grease a 12-hole muffin pan. Sift together the flour, baking powder, ginger, cinnamon, and salt into a large bowl. Stir in the sugar and preserved ginger.

Place the eggs in a large pitcher or bowl and beat lightly, then beat in the milk, oil, and corn syrup. Make a well in the center of the dry ingredients and pour in the beaten liquid ingredients. Stir gently until just combined; do not overmix. Spoon the batter into the muffin pan.

Bake in the preheated oven for 20 minutes, or until well risen, golden brown, and firm to the touch. Let cool in the pan for 5 minutes, then serve warm or transfer to a wire rack to cool completely.

756 With lemon icing

Sift 1⅓ cups confectioners' sugar into a bowl, add 1 tablespoon of lemon juice, and mix until smooth, then spread over the muffins and let set.

757 Moist orange & almond muffins

MAKES 12

2 oranges
about ⅓ cup milk
1⅔ cups all-purpose flour
1 tbsp baking powder
pinch of salt
heaping ½ cup superfine sugar
⅔ cup ground almonds
2 eggs
6 tbsp sunflower oil or 6 tbsp butter, melted and cooled
½ tsp almond extract
scant ¼ cup raw brown sugar

Preheat the oven to 400°F/200°C. Line a 12-hole muffin pan with 12 paper liners. Finely grate the rind from the oranges and squeeze the juice. Add enough milk to make the juice up to a generous 1 cup, then stir in the orange rind. Sift together the flour, baking powder, and salt into a large bowl. Stir in the superfine sugar and ground almonds.

Place the eggs in a bowl and beat lightly, then beat in the orange mixture, oil, and almond extract. Make a well in the center of the dry ingredients, pour in the liquid ingredients, and mix. Spoon the batter into the paper liners. Sprinkle the raw brown sugar over the tops.

Bake in the preheated oven for 20 minutes, or until well risen, golden brown, and firm to the touch. Let cool in the pan for 5 minutes, then serve warm or transfer to a wire rack to cool completely.

758 With slivered almond topping

Scatter 1 cup slivered almonds over the muffins before they are baked.

759 Orange, walnut & rosemary muffins

MAKES 12

2 cups all-purpose flour
1 tbsp baking powder
½ tsp baking soda
pinch of salt
heaping ½ cup superfine sugar
½ cup walnuts, coarsely chopped
2 eggs
heaping 1 cup plain yogurt
6 tbsp sunflower oil or 6 tbsp butter, melted and cooled
finely grated rind of 2 oranges
1 tbsp finely chopped fresh rosemary leaves, plus extra sprigs for decorating

ICING
1½ cups confectioners' sugar
3–4 tsp fresh orange juice
finely grated rind of ½ orange

Preheat the oven to 400°F/200°C. Line a 12-hole muffin pan with 12 paper liners. Sift together the flour, baking powder, baking soda, and salt into a large bowl. Stir in the superfine sugar and walnuts.

Place the eggs in a large pitcher or bowl then beat in the yogurt, oil, orange rind, and chopped rosemary leaves. Make a well in the center of the dry ingredients and pour in the beaten liquid ingredients. Stir gently until just combined; do not overmix. Spoon the batter into the paper liners.

Bake in the preheated oven for 20 minutes, or until well risen, golden brown, and firm to the touch. Let cool in the pan for 5 minutes, then transfer to a wire rack to cool completely.

When the muffins are cold, make the icing. Sift the confectioners' sugar into a bowl. Add the orange juice and orange rind and stir until the mixture is smooth and thick enough to coat the back of a wooden spoon.

Spoon the icing on top of each muffin. Decorate with a rosemary sprig and let set for about 30 minutes before serving.

760 Marbled chocolate muffins

MAKES 12

6 tbsp sunflower oil or 6 tbsp butter, melted and cooled, plus extra for greasing
2 cups all-purpose flour
1 tbsp baking powder
pinch of salt
heaping ½ cup superfine sugar
2 eggs
generous 1 cup milk
1 tsp vanilla extract
2 tbsp unsweetened cocoa

Preheat the oven to 400°F/200°C. Grease a 12-hole muffin pan. Sift together the flour, baking powder, and salt into a large bowl. Stir in the sugar.

Place the eggs in a large pitcher or bowl and beat lightly, then beat in the milk, oil, and vanilla extract. Make a well in the center of the dry ingredients and pour in the beaten liquid ingredients. Stir gently until just combined; do not overmix.

Divide the batter between 2 bowls. Sift the cocoa into one bowl and mix together. Using teaspoons, spoon the batters into the muffin pan, alternating the chocolate batter and the plain batter.

Bake in the preheated oven for 20 minutes, or until well risen, golden brown, and firm to the touch. Let cool in the pan for 5 minutes, then serve warm or transfer to a wire rack to cool completely.

761 Marbled coffee muffins

Replace the cocoa with espresso coffee powder.

762 Raspberry crumble muffins

Makes 12

6 tbsp sunflower oil or 6 tbsp butter, melted and cooled, plus extra for greasing
2 cups all-purpose flour
1 tbsp baking powder
½ tsp baking soda
pinch of salt
heaping ½ cup superfine sugar
2 eggs
heaping 1 cup plain yogurt
1 tsp vanilla extract
1 cup frozen raspberries

CRUMBLE TOPPING
⅓ cup all-purpose flour
2½ tbsp butter, cut into pieces
2 tbsp superfine sugar

Preheat the oven to 400°F/200°C. Grease a 12-hole muffin pan.

To make the crumble topping, place the flour into a bowl. Add the butter and rub it in with your fingertips until the mixture resembles fine breadcrumbs. Stir in the sugar and set aside.

To make the muffins, sift together the flour, baking powder, baking soda, and salt into a large bowl. Stir in the sugar. Place the eggs in a large pitcher or bowl and beat lightly, then beat in the yogurt, oil, and vanilla extract. Make a well in the center of the dry ingredients, pour in the beaten liquid ingredients, and add the raspberries.

Stir gently until just combined; do not overmix. Spoon the batter into the muffin pan. Scatter the crumble topping over each muffin and then press down lightly.

Bake in the preheated oven for 20 minutes, or until well risen, golden brown, and firm to the touch. Let cool in the pan for 5 minutes, then serve warm or transfer to a wire rack to cool completely.

763 With almond crunch topping

Add ⅓ cup chopped toasted slivered almonds and 6 crushed amaretti cookies to the crumble topping before scattering over the muffins.

764 Sour cream & pineapple muffins

Makes 12

6 tbsp sunflower oil or 6 tbsp butter, melted and cooled, plus extra for greasing
2 slices canned pineapple slices in natural juice, plus 2 tbsp juice from the can
2 cups all-purpose flour
1 tbsp baking powder
pinch of salt
heaping ½ cup superfine sugar
2 eggs
heaping ¾ cup sour cream
1 tsp vanilla extract

Preheat the oven to 400°F/200°C. Grease a 12-hole muffin pan. Drain and finely chop the pineapple slices.

Sift together the flour, baking powder, and salt into a large bowl. Stir in the sugar and chopped pineapple.

Place the eggs in a large pitcher or bowl and beat lightly, then beat in the sour cream, oil, pineapple juice, and vanilla extract. Make a well in the center of the dry ingredients and pour in the beaten liquid ingredients. Stir gently until just combined; do not overmix. Spoon the batter into the muffin pan.

Bake in the preheated oven for 20 minutes, or until well risen, golden brown, and firm to the touch. Let cool in the pan for 5 minutes, then serve warm or transfer to a wire rack to cool completely.

765 With pineapple frosting

Beat scant ½ cup cream cheese with 2 tablespoons of confectioners' sugar and 1 tablespoon of pineapple juice, then spread over the cooled muffins.

766 Spicy apple & oat muffins

Makes 12

6 tbsp sunflower oil, plus extra for greasing
1 cup all-purpose flour
1 tbsp baking powder
1 tsp apple pie spice
heaping ½ cup light brown sugar
2 cups rolled oats
1 large apple
2 eggs
½ cup skim milk
½ cup fresh apple juice

Preheat the oven to 400°F/200°C. Grease a 12-hole muffin pan. Sift together the flour, baking powder, and apple pie spice into a large bowl. Stir in the sugar and 1⅔ cups of the oats.

Finely chop the unpeeled apple, discarding the core. Add to the flour mixture and stir together.

Place the eggs in a large pitcher or bowl and beat lightly, then beat in the milk, apple juice, and oil. Make a well in the center of the dry ingredients and pour in the beaten liquid ingredients. Stir gently until just combined; do not overmix. Spoon the batter into the muffin pan and sprinkle the tops with the remaining oats.

Bake in the preheated oven for 20 minutes, or until well risen, golden brown, and firm to the touch. Let cool in the pan for 5 minutes, then serve warm or transfer to a wire rack to cool completely.

767 Pear, oat & nutmeg muffins

Replace the apple and apple juice with 2 medium peeled, cored, and chopped pears and pear juice, and add ½ teaspoon of ground nutmeg.

768 Spicy dried fruit muffins

Makes 12

6 tbsp sunflower oil or 6 tbsp butter, melted and cooled
2 cups all-purpose flour
1 tbsp baking powder
1 tbsp apple pie spice
pinch of salt
heaping ½ cup superfine sugar
heaping 1 cup mixed dried fruit
2 eggs
generous 1 cup milk

Preheat the oven to 400°F/200°C. Line a 12-hole muffin pan with 12 paper liners. Sift together the flour, baking powder, apple pie spice, and salt into a large bowl. Stir in the sugar and dried fruit.

Place the eggs in a large pitcher or bowl and beat lightly, then beat in the milk and oil. Make a well in the center of the dry ingredients and pour in the beaten liquid ingredients. Stir gently until just combined; do not overmix. Spoon the batter into the paper liners.

Bake in the preheated oven for 20 minutes, or until well risen, golden brown, and firm to the touch. Let cool in the pan for 5 minutes, then serve warm or transfer to a wire rack to cool completely.

769 With brandy cream

Whip heaping ¾ cup heavy cream with 1 tablespoon of brandy and 1 tablespoon of superfine sugar until stiff, then spoon onto the cooled muffins.

770 Chocolate muffins

MAKES 12

1⅔ cups all-purpose flour
½ cup unsweetened cocoa
1 tbsp baking powder
pinch of salt
heaping ½ cup light brown sugar
2 eggs
heaping ¾ cup sour cream
6 tbsp sunflower oil or 6 tbsp butter, melted and cooled
3 tbsp dark corn syrup

Preheat the oven to 400°F/200°C. Line a 12-hole muffin pan with 12 paper liners. Sift together the flour, cocoa, baking powder, and salt into a large bowl. Stir in the sugar.

Place the eggs in a large pitcher or bowl and beat lightly, then beat in the sour cream, oil, and dark corn syrup. Make a well in the center of the dry ingredients and pour in the beaten liquid ingredients. Stir gently until just combined; do not overmix. Spoon the batter into the paper liners.

Bake in the preheated oven for 20 minutes, or until well risen and firm to the touch. Let cool in the pan for 5 minutes, then serve warm or transfer to a wire rack to cool completely.

771 With chocolate topping

Spread the cooled muffins with 7 oz/200 g chocolate hazelnut spread.

772 Sticky toffee muffins

MAKES 12

6 tbsp sunflower oil or 6 tbsp butter, melted and cooled, plus extra for greasing
scant 1½ cups pitted dates
generous 1 cup water
2 cups all-purpose flour
1 tbsp baking powder
pinch of salt
heaping ½ cup dark brown sugar
2 eggs
4 tbsp dulce de leche (from a jar), for serving

Preheat the oven to 400°F/200°C. Grease a 12-hole muffin pan. Put the dates and water in a food processor and blend to form a coarse purée. Sift together the flour, baking powder, and salt into a large bowl. Stir in the sugar.

Place the eggs in a large pitcher or bowl and beat lightly, then beat in the date purée and oil. Make a well in the center of the dry ingredients and pour in the beaten liquid ingredients. Stir gently until just combined; do not overmix. Spoon the batter into the muffin pan.

Bake in the preheated oven for 20 minutes, or until golden brown and firm to the touch. Let cool in the pan for 5 minutes, then serve warm or transfer to a wire rack to cool completely. Spread a teaspoon of dulce de leche over the top of each muffin before serving.

773 Toasted almond & apricot muffins

Makes 12

heaping ½ cup dried apricots, cut into small pieces
3 tbsp fresh orange juice
⅓ cup blanched almonds
2 cups all-purpose flour
1 tbsp baking powder
pinch of salt
heaping ½ cup superfine sugar
2 eggs
generous ¾ cup buttermilk
6 tbsp sunflower oil or 6 tbsp butter, melted and cooled
¼ tsp almond extract
scant ½ cup slivered almonds

Place the apricots in a bowl, add the orange juice, and let soak for 1 hour.

Preheat the oven to 400°F/200°C. Line a 12-hole muffin pan with 12 paper liners. Preheat the broiler and line a broiler pan with foil. Spread out the almonds on the broiler pan and toast until golden, turning frequently. Cool then chop coarsely.

Sift together the flour, baking powder, and salt into a large bowl. Stir in the sugar and almonds.

Place the eggs in a large pitcher or bowl and beat lightly, then beat in the buttermilk, oil, and almond extract. Make a well in the center of the dry ingredients, pour in the beaten liquid ingredients, and add the soaked apricots. Stir gently until just combined; do not overmix. Spoon the batter into the paper liners. Scatter the slivered almonds on top of each muffin.

Bake in the preheated oven for 20 minutes, or until well risen, golden brown, and firm to the touch. Let cool in the pan for 5 minutes, then serve warm or transfer to a wire rack to cool completely.

774 With apricot centers

Fill each muffin liner halfway with batter and spoon in a little apricot preserve in the middle, then cover with the remaining batter.

775 Tropical banana & passion fruit muffins

Makes 12

2 bananas
about ⅔ cup milk
2 cups all-purpose flour
1 tbsp baking powder
pinch of salt
heaping ½ cup light brown sugar
2 eggs
6 tbsp sunflower oil or 6 tbsp butter, melted and cooled
1 tsp vanilla extract
2 passion fruits
2 tbsp honey

Preheat the oven to 400°F/200°C. Line a 12-hole muffin pan with 12 paper liners. Mash the bananas and put in a pitcher. Add enough milk to make the purée up to a heaping 1 cup.

Sift together the flour, baking powder, and salt into a large bowl. Stir in the sugar.

Place the eggs in a large pitcher or bowl and beat lightly, then beat in the banana and milk mixture, oil, and vanilla extract. Make a well in the center of the dry ingredients and pour in the beaten liquid ingredients. Stir gently until just combined; do not overmix. Spoon the batter into the paper liners.

Bake in the preheated oven for 20 minutes, or until well risen, golden brown, and firm to the touch. Let cool in the pan for 5 minutes, then transfer to a wire rack to cool completely.

Meanwhile, halve the passion fruits and spoon the pulp into a small saucepan. Add the honey and heat very gently until warmed through. Spoon on top of the muffins before serving.

776 Walnut & cinnamon muffins

Makes 12

2 cups all-purpose flour
1 tbsp baking powder
1 tsp ground cinnamon
pinch of salt
heaping ½ cup light brown sugar
⅔ cup walnuts, coarsely chopped
2 eggs
generous 1 cup milk
6 tbsp sunflower oil or 6 tbsp butter, melted and cooled
1 tsp vanilla extract

Preheat the oven to 400°F/200°C. Line a 12-hole muffin pan with 12 paper liners. Sift together the flour, baking powder, cinnamon, and salt into a large bowl. Stir in the sugar and walnuts.

Place the eggs in a large pitcher or bowl and beat lightly, then beat in the milk, oil, and vanilla extract. Make a well in the center of the dry ingredients and pour in the beaten liquid ingredients. Stir gently until just combined; do not overmix. Spoon the batter into the paper liners.

Bake in the preheated oven for 20 minutes, or until well risen, golden brown, and firm to the touch. Let cool in the pan for 5 minutes, then serve warm or transfer to a wire rack to cool completely.

777 Hazelnut & vanilla seed muffins

Replace the walnuts and cinnamon with ⅔ cup chopped toasted hazelnuts and the seeds from a vanilla bean.

778 Lemon & poppy seed muffins

Makes 12

2½ cups all-purpose flour
1 tbsp baking powder
heaping ½ cup superfine sugar
2 tbsp poppy seeds
4 tbsp butter
1 large egg, lightly beaten
1 cup milk
finely grated rind and juice of 1 lemon

Preheat the oven to 375°F/190°C. Line a 12-hole muffin pan with 12 paper liners. Sift the flour and baking powder into a large bowl and stir in the sugar.

Heat a heavy-bottom skillet over medium–high heat and add the poppy seeds, then toast for about 30 seconds, shaking the skillet to prevent them burning. Remove from the heat and add to the flour mixture.

Place the butter in a saucepan and heat over low heat until melted. Transfer to a bowl and beat with the egg, milk, lemon rind and juice. Pour into the dry mixture and stir well to form a soft, sticky dough. Add a little more milk if it is too dry. Spoon the batter into the paper liners.

Bake in the preheated oven for 25–30 minutes, or until risen, golden brown, and firm to touch. Transfer to a wire rack to cool completely.

779 Cream & spice muffins

MAKES 12

6 tbsp sunflower oil or 6 tbsp butter, melted and cooled, plus extra for greasing
2 cups all-purpose flour
1 tbsp baking powder
1 tsp ground cinnamon
½ tsp ground allspice
½ tsp freshly grated nutmeg
pinch of salt
heaping ½ cup light brown sugar
2 eggs
generous 1 cup heavy cream
confectioners' sugar, for dusting

Preheat the oven to 400°F/200°C. Grease a 12-hole muffin pan. Sift together the flour, baking powder, cinnamon, allspice, nutmeg, and salt into a large bowl. Stir in the brown sugar.

Place the eggs in a large pitcher or bowl and beat lightly, then beat in the cream and oil. Make a well in the center of the dry ingredients and pour in the beaten liquid ingredients. Stir gently until just combined; do not overmix. Spoon the batter into the muffin pan.

Bake in the preheated oven for 20 minutes, or until well risen, golden brown, and firm to the touch. Let cool in the pan for 5 minutes, then serve warm or transfer to a wire rack to cool completely. Dust with sifted confectioners' sugar before serving.

780 With spice butter topping

Blend heaping ⅔ cup butter with 3 tablespoons of confectioners' sugar and 1 teaspoon of pumpkin pie spice, then spread over the cooled muffins.

781 Triple chocolate muffins

MAKES 12

heaping 1¾ cups all-purpose flour
¼ cup unsweetened cocoa
2 tsp baking powder
½ tsp baking soda
½ cup semisweet chocolate chips
½ cup white chocolate chips
scant ½ cup light brown sugar
2 eggs, lightly beaten
1¼ cups sour cream
6 tbsp butter, melted

Preheat the oven to 400°F/200°C. Line a 12-hole muffin pan with 12 paper liners. Sift the flour, cocoa, baking powder, and baking soda into a large bowl, then stir in the semisweet and white chocolate chips. Stir in the sugar.

Place the eggs, sour cream, and butter in a separate bowl and mix well. Add the wet ingredients to the dry ingredients and stir gently until just combined. Spoon the batter into the paper liners.

Bake in the preheated oven for 20 minutes, or until well risen and firm to the touch. Let cool in the pan for 5 minutes, then serve warm or transfer to a wire rack to cool completely.

782 Chocolate & cherry muffins

Replace the white chocolate chips with 3 oz/85 g chopped candied cherries.

783 Easter muffins

MAKES 12

6 tbsp sunflower oil or 6 tbsp butter, melted and cooled, plus extra for greasing
1⅔ cups all-purpose flour
½ cup unsweetened cocoa
1 tbsp baking powder
pinch of salt
heaping ½ cup light brown sugar
2 eggs
generous 1 cup buttermilk

TOPPING
1 quantity buttercream (page 10)
9 oz/250 g sugar-coated mini chocolate eggs, for decorating

Preheat the oven to 400°F/200°C. Grease a 12-hole muffin pan. Sift together the flour, cocoa, baking powder, and salt into a large bowl. Stir in the brown sugar.

Place the eggs in a large pitcher or bowl and beat lightly, then beat in the buttermilk and oil. Make a well in the center of the dry ingredients and pour in the beaten liquid ingredients. Stir gently until just combined; do not overmix. Spoon the batter into the muffin pan.

Bake in the preheated oven for 20 minutes, or until well risen and firm to the touch. Let cool in the pan for 5 minutes, then transfer to a wire rack to cool.

Place the frosting in a pastry bag fitted with a large star tip and pipe a circle around the top of each muffin to form a "nest." Place the eggs in the center of each muffin for decorating.

784 Easter fruit muffins

Omit the frosting. Roll out 3½ oz/100 g marzipan and cut out twelve 1½-inch/3-cm circles. Brush each muffin with a little apricot jam and press a marzipan circle onto the top of each muffin. Using 3 oz/85 g marzipan, roll out 12 balls and press one on top of each muffin, then use a kitchen blow torch to toast the tops.

785 Thanksgiving cranberry & orange muffins

MAKES 12

1¾ cups dried cranberries
3 tbsp fresh orange juice
6 tbsp sunflower oil or 6 tbsp butter, melted and cooled, plus extra for greasing
2 cups all-purpose flour
1 tbsp baking powder
pinch of salt
heaping ½ cup superfine sugar
2 eggs
generous ¾ cup milk
finely grated rind of 1 orange

Put the cranberries in a bowl, add the orange juice, and let soak for 1 hour. Preheat the oven to 400°F/200°C. Grease a 12-hole muffin pan. Sift together the flour, baking powder, and salt into a large bowl. Stir in the sugar.

Place the eggs in a large pitcher or bowl and beat lightly, then beat in the milk, oil, and orange rind. Make a well in the center of the dry ingredients, pour in the beaten liquid ingredients, and add the cranberries and orange juice. Stir gently until just combined; do not overmix. Spoon the batter into the muffin pan.

Bake in the preheated oven for 20 minutes, or until well risen, golden brown, and firm to the touch. Let cool in the pan for 5 minutes, then serve warm or transfer to a wire rack to cool completely.

786 Cranberry, orange & pecan muffins

Add ½ cup chopped pecans to the batter for an extra crunch.

787 Halloween pumpkin muffins

MAKES 12

2 cups all-purpose flour
1 tbsp baking powder
1 tsp pumpkin pie spice
pinch of salt
heaping ½ cup dark brown sugar
2 eggs
generous ¾ cup milk
6 tbsp sunflower oil or 6 tbsp butter, melted and cooled
15 oz/425 g canned pumpkin flesh
4 tbsp dulce de leche (from a jar)

Preheat the oven to 400°F/200°C. Line a 12-hole muffin pan with 12 paper liners. Sift together the flour, baking powder, pumpkin pie spice, and salt into a large bowl. Stir in the sugar.

Place the eggs in a large pitcher or bowl and beat lightly, then beat in the milk and oil. Make a well in the center of the dry ingredients, pour in the beaten liquid ingredients, and add the pumpkin flesh. Stir until combined; do not overmix. Spoon the batter into the paper liners.

Bake in the preheated oven for 20 minutes, or until well risen, golden brown, and firm to the touch. Let cool in the pan for 5 minutes, then serve warm or transfer to a wire rack to cool. Spread a teaspoon of dulce de leche over the top of each muffin before serving.

788 With maple butter frosting

Omit the dulce de leche and make a butter frosting by beating ¾ cup butter with 3 tablespoons of maple syrup and 2 tablespoons of confectioners' sugar. Spread over the cooled muffins.

789 Christmas snowflake muffins

MAKES 12

2 cups all-purpose flour
1 tbsp baking powder
1 tsp ground allspice
pinch of salt
heaping ½ cup dark brown sugar
2 eggs
generous ⅓ cup milk
6 tbsp sunflower oil or 6 tbsp butter, melted and cooled
⅔ cup mixed dried fruit with cherries and nuts

TOPPING
1 lb/450 g ready-to-roll fondant
confectioners' sugar, for dusting
2½ tsp apricot jam
silver dragées, for decorating

Preheat the oven to 400°F/200°C. Line a 12-hole muffin pan with 12 paper liners. Sift together the flour, baking powder, allspice, and salt into a large bowl. Stir in the brown sugar.

Place the eggs in a large pitcher or bowl and beat lightly, then beat in the milk and oil. Make a well in the center of the dry ingredients and pour in the liquid ingredients and dried fruit. Stir until combined; do not overmix. Spoon the batter into the paper liners.

Bake in the preheated oven for 20 minutes, or until well risen, golden brown, and firm to the touch. Let cool in the pan for 5 minutes, then transfer to a wire rack and let cool completely.

Knead the frosting until pliable. Roll out the frosting on a surface dusted with confectioners' sugar to a thickness of ¼ inch/5 mm. Using a 2¾-inch/7-cm fluted cutter, cut out 12 "snowflakes."

Heat the apricot jam until runny, then brush over the tops of the muffins. Place a snowflake on top of each one, then decorate with silver dragées.

790 Christmas holly muffins

Tint 1¾ oz/50 g royal icing with green food coloring and roll out, then cut out holly leaves and use for decorating the muffins. Add cranberries for the holly berries.

791 Rose-topped wedding muffins

MAKES 12

2 cups all-purpose flour
1 tbsp baking powder
pinch of salt
heaping ½ cup superfine sugar
2 eggs
generous 1 cup milk
6 tbsp sunflower oil or 6 tbsp butter, melted and cooled
1 tsp vanilla extract
12 store-bought sugar roses or fresh rose petals or buds, for decorating

ICING
1½ cups confectioners' sugar
3–4 tsp hot water

Preheat the oven to 400°F/200°C. Increase the quantity of ingredients according to the number of wedding guests invited, double quantities each time to make 24 muffins. Line the appropriate number of muffin pans with paper liners.

Sift together the flour, baking powder, and salt into a large bowl. Stir in the sugar. Place the eggs in a large pitcher or bowl and beat lightly, then beat in the milk, oil, and vanilla extract. Make a well in the center of the dry ingredients and pour in the beaten liquid ingredients. Stir gently until just combined; do not overmix. Spoon the batter into the paper liners.

Bake in the preheated oven for 20 minutes, or until well risen, golden brown, and firm to the touch. Let cool in the pan or pans for 5 minutes, then transfer to a wire rack to cool completely. Store in the freezer until required.

On the day of serving, if using fresh flowers, rinse and dry on paper towels. For the icing, sift the confectioners' sugar into a bowl. Add the water and stir until the mixture is smooth and thick enough to coat the back of a wooden spoon. Spoon the icing on top of each muffin, then top with a rose petal, rose bud, or sugar rose.

792 Berry-topped wedding muffins

Instead of the sugar roses, top with piles of jewel berries: Mix pomegranate seeds and tiny wild strawberries and spoon onto the icing, then sift over a little confectioners' sugar to finish.

793 Anniversary muffins

MAKES 12

6 tbsp sunflower oil or 6 tbsp butter, melted and cooled, plus extra for greasing
2 cups all-purpose flour
1 tbsp baking powder
pinch of salt
heaping ½ cup superfine sugar
2 eggs
generous 1 cup buttermilk
finely grated rind of 1 lemon

TOPPING
6 tbsp butter, softened
1½ cups confectioners' sugar
gold or silver dragées, for decorating

Preheat the oven to 400°F/200°C. Grease a 12-hole muffin pan. Sift together the flour, baking powder, and salt into a large bowl. Stir in the superfine sugar.

Place the eggs in a large pitcher or bowl and beat lightly, then beat in the buttermilk, oil, and lemon rind. Make a well in the center of the dry ingredients and pour in the beaten liquid ingredients. Stir gently until just combined; do not overmix. Spoon the batter into the muffin pan.

Bake in the preheated oven for 20 minutes, or until well risen, golden brown, and firm to the touch. Let cool in the pan for 5 minutes, then transfer to a wire rack to cool completely.

To make the frosting, place the butter in a large bowl and beat until fluffy. Sift in the confectioners' sugar and beat together until smooth and creamy.

When the muffins are cold, place the frosting in a pastry bag fitted with a large star tip and pipe circles on top of each muffin to cover the top. Sprinkle with the gold or silver dragées for decorating.

794 Anniversary hearts

Tint 3½ oz/100 g royal icing with red food coloring and roll out thinly, then use a small heart-shaped cutter to cut out heart shapes and decorate the topping with 3 hearts set upright on each muffin.

795 Mother's day breakfast muffins

MAKES 12

2 cups all-purpose flour
1 tbsp baking powder
pinch of salt
heaping ½ cup superfine sugar
2 eggs
generous 1 cup milk
6 tbsp sunflower oil or 6 tbsp butter, melted and cooled
1 tsp orange extract
fresh strawberries, for serving
confectioners' sugar, for dusting

Preheat the oven to 400°F/200°C. Line a 12-hole muffin pan with 12 paper liners. Sift together the flour, baking powder, and salt into a large bowl. Stir in the superfine sugar.

Place the eggs in a large pitcher or bowl and beat lightly, then beat in the milk, oil, and orange extract. Make a well in the center of the dry ingredients and pour in the beaten liquid ingredients. Stir gently until just combined; do not overmix. Spoon the batter into the paper liners.

Bake in the preheated oven for 20 minutes, or until well risen, golden brown, and firm to the touch. Let cool in the pan for 5 minutes. Meanwhile, arrange the strawberries in a bowl. Dust the muffins with sifted confectioners' sugar and serve warm.

796 With malted chocolate butter

Omit the strawberries and make honeycomb butter by beating scant 1 cup butter until soft, then crush 3½ oz/100 g malted chocolate balls and mixing into the butter. Serve with the muffins.

797 Valentine heart muffins

MAKES 12

6 tbsp sunflower oil or 6 tbsp butter, melted and cooled, plus extra for greasing
1⅔ cups all-purpose flour
½ cup unsweetened cocoa
1 tbsp baking powder
pinch of salt
heaping ½ cup light brown sugar
2 eggs
generous 1 cup buttermilk

MARZIPAN HEARTS
confectioners' sugar, for dusting
2½ oz/70 g marzipan, colored with a few drops of red food coloring

FROSTING
2 oz/55 g semisweet chocolate, broken into pieces
8 tbsp butter, softened
2 cups confectioners' sugar

To make the marzipan hearts, dust a work surface with confectioners' sugar and roll the marzipan to a thickness of ¼ inch/5 mm. Using a small heart-shaped cutter, cut out 12 hearts. Line a baking sheet with parchment paper, dust with confectioners' sugar, and place the hearts on it. Let stand for 3–4 hours, or until the marizpan hearts are dry.

Preheat the oven to 400°F/200°C. Grease a 12-hole heart-shaped muffin pan. Sift together the flour, cocoa, baking powder, and salt into a large bowl. Stir in the brown sugar. Place the eggs in a pitcher or bowl and beat lightly, then beat in the buttermilk and oil. Make a well in the center of the dry ingredients and pour in the beaten liquid ingredients. Stir until combined. Spoon the batter into the muffin pan.

Bake in the preheated oven for 20 minutes, or until well risen and firm to the touch. Leave for 5 minutes, then transfter to a wire rack to cool completely.

Melt the chocolate. Beat the butter in a bowl until fluffy, sift in the confectioners' sugar, and beat until smooth. Add the chocolate and beat. Spread the frosting on top of the muffins, then decorate with a marzipan heart.

798 White heart muffins

Omit the cocoa from the muffin batter and bake as before. Make the frosting with white chocolate and cut the hearts from white marzipan.

799 Marshmallow muffins

Makes 12

6 tbsp sunflower oil or 6 tbsp butter, melted and cooled, plus extra for greasing
3½ oz/100 g mini white marshmallows
1⅔ cups all-purpose flour
½ cup unsweetened cocoa
1 tbsp baking powder
pinch of salt
heaping ½ cup light brown sugar
2 eggs
generous 1 cup milk

Preheat the oven to 400°F/200°C. Grease a 12-hole muffin pan. Using scissors, cut the marshmallows in half. Sift together the flour, cocoa, baking powder, and salt into a large bowl. Stir in the sugar and marshmallows.

Place the eggs in a large pitcher or bowl and beat lightly, then beat in the milk and oil. Make a well in the center of the dry ingredients and pour in the beaten liquid ingredients. Stir gently until just combined; do not overmix. Spoon the batter into the muffin pan.

Bake in the preheated oven for 20 minutes, or until well risen and firm to the touch. Let cool in the pan for 5 minutes, then serve warm or transfer to a wire rack to cool completely.

800 Chocolate chunk muffins

Makes 12

2 cups all-purpose flour
1 tbsp baking powder
pinch of salt
heaping ½ cup superfine sugar
6 oz/175 g chocolate chunks
2 eggs
generous 1 cup milk
6 tbsp sunflower oil or 6 tbsp butter, melted and cooled
1 tsp vanilla extract

Preheat the oven to 400°F/200°C. Line a 12-hole muffin pan with 12 paper liners. Sift together the flour, baking powder, and salt into a large bowl. Stir in the sugar and chocolate chunks.

Place the eggs in a large pitcher or bowl and beat lightly, then beat in the milk, oil, and vanilla extract. Make a well in the center of the dry ingredients and pour in the beaten liquid ingredients. Stir gently until just combined; do not overmix. Spoon the batter into the paper liners.

Bake in the preheated oven for 20 minutes, or until well risen, golden brown, and firm to the touch. Let cool in the pan for 5 minutes, then serve warm or transfer to a wire rack to cool completely.

801 Chocolate chunk & peanut muffins

Use 3½ oz/100 g chocolate chunks and ½ cup chopped salted peanuts.

802 Children's party muffins

MAKES 12

2 cups all-purpose flour
1 tbsp baking powder
½ tsp salt
heaping ½ cup superfine sugar
2 eggs
generous 1 cup milk
6 tbsp sunflower oil or 6 tbsp butter, melted and cooled
1 tsp vanilla extract

TOPPING
1½ cups confectioners' sugar
3–4 tsp hot water
variety of small candies, for decorating

Preheat the oven to 400°F/200°C. Line a 12-hole muffin pan with 12 paper liners. Sift together the flour, baking powder, and salt into a large bowl. Stir in the superfine sugar.

Place the eggs in a large pitcher or bowl and beat lightly, then beat in the milk, oil, and vanilla extract. Make a well in the center of the dry ingredients and pour in the beaten liquid ingredients. Stir until combined. Spoon the batter into the paper liners.

Bake in the preheated oven for 20 minutes, or until well risen, golden brown, and firm to the touch. Let cool in the pan for 5 minutes, then transfer to a wire rack to cool completely.

When the muffins are cold, make the icing. Sift the confectioners' sugar into a bowl. Add the water and stir until the mixture is smooth and thick enough to coat the back of a wooden spoon. Spoon the icing on top of each muffin, then add the decoration of your choice. Let set for about 30 minutes before serving.

803 Signature muffins

Spread each muffin with the white icing and when set, write each child's name on a muffin with a tube of decorating icing.

804 Birthday muffins

MAKES 12

6 tbsp sunflower oil or 6 tbsp butter, melted and cooled, plus extra for greasing
2 cups all-purpose flour
1 tbsp baking powder
pinch of salt
heaping ½ cup superfine sugar
2 eggs
generous 1 cup milk
finely grated rind of 1 lemon
12 candles and candleholders, for decorating

FROSTING
6 tbsp butter, softened
1½ cups confectioners' sugar

Preheat the oven to 400°F/200°C. Grease a 12-hole muffin pan. Sift together the flour, baking powder, and salt into a large bowl. Stir in the sugar.

Place the eggs in a large pitcher or bowl and beat lightly, then beat in the milk, oil, and lemon rind. Make a well in the center of the dry ingredients and pour in the beaten liquid ingredients. Stir gently until just combined; do not overmix. Spoon the batter into the muffin pan.

Bake in the preheated oven for 20 minutes, or until well risen and golden brown. Let cool in the pan for 5 minutes then, transfer to a wire rack to cool completely.

To make the frosting, place the butter in a large bowl and beat until fluffy. Sift in the confectioners' sugar and beat together until smooth and creamy. When the muffins are cold, spread each one with a little of the frosting, then place a candleholder and candle on top.

805 Multicolored muffins

Divide the butter frosting into 4 portions and tint each one with a different food coloring. Spread over the muffins and match the candle color to the frosting color.

806 Rocky road chocolate muffins

Makes 12

6 tbsp sunflower oil or 6 tbsp butter, melted and cooled, plus extra for greasing
1⅔ cups all-purpose flour
½ cup unsweetened cocoa
1 tbsp baking powder
pinch of salt
heaping ½ cup superfine sugar
heaping ½ cup white chocolate chips
1¾ oz/50 g white mini marshmallows, cut in half
2 eggs
generous 1 cup milk

Preheat the oven to 400°F/200°C. Grease a 12-hole muffin pan. Sift together the flour, cocoa, baking powder, and salt into a large bowl. Stir in the sugar, chocolate chips, and marshmallows.

Place the eggs in a large pitcher or bowl and beat lightly, then beat in the milk and oil. Make a well in the center of the dry ingredients and pour in the beaten liquid ingredients. Stir gently until just combined; do not overmix. Spoon the batter into the muffin pan.

Bake in the preheated oven for 20 minutes, or until risen and firm to the touch. Let cool in the pan for 5 minutes, then serve warm or transfer to a wire rack to cool completely.

807 Extra rocky muffins

Use ⅓ cup white chocolate chips and add heaping ½ cup chopped Brazil nuts to the muffin batter for extra texture.

808 Brie & cranberry muffins

MAKES 12

6 tbsp sunflower oil or 6 tbsp butter, melted and cooled, plus extra for greasing
2 cups all-purpose flour
1 tbsp baking powder
½ tsp baking soda
pinch of salt
freshly ground black pepper
5½ oz/150 g Brie, finely cubed
2 eggs
heaping 1 cup plain yogurt
4 tbsp cranberry sauce

Preheat the oven to 400°F/200°C. Grease a 12-hole muffin pan. Sift together the flour, baking powder, baking soda, salt, and pepper to taste into a large bowl. Stir in the Brie.

Place the eggs in a large pitcher or bowl and beat lightly, then beat in the yogurt and oil. Make a well in the center of the dry ingredients and pour in the liquid ingredients. Stir until combined; do not overmix. Spoon half of the batter into the muffin pan. Add a teaspoon of cranberry sauce to the center of each, then spoon in the remaining batter.

Bake in the preheated oven for 20 minutes, or until well risen, golden brown, and firm to the touch. Let cool in the pan for 5 minutes, then serve warm.

809 Fontina & pesto muffins

Replace the Brie with Fontina cheese and replace the cranberry sauce with red pesto.

810 Caramelized onion muffins

MAKES 12

7 tbsp sunflower oil
3 onions, finely chopped
1 tbsp red wine vinegar
2 tsp sugar
2 cups all-purpose flour
1 tbsp baking powder
pinch of salt
freshly ground black pepper
2 eggs
generous 1 cup buttermilk

Preheat the oven to 400°F/200°C. Line a 12-hole muffin pan with 12 paper liners. Heat 2 tablespoons of the oil in a skillet. Add the onions and cook for 3 minutes, or until beginning to soften. Add the vinegar and sugar and cook, stirring occasionally, for an additional 10 minutes, or until golden brown. Remove from the heat and let cool.

Meanwhile, sift together the flour, baking powder, and salt and pepper to taste into a large bowl.

Place the eggs in a large pitcher or bowl and beat lightly, then beat in the buttermilk and the remaining oil. Make a well in the center of the dry ingredients, pour in the beaten liquid ingredients, and add the onion mixture, reserving 4 tablespoons for the topping. Stir gently until just combined; do not overmix. Spoon the batter into the paper liners. Sprinkle the reserved onion mixture on top of the muffins. Bake in the preheated oven for 20 minutes, or until well risen, golden brown, and firm to the touch. Let cool in the pan for 5 minutes, then serve warm.

811 Caramelized red onion muffins

Replace the onion with red onions and use balsamic vinegar instead of wine vinegar.

812 Carrot & cilantro muffins

MAKES 12

6 tbsp sunflower oil or 6 tbsp butter, melted and cooled, plus extra for greasing
2 cups all-purpose flour
1 tbsp baking powder
pinch of salt
freshly ground black pepper
heaping 1 cup grated carrot
2 eggs
generous 1 cup buttermilk
3 tbsp chopped fresh cilantro, plus extra sprigs for garnishing

Preheat the oven to 400°F/200°C. Grease a 12-hole muffin pan. Sift together the flour, baking powder, and salt and pepper to taste into a large bowl. Stir in the grated carrot.

Place the eggs in a large pitcher or bowl and beat lightly, then beat in the buttermilk, oil, and chopped cilantro. Make a well in the center of the dry ingredients and pour in the beaten liquid ingredients. Stir until just combined; do not overmix. Spoon the batter into the muffin pan.

Bake in the preheated oven for 20 minutes, or until well risen, golden brown, and firm to the touch. Let cool in the pan for 5 minutes, then serve warm, garnished with sprigs of cilantro.

813 Carrot, cilantro & onion muffins

Add 2 finely chopped scallions to the batter along with the carrot.

814 Cheese & ham muffins

MAKES 12

2 cups all-purpose flour
1 tbsp baking powder
pinch of salt
3½ oz/100 g sliced ham, finely chopped
1¼ cups coarsely grated sharp cheddar cheese
2 eggs
generous 1 cup milk
6 tbsp sunflower oil or 6 tbsp butter, melted and cooled
freshly ground black pepper

Preheat the oven to 400°F/200°C. Line a 12-hole muffin pan with 12 paper liners. Sift together the flour, baking powder, and salt and pepper to taste into a large bowl. Stir in the ham and 1 cup of the cheddar cheese.

Place the eggs in a large pitcher or bowl and beat lightly, then beat in the milk and oil. Make a well in the center of the dry ingredients and pour in the beaten liquid ingredients. Stir gently until just combined; do not overmix. Spoon the batter into the paper liners. Scatter the remaining cheese over the tops of the muffins.

Bake in the preheated oven for 20 minutes, or until well risen, golden brown, and firm to the touch. Let cool in the pan for 5 minutes, then serve warm.

815 Double cheese muffins

Cut 6 oz/175 g mozzarella cheese into cubes, omit the ham, and add a cube of mozzarella cheese to the middle of each muffin, then bake.

816 Chicken & corn muffins

MAKES 12

7 tbsp sunflower oil, plus extra for greasing
1 onion, finely chopped
1 skinless chicken breast, about 6 oz/175 g, finely chopped
2 cups all-purpose flour
1 tbsp baking powder
pinch of salt
freshly ground black pepper
2 eggs
generous 1 cup buttermilk
½ cup frozen corn kernels
ground paprika, for garnishing

Preheat the oven to 400°F/200°C. Grease a 12-hole muffin pan. Heat 1 tablespoon of the oil in a skillet. Add the onion and cook for 2 minutes. Add the chicken and cook for about 5 minutes, stirring occasionally, until tender. Remove from the heat and let cool. Meanwhile, sift together the flour, baking powder, and salt and pepper to taste into a large bowl.

Place the eggs in a large pitcher or bowl and beat lightly, then beat in the buttermilk and remaining oil. Make a well in the center of the dry ingredients, pour in the beaten liquid ingredients, and add the chicken mixture and corn. Stir gently until just combined; do not overmix. Spoon the batter into the muffin pan.

Bake in the preheated oven for 20 minutes, or until well risen, golden brown, and firm to the touch. Let cool in the pan for 5 minutes, sprinkle with paprika then serve warm.

817 Turkey & cranberry muffins

Replace the chicken breast with 6 oz/175 g turkey scallop and replace the corn with scant 1 cup frozen cranberries.

818 Zucchini & sesame seed muffins

MAKES 12

6 tbsp sunflower oil or 6 tbsp butter, melted and cooled, plus extra for greasing
1 large zucchini
2 cups all-purpose flour
1 tbsp baking powder
pinch of salt
freshly ground black pepper
2 tbsp sesame seeds
½ tsp dried mixed herbs
2 eggs
generous 1 cup buttermilk

Preheat the oven to 400°F/200°C. Grease a 12-hole muffin pan. Grate the zucchini, squeezing out any excess moisture.

Sift together the flour, baking powder, and salt and pepper to taste into a large bowl. Stir in 4 teaspoons of the sesame seeds and the mixed herbs. Place the eggs in a large pitcher or bowl and beat lightly, then beat in the buttermilk and oil. Make a well in the center of the dry ingredients, pour in the beaten liquid ingredients, and add the zucchini. Stir gently until just combined; do not overmix. Spoon the batter into the muffin pan. Scatter the remaining 2 teaspoons of sesame seeds over the tops of the muffins.

Bake in the preheated oven for 20 minutes, or until well risen, golden brown, and firm to the touch. Let cool in the pan for 5 minutes, then serve warm.

819 Zucchini & feta cheese muffins

Add 5½ oz/150 g crumbled feta with the zucchini, then add a thin slice of zucchini to the top of each muffin before scattering over the seeds.

820 Crispy bacon muffins

MAKES 12

9 oz/250 g rindless, smoked bacon
7 tbsp sunflower oil
1 onion, finely chopped
2 cups all-purpose flour
1 tbsp baking powder
pinch of salt
freshly ground black pepper
2 eggs
generous 1 cup buttermilk

Preheat the oven to 400°F/200°C. Line a 12-hole muffin pan with 12 paper liners. Chop the bacon, reserving 3 slices for garnishing. Cut each of the reserved slices into 4 pieces and set aside.

Heat 1 tablespoon of the oil in a skillet. Add the onion and cook for 2 minutes.

Add the chopped bacon and cook for 5 minutes, stirring occasionally, until crispy. Let cool.

Meanwhile, sift together the flour, baking powder, and salt and pepper to taste into a large bowl.

Place the eggs in a large pitcher or bowl and beat lightly, then beat in the buttermilk and remaining oil. Make a well in the center of the dry ingredients, pour in the beaten liquid ingredients, and add the bacon mixture. Stir gently until just combined; do not overmix. Spoon the batter into the paper liners. Place one of the reserved pieces of bacon on top of each muffin.

Bake in the preheated oven for 20 minutes, or until well risen, golden brown, and firm to the touch. Let cool in the pan for 5 minutes, then serve warm.

821 Crispy bacon & spinach muffins

Melt 1 tablespoon of butter in a skillet, add 3 oz/85 g fresh baby spinach leaves and stir for 1–2 minutes, until wilted. Transfer to a strainer, press all the liquid out, and chop, then add to the batter before baking.

822 Crumble-topped cheese & chive muffins

MAKES 12

6 tbsp sunflower oil or 6 tbsp butter, melted and cooled, plus extra for greasing
2 cups all-purpose flour
1 tbsp baking powder
pinch of salt
freshly ground black pepper
1⅓ cups coarsely grated sharp cheddar cheese
4 tbsp snipped fresh chives
2 eggs
generous 1 cup buttermilk

CRUMBLE TOPPING
heaping ⅓ cup all-purpose flour
2½ tbsp butter, cut into pieces
¼ cup finely grated cheddar cheese
salt and freshly ground black pepper

Preheat the oven to 400°F/200°C. Grease a 12-hole muffin pan.

To make the crumble topping, place the flour into a bowl. Add the butter and rub it in with your fingertips until the mixture resembles fine breadcrumbs. Stir in the cheddar cheese and season to taste with salt and pepper.

To make the muffins, sift together the flour, baking powder, and salt and pepper to taste into a large bowl. Stir in the cheddar cheese and chives.

Place the eggs in a large pitcher or bowl and beat lightly, then beat in the buttermilk and oil. Make a well in the center of the dry ingredients and pour in the beaten liquid ingredients. Stir gently until just combined; do not overmix. Spoon the batter into the muffin pan. Scatter the topping over the muffins.

Bake in the preheated oven for 20 minutes, or until well risen, golden brown, and firm to the touch. Let cool in the pan for 5 minutes, then serve warm.

823 Parmesan & sage muffins

Replace the cheddar cheese with 1 cup finely grated Parmesan cheese and replace the chives with 2 tablespoons of finely shredded sage leaves.

824 *Italian pesto muffins*

MAKES 12

2 cups all-purpose flour
1 tbsp baking powder
pinch of salt
freshly ground black pepper
½ cup pine nuts
2 eggs
⅔ cup buttermilk
6 tbsp sunflower oil or 6 tbsp butter, melted and cooled
6 tbsp pesto
scant 2 tbsp freshly grated Parmesan cheese

Preheat the oven to 400°F/200°C. Line a 12-hole muffin pan with 12 paper liners. Sift together the flour, baking powder, and salt and pepper to taste into a large bowl. Stir in the pine nuts.

Place the eggs in a large pitcher or bowl and beat lightly, then beat in the buttermilk, oil, and pesto. Make a well in the center of the dry ingredients and pour in the beaten liquid ingredients. Stir gently until just combined; do not overmix. Spoon the batter into the paper liners. Scatter the Parmesan cheese over the tops of the muffins.

Bake in the preheated oven for 20 minutes, or until well risen, golden brown, and firm to the touch. Let cool in the pan for 5 minutes, then serve warm.

825 *With ricotta cheese topping*

Beat 7 oz/200 g ricotta cheese with a pinch of salt and some freshly ground black pepper, pile into a serving bowl, and drizzle over a little extra virgin olive oil, then use to spread on the warm muffins.

826 *Mini bleu cheese & pear muffins*

MAKES 48

6 tbsp sunflower oil or 6 tbsp butter, melted and cooled, plus extra for greasing
14 oz/400 g canned pear halves in natural juice, drained
2 cups all-purpose flour
1 tbsp baking powder
pinch of salt
freshly ground black pepper
3½ oz/100 g bleu cheese, finely crumbled
2 eggs
generous 1 cup milk
scant ½ cup walnut pieces

Preheat the oven to 400°F/200°C. Grease two 24-hole mini muffin pans. Chop the pears into small pieces. Sift together the flour, baking powder, and salt and pepper to taste into a large bowl. Stir in the bleu cheese and pears.

Place the eggs in a large pitcher or bowl and beat lightly, then beat in the milk and oil. Make a well in the center of the dry ingredients and pour in the beaten liquid ingredients. Stir gently until just combined; do not overmix. Spoon the batter into the muffin pans. Scatter the walnuts over the tops of the muffins.

Bake in the preheated oven for 15 minutes, or until well risen and golden brown. Let cool in the pans for 5 minutes, then serve warm.

827 *Mini bleu cheese & onion muffins*

Replace the pears with 3 finely chopped scallions.

828 Mini shrimp & parsley muffins

MAKES 48

6 tbsp sunflower oil or 6 tbsp butter, melted and cooled, plus extra for greasing
9 oz/250 g cooked peeled shrimp
2 cups all-purpose flour
1 tbsp baking powder
pinch of salt
freshly ground black pepper
2 eggs
generous 1 cup buttermilk
3 tbsp chopped fresh parsley

Preheat the oven to 400°F/200°C. Grease two 24-hole mini muffin pans. Chop the shrimp into small pieces. Sift together the flour, baking powder, and salt and pepper to taste into a large bowl. Stir in the chopped shrimp.

Place the eggs in a large pitcher or bowl and beat lightly, then beat in the buttermilk, oil, and parsley. Make a well in the center of the dry ingredients and pour in the beaten liquid ingredients. Stir gently until just combined; do not overmix. Spoon the batter into the muffin pan.

Bake in the preheated oven for 15 minutes, or until well risen, golden brown, and firm to the touch. Let cool in the pan for 5 minutes, then serve warm.

829 Mini shrimp & dill muffins

Stir 1 teaspoon of creamed horseradish into the buttermilk and replace the parsley with 2 tablespoons of finely chopped dill.

830 Parmesan & pine nut muffins

MAKES 12

2 cups all-purpose flour
1 tbsp baking powder
pinch of salt
freshly ground black pepper
heaping ¾ cup freshly grated Parmesan cheese
½ cup pine nuts
2 eggs
generous 1 cup buttermilk
6 tbsp sunflower oil or 6 tbsp butter, melted and cooled

TOPPING
2 tbsp freshly grated Parmesan cheese
⅓ cup pine nuts

Preheat the oven to 400°F/200°C. Line a 12-hole muffin pan with 12 paper liners. To make the topping, mix together the Parmesan cheese and pine nuts and set aside.

To make the muffins, sift together the flour, baking powder, and salt and pepper to taste into a large bowl. Stir in the Parmesan cheese and pine nuts.

Place the eggs in a large pitcher or bowl and beat lightly, then beat in the buttermilk and oil. Make a well in the center of the dry ingredients and pour in the beaten liquid ingredients. Stir gently until just combined; do not overmix. Spoon the batter into the paper liners, then scatter the topping over the muffins.

Bake in the preheated oven for 20 minutes, or until well risen, golden brown, and firm to the touch. Leave for 5 minutes, then serve warm.

831 Pepperoni & sun-dried tomato muffins

MAKES 12

sunflower oil, for greasing
2 cups all-purpose flour
1 tbsp baking powder
pinch of salt
freshly ground black pepper
1 tsp dried oregano
2¾ oz/75 g sun dried tomatoes in oil, drained (oil reserved) and finely chopped
3½ oz/100 g pepperoni slices, finely chopped
2 eggs
generous 1 cup buttermilk
1 garlic clove, crushed

Preheat the oven to 400°F/200°C. Grease a 12-hole muffin pan. Sift together the flour, baking powder, and salt and pepper to taste into a large bowl. Stir in the oregano, tomatoes, and pepperoni.

Place the eggs in a large pitcher or bowl and beat lightly, then beat in the buttermilk, 6 tablespoons of the reserved oil from the tomatoes, and the garlic. Make a well in the center of the dry ingredients and pour in the beaten liquid ingredients. Stir gently until just combined; do not overmix. Spoon the batter into the muffin pan.

Bake in the preheated oven for 20 minutes, or until well risen, golden brown, and firm to the touch. Let cool in the pan for 5 minutes, then serve warm.

832 Anchovy & caper muffins

Omit the pepperoni and add 3 chopped, drained anchovies and 2 teaspoons of chopped capers.

833 Shredded vegetable muffins

MAKES 12

6 tbsp sunflower oil, plus extra for greasing
1 small zucchini
2 medium carrots
1 cup whole wheat flour
1 cup all-purpose flour
1 tbsp baking powder
heaping ½ cup superfine sugar
heaping ¼ cup golden raisins
2 eggs
generous 1 cup buttermilk

Preheat the oven to 400°F/200°C. Grease a 12-hole muffin pan. Grate the zucchini and squeeze out any excess moisture. Place in a bowl and grate in the carrots.

Sift together both flours and the baking powder into a large bowl, adding any bran left in the strainer. Stir in the sugar and golden raisins.

Place the eggs in a large pitcher or bowl and beat lightly, then beat in the buttermilk and oil. Make a well in the center of the dry ingredients, pour in the beaten liquid ingredients, and add the grated vegetables. Stir gently until just combined; do not overmix. Spoon the batter into the muffin pan.

Bake in the preheated oven for 20 minutes, or until well risen, golden brown, and firm to the touch. Let cool in the pan for 5 minutes, then serve warm or transfer to a wire rack to cool completely.

834 Shredded vegetable & cheese muffins

Omit the golden raisins and sugar. Add 2 finely chopped scallions and 3 tablespoons of finely grated Parmesan cheese.

835 Smoked salmon & dill muffins

Makes 12

6 tbsp sunflower oil or 6 tbsp butter, melted and cooled, plus extra for greasing
2 cups all-purpose flour
1 tbsp baking powder
pinch of salt
freshly ground black pepper
2 eggs
generous 1 cup buttermilk
5½ oz/150 g smoked salmon, finely chopped, plus extra for garnishing
2 tbsp chopped fresh dill, plus extra sprigs for garnishing

Preheat the oven to 400°F/200°C. Grease a 12-hole muffin pan. Sift together the flour, baking powder, and salt and pepper to taste into a large bowl.

Place the eggs in a large pitcher or bowl and beat lightly, then beat in the buttermilk and oil. Make a well in the center of the dry ingredients, pour in the beaten liquid ingredients, and add the smoked salmon and chopped dill. Stir gently until just combined; do not overmix. Spoon the batter into the muffin pan.

Bake in the preheated oven for 20 minutes, or until well risen, golden brown, and firm to the touch. Let cool in the pan for 5 minutes, then serve warm. Serve garnished with smoked salmon and dill.

836 With caviar topping

Top each cooled muffin with a spoonful of sour cream, a strip of smoked salmon, and ½ teaspoon of caviar. Finish with a dill sprig.

837 Soft cheese & garlic muffins

Makes 12

6 tbsp sunflower oil or 6 tbsp butter, melted and cooled, plus extra for greasing
2 cups all-purpose flour
1 tbsp baking powder
½ tsp baking soda
pinch of salt
freshly ground black pepper
2 eggs
⅔ cup plain yogurt
⅔ cup soft cheese, flavored with garlic and herbs

Preheat the oven to 400°F/200°C. Grease a 12-hole muffin pan. Sift together the flour, baking powder, baking soda, and salt and pepper to taste into a large bowl.

Place the eggs in a large pitcher or bowl and beat lightly, then beat in the yogurt, oil, and soft cheese until smooth. Make a well in the center of the dry ingredients and pour in the beaten liquid ingredients. Stir until just combined; do not overmix. Spoon the batter into the muffin pan.

Bake in the preheated oven for 20 minutes, or until well risen, golden brown, and firm to the touch. Let cool in the pan for 5 minutes, then serve warm.

838 Bleu cheese & walnut muffins

Omit the soft cheese and use 5½ oz/150 g soft bleu cheese, such as Gorgonzola, and add 2 tablespoons of chopped walnuts.

839 Spicy chorizo muffins

Makes 12

2 cups all-purpose flour
1 tbsp baking powder
pinch of salt
1 tsp ground paprika, plus extra for garnishing
3½ oz/100 g chorizo sausage, outer casing removed, finely chopped
1 small red bell pepper, cored, seeded, and finely chopped
2 eggs
generous 1 cup buttermilk
6 tbsp sunflower oil or 6 tbsp butter, melted and cooled
1 garlic clove, crushed

Preheat the oven to 400°F/200°C. Line a 12-hole muffin pan with 12 paper liners. Sift together the flour, baking powder, salt, and paprika into a large bowl. Stir in the chorizo sausage and red bell pepper.

Place the eggs in a large pitcher or bowl and beat lightly, then beat in the buttermilk, oil, and garlic. Make a well in the center of the dry ingredients and pour in the beaten liquid ingredients. Stir gently until just combined; do not overmix. Spoon the batter into the paper liners.

Bake in the preheated oven for 20 minutes, or until well risen, golden brown, and firm to the touch. Let cool in the pan for 5 minutes, sprinkle with paprika, then serve warm.

840 Spicy chorizo & green olive muffins

Omit the red bell pepper and add 15 chopped, pitted green olives to the batter. Top each muffin with 1 whole pitted green olive before baking.

841 Asparagus & sour cream muffins

Makes 12

7 tbsp sunflower oil, plus extra for greasing
8 oz/225 g fresh asparagus
2 cups all-purpose flour
1 tbsp baking powder
pinch of salt
freshly ground black pepper
2 eggs
heaping 1 cup sour cream
heaping ¼ cup finely grated cheddar cheese

Preheat the oven to 400°F/200°C. Grease a 12-hole muffin pan. Place 1 tablespoon of the oil in a roasting pan. Add the asparagus and turn in the oil. Roast in the oven for 10 minutes, or until tender. When cool enough to handle, coarsely chop the asparagus.

Sift together the flour, baking powder, and salt and pepper to taste into a large bowl. Stir in the asparagus. Place the eggs in a large pitcher or bowl and beat lightly, then beat in the sour cream and remaining oil. Make a well in the center of the dry ingredients and pour in the beaten liquid ingredients. Stir gently until just combined; do not overmix. Spoon the batter into the muffin pan. Scatter the cheese over the tops.

Bake in the preheated oven for 20 minutes, or until well risen and firm to the touch. Let cool in the pan for 5 minutes, then serve warm.

842 With asparagus tip topping

Roll 12 asparagus tips in olive oil and place one on the center of each muffin before baking.

843 Spinach & nutmeg muffins

Makes 12

- 8 tbsp sunflower oil, plus extra for greasing
- 9 oz/250 g frozen chopped spinach, thawed
- 1 onion, finely chopped
- 1 garlic clove, finely chopped
- 2 cups all-purpose flour
- 1 tbsp baking powder
- ½ tsp freshly grated nutmeg
- pinch of salt
- freshly ground black pepper
- 2 eggs
- generous 1 cup buttermilk
- ⅓ cup pine nuts

Preheat the oven to 400°F/200°C. Grease a 12-hole muffin pan. Place the spinach in a strainer and drain well, squeezing out as much of the moisture as possible.

Heat 2 tablespoons of the oil in a skillet. Add the onion and cook for about 3 minutes, or until beginning to soften. Add the garlic and cook for 1 minute. Add the spinach and cook for an addiitonal 2 minutes, stirring all the time. Remove from the heat and let cool.

Meanwhile, sift together the flour, baking powder, nutmeg, and salt and pepper to taste into a large bowl.

Place the eggs in a large pitcher or bowl and beat lightly, then beat in the buttermilk and remaining oil. Make a well in the center of the dry ingredients, pour in the beaten liquid ingredients, and add the spinach mixture. Stir gently until just combined; do not overmix. Spoon the batter into the muffin pan. Scatter the pine nuts over the tops.

Bake in the preheated oven for 20 minutes, or until well risen, golden brown, and firm to the touch. Let cool in the pan for 5 minutes, then serve warm.

844 Scallion & goat cheese muffins

Makes 12

- 6 tbsp sunflower oil or 6 tbsp butter, melted and cooled, plus extra for greasing
- 2 cups all-purpose flour
- 1 tbsp baking powder
- pinch of salt
- 1 bunch scallions, finely sliced
- 5½ oz/150 g goat cheese, finely diced
- 2 eggs
- generous 1 cup buttermilk
- freshly ground black pepper

Preheat the oven to 400°F/200°C. Grease a 12-hole muffin pan. Sift together the flour, baking powder, and salt and pepper to taste into a large bowl. Stir in the scallions and goat cheese.

Place the eggs in a large pitcher or bowl and beat lightly, then beat in the buttermilk and oil. Make a well in the center of the dry ingredients and pour in the beaten liquid ingredients. Stir gently until just combined; do not overmix. Spoon the batter into the muffin pan.

Bake in the preheated oven for 20 minutes, or until well risen, golden brown, and firm to the touch. Let cool in the pan for 5 minutes, then serve warm.

845 Goat cheese & leek muffins

Omit the scallions and sauté 1 finely chopped leek in 2 tablespoons of butter until soft. Cool and add to the muffin batter along with ½ teaspoon of English mustard powder and a pinch of cayenne pepper, then bake, as before.

846 Tomato & basil muffins

MAKES 12

sunflower oil, for greasing
2 cups all-purpose flour
1 tbsp baking powder
pinch of salt
freshly ground black pepper
3½ oz/100 g sun-dried tomatoes in oil, drained (oil reserved) and finely chopped
2 eggs
generous 1 cup buttermilk
4 tbsp chopped fresh basil leaves
1 garlic clove, crushed
2 tbsp freshly grated Parmesan cheese

Preheat the oven to 400°F/200°C. Grease a 12-hole muffin pan. Sift together the flour, baking powder, and salt and pepper to taste into a large bowl. Stir in the sun-dried tomatoes.

Place the eggs in a large pitcher or bowl and beat lightly, then beat in the buttermilk, 6 tablespoons of the reserved oil from the tomatoes, the basil, and garlic. Make a well in the center of the dry ingredients and pour in the beaten liquid ingredients. Stir gently until just combined; do not overmix. Spoon the batter into the muffin pan. Scatter the Parmesan cheese over the tops of the muffins.

Bake in the preheated oven for 20 minutes, or until well risen, golden brown, and firm to the touch. Let cool in the pan for 5 minutes then serve warm.

847 Tomato, basil & black olive muffins

Use 5 tablespoons of oil, as before, plus 1 tablespoon of black olive tapenade.

848 Tuna & olive muffins

MAKES 12

6 tbsp sunflower oil or 6 tbsp butter, melted and cooled, plus extra for greasing
½ cup pitted black olives
2 cups all-purpose flour
1 tbsp baking powder
pinch of salt
freshly ground black pepper
2 eggs
generous 1 cup buttermilk
14 oz/400 g canned tuna in olive oil, drained and flaked

Preheat the oven to 400°F/200°C. Grease a 12-hole muffin pan. Coarsely chop the olives, reserving 12 whole ones for garnishing.

Sift together the flour, baking powder, and salt and pepper to taste into a large bowl. Stir in the chopped olives. Place the eggs in a large pitcher or bowl and beat lightly, then beat in the buttermilk and oil. Make a well in the center of the dry ingredients, pour in the beaten liquid ingredients, and add the tuna. Stir gently until just combined; do not overmix. Spoon the batter into the muffin pan. Top each muffin with one of the reserved olives.

Bake in the preheated oven for 20 minutes, or until well risen, golden brown, and firm to the touch. Leave for 5 minutes, then serve warm.

849 Tuna, olive & caper muffins

For extra piquancy, add 2 teaspoons of chopped, drained capers to the batter.

Tempting Treats

850 Cream puffs

MAKES ABOUT 24

CHOUX PASTRY
5 tbsp butter, plus extra for greasing
¾ cup all-purpose flour
generous ¾ cup water
3 eggs, lightly beaten

CREAM FILLING
1¼ cups heavy cream
3 tbsp superfine sugar
1 tsp vanilla extract

CHOCOLATE SAUCE
4½ oz/125 g semisweet chocolate, broken into small pieces
2 heaping tbsp butter
6 tbsp water
2 tbsp brandy

Preheat the oven to 400°F/200°C. Grease a large baking sheet. Sift the flour. Place the butter and water into a pan and heat gently until the butter has melted. Bring to a boil, then remove from the heat and immediately add all the flour, beating well until the mixture leaves the sides of the saucepan and forms a ball. Let cool slightly. Beat in enough of the eggs to give the mixture a soft dropping consistency. Transfer the mixture to a pastry bag fitted with a ½-inch/1-cm plain tip and pipe small balls onto the baking sheet.

Bake in the preheated oven for 25 minutes. Remove from the oven and pierce each ball with a skewer to let the steam to escape.

For the filling, place the cream, sugar, and vanilla extract in a bowl and whip together. Cut the pastry balls almost in half and fill with the cream.

To make the sauce, place the chocolate, butter, and water in a heatproof bowl, set the bowl over a saucepan of gently simmering water, and heat until smooth. Stir in the brandy. Pile the cream puffs into individual serving dishes or into a pyramid on a raised cake stand. Pour over the sauce and serve.

851 Chocolate & banana cream puffs

Make the cream puffs and sauce. Just before serving, whip the cream, sugar, and vanilla until just holding soft peaks. Mash 1 large ripe banana with a fork until smooth, then fold into the cream. Fill the cream puffs and serve immediately.

852 With strawberry coulis

Whiz 1¾ cups strawberries in a food processor, then push through a strainer to remove the seeds. Stir in ¼ cup confectioners' sugar and 2 tablespoons of framboise or peach schnapps. Serve with the cream puffs.

853 Cream-filled turnovers

MAKES 8

1 lb/450 g puff pastry, thawed if frozen	*generous 1 cup heavy cream or whipping cream*
all-purpose flour, for dusting	*1 tsp vanilla extract*
1 egg	*¼ cup raspberry or strawberry jam*
1 tbsp water	
4 tbsp superfine sugar	

Preheat the oven to 425°F/220°C. Line a large baking sheet with parchment paper. Roll the pastry out on a lightly floured work surface to a little larger than 10 inches/25 cm square. Using a sharp knife, trim the edges and cut out four 5-inch/13-cm squares. Cut each square in half diagonally to produce 8 triangles and place on the lined baking sheet.

Beat the egg with the water and brush over the tops of the triangles, being careful not to let it run down the sides. Sprinkle the tops with half the sugar.

Bake in the preheated oven for 15 minutes, or until risen, crisp, and golden. Transfer to a wire rack to cool completely.

Place the cream, remaining sugar, and vanilla extract in a large bowl and whip until peaks form. Spoon into a pastry bag fitted with a star tip. Split the puff pastry triangles in half horizontally and spread jam on the bottom halves. Pipe the cream on top of the jam and sandwich the 2 halves back together. Chill in the refrigerator until required.

854 Apple & cream turnovers

While the pastry is cooking, peel, core, and slice 4 apples. Place in a saucepan with 2 tablespoons of butter, 2 tablespoons of light brown sugar, and ½ teaspoon of apple pie spice and cook gently for 2–3 minutes, or until softened. Let cool. Whip the cream, omitting the sugar and vanilla. Spoon the apple into the pastry and top with cream to sandwich the pastry back together.

855 Cinnamon knots

MAKES 14

4 tbsp butter, plus extra for greasing	*2 tbsp confectioners' sugar*
½ tsp ground cinnamon	*6 sheets filo dough (total weight about 3¼ oz/90 g)*
1 tsp superfine sugar	

Preheat the oven to 350°F/180°C. Grease a large baking sheet. Place the butter in a saucepan and heat gently until melted, then cool.

Place the cinnamon and sugars in a large bowl and stir together. Brush 1 sheet of filo dough with melted butter. Cover the remaining sheets with a damp dish towel. Sprinkle a little of the cinnamon mixture over the dough. Lay a second sheet of dough on top and repeat until the dough and cinnamon mix have been used, reserving a little of the cinnamon mix for decorating. Cut the dough widthwise into ¾-inch/2-cm strips and tie each strip into a knot. Place on the baking sheet.

Bake in the preheated oven for 15–20 minutes, or until golden brown. Let cool. Dust with the reserved cinnamon mixture.

856 Chocolate éclairs

MAKES 12

CHOUX PASTRY
5 tbsp butter, diced, plus extra for greasing
¾ cup all-purpose flour
⅔ cup water
2 eggs

PASTRY CREAM
2 eggs, lightly beaten
4 tbsp superfine sugar
2 tbsp cornstarch
1¼ cups milk
¼ tsp vanilla extract

TOPPING
2 tbsp butter
1 tbsp milk
1 tbsp unsweetened cocoa
½ cup confectioners' sugar
1¾ oz/50 g white chocolate, broken into pieces

Preheat the oven to 400°F/200°C. Grease a baking sheet. Sift the flour. Place the butter and water in a saucepan and heat gently until the butter has melted. Bring to a boil, then remove from the heat and immediately add all the flour, beating well until the mixture leaves the sides of the saucepan and forms a ball.

Let cool slightly, then gradually beat in the eggs to form a smooth, glossy mixture. Spoon into a large pastry bag fitted with a ½-inch/1-cm plain tip. Sprinkle the baking sheet with a little water and pipe éclairs 3 inches/7.5 cm long, spaced well apart.

Bake in the preheated oven for 30–35 minutes, or until crisp and golden. Make a small slit in the side of each éclair, then transfer to a wire rack to cool. Meanwhile, to make the pastry cream, place the eggs and sugar in a large bowl and whisk together until thick and creamy. Fold in the cornstarch. Heat the milk in a pan until almost boiling, then pour onto the egg mixture, whisking. Transfer to the pan and cook gently, stirring until thick. Remove from the heat and stir in the vanilla extract. Cover and let cool.

To make the frosting, melt the butter and milk in a separate pan. Remove from the heat and stir in the cocoa and confectioners' sugar. Split the éclairs lengthwise and pipe in the pastry cream. Spread the frosting over the top of the éclairs. Place the white chocolate in a heatproof bowl, set the bowl over a pan of gently simmering water, and heat until melted, then drizzle over the chocolate frosting and let set.

857 Double choc éclairs

To make a chocolate pastry cream, add 3 oz/85 g finely chopped milk or semisweet chocolate to the hot milk and stir until the chocolate has melted to produce a chocolate milk.

858 Coffee éclairs

To make a coffee pastry cream, stir 2 tablespoons of instant coffee into the hot milk. To make coffee frosting, melt the butter with the milk and 1 tablespoon of instant coffee.

859 Toffee chocolate puff tarts

MAKES 12

13 oz/375 g ready-rolled puff pastry
5 oz/140 g semisweet chocolate, broken into pieces
1¼ cups heavy cream
¼ cup superfine sugar
4 egg yolks
4 tbsp ready-made toffee sauce
whipped cream, for serving
unsweetened cocoa, for dusting

Line the bottoms of a 12-hole muffin pan with disks of parchment paper. Cut out twelve 2-inch/5-cm rounds from the edge of the pastry and cut the remainder into 12 strips. Roll the strips to half their thickness and line the sides of each hole with 1 strip. Place a disk of pastry in each bottom and press together to seal and make a tart case. Prick the bottoms and let chill in the refrigerator for 30 minutes.

Preheat the oven to 400°F/200°C. While the pastry is chilling, place the chocolate in a heatproof bowl, set the bowl over a saucepan of gently simmering water, and heat until melted. Let cool slightly, then stir in the cream.

Place the sugar and egg yolks in a bowl and beat together, then mix well with the melted chocolate. Place a teaspoonful of the toffee sauce into each tart shell, then divide the chocolate mixture evenly among the tarts.

Bake in the preheated oven for 20–25 minutes, turning the pan around halfway through cooking, until just set. Let cool in the pan, then remove carefully and serve with whipped cream, dusted with cocoa.

860 Cherry chocolate puff tarts

Replace the toffee sauce with black cherry jam.

861 Toffee nut chocolate puff tarts

Stir heaping ⅓ cup chopped hazelnuts or pecans into the melted chocolate, before stirring in the cream.

862 Crown loaf

MAKES 6

2 tbsp butter, diced, plus extra for greasing
1⅔ cups white bread flour, plus extra for dusting
½ tsp salt
1 envelope or scant 1 tbsp active dry yeast
½ cup tepid milk
1 egg, lightly beaten

FILLING
4 tbsp butter, softened
¼ cup light brown sugar
2 tbsp chopped hazelnuts
1 tbsp chopped preserved ginger
½ cup chopped candied peel
1 tbsp dark rum or brandy

ICING
1 cup confectioners' sugar
1–2 tbsp lemon juice

Grease a large baking sheet. Sift the flour and salt into a bowl, then stir in the yeast. Add the butter and rub it in with your fingertips. Add the milk and egg and mix to form a dough. Place the dough in a greased bowl, cover, and stand in a warm place for 40 minutes, until doubled in size. Punch down the dough lightly for 1 minute, then roll out on a lightly floured work surface to a rectangle measuring 12 x 9 inches/30 x 23 cm.

For the filling, place the butter and sugar in a large bowl and beat together until light and fluffy. Stir in the hazelnuts, ginger, candied peel, and rum and spread the filling over the dough, leaving a 1-inch/2.5-cm border. Roll up the dough, starting from one of the long edges, into a sausage shape. Cut into slices at 2-inch/5-cm intervals and place, cut-side down, in a circle on the baking sheet with the slices just touching. Cover and let stand in a warm place for 30 minutes.

Preheat the oven to 375°F/190°C. Bake the loaf for 20–30 minutes, or until golden. Meanwhile, mix the confectioners' sugar with enough lemon juice to form a thin icing.

Let the loaf cool slightly before drizzling with the icing. Let set before serving.

863 Cherry & almond crown

Replace the hazelnuts with chopped almonds and the preserved ginger and candied peel with heaping ⅓ cup chopped candied cherries.

864 *Pain au chocolat*

Makes 12

¾ cup butter, softened, plus extra for greasing
heaping 3 ½ cups white bread flour, plus extra for dusting
½ tsp salt
1 envelope or scant 1 tbsp active dry yeast
2 tbsp lard or white vegetable fat
1 egg, lightly beaten
1 cup tepid water
3½ oz/100 g semisweet chocolate, broken into 12 squares
beaten egg, for glazing

Grease a large baking sheet. Sift the flour and salt into a bowl and stir in the yeast. Add the lard and rub it in with your fingertips. Add the egg and enough of the water to form a soft dough. Knead for 10 minutes, until the dough is smooth and elastic.

Roll the dough out on a lightly floured work surface to a 15 x 8-inch/38 x 20-cm rectangle and mark it vertically into thirds. Divide the butter into 3 portions and dot one portion over the first two thirds of the rectangle, leaving a small border around the edge. Fold the rectangle into 3 by first folding over the plain part of the dough, then folding over the other side. Seal the edges of the dough by pressing with a rolling pin. Give the dough a quarter turn and roll out as big as the original rectangle. Fold again (without adding butter), then wrap in plastic wrap and chill for 30 minutes. Repeat this rolling, folding, and turning twice more until all of the butter has been used, chilling the dough each time. Re-roll and fold twice more without butter. Chill for a final 30 minutes.

Roll the dough out on a lightly floured work surface to 18 x 12 inches/45 x 30 cm and halve lengthwise. Cut each half into 6 rectangles and brush with beaten egg. Place a chocolate square at one end of each rectangle and roll up to form a sausage. Press the ends together and place, seam-side down, on the baking sheet. Cover and leave in a warm place for 40 minutes.

Preheat the oven to 425°F/220°C. Brush each pastry with egg and bake in the preheated oven for 20–25 minutes, or until golden. Cool on a wire rack. Serve warm or cold.

865 *Pain au chocolat et noisette*

Place a rounded teaspoon of chocolate hazelnut spread instead of the chocolate in each pastry.

866 *Pain au apricot*

Mix ½ cup chopped plumped dried apricots with 3 tablespoons of ground almonds and 1 tablespoon of superfine sugar and use to fill the pastries.

867 Fresh croissants

Makes 12

heaping 3½ cups white bread flour, plus extra for dusting
3 tbsp superfine sugar
1 tsp salt
2 tsp active dry yeast
1¼ cups lukewarm milk
heaping 1¼ cups butter, softened, plus extra for greasing
1 egg, lightly beaten with 1 tbsp milk, for glazing

Sift the dry ingredients into a large bowl, make a well in the center and add the milk. Mix to form a soft dough, adding more milk if too dry, then knead on a lightly floured surface for 5–10 minutes, or until smooth and elastic. Place in a large, greased bowl, cover, and leave in a warm place until doubled in size.

Meanwhile, place the butter between 2 sheets of parchment paper and flatten with a rolling pin to form a rectangle about ¼ inch/5 mm thick. Let chill in the refrigerator.

Knead the dough for 1 minute. Remove the butter from the refrigerator and let soften slightly. Roll the dough out on a well-floured work surface to 18 x 6 inches/46 x 15 cm.

Place the butter in the center, folding up the sides and squeezing the edges together gently. With the short end of the dough toward you, fold the top third down toward the center, then fold the bottom third up. Give the dough a quarter turn, roll out as big as the original rectangle, and fold again. If the butter feels soft, wrap the dough in plastic wrap and chill. Repeat the rolling process twice more. Cut the dough in half.

Roll out each half into a rectangle about ¼ inch/5 mm thick. To cut out the croissants, use a cardboard triangular template, with a 7-inch/18-cm bottom and 8-inch/20-cm side.

Brush the triangles lightly with the egg glaze. Roll into croissant shapes, starting at the bottom and tucking the point underneath to prevent the croissants from unrolling while cooking. Brush again with the egg glaze. Place on a baking sheet and leave to double in size.

Preheat the oven to 400°F/200°C. Bake the croissants in the preheated oven for 15–20 minutes, or until golden brown. Transfer to a wire rack to cool and serve warm.

868 Ham & cheese croissants

Make and roll out the croissants as before. Sprinkle the dough triangles with grated cheese and chopped ham before rolling into croissant shapes.

869 Sun-dried tomato croissants

Spread the dough triangles with sun-dried tomato paste before rolling up and shaping the croissants.

870 Almond croissants

Roll a walnut-size piece of marzipan into a sausage shape a little shorter than the long side of each triangle of dough and roll up the croissants around the marzipan. After baking, dust with confectioners' sugar to serve.

871 Apple danish

Makes 16

DANISH PASTRY DOUGH
2 cups white bread flour, plus extra for dusting
¾ cup butter, well chilled, plus extra for greasing
¼ tsp salt
1 envelope or scant 1 tbsp active dry yeast
2 tbsp superfine sugar
1 egg
1 tsp vanilla extract
6 tbsp lukewarm water
milk, for glazing

FILLING
2 baking apples, peeled, cored, and chopped
grated rind of 1 lemon
4 tbsp sugar

Place the flour in a bowl, add 2 tablespoons of the butter, and rub it in with your fingertips. Chill the remaining butter in the freezer until hard but not frozen. Dust with flour and grate coarsely into a bowl. Let chill in the refrigerator. Stir the salt, yeast, and sugar into the flour mixture.

Place the egg, vanilla extract, and water in a bowl and beat together, then add to the flour mixture and mix to form a dough. Knead for 10 minutes on a floured work surface, then chill for 10 minutes. Roll the dough out on a lightly floured work surface to 12 x 8 inches/30 x 20 cm and mark it into thirds lengthwise. Sprinkle the grated butter over the top two thirds, leaving a ½–¾-inch/1–2-cm border around the edge. Fold the bottom third of dough over the center, then fold down the top third. Give the dough a quarter turn and roll out as big as the original rectangle. Fold the bottom third up and the top third down again. Wrap and chill for 30 minutes. Repeat this rolling, folding, and turning 4 times, chilling each time. Chill the dough overnight.

Preheat the oven to 400°F/200°C. Grease 2 baking sheets. Mix together the apples, lemon rind, and 3 tablespoons of the sugar. Roll the dough out into a 16-inch/40-cm square and cut into 16 squares. Pile a little of the filling in the center of each square. Brush the edges with milk and fold the corners together into the center. Chill on the baking sheets for 15 minutes.

Brush the pastries with milk and sprinkle with the remaining sugar. Bake in the preheated oven for 10 minutes. Reduce the oven temperature to 350°F/180°C and bake for an additional 10–15 minutes.

872 Apple & golden raisin danish

Replace the baking apples with 2 apples and add ½ cup golden raisins.

873 Apricot danish

For the filling, drain and chop 14 oz/400 g canned apricots in natural juice. Toss with the lemon rind, sugar, and ½ teaspoon of ground nutmeg.

874 Cherry & almond danish

For the filling, drain and chop 14 oz/400 g canned cherries. Toss with the lemon rind, sugar, ⅔ cup ground almonds, and 2 tablespoons of the cherry juice from the can.

875 Pear & raisin danish

For the filling, replace the apples with 2 pears and add ⅓ cup raisins.

876 Strawberry petits choux

MAKES 12

FILLING AND TOPPING
2 tsp powdered gelatin
2 tbsp water
2½ cups strawberries
1 cup ricotta cheese
1 tbsp superfine sugar
2 tsp crème de fraises de bois
confectioners' sugar, for dusting

PETITS CHOUX
¾ cup all-purpose flour
2 tbsp unsweetened cocoa
pinch of salt
6 tbsp butter
1 cup water
2 eggs, plus 1 egg white, lightly beaten

Sprinkle the gelatin over the water in a heatproof bowl and let soften for 2 minutes, then place the bowl over a saucepan of simmering water and stir until the gelatin dissolves. Remove from the heat.

Place 1½ cups of the strawberries in a blender with the ricotta, sugar, and liqueur and process until blended. Add the gelatin and process briefly. Transfer the mousse to a bowl, cover with plastic wrap, and chill in the refrigerator for 1–1½ hours, or until set.

Preheat the oven to 425°F/ 220°C. Line a large baking sheet with parchment paper.

To make the petits choux, sift together the flour, cocoa, and salt. Place the butter and water in a saucepan and heat gently until the butter has melted. Bring to a boil, then remove from the heat and immediately add all the flour mixture, beat the mixture well until it leaves the sides of the saucepan and forms a ball. Let cool slightly.

Gradually beat the eggs and egg white into the flour paste and continue beating until it is smooth and glossy, then drop 12 rounded tablespoonfuls of the mixture onto the baking sheet. Bake in the preheated oven for 20–25 minutes, or until puffed up and crisp.

Make a slit in the side of each petit chou, then return to the oven for an additional 5 minutes. Transfer the petits choux to a wire rack to cool.

Slice the other strawberries. Cut the petits choux in half and divide the mousse and strawberries among them. Replace the tops and dust with sifted confectioners' sugar. Chill in the refrigerator until required, but eat within 1½ hours of making.

877 Raspberry petits choux

Replace the strawberries with raspberries and place whole raspberries into the filled pastries with the mousse.

878 Apricot petits choux

Drain two 14 oz/400 g canned apricots in natural juice and use in place of the strawberries.

879 Raspberry chocolate boxes

MAKES 12

MOCHA MOUSSE
7 oz/200 g semisweet chocolate, broken into pieces
1½ tsp cold, strong black coffee
1 egg yolk
1½ tsp Kahlùa or other coffee liqueur
2 egg whites
1⅔ cups raspberries

SPONGE CAKE
2 tbsp butter, for greasing
1 egg, plus 1 egg white
4 tbsp superfine sugar
5 tbsp all-purpose flour

To make the mocha mousse, place 2 oz/55 g of the chocolate in a heatproof bowl, set the bowl over a saucepan of gently simmering water, and heat until melted. Add the coffee and stir over low heat until smooth, then let cool slightly. Stir in the egg yolk and the coffee liqueur. Place the egg whites in a separate bowl and whisk until stiff peaks form. Fold into the chocolate mixture, cover with plastic wrap, and chill for 2 hours, or until set.

For the sponge cake, lightly grease an 8-inch/20-cm square cake pan and line the bottom with parchment paper. Place the egg and extra white with the sugar in a heatproof bowl set over a saucepan of gently simmering water. Whisk for 5–10 minutes, or until pale and thick. Remove from the heat and continue whisking for 10 minutes, until cold and a trail is left when the whisk is dragged across the surface.

Preheat the oven to 350°F/180°C. Sift the flour over the egg mixture and fold it in. Pour the batter into the pan and spread evenly. Bake in the preheated oven for 20–25 minutes, or until firm to the touch. Cool on a wire rack, then invert the cake, leaving the paper in place.

To make the chocolate boxes, grease a 12 x 9-inch/30 x 23-cm jelly roll pan and line with parchment paper. Place the remaining chocolate in a heatproof bowl, set the bowl over a pan of gently simmering water, and heat until melted, but not too runny. Pour into the pan and spread evenly with a spatula. Let set in a cool place for 30 minutes.

Turn out the set chocolate onto parchment paper. Cut it into 36 rectangles, measuring about 3 x 1 inches/7.5 x 2.5 cm. Cut 12 of these rectangles in half to make 24 rectangles measuring about 1½ x 1 inches/4 x 2.5 cm.

Trim the edges off the sponge cake, then cut it into 12 slices, measuring about 3 x 1¼-inches/7.5 x 3 cm. Spread a little of the mocha mousse along the sides of each sponge rectangle and press 2 long and 2 short chocolate rectangles onto the sides to make boxes. Divide the remaining mousse among the boxes and top with raspberries. Chill in the refrigerator until ready to serve.

880 Strawberry chocolate boxes

Make as before but omit the coffee and replace the coffee liqueur with cassis. Use fresh strawberries instead of raspberries.

881 White chocolate & raspberry boxes

To make the mousse, melt 3 oz/85 g white chocolate. Remove from the heat then stir in 2 egg yolks and 2 tablespoons of heavy cream. Whisk 2 egg whites until they form stiff peaks and fold into the chocolate mixture. Cover and let set. Complete as before using 5 oz/150 g semisweet chocolate.

882 Strawberry tartlets

Makes 4

PIE DOUGH
1 cup all-purpose flour
2 tbsp confectioners' sugar
5 tbsp butter, at room temperature, cut into small pieces
1 egg yolk
1–2 tbsp water

FILLING
1 vanilla bean, split
generous ¾ cup milk
2 egg yolks
3 tbsp superfine sugar
1 tbsp all-purpose flour
1 tbsp cornstarch
½ cup heavy cream, lightly whipped
2¼ heaping cups strawberries, hulled
4 tbsp strawberry jam, melted

To make the dough, sift the flour and confectioners' sugar into a bowl. Add the butter and egg yolk and mix with your fingertips, adding a little water, if necessary, to form a soft dough. Cover with plastic wrap and chill in the refrigerator for 15 minutes.

Preheat the oven to 400°F/ 200°C. Roll the dough out on a lightly floured surface and use to line four 3½-inch/9-cm tartlet pans. Prick the bottoms with a fork, line with parchment paper, and fill with baking beans. Bake in the preheated oven for 10 minutes. Remove the paper and beans and bake unfilled for an additional 5 minutes, or until golden brown. Let cool.

To make the filling, place the vanilla bean in a saucepan with the milk and set on a low heat to steep, without boiling, for 10 minutes. Place the egg yolks, sugar, flour, and cornstarch in a large bowl and whisk together until smooth. Strain the milk into the bowl and whisk until smooth.

Pour the mixture back into the pan and stir over medium heat until boiling, then cook, stirring continuously, for about 2 minutes, or until thickened and smooth. Remove from the heat and fold in the whipped cream. Spoon the mixture into the pastry shells.

When the filling has set slightly, top with strawberries, sliced if large, then spoon over a little strawberry jam to glaze.

883 Kiwi tartlets

Replace the strawberries with sliced kiwi and brush with apricot jam.

884 Grape tartlets

Replace the strawberries with red and green grapes and arrange in circles on top of the filling, then brush with warm apricot jam.

885 Berry tartlets

Replace the strawberries with raspberries or blueberries.

886 Apple strudel with cider sauce

MAKES 4

8 apples
1 tbsp lemon juice
¾ cup golden raisins
1 tsp ground cinnamon
½ tsp ground nutmeg
1 tbsp light brown sugar
6 sheets filo dough thawed, if frozen
vegetable oil spray
confectioners' sugar, for serving

SAUCE
1 tbsp cornstarch
2 cups hard cider

Preheat the oven to 375°F/190°C. Line a baking sheet with parchment paper. Peel and core the apples and chop them into ½-inch/1-cm dice. Toss the apples in a bowl with the lemon juice, golden raisins, cinnamon, nutmeg, and brown sugar.

Lay out a sheet of filo dough, spray with vegetable oil, and lay a second sheet on top. Repeat with a third sheet. Spread over half the apple mixture and roll up lengthwise, tucking in the ends to enclose the filling. Repeat to make a second strudel, then slide onto the baking sheet and spray with oil. Bake in the preheated oven for 15–20 minutes.

To make the sauce, blend the cornstarch in a saucepan with a little cider until smooth. Add the remaining cider and heat gently, stirring, until the mixture boils and thickens. Slice the strudel and serve warm or cold, dredged with confectioners' sugar, and accompanied by the cider sauce.

887 With toffee sauce

For the sauce, place generous ⅓ cup heavy cream, 3 tablespoons of butter, ¼ cup dark brown sugar, and 1 tablespoon of dark corn syrup in a saucepan and heat, stirring, until the sauce comes to a boil. Let cool slightly.

888 With sabayon sauce

For the sauce, whisk 3 egg yolks with 2 tablespoons of superfine sugar in a heatproof bowl until thick, then set over a pan of simmering water. Add ¼ cup sweet white wine and whisk until thick. Serve warm with the strudel.

889 Pear strudel with cider sauce

Replace the apples with pears and the golden raisins with raisins.

890 Chocolate blueberry tarts

Makes 10

1¼ cups all-purpose flour, plus extra for dusting
½ cup unsweetened cocoa
¼ cup superfine sugar
pinch of salt
9 tbsp butter
1 large egg yolk
1⅓ cups blueberries
2 tbsp crème de cassis
3 tsp confectioners' sugar, plus extra for dusting

FILLING
5 oz/140 g semisweet chocolate, broken into pieces
1 cup heavy cream
⅔ cup sour cream

To make the dough, place the flour, cocoa, sugar, and salt in a food processor and pulse to mix. Add the butter, pulse again, then add the egg yolk and a little cold water to form a dough. Alternatively, place the flour, cocoa, sugar, and salt in a large bowl, add the butter, and rub it in with your fingertips until the mixture resembles breadcrumbs. Add the egg yolk and a little cold water to form a dough. Cover the dough with plastic wrap and chill in the refrigerator for 30 minutes.

Preheat the oven to 350°F/180°C. Roll the dough out on a floured work surface and use to line ten 4-inch/10-cm tartlet pans. Freeze for 30 minutes.

Bake in the preheated oven for 15–20 minutes. Let cool.

Place the blueberries, crème de cassis, and sift the confectioners' sugar into a saucepan and warm through so the berries become shiny, but do not burst. Remove from the heat and let cool.

For the filling, place the chocolate in a heatproof bowl, set the bowl over a saucepan of gently simmering water, and heat until melted, then cool slightly. Place the cream in a large bowl and whip until stiff, then fold in the sour cream and chocolate.

Divide the chocolate filling evenly among the tart shells, smoothing the surface, and top with the blueberries. Dust with sifted confectioners' sugar.

891 Chocolate orange tarts

Make the pastry shells, and bake unfilled. Replace the sour cream with heavy cream and whip with the grated rind of 1 orange, then stir in 2 tablespoons of orange flavored liqueur and add to the chocolate. Pour the filling into the pastry shells, then top with orange segments.

892 Chocolate raspberry tarts

Make the pastry shells and filling as before. Replace the blueberries with raspberries and substitute the crème de cassis with framboise.

893 Fresh black cherry tarts

MAKES 8

1⅔ cups all-purpose flour, plus extra for dusting
8 tbsp butter, cut into cubes
2 tbsp confectioners' sugar
1 tsp vanilla extract
1 egg yolk
2–3 tbsp cold water

FILLING
1 heaping cup mascarpone
½ cup confectioners' sugar
2 eggs
⅔ cup heavy cream
9 oz/250 g black cherries
3 tbsp black cherry jam
1 tbsp water

Place the flour in a large bowl. Add the butter to the flour and rub it in with your fingertips until the mixture resembles fine breadcrumbs. Add the confectioners' sugar, vanilla extract, egg yolk, and enough water to form a soft dough. Cover with plastic wrap and chill in the refrigerator for 15 minutes.

Roll the dough out on a floured work surface and use to line eight 4-inch/10-cm shallow tartlet pans. Chill in the refrigerator for 30 minutes.

Preheat the oven to 400°F/200°C. Prick the bottom of the shells, then line with parchment paper and fill with baking beans. Bake in the preheated oven for 10 minutes, then remove the paper and beans and bake for an additional 5–10 minutes, or until crisp and golden.

Transfer the pans to a wire rack to cool. Reduce the oven temperature to 350°F/180°C.

To make the filling, place the mascarpone, confectioners' sugar, and eggs in a large bowl and whisk together until well combined, then stir in the heavy cream. Remove the pastry shells from the pans and place on a baking sheet.

Fill each pastry shell with the mascarpone mixture and bake in the oven for 10 minutes, or until the mixture begins to set. Let cool, then chill for 2 hours.

Pit the cherries and halve, then arrange on top of the tarts. Melt the jam with the water in a small saucepan, then drizzle over the fruit. Chill until required.

894 Fresh berry tartlets

Stir 2 tablespoons of framboise into the mascarpone mixture before filling the tartlet shells. Top the chilled shells with 1¾ cups fresh raspberries and use apricot jam or seedless raspberry jam to make the glaze.

895 Chocolate candied orange peels

MAKES 48

2 thick-skinned oranges
¾ cup granulated sugar
⅔ cup water
⅓ cup superfine sugar
2¼ oz/60 g semisweet chocolate, broken into pieces

Cut the oranges into quarters and remove the flesh. Cut each piece of orange peel into about 6 triangular shapes measuring about ½ inch/1 cm thick.

Place the peels into a large saucepan, just cover with cold water, and bring to a boil. Drain, then cover with fresh water and bring to a boil again. Repeat the process 3 more times. Finally, drain the orange peels.

Place the granulated sugar and water in the pan and heat gently, stirring all the time, until the sugar has dissolved. Add the orange peels, bring to a boil, and boil gently, stirring occasionally, until the syrup has almost evaporated and the peel has softened. Let cool.

When the mixture is cold, drain the peels well. Spread the superfine sugar on a large plate and, working in batches, turn the peel in the sugar until coated on both sides. Place the peel on a wire rack, in a single layer, over a baking sheet.

Sprinkle any remaining sugar over the top of the peel and let dry for at least 12 hours, or overnight.

When the peel is dry, line a baking sheet with parchment paper. Place the chocolate in a heatproof bowl, set the bowl over a saucepan of gently simmering water, and heat until melted. Remove from the heat and stir until smooth.

Dip the pieces of peel into the melted chocolate and then place on the baking sheet. Leave in a cool place for 2–3 hours, or until the chocolate is set.

896 Really rich chocolate tarts

MAKES 8

1⅔ cups all-purpose flour, plus extra for dusting
8 tbsp butter, cut into cubes
2 tbsp confectioners' sugar
1 egg yolk
2–3 tbsp cold water

FILLING
9 oz/250 g semisweet chocolate, broken into pieces, plus extra, grated, for decorating
8 tbsp butter
½ cup confectioners' sugar
1¼ cups heavy cream

Place the flour in a large bowl. Add the butter and rub it in with your fingertips until the mixture resembles breadcrumbs. Add the confectioners' sugar, egg yolk, and enough water to form a soft dough. Cover and chill in the refrigerator for 15 minutes.

Roll the dough out on a lightly floured work surface and use to line eight 4-inch/10-cm shallow tartlet pans. Chill for 30 minutes.

Preheat the oven to 400°F/200°C. Prick the bottom of the shells with a fork and line with a little crumpled foil. Bake in the preheated oven for 10 minutes, then remove the foil and bake for 5–10 minutes, until crisp. Transfer to a wire rack to cool. Reduce the oven temperature to 325°F/160°C.

To make the filling, place the chocolate, butter, and confectioners' sugar in a heat-proof bowl set over a saucepan of simmering water and heat until melted. Remove from the heat and stir in a generous ¾ cup heavy cream. Remove the shells from the pans and place on a baking sheet. Fill each shell with the chocolate. Bake for 5 minutes. Cool, then chill until required.

To serve, whip the remaining cream and pipe or spoon into the center of each tart. Decorate with grated chocolate.

897 Rich lemon tarts

For a tangy lemon filling, preheat the oven to 350°F/180°C. Place 4 eggs and ½ cup superfine sugar into a bowl and whisk together. Add the grated rind of 2 lemons and ⅔ cup lemon juice and whisk together, then finally whisk in ⅔ cup heavy cream. Pour into the baked pastry shells and bake for 15–20 minutes, or until just set. Cool, then chill in the refrigerator. Serve on their own or with fresh raspberries.

898 Dates & figs with an almond filling

MAKES 48

1⅔ cups ground almonds
1⅓ cups confectioners' sugar
2 tsp rum or brandy
1 egg white, lightly beaten
24 pitted dates
24 plumped dried figs

Place the almonds and sugar in a bowl and stir until well combined. Add the rum and egg white and mix to a firm paste.

Cut the dates almost in half lengthwise, then cut a cross into the center of the figs. Divide the almond paste in half, then divide one half into 24 pieces and roll into small sausage shapes. Place in the center of each date, then place the date into paper petit four cases.

Divide the remaining paste into 24 pieces and roll into balls, then use to fill the center of each fig and place in petit four cases. Chill in the refrigerator until required.

899 Marzipan-stuffed dates & figs

Produce this delicious recipe in half the time by replacing the filling with ready-made marzipan.

900 *Fruit & nut fudge*

Makes 36 Pieces

2 tbsp butter, plus extra for greasing
9 oz/250 g semisweet chocolate, broken into pieces
4 tbsp evaporated milk
scant 4 cups confectioners' sugar
1/3 cup coarsely chopped hazelnuts
1/4 cup golden raisins

Lightly grease an 8-inch/20-cm square cake pan. Place the chocolate, butter, and evaporated milk in a heatproof bowl, set the bowl over a saucepan of gently simmering water, and stir until the chocolate and butter have melted and the mixture is well blended.

Remove from the heat, sift in the confectioners' sugar a little at a time, beating to incorporate. Stir the hazelnuts and golden raisins into the mixture, then press the fudge into the pan and smooth the top. Chill in the refrigerator until firm.

Tip the fudge out onto a cutting board and cut into squares with a sharp knife. Chill in the refrigerator until required.

901 *Cranberry & pecan fudge*

Replace the golden raisins with dried cranberries and the hazelnuts with pecans.

902 *Mocha walnut fudge*

Add 1 tablespoon of instant coffee to the chocolate and evaporated milk and replace the golden raisins and hazelnuts with 3/4 cup chopped walnuts.

903 Ginger chocolate fudge

Makes 49 Pieces

8 tbsp butter, plus extra for greasing
6 pieces preserved ginger
1¼ cups milk
5½ oz/150 g semisweet chocolate, broken into pieces
2¼ cups granulated sugar

Grease a shallow 7-inch/18-cm square pan or a shallow 8 x 6-inch/20 x 15-cm rectangular pan. Dry the syrup off the pieces of preserved ginger on paper towels, then chop finely.

Pour the milk into a large saucepan and add the chocolate, butter, and sugar. Heat gently, stirring all the time, until the chocolate and butter have melted and the sugar has completely dissolved. Bring to a boil and boil for about 10–15 minutes, stirring occasionally, until a little of the mixture, when dropped into a small bowl of cold water, forms a soft ball when rolled between the fingers. The temperature on a sugar thermometer should reach 240°F/116°C (soft ball stage). Remove from the heat and stir in the chopped ginger. Let cool for 5 minutes.

Using a wooden spoon, beat the fudge until it begins to lose its shine and is thick and creamy. Immediately turn the mixture into the pan and let cool. When the mixture is cool, mark the surface into 1-inch/2.5-cm squares and leave until set. When set, cut the fudge into squares with a sharp knife.

904 Cherry chocolate fudge

Replace the preserved ginger with ¾ cup chopped candied cherries.

905 Brown sugar fudge

Makes 49 Pieces

7 tbsp butter, cut into cubes, plus extra for greasing
1¼ cups whole-milk
4 cups light brown sugar
1 tsp vanilla extract

Grease a shallow 7-inch/18-cm square pan. Place the milk, sugar, and butter into a large saucepan and bring slowly to a boil, stirring continuously, until the butter has melted. Bring to a boil, then cover the pan with a lid and boil gently for 2 minutes. Uncover and continue to boil, stirring occasionally, until a little of the mixture, dropped into a small bowl of cold water, forms a soft ball when rolled between your fingers. The temperature on a sugar thermometer should reach 240°F/116°C (soft ball stage). Remove from the heat and stir in the vanilla extract. Let cool for 5 minutes.

Using a wooden spoon, beat the fudge until it begins to lose its shine and is thick and creamy. Immediately turn the mixture into the pan and let cool. When the mixture is cool, mark the surface into 1-inch/2.5-cm squares and leave until set. When set, cut the fudge into squares with a sharp knife.

906 Rich chocolate fudge

MAKES 49 PIECES

6 tbsp utter, plus extra for greasing
$2^1/_4$ cups granulated sugar
$^2/_3$ cup evaporated milk
$5^1/_2$ oz/150 g semisweet chocolate, broken into pieces
2 tbsp unsweetened cocoa

Grease and line a 7-inch/18-cm square cake pan. Place all the ingredients in a large saucepan and heat gently, stirring over low heat until the sugar dissolves and the chocolate melts to form a smooth mixture.

Bring to a boil and boil for about 10–15 minutes, stirring occasionally, until a little of the mixture, when dropped into a small bowl of cold water, forms a soft ball when rolled between the fingers. The temperature on a sugar thermometer should reach 240°F/116°C (soft ball stage). Let cool for 5–10 minutes, then beat vigorously with a wooden spoon until the mixture thickens and begins to "grain" (form small crystals). Pour into the pan and mark into squares.

Let cool and set before cutting into squares to serve.

907 Vanilla fudge

Heat $2^1/_4$ cups granulated sugar, 6 tablespoons of butter, $^2/_3$ cup evaporated milk, and $^2/_3$ cup milk together in a saucepan until the sugar dissolves. Bring to a boil and boil as before. Add 1 teaspoon of vanilla extract to the mixture before beating with a wooden spoon. Stir the mixture occasionally because it burns very easily.

908 Mocha fudge

Add 4 tablespoons of instant coffee in place of the cocoa.

909 Rum & raisin choc fudge

Gently heat 2 tablespoons of rum until hot in a small saucepan, then add $^3/_4$ cup raisins. Let cool while preparing the fudge, then add to the fudge when beating the mixture with a wooden spoon.

910 Chocolate orange fudge

Omit the cocoa and add the finely grated rind and juice of $^1/_2$ orange.

911 Nutty chocolate clusters

MAKES 30

6 oz/175 g white chocolate, broken into pieces
3½ oz/100 g graham crackers
⅔ cup chopped macadamia nuts or Brazil nuts
1 oz/25 g preserved ginger, chopped (optional)
6 oz/175 g semisweet chocolate, broken into pieces

Line a large baking sheet with a sheet of parchment paper. Place the white chocolate in a large heatproof bowl, set the bowl over a saucepan of gently simmering water, and heat until melted.

Break the graham crackers into small pieces. Stir the crumbs into the melted chocolate with the chopped nuts and preserved ginger, if using, then place heaping teaspoons of the mixture on the baking sheet. Chill the mixture in the refrigerator until set, then remove from the parchment paper.

Melt the semisweet chocolate and let cool slightly. Dip the clusters into the melted chocolate, letting the excess to drip back into the bowl. Chill the clusters on the baking sheet until set.

912 Cherry & walnut clusters

Replace the macadamia or Brazil nuts with walnuts and the ginger with chopped candied cherries.

913 Date & nut clusters

Replace the preserved ginger with ⅓ cup chopped dates and reduce the crackers to 3 oz/85 g.

914 Apricot & almond clusters

MAKES ABOUT 24

4 oz/115 g semisweet chocolate, broken into pieces
2 tbsp honey
⅔ cup plumped dried apricots, chopped
⅓ cup blanched almonds, chopped

Place the chocolate and honey in a heatproof bowl, set the bowl over a saucepan of gently simmering water, and heat until melted and smooth.

Stir in the apricots and almonds, then drop teaspoonfuls of the mixture into paper candy cases. Let set.

915 Date & almond clusters

Replace the apricots with plumped dried dates.

916 Apricot & hazelnut clusters

Replace the almonds with chopped toasted hazelnuts.

917 Fig & almond clusters

Replace the apricots with chopped dried figs.

918 *Nutty palmiers*

MAKES ABOUT 20

butter, for greasing
6 oz/175 g ready-made puff pastry, thawed if frozen
all-purpose flour, for dusting
¼ cup finely chopped roasted hazelnuts or pecans
2 tbsp raw brown sugar
1 egg white, lightly beaten

Preheat the oven to 400°F/200°C. Grease 2 large baking sheets. Roll out the pastry on a lightly floured work surface to form an 8 x 12-inch/20 x 30-cm rectangle. Trim the edges with sharp knife.

Place the nuts and sugar in a bowl and mix together. Brush the pastry with egg white and sprinkle with three quarters of the nuts and sugar. Fold the long sides of the pastry so that they reach halfway toward the center. Fold again so that they just meet in the center and roll gently with a rolling pin to flatten very slightly. Brush with a little more egg white and sprinkle the remaining sugar and nuts over the surface. Fold in half down the center and gently flatten again with the rolling pin.

Using a sharp knife, cut the roll into about 20 thin slices and place cut side down on the baking sheets, spaced well apart.

Bake in the preheated oven for 10 minutes. Remove from the oven and turn the palmiers over. Return to the oven and bake for an additional 5 minutes, or until golden and crisp. Transfer to a wire rack to cool completely.

919 *Chocolate palmiers*

Replace the sugar and nuts with 4 tablespoons of grated chocolate and 2 teaspoons of superfine sugar. Chill in the refrigerator for 15 minutes before baking.

920 *Cheesy palmiers*

Replace the sugar and nuts with ¾ cup grated cheddar cheese and 2 finely chopped scallions.

921 *Cinnamon palmiers*

Replace the sugar and nuts with a mixture of 4 tablespoons of superfine sugar mixed with 1 teaspoon of ground cinnamon.

922 *Pesto & tomato palmiers*

Roll out the pastry and spread with 2 tablespoons of pesto. Finely chop 2 sun-dried tomatoes and sprinkle most of the tomato over the pastry. Fold as before, spreading the pastry with a little more pesto and the remaining tomato before the final fold.

923 *Sacristons*

Roll out the pastry, then brush the pastry with a little beaten egg white and sprinkle over 4 tablespoons of superfine sugar and ⅓ cup chopped almonds. Lightly press the almonds into the pastry with a rolling pin. Cut into fingers measuring about 2½ x ½ inch/6 x 1 cm. Twist each finger and place on the baking sheets, spaced well apart. Bake in the preheated oven for 10–12 minutes, or until golden and crisp. Transfer to a wire rack to cool completely.

924 Chocolate mendiants

MAKES ABOUT 30

¼ cup plumped dried figs, dates or apricots, or candied orange peel
¼ cup raisins, golden raisins, or cranberries
1 tbsp pistachios or blanched hazelnuts
¼ cup blanched almonds
5½ oz/150 g semisweet chocolate, broken into pieces

Line several baking sheets with parchment paper. If using figs, coarsely snip into small pieces using scissors and place in a pile or in a small bowl. Place the remaining fruits and nuts in piles or in small bowls.

Place the chocolate in a heatproof bowl, set the bowl over a saucepan of gently simmering water, and heat until melted. Remove from the heat and stir until smooth.

Place 4–5 heaping teaspoons of the chocolate on a baking sheet and spread into disks measuring about 2 inches/5 cm in diameter. Place equal amounts of the fruits and nuts on each disk, then repeat with the remaining chocolate, fruit, and nuts. Leave in a cool place for 2–3 hours, or until set.

925 Almond macaroons

MAKES ABOUT 12

1 egg white
1 cup ground almonds
½ cup superfine sugar, plus extra for rolling
½ tsp almond extract
6–7 blanched almonds, split in half

Preheat the oven to 350°F/180°C. Line 2 large baking sheets with parchment paper. Place the egg white in a bowl and beat with a fork until frothy, then stir in the ground almonds, sugar, and almond extract, mixing to form a sticky dough.

Using lightly sugared hands, roll the dough into small balls and place on the baking sheets. Press an almond half into the center of each.

Bake in the preheated oven for 15–20 minutes, or until pale golden. Transfer to a wire rack to cool completely.

926 Hazelnut macaroons

Grind ½ cup hazelnuts very finely in a food processor and use instead of the ground almonds. Decorate with halved hazelnuts.

927 Coconut macaroons

Replace the ground almonds with ⅔–¾ cup dry unsweetened coconut. Decorate with halved candied cherries.

928 *Walnut & honey triangles*

MAKES 18

3½ tbsp butter
½ cup cream cheese
1 tbsp honey
2 tbsp superfine sugar
1 cup walnut halves, finely chopped
finely grated rind of 1 lemon
6 sheets filo dough (total weight about 3¼ oz/90 g)
confectioners' sugar, for decorating

Preheat the oven to 350°F/180°C. Grease a large baking sheet. Place the butter in a saucepan and heat gently until melted, then let cool slightly. Meanwhile, place the cream cheese, honey, and sugar in a large bowl and beat together until combined. Add the chopped walnuts and lemon rind and stir together.

Brush 1 sheet of filo dough with melted butter and cut into 3 equal strips. Cover the remaining sheets with a clean damp dish cloth. Place 1 heaping teaspoon of the walnut mixture at the end of each strip. Fold over the end at a diagonal to form a triangle, then continue to fold up the filo, maintaining the triangle shape.

Place on the baking sheet and brush with melted butter. Repeat with the remaining filo and walnut mixture. Bake in the preheated oven for 10–15 minutes, or until golden brown. Let cool. For decorating, sift confectioners' sugar lightly over the triangles and serve immediately.

929 *Chocolate almond petits fours*

MAKES 16

½ cup ground almonds
½ cup granulated sugar
5 tsp unsweetened cocoa
1 egg white
8 blanched almonds, halved
2 oz/55 g semisweet chocolate, broken into pieces

Preheat the oven to 375°F/190°C. Line a large baking sheet with parchment paper. Place the ground almonds, sugar, and cocoa in a bowl and mix together well. Add the egg white and mix to form a firm mixture. Fill a pastry bag, fitted with a small plain tip, with the mixture and pipe 2-inch/5-cm lengths, spaced well apart, onto the baking sheet. Place an almond half on top of each.

Bake in the preheated oven for 5 minutes, or until firm. Transfer to a wire rack to cool.

When the petits fours are cold, place the chocolate in a heatproof bowl, set the bowl over a saucepan of gently simmering water, and heat until melted. Dip each end of the petits fours into the melted chocolate and let set.

930 *Chocolate hazelnut petits fours*

Grind ¼ cup hazelnuts in a food processor and use instead of the ground almonds. Place a halved hazelnut in the center of each instead of the almond.

931 *Coffee almond petits fours*

Add 2 tablespoons of coffee powder instead of the cocoa. Dip the petits fours into the melted chocolate or leave them undipped.

932 Golden apricot & almond tarts

MAKES 12

1½ tbsp butter, plus extra for greasing
6 sheets filo dough (total weight about 3¼ oz/90 g)
2 tbsp apricot jam
2 large egg whites
4 tbsp superfine sugar
½ cup ground almonds
¼ cup slivered almonds

Preheat the oven to 350°F/180°C. Grease a 12-hole muffin pan. Place the butter in a saucepan and heat gently until melted, then let cool slightly. Brush 1 sheet of filo dough with melted butter. Cover the remaining sheets with a clean damp dish cloth. Lay a second sheet of filo dough on top, brush with butter, and repeat with a third sheet.

Using a 3¼-inch/8-cm round cutter, cut the filo into 6 rounds and place in the muffin pan. Repeat with the remaining filo dough sheets and butter. Spoon the jam equally into the pastry shells.

Place the egg whites in a large bowl and whisk until stiff. Add the sugar and ground almonds and, using a large metal spoon, fold in until combined. Spoon the mixture into the tarts and spread out to cover the jam. Sprinkle the slivered almonds over the top.

Bake in the preheated oven for 25 minutes, or until golden brown. Serve warm or transfer to a wire rack to cool.

933 Tiny chocolate cupcakes with ganache frosting

MAKES 20

4 tbsp butter, softened
¼ cup superfine sugar
1 large egg, lightly beaten
heaping ¼ cup self-rising flour
2 tbsp unsweetened cocoa
1 tbsp milk
20 chocolate-coated coffee beans, for decorating

FROSTING
3½ oz/100 g semisweet chocolate, broken into pieces
generous ⅓ cup heavy cream

Preheat the oven to 375°F/190°C. Place 20 double-layer mini paper liners on 2 large baking sheets. Place the butter and sugar in a large bowl and beat together until light and fluffy, then gradually beat in the egg. Sift in the flour and cocoa and fold into the mixture. Stir in the milk.

Fill a pastry bag fitted with a large plain tip with the batter and pipe it into the paper liners, filling each one half full.

Bake in the preheated oven for 10–15 minutes, or until well risen and firm to the touch. Transfer to a wire rack to cool.

To make the frosting, place the chocolate and cream in a saucepan and heat gently, stirring continuously, until the chocolate has melted. Pour into a large heatproof bowl and, using an electric hand-held mixer, beat the mixture for 10 minutes, or until thick, glossy and cool.

Fill a pastry bag fitted with a large star tip with the frosting and pipe a swirl on top of each cupcake. Alternatively, spoon the frosting over the top of each cupcake. Chill in the refrigerator for 1 hour, then serve decorated with a chocolate-coated coffee bean.

934 With milk chocolate ganache

Replace the semisweet chocolate with milk chocolate and decorate with a white chocolate disk or white chocolate curls made with a vegetable peeler.

935 Tiny coffee & hazelnut cupcakes

Replace the cocoa and milk with 2 tablespoons of instant coffee dissolved in 2 tablespoons of milk. Add ¼ cup chopped hazelnuts to the cake batter and decorate with toasted hazelnuts instead of coffee beans.

936 Persian almond rolls

MAKES 15

7 tbsp butter, plus extra for greasing
1½ cups blanched almonds, chopped
4 tbsp superfine sugar
1 tsp ground cinnamon
12 sheets filo dough (total weight about 6½ oz/190 g)

SYRUP
heaping ⅓ cup granulated sugar
4 tbsp water
1½ tsp lemon juice

Preheat the oven to 350°F/180°C. Grease a large baking sheet. Place the butter in a saucepan and heat gently until melted, then let cool slightly. Place the almonds, sugar, and cinnamon in a bowl and stir together.

Brush 1 sheet of filo dough with melted butter. Lay a second sheet of filo on top and brush with butter. Cover the remaining sheets with a damp dish cloth. Spoon a little of the almond mixture along the long edge of the filo, leaving a ¾-inch/2-cm border at each end. Fold in the sides and roll up. Place the rolls on the baking sheet and brush with melted butter. Repeat with the remaining filo and almond mixture. Bake in the preheated oven for 15–20 minutes, or until golden brown.

Place the granulated sugar, water, and lemon juice in a pan and heat gently, stirring continuously until the sugar has dissolved. Bring to a boil and boil for 5 minutes, then let cool. Pour the syrup over the top of the rolls and let cool, then cut each roll into 2-inch/5-cm rolls.

937 Chocolate Easter egg nests

MAKES 12

5 tbsp butter
4 oz/115 g milk chocolate, broken into pieces
3 tbsp dark corn syrup
1 tbsp unsweetened cocoa
7 cups puffed rice cereal or flaked corn cereal, or shredded wheat cereal broken into strands
mini chocolate or marzipan Easter eggs, for decorating

Place 12 paper liners in a 12-hole muffin pan. Place the butter, chocolate, dark corn syrup, and cocoa in a saucepan and heat gently, stirring continuously, until melted and combined. Remove from the heat and carefully stir the cereal into the mixture, being careful not to break it too much. Stir until well coated.

Spoon the chocolate mixture into the paper cake liners and make a dip in the center so that they form "nests." Chill in the refrigerator until set. Remove from the paper liners, then arrange the eggs inside each of the nests.

938 *Baklava*

MAKES 25

2¼ cups walnut halves
1½ cups shelled pistachios
⅔ cup blanched almonds
4 tbsp pine nuts, finely chopped
finely grated rind of 2 large oranges
6 tbsp sesame seeds
1 tbsp superfine sugar
½ tsp ground cinnamon
½ tsp pumpkin pie spice
generous 1 cup butter, melted, plus extra for greasing
23 sheets filo dough, thawed, if frozen

SYRUP
2¼ cups superfine sugar
2 cups water
5 tbsp honey
3 cloves
2 large strips lemon zest

To make the filling, place the walnuts, pistachios, almonds, and pine nuts in a food processor and process gently, until finely chopped but not ground. Transfer the chopped nuts to a bowl and stir in the orange rind, sesame seeds, sugar, cinnamon, and pumpkin pie spice.

Preheat the oven to 325°F/160°C. Grease a square 10-inch/25-cm ovenproof dish, about 2 inches/5 cm deep. Cut the stacked filo sheets to size, using a ruler. Keep the sheets covered with a damp dish towel. Place a sheet of filo on the bottom of the dish and brush with melted butter. Top with 7 more sheets, brushing with butter between each layer.

Sprinkle with a generous one fifth of the filling. Top with 3 sheets of filo dough, brushing each one with butter. Continue layering until you have used up all the filo and filling, ending with a top layer of 3 filo sheets. Brush with butter.

Cut the baklava into 2-inch/5-cm squares with a sharp knife and brush again with butter. Bake in the preheated oven for 1 hour.

Meanwhile, place all the ingredients for the syrup in a saucepan and slowly bring to a boil, stirring to dissolve the sugar. Reduce the heat and simmer for 15 minutes, without stirring, until a thin syrup forms. Let cool.

Strain the cooled syrup over the top of the baklava, let cool in the dish, and cut out the squares to serve.

939 *Filo Christmas crackers*

MAKES 12

heaping ¼ cup plumped dried apricots
½ cup mixed dried fruit
⅓ cup blanched almonds, chopped
2 tbsp sherry
3½ tbsp butter, plus extra for greasing
6 sheets filo dough (total weight about 3¼ oz/90 g)
confectioners' sugar, for dusting

Cut the apricots finely with scissors and place in a large bowl. Add the dried fruit, almonds, and sherry and let soak for 1–2 hours.

Preheat the oven to 350°F/180°C. Grease a large baking sheet. Place the butter in a saucepan and heat gently until melted, then let cool slightly. Meanwhile, cut 1 sheet of filo in half widthwise and brush each half with melted butter. Cover the remaining sheets with a damp dish towel. Spoon a little of the dried fruit mixture along the long edge of the filo sheets, leaving a 2½-inch/6-cm border at each end. Roll up, pinching the ends together to form a cracker shape. Place on the baking sheet and brush with melted butter. Repeat with the remaining filo and filling. Bake in the preheated oven for 15–20 minutes, or until golden brown. Dust with sifted confectioners' sugar to serve.

940 Galaktoboureko

Makes 20

1scant ⅔ cup butter
4 large eggs
⅔ cup superfine sugar
4 cups milk
¾ cup semolina
finely grated rind 1 lemon and 1½ tsp lemon juice
7 oz/200 g filo dough
heaping ⅓ cup granulated sugar
4 tbsp water

Preheat the oven to 350°F/180°C. Place 8 tablespoons of the butter in a saucepan and heat gently until melted, then let cool slightly. Use a little of the melted butter to grease a shallow 10 x 7-inch/35 x 18 cm roasting pan.

Place the eggs and superfine sugar in a large bowl and whisk together until pale and creamy. Heat the milk in a large pan until warm, then stir into the egg mixture. Return the mixture to the pan and add the semolina and lemon rind. Heat gently, stirring, until the mixture boils and thickens. Remove from the heat and stir in the remaining butter.

Line the roasting pan with a sheet of filo dough and brush with melted butter. Cover the remaining sheets with a damp dish cloth. Lay a second sheet of filo on top, bringing it up the sides of the pan, and brush with butter. Continue until half of the filo sheets have been used, bringing it up the sides of the pan each time. Spoon the milk mixture into the pan and spread out evenly. Cover with the remaining filo sheets, brushing each sheet with butter and tucking down the edges. Cut the top layers of the filo into 20 square shapes.

Bake in the preheated oven for 35–40 minutes, or until golden brown. Meanwhile, place the granulated sugar, water, and lemon juice in a pan and heat, stirring until the sugar has dissolved. Bring to a boil, without stirring, and boil for 5 minutes.

Let cool, then pour the syrup over the top of the filo. Cut along the lines to divide into pieces.

941 French beignets

Makes About 24

6 tbsp butter, cut into pieces
generous ¾ cup water
¾ cup white bread flour
2 eggs, lightly beaten
sunflower oil, for deep frying

RASPBERRY SAUCE
1 lb/450 g raspberries
heaping ⅓ cup superfine sugar, plus extra for sprinkling
1 tbsp water

To make the sauce, place the raspberries, sugar, and water in a saucepan and heat gently until soft. Push through a strainer and set aside.

To make the beignets, place the butter and water in a pan and heat gently until the butter melts. Increase the heat and bring to a rapid boil. Remove from the heat, then add the flour and beat until the mixture forms a ball. Cool slightly, then gradually beat in the eggs until smooth and glossy.

Heat the oil in a suitable pan to 375°F/190°C. Drop rounded teaspoons of the mixture in batches into the oil and deep-fry until the beignets rise to the top and are golden and crisp. Remove with a slotted spoon and drain on paper towels. Repeat until all the mixture has been used. Drizzle the sauce over the beignets and sprinkle with sugar.

942 With rum sauce

To make the rum sauce, grate the rind from ½ orange and squeeze the juice from 2 oranges. Mix 1 teaspoon of cornstarch with a little orange juice, then add the remaining juice. Add ¼ cup raw brown sugar and heat until thick. Whisk in 2 tablespoons of butter, cut into cubes, stir in the orange rind and 4 tablespoons of rum and simmer for 1 minute, then serve with the beignets.

943 Jewish rugelach

Makes 24

8 tbsp butter, softened
½ cup cream cheese
3 tbsp superfine sugar
½ cup sour cream
1 tsp vanilla extract
heaping 1¾ cups all-purpose flour

FILLING
¼ cup light brown sugar
1½ tsp ground cinnamon
½ cup raisins, chopped
heaping ½ cup walnuts, chopped
beaten egg, for glazing

Place the butter in a large bowl and beat until creamy, then beat in the cream cheese, sugar, sour cream, and vanilla extract until well combined. Beat in the flour, then bring the mixture together with your fingertips to form a soft dough. Cover with plastic wrap and chill in the refrigerator.

Preheat the oven to 350°F/180°C. Line 2 large baking sheets with parchment paper. To make the filling, place the sugar, cinnamon, raisins, and walnuts in a bowl and mix together.

Divide the dough into 4 pieces and roll each piece into an 8-inch/20-cm round between 2 sheets of parchment paper. (Keep the dough balls chilled until you roll them out.) Cut each round into 6 wedges and sprinkle evenly with one quarter of the filling. Starting at the wide end, roll toward the point, then curve into a crescent and place on the baking sheets. Repeat with the remaining dough, then brush the crescents with beaten egg.

Bake in the preheated oven for 15–20 minutes, or until golden brown. Transfer to a wire rack to cool.

944 Apricot & pecan rugelach

On each round of dough spread 2–3 tablespoons of apricot jam then sprinkle with 1–2 tablespoons of finely chopped pecans before cutting into wedges and shaping.

945 Chocolate rugelach

Sprinkle each round of dough with 3 tablespoons of chopped milk or semisweet chocolate before cutting into wedges and shaping.

946 Raspberry & golden raisin rugelach

On each round of dough spread 2–3 tablespoons of raspberry jam then sprinkle with 1–2 tablespoons of chopped golden raisins before cutting into wedges and shaping.

947 Chocolate & hazelnut rugelach

On each round of dough spread 2–3 tablespoons of chocolate hazelnut spread then sprinkle with 1–2 tablespoons of finely chopped, toasted hazelnuts before cutting into wedges and shaping.

948 Marzipan rugelach

Coarsely grate 4 oz/115 g marzipan and sprinkle one quarter over each round. Sprinkle a few poppy seeds over the marzipan, if liked, then cut into wedges and shape.

949 Tunisian almond cigars

MAKES 36

6 tbsp butter
2¼ cups ground almonds
1 cup superfine sugar
2 tbsp orange blossom water
1 egg white, lightly beaten
12 sheets filo dough, about 11 x 15 inches/28 x 38 cm
generous ⅓ cup honey

Preheat the oven to 400°F/200°C. Place the butter in a saucepan and heat gently until melted, then let cool slightly.

Place the almonds and sugar in a bowl and stir until well combined. Add the orange blossom water and egg white and mix to form a firm paste. Divide the mixture into 6 pieces and roll each piece into a long sausage about 11 inches/28 cm long. Place a sheet of filo dough on the work surface and brush with melted butter. Place another sheet on top and brush with butter. Place a strip of almond paste on one end and roll up to enclose in layers of filo. Trim the ends and cut into 6 pieces, then place on a baking sheet. Repeat with the remaining filo and paste.

Bake in the preheated oven for 25–30 minutes, or until crisp and golden. Warm the honey in a saucepan and pour over the cooked pastries, then let cool before serving.

950 Tunisian hazelnut cigars

Replace the ground almonds with finely ground hazelnuts.

951 Tunisian pistachio cigars

Replace the almonds with very finely chopped pistachios.

952 Italian baked sweet ravioli

MAKES 48

3 tbsp extra virgin olive oil, plus extra for greasing
scant 1½ cups all-purpose flour, plus extra for dusting
scant ½ cup superfine sugar
3 egg yolks
3–4 tbsp water

FILLING
½ cup ricotta cheese
1½ tbsp superfine sugar
grated rind of ½ lemon
1 tbsp lemon juice

GLAZE
1 egg white, lightly beaten
superfine sugar

Preheat the oven to 350°F/180°C. Lightly grease a large baking sheet. Place the flour and sugar in a large bowl and make a well in the center. Add the egg yolks, oil, and 3 tablespoons of water and mix to form a firm dough, adding a little extra water if required. Knead for a few minutes. Let stand for 15 minutes.

Meanwhile, make the filling by combining all the ingredients in a small bowl. Divide the dough into 2 pieces and roll each piece out on a lightly floured work surface to a rectangle about 16 x 12 inches/ 40 x 30 cm. Cut into 2-inch/5-cm squares and place 1 teaspoon of filling on one square of dough. Moisten the edges of the dough with water, top with the second square, and seal well with the tines of a fork. Place on the baking sheet and repeat with the remaining filling and dough.

Brush the tops of the ravioli with egg white and dust lightly with sugar. Bake in the preheated oven for 20–25 minutes, or until crisp and golden. Let cool slightly before serving.

953 Chocolate orange ravioli

For the filling, place 1 oz/25 g chocolate in a heatproof bowl, set the bowl over a saucepan of gently simmering water, and heat until melted. Let cool, then beat into the ricotta with 1 tablespoon of orange-flavored liqueur and the grated rind of ½ orange.

954 *Bakewell slices*

Makes 12

1¼ cups all-purpose flour, plus extra for dusting
9 tbsp butter
2 tbsp superfine sugar
1 egg yolk
about 1 tbsp cold water

FILLING
8 tbsp butter
heaping ½ cup superfine sugar
1¼ cups ground almonds
3 eggs, beaten
½ tsp almond extract
4 tbsp raspberry jam
2 tbsp slivered almonds

Sift the flour into a bowl, add the butter, and rub it in with your fingertips until the mixture resembles fine breadcrumbs. Stir in the sugar, then mix the egg yolk with the water and stir in to form a firm dough, adding a little more water if necessary. Wrap in plastic wrap and chill in the refrigerator for 15 minutes.

Preheat the oven to 400°F/200°C Roll the dough out on a floured work surface and use to line a 9-inch/23-cm square tart pan or shallow cake pan. Prick the bottom and chill for 15 minutes.

Place the butter and sugar in a large bowl and beat together until light and fluffy, then beat in the ground almonds, eggs, and almond extract. Spread the jam over the dough bottom and top with the almond mixture, spreading evenly. Sprinkle with the slivered almonds.

Bake in the preheated oven for 10 minutes, then reduce the oven temperature to 350°F/180°C and bake for 25–30 minutes, or until the filling is golden brown. Let cool, then cut into bars.

955 *Apricot & almond slices*

Add ⅓ cup chopped plumped dried apricots to the filling mixture and replace the raspberry jam with apricot jam.

956 *Filo chocolate triangles*

Makes 32

6 tbsp butter, melted, plus extra for greasing
5½ oz/150 g semisweet chocolate, coarsely chopped
4 oz/115 g chocolate cake crumbs
2 tbsp toasted hazelnuts, chopped
2 tbsp light brown sugar
5 large sheets filo dough
confectioners' sugar, for dusting

Preheat the oven to 400°F/200°C. Lightly grease a large baking sheet. Place the butter in a saucepan and heat gently until melted, then let cool slightly. Place the chocolate, cake crumbs, hazelnuts, sugar, and brandy in a large bowl and mix together.

Lay one sheet of filo dough on the work surface and brush with melted butter. Cut in half widthwise, then cut each half into 4 strips lengthwise. Place a little of the chocolate mixture at one end of a strip of filo dough. Fold over the end at a diagonal to form a triangle, then continue to fold up the filo, maintaining the triangle shape. Place on the baking sheet and brush with butter. Repeat with the remaining strips of filo, to make 8 triangles. Cut the remaining sheets of filo and make additional triangles. Bake in the preheated oven for 8–10 minutes, or until golden. Let cool. Dust with confectioners' sugar before serving.

957 *Cherry & coconut triangles*

For a fruity filling, drain and coarsely chop 15 oz/425 g canned black cherries and mix in a bowl with ⅔ cup dry unsweetened coconut, 2 oz/55 g cake broken into crumbs, 2 tbsp light brown sugar, ¼ teaspoon of ground cinnamon, and 1 tablespoon of rum.

958 Rum & chocolate cups

MAKES 12

2 oz/55 g semisweet chocolate, broken into pieces
12 toasted hazelnuts, for decorating

FILLING
4 oz/115 g semisweet chocolate, broken into pieces
1 tbsp dark rum
4 tbsp mascarpone cheese

To make the chocolate cups, place the chocolate in a heatproof bowl, set the bowl over a saucepan of gently simmering water, and heat until just melted, but not too runny. Spoon about ½ teaspoon of melted chocolate into a foil candy case and brush it over the bottom and up the sides. Coat 11 more foil cases in the same way and let set for 30 minutes. Chill in the refrigerator for 15 minutes. If necessary, reheat the chocolate in the heatproof bowl until melted, then coat the foil cases with a second, slightly thinner coating. Chill for an additional 30 minutes.

Meanwhile, to make the filling, melt the chocolate as before, then let cool slightly. Stir in the rum and beat in the mascarpone cheese until fully incorporated and smooth, then let cool completely, stirring occasionally.

Spoon the filling into a pastry bag fitted with a ½-inch/1-cm star tip and pipe the filling into the cups. Top each one with a toasted hazelnut.

959 Brandy & almond chocolate cups

Replace the rum with brandy and top the cups with a toasted almond.

960 Peppermint creams

MAKES ABOUT 30

2⅔ cups confectioners' sugar, plus extra for dusting
1 egg white
peppermint extract, to taste
green food coloring (optional)

Line a large baking sheet with parchment paper. Sift the confectioners' sugar. Place the egg white in a large bowl and whisk with a fork until just frothy. Add half the confectioners' sugar and beat in. Add a few drops of peppermint extract, then gradually add enough confectioners' sugar to mix to a firm paste, ading a little more confectioners' sugar, if necessary. Knead in extra peppermint extract to taste.

Divide the paste in half and color one half pale green with a few drops of food coloring, if liked.

Sprinkle a little confectioners' sugar on the work surface, then roll out the paste until it is about ¼ inch/5 mm thick. Cut out rounds or other shapes with a cutter and place on the parchment paper. Let dry out in a cool, dry place for a few hours.

961 Bitter chocolate mint creams

Put 4 oz/115 g semisweet chocolate in a heatproof bowl, set the bowl over a saucepan of gently simmering water, and heat until melted. Let cool slightly, then dip the peppermint creams into the chocolate to cover half of the mint. Replace on the parchment paper and let set.

962 Chocolate creams

MAKES ABOUT 30

7 oz/200 g semisweet chocolate, broken into pieces
2 tbsp light cream
2 cups confectioners' sugar
drinking chocolate powder, for dusting

Line a large baking sheet with parchment paper. Place 2 oz/55 g of the chocolate in a large heatproof bowl, set the bowl over a saucepan of gently simmering water, and heat until melted. Stir in the cream and remove the bowl from the heat.

Sift the confectioners' sugar into the melted chocolate and, using a fork, mix together, then knead to form a firm, smooth and pliable mixture.

Lightly dust a work surface with drinking chocolate powder, and roll the mixture out until it is about ¼-inch/5-mm thick. Cut into rounds using a 1-inch/2.5-cm plain round cutter and place on the baking sheet. Let stand for about 12 hours, or overnight, until set and dry.

When the chocolate creams have set, line another baking sheet with parchment paper. Melt the remaining chocolate as before and, using 2 forks, carefully dip each chocolate cream into the melted chocolate. Lift it out quickly, letting any excess chocolate drain back into the bowl, and place on the parchment paper. Let set.

963 Coffee lovers' creams

MAKES 30

3 cups confectioners' sugar
2 tbsp condensed milk
2 tbsp strong black coffee
4 oz/115 g milk chocolate, broken into pieces

Line a large baking sheet with parchment paper. Sift the confectioners' sugar. Place half the confectioners' sugar, condensed milk, and coffee in a large bowl and mix well, then knead in enough confectioners' sugar to mix to a firm paste. Take small pieces of the paste and roll into a ball. Place on the parchment paper and flatten with the tines of a fork. Let dry out in a cool, dry place for a few hours.

Place the chocolate in a heatproof bowl, set the bowl over a saucepan of gently simmering water, and heat until melted. Let cool slightly, then dip the creams halfway into the chocolate. Allow the excess to run off and replace on the parchment paper. Drizzle any remaining chocolate, backward and forward, over the tops of the cream and let set.

964 Brandy snaps

MAKES ABOUT 20

6 tbsp butter
scant ½ cup superfine sugar
3 tbsp dark corn syrup
⅔ cup all-purpose flour
1 tsp ground ginger
1 tbsp brandy
finely grated rind of ½ lemon

FILLING
⅔ cup heavy cream or whipping cream
1 tbsp brandy (optional)
1 tbsp confectioners' sugar

Preheat the oven to 325°F/160°C. Line 3 large baking sheets with parchment paper. Place the butter, sugar, and dark corn syrup in a saucepan and heat gently, stirring occasionally, until melted. Let cool slightly, then sift the flour and ginger into the pan and beat until smooth. Stir in the brandy and lemon rind. Drop small spoonfuls of the mixture onto the baking sheets, leaving plenty of room for spreading.

Bake one baking sheet at a time in the preheated oven for 10–12 minutes, or until the snaps are golden brown. Remove the first baking sheet from the oven and let cool for about 30 seconds, then lift each round with a spatula and wrap around the handle of a wooden spoon. If the brandy snaps start to become too firm to wrap, return them to the oven for about 30 seconds to soften again. When firm, remove from the handles and cool on a wire rack. Repeat with the remaining baking sheets.

For the filling, place the cream, brandy, if using, and confectioners' sugar in a bowl and whip until thick. Just before serving, pipe the cream mixture into each end of the brandy snaps.

965 With coffee cream

Dissolve 2 tablespoons of instant coffee in 2 tablespoons of hot milk. Add to the cream with the confectioners' sugar and brandy, if using, and whip until thick. Use to fill the brandy snaps.

966 With vanilla mascarpone cream

Place 1 lb 2 oz/500 g mascarpone with 1 tablespoon of superfine sugar in a bowl. Split a vanilla bean lengthwise and scoop out the seeds, add to the mascarpone, and beat until combined. Use to fill the brandy snaps.

967 Brandy snap cups

Grease the outside of a teacup. Make and bake as before. After removing from the oven, let cool for 30 seconds, then lift each with a spatula and place over the upturned teacup, gently shaping the edges into a cup shape. When firm, after a few seconds, remove from the cup and place on a wire rack. Serve filled with whipped cream and fruit or with spoonfuls of ice cream or other creamy desserts. Fill just before serving.

968 Rum truffles

Makes 24

6 oz/175 g semisweet chocolate, broken into pieces
4 tbsp heavy cream
2 tbsp butter
2 tbsp confectioners' sugar
3 tbsp rum
scant 1 cup ground almonds
2–3 tbsp unsweetened cocoa

Place the chocolate, cream, and butter in a heatproof bowl, set the bowl over a saucepan of gently simmering water, and heat until melted. Remove from the heat and stir in the confectioners' sugar, the rum, and the almonds.

Let cool until firm enough to roll into 24 balls. Sift the cocoa onto a plate and roll the truffles in it. Place in small paper cases and chill until they are required.

969 Almond truffles

For a nonalcoholic truffle, omit the rum and add 1 teaspoon of almond extract. Roll in a little grated chocolate or dip in white chocolate to complete.

970 Brandy truffles

Replace the ground almonds with very finely chopped hazelnuts and add 3 tablespoons of brandy instead of the rum.

971 Chocolate liqueurs

Makes 40

3½ oz/100 g semisweet chocolate, broken into pieces
20 candied cherries
20 hazelnuts or macadamia nuts
1¾ oz/50 g semisweet chocolate and chocolate shavings, for decorating

FILLING
⅔ cup heavy cream
2 tbsp confectioners' sugar
4 tbsp liqueur

Line a large baking sheet with parchment paper. Place the semisweet chocolate in a heatproof bowl, set the bowl over a saucepan of gently simmering water, and heat until melted. Spoon the chocolate into 40 small paper cases, spreading up the sides with a spoon or brush, then place upside down on the baking sheet and let set.

Carefully peel away the paper cases and place a cherry or nut in each cup.

To make the filling, place the heavy cream in a bowl and sift the confectioners' sugar on top. Whip the cream until it is just holding its shape, then whip in the liqueur.

Place the cream in a pastry bag fitted with a ½-inch/1-cm plain tip and pipe a little into each chocolate case. Let chill for 20 minutes.

For decorating, melt the chocolate as before, then spoon the melted chocolate over the cream to cover it. Add the shavings and let harden before serving.

972 Chocolate whiskey cups

Replace the liqueur with whiskey and add a little strong coffee to the cream.

973 White chocolate truffles

Makes 20

2 tbsp butter
5 tbsp heavy cream
11½ oz/325 g white chocolate, broken into pieces
1 tbsp orange liqueur (optional)

Line a jelly roll pan with parchment paper. Place the butter and cream in a small saucepan. Bring slowly to a boil, stirring continuously, and boil for 1 minute, then remove from the heat. Add 8 oz/225 g of the chocolate to the cream and stir until melted, then beat in the liqueur, if using. Pour into the pan and chill for 2 hours, until firm.

Break off pieces of the mixture and roll them into balls. Chill for an additional 30 minutes before finishing the truffles.

To finish, place the remaining white chocolate in a heatproof bowl, set the bowl over a saucepan of gently simmering water, and heat until melted. Dip the balls in the chocolate, letting the excess drip back into the bowl, and place on parchment paper. Swirl the chocolate with the tines of a fork and let harden.

974 White & dark chocolate truffles

Replace the white chocolate for the coating with semisweet chocolate.

975 Milk chocolate truffles

Replace the white chocolate for the filling with milk chocolate and replace the orange liqueur with brandy or amaretto. Coat in white or milk chocolate.

976 Italian chocolate truffles

Makes 24

6 oz/175 g semisweet chocolate, broken into pieces
2 tbsp amaretto or orange liqueur
3 tbsp butter
4 tbsp confectioners' sugar
½ cup ground almonds
1¾ oz/50 g semisweet chocolate, grated

Place the chocolate and liqueur in a heatproof bowl, set the bowl over a saucepan of gently simmering water, and heat until the chocolate has melted. Add the butter and stir until it has melted. Stir in the confectioners' sugar and the ground almonds. Leave the mixture in a cool place until firm enough to roll into 24 balls.

Place the grated chocolate on a plate and roll the truffles in the chocolate to coat them. Place the truffles in 24 paper candy cases and chill in the refrigerator until ready to serve.

977 Rocky road bites

MAKES 18

4½ oz/125 g milk chocolate, broken into pieces
1½ oz/40 g mini multicolored marshmallows
scant ¼ cup chopped walnuts
scant ¼ cup plumped dried apricots, chopped

Line a large baking sheet with parchment paper. Place the milk chocolate in a large heatproof bowl, set the bowl over a saucepan of gently simmering water, and heat until melted. Stir in the marshmallows, walnuts, and apricots and toss in the melted chocolate until well covered.

Place heaping teaspoonfuls of the mixture on the baking sheet, then chill in the refrigerator until set.

Once set, carefully remove the bites from the parchment paper and place in small paper cases to serve, if liked.

978 Peanut & cherry bites

Replace the walnuts with coarsely chopped peanuts and the apricots with quartered, candied cherries.

979 Chocolate ice cream bites

MAKES ABOUT 6

Line a baking sheet with plastic wrap. Scoop out balls of ice cream with a melon baller and place them on the baking sheet. Alternatively, cut the ice cream into bite-size cubes. Stick a toothpick in each piece and return to the freezer until very hard.

Place the chocolate and butter in a heatproof bowl, set the bowl over a saucepan of gently simmering water, and heat until melted. Quickly dip the frozen ice cream balls or cubes into the warm chocolate and return to the freezer. Freeze until ready to serve.

1 lb 5 oz/600 g good-quality ice cream
7 oz/200 g semisweet chocolate, broken into pieces
2 tbsp butter

980 Peanut blossoms

Makes 24

6 tbsp butter, plus extra for greasing
scant ½ cup superfine sugar
scant ½ cup peanut butter
1 egg
3 tbsp dark corn syrup
1¼ cups all-purpose flour

FILLING
2 oz/55 g milk chocolate or semisweet chocolate, broken into pieces
2 tbsp butter
scant ¼ cup confectioners' sugar

Place the butter and sugar in a large bowl and beat together until pale and fluffy. Add the peanut butter, egg, and dark corn syrup, and beat until well combined. Sift the flour and work into the mixture to form a soft dough, then chill in the refrigerator for 30 minutes.

Preheat the oven to 350°F/180°C. Grease a large baking sheet. Shape the dough into 1-inch/2.5-cm balls, place on the baking sheet, spaced well apart, and flatten slightly with a spatula. Press your finger into the center of each ball to form a dip. Bake in the preheated oven for about 10 minutes, or until golden brown. Let cool for a few minutes on the baking sheet, then transfer to a wire rack.

For the filling, place the chocolate and butter in a heatproof bowl, set the bowl over a saucepan of gently simmering water, and heat until melted. Beat in the confectioners' sugar. Spoon or pipe the filling into the center of the cookies and let set.

981 Jam blossoms

Replace the chocolate center with a little jam of your choice and spoon into the dip of the cookie before baking.

982 Brazil nut brittle

Makes About 20 Pieces

sunflower oil, for greasing
12 oz/350 g semisweet chocolate, broken into pieces
⅔ cup shelled Brazil nuts, chopped
6 oz/175 g white chocolate, coarsely chopped
6 oz/175 g fudge, coarsely chopped

Brush the bottom of a square 8-inch/20-cm cake pan with oil to grease and line with parchment paper. Place half the semisweet chocolate in a heatproof bowl, set the bowl over a saucepan of gently simmering water, and heat until melted, then spread in the pan. Sprinkle with the chopped Brazil nuts, white chocolate, and fudge.

Melt the remaining semisweet chocolate pieces and pour over the top. Let the brittle set, then break up into jagged pieces with the tip of a strong knife.

983 Macadamia nut brittle

Replace the Brazil nuts with macadamia nuts and replace the white chocolate with milk chocolate, if liked.

984 Honeycomb toffee

MAKES ABOUT 50 PIECES

butter, for greasing
2½ cups granulated sugar
1¼ cups water
4 tbsp malt vinegar
½ tsp baking soda

Grease a shallow 7-inch/18-cm square pan. Place the sugar, water, and vinegar into a large saucepan and heat gently, stirring continuously, until the sugar has dissolved. Bring the mixture to a boil and boil, without stirring, until a little of the mixture, dropped into a cup of cold water, separates into hard threads. The temperature on a sugar thermometer should reach 280°F/138°C (soft crack stage).

Remove the pan from the heat, then immediately add the baking soda and stir until mixed together. (The mixture will bubble and rise in the pan.) When the mixture stops bubbling, immediately pour it into the pan and let set.

When the toffee has set, turn out of the pan onto a board and break into pieces with the end of a rolling pin.

985 Almond stars

MAKES ABOUT 20

3 egg whites
1 cup superfine sugar
½ tsp almond extract
2¼ cups ground almonds
10–12 candied cherries, halved

Preheat the oven to 325°F/160°C. Line 2 large baking sheets with parchment paper. Place the egg whites in a large bowl and whisk until stiff peaks form. Gradually whisk in the sugar, then add the almond extract. Fold in the ground almonds until well combined.

Spoon the mixture into a pastry bag fitted with a large star tip and pipe large stars onto the baking sheets, spaced well apart. Top each star with half a cherry.

Bake in the preheated for 25–30 minutes, or until lightly browned and crisp. Let cool on the baking sheet.

986 Coconut mounds

Replace the ground almonds with dry unsweetened coconut. Chop the cherries and fold in with the coconut. Pile spoonfuls of the mixture onto the baking sheets and bake as before.

987 Chocolate meringues

Makes 8

4 egg whites
1 cup superfine sugar
1 tsp cornstarch
1½ oz/40 g semisweet chocolate, grated

FILLING
3½ oz/100 g semisweet chocolate, broken into pieces
⅔ cup heavy cream
1 tbsp confectioners' sugar
1 tbsp brandy (optional)

Preheat the oven to 275°F/140°C. Line 2 large baking sheets with parchment paper. Place the egg whites in a large bowl and whisk until soft peaks form, then gradually whisk in half the sugar. Continue whisking until the mixture is very stiff and glossy. Carefully fold in the remaining sugar, cornstarch, and grated chocolate. Spoon the mixture into a pastry bag fitted with a large star or plain tip and pipe 16 large rosettes or mounds onto the baking sheets.

Bake in the preheated oven for about 1 hour, changing the position of the baking sheets after 30 minutes. Without opening the oven door, turn off the oven and let the meringues cool in the oven. Once cold, carefully peel off the parchment paper.

To make the filling, place the chocolate in a heatproof bowl, set the bowl over a saucepan of gently simmering water, and heat until melted. Carefully spread it over the bottoms of the meringues and stand them upside down on a wire rack until the chocolate has set. Place the cream, confectioners' sugar, and brandy, if using, in a bowl and whip until the cream holds its shape, then use to sandwich the chocolate-coated meringues together in pairs.

988 Ladies' kisses

Makes 20

¾ cup butter
heaping ½ cup superfine sugar
1 egg yolk
heaping 1 cup ground almonds
1¼ cups all-purpose flour
2 oz/55 g semisweet chocolate, broken into pieces

Place the butter and sugar in a large bowl and beat together until pale and fluffy. Beat in the egg yolk, then beat in the ground almonds and flour. Continue beating until thoroughly mixed. Shape the dough into a ball, wrap in plastic wrap, and chill in the refrigerator for 1½–2 hours.

Preheat the oven to 325°F/160°C. Line 3 large baking sheets with parchment paper.

Break off walnut-size pieces of dough and roll them into balls between the palms of your hands, then place the dough balls on the baking sheets, spaced well apart. Bake in the preheated oven for 20–25 minutes, or until golden brown. Carefully transfer to wire racks to cool.

Place the chocolate in a heatproof bowl, set the bowl over a saucepan of gently simmering water, and heat until melted. Spread the melted chocolate on the flat sides of the cookies and sandwich them together in pairs. Return to the wire racks to cool.

989 Baby meringues

Makes About 13

4 egg whites
pinch of salt
scant ⅔ cup granulated sugar
scant ⅔ cup superfine sugar
1¼ cups heavy cream, lightly whipped, for serving

Preheat the oven to 250°F/120°C. Line 3 large baking sheets with parchment paper. Place the egg whites and salt in a large bowl and whisk until stiff. (You should be able to turn the bowl upside down without any movement from the whisked egg whites.) Whisk in the granulated sugar, a little at a time; the meringue should begin to look glossy at this stage. Sprinkle in the superfine sugar, a little at a time, and continue whisking until all the sugar has been incorporated and the meringue forms thick peaks.

Transfer the meringue mixture to a pastry bag fitted with a ¾-inch/2-cm star tip and carefully pipe about 26 small whirls of the mixture onto the baking sheets.

Bake in the preheated oven for 1½ hours, or until the meringues are pale golden and can be easily lifted off the paper. Without opening the oven door, turn off the oven and let the meringues cool in the oven.

Just before serving, sandwich the meringues together in pairs with the lightly whipped cream.

990 Brown sugar meringues

Replace the granulated and superfine sugar with light brown sugar for a delicious, slightly chewy meringue.

991 Nutty meringues

Carefully fold in ⅓ cup finely chopped pistachios or toasted hazelnuts after all the sugar has been added.

992 Chewy date crunchies

Makes 16

scant ⅔ cup butter, plus extra for greasing
scant ½ cup light brown sugar
¼ cup honey
5 ½ cups toasted oat cereal
1 cup rolled oats
⅔ cup chopped dates

Preheat the oven to 375°F/190°C. Grease and line the bottom of an 8-inch/20-cm square cake pan. Place the butter, sugar, and honey in a saucepan and heat gently, stirring continuously, until the butter is melted and everything is well combined. Remove from the heat.

Lightly crush the oat cereals with a rolling pin to remove any large lumps and add to the pan, then stir in the dates. Spoon the mixture into the cake pan and press down lightly.

Bake in the preheated oven for 20 to 25 minutes. Let cool for a few minutes in the pan, then cut into 16 squares and finish cooling completely in the pan.

993 Chewy apricot crunchies

Replace the dates with chopped plumped dried apricots and add ¼ cup lightly toasted slivered almonds for an extra nutty flavor.

994 *Mini florentines*

MAKES 40

5½ tbsp butter
heaping ⅓ cup superfine sugar
scant ¼ cup golden raisins or raisins
3 tbsp chopped candied cherries
3 tbsp chopped candied ginger
scant 2 tbsp sunflower seeds
1 cup slivered almonds
2 tbsp heavy cream
6 oz/175 g semisweet or milk chocolate, broken into pieces

Preheat the oven to 350°F/180°C. Line 2 large baking sheets with parchment paper. Place the butter in a saucepan and heat gently until melted. Add the sugar, stir until dissolved, then bring the mixture to a boil. Remove from the heat and stir in the golden raisins, candied cherries, candied ginger, sunflower seeds, and almonds. Mix well, then beat in the cream. Place small teaspoons of mixture on the baking sheets, spaced well apart. You will need to do more than one batch.

Bake in the preheated oven for 10–12 minutes, or until light golden in color. Remove from the oven and, while still hot, use a round cookie cutter to pull in the edges to form perfect circles. Let cool and become crisp before removing from the baking sheets.

Place the chocolate in a heatproof bowl, set the bowl over a saucepan of gently simmering water, and heat until melted. Spread most of the chocolate onto a sheet of parchment paper, and when the chocolate is nearly setting, place the cookies flat-side down on the chocolate and let harden. Cut around the florentines and remove from the parchment paper. Spread the remaining melted chocolate on the coated side of the florentines and use a fork to mark waves in the chocolate. Let set.

995 *Italian chocolate salami*

MAKES 18 SLICES

3½ oz/100 g plain butter cookies
2¾ oz/75 g amaretti cookies
7 oz/200 g semisweet chocolate
¾ cup butter, cut into cubes, plus extra for greasing
3 tbsp amaretto, rum, or brandy
1 large egg yolk
⅓ cup blanched almonds, chopped
confectioners' sugar, for dusting

Place the butter cookies and amaretti cookies in a food processor and pulse until finely chopped. Transfer the cookies to a large bowl.

Place the chocolate in a heatproof bowl, set the bowl over a saucepan of gently simmering water, add the butter and amaretto, and heat gently until melted. Remove from the heat and stir together. Add the crushed cookies, egg yolk, and almonds to the chocolate mixture and mix well. Leave in a cool place for about 2 hours, or until cold.

Grease a large sheet of foil. Turn the chocolate mixture onto the foil and, using your hands and a spatula, shape into a log shape about 12 inches/30 cm long with tapered ends to resemble an Italian salami. Wrap in the foil and chill in the freezer for at least 4 hours, or until firm.

Dust a sheet of parchment paper generously with confectioners' sugar. Remove the chocolate log from the foil and turn onto the parchment paper. Roll the log in the confectioners' sugar until it is evenly coated and looks like an Italian salami. Leave in a cool place for 1 hour, then cut into slices to serve.

996 *Chocolate sparkles*

MAKES ABOUT 5

10½ oz/300 g milk chocolate, broken into pieces
generous ⅓ cup heavy cream
1 tsp vanilla extract
1 tbsp confectioners' sugar
1½ tbsp butter

FOR DECORATING
colored sprinkles
silver or pink stars
grated or flaked white chocolate, or your favorite colorful decorations

Place the chocolate and cream in a heatproof bowl, set the bowl over a saucepan of gently simmering water, and heat, stirring occasionally, until the chocolate is melted. Let cool slightly, then stir in the vanilla extract, confectioners' sugar, and butter until well combined. Chill the mixture in the refrigerator until firm.

Use a teaspoon to scoop up some of the mixture and roll into a ball shape. Repeat until the mixture is used up.

Dip the chocolate balls into your favorite coatings for decorating, turning them until they are evenly coated, and arrange the chocolates in small paper cases.

997 *Alphabet apple pie*

MAKES 4

1⅔ cups all-purpose flour, plus extra for dusting
pinch of salt
2 tbsp confectioners' sugar
heaping 8 tbsp cold butter (or half butter and half vegetable fat), cut into small pieces
1 egg, separated
1–2 tbsp cold water

FILLING
1 lb 8 oz/675 g apples, peeled, halved, cored, and thinly sliced
2 tbsp orange juice
1 tsp ground cinnamon
3 tbsp superfine sugar

Sift the flour, salt, and confectioners' sugar into a bowl. Add the butter and rub it in until the mixture resembles breadcrumbs. Mix in the egg yolk and water and form the dough into a ball. Cover and chill in the refrigerator for 30 minutes.

Preheat the oven to 400°F/200°C. Place the apple, orange juice, cinnamon, and sugar in a bowl and mix together, then divide among 4 heatproof ramekin-style dishes. Wet the rim of each dish.

Roll the dough out on a floured surface, cut 4 rounds, and use to top each pie. Trim the edges and crimp with a fork. Brush with egg white and make a slit in the top. Cut out letters from the trimmings, place on a baking sheet, and bake in the preheated oven for 30–35 minutes.

998 Chocolate & vanilla creams

Makes 4

2 cups heavy cream
6 tbsp superfine sugar
1 vanilla bean
heaping ¾ cup sour cream
2 tsp powdered gelatin
3 tbsp water
1¾ oz/50 g semisweet chocolate, broken into pieces
chocolate shavings, for decorating

Place the cream and sugar in a saucepan and add the vanilla bean. Heat gently, stirring until the sugar has dissolved, then bring to a boil. Reduce the heat and simmer for 2–3 minutes. Remove from the heat and take out the vanilla bean. Stir in the sour cream.

Sprinkle the gelatin over the water in a small heatproof bowl and leave until spongy, then set over a pan of hot water and stir until dissolved. Stir into the cream mixture and pour half of this mixture into another bowl.

Place the semisweet chocolate in a heatproof bowl, set the bowl over a pan of simmering water, and heat until melted, then stir into one half of the cream mixture. Pour the chocolate mixture into 4 individual glasses and chill for 15–20 minutes, or until just set. While the chocolate mixture is chilling, keep the vanilla mixture at room temperature.

Spoon the vanilla mixture on top of the chocolate mixture and chill until the vanilla cream is set. Before serving, decorate with the shavings.

999 Chocolate rum pots

Makes 6

8 oz/225 g semisweet chocolate
4 eggs, separated
6 tbsp superfine sugar
4 tbsp dark rum
4 tbsp heavy cream

FOR DECORATING
whipped cream
marbled chocolate shapes

Place the chocolate in a heatproof bowl, set the bowl over a saucepan of gently simmering water, and heat until melted. Let cool slightly.

Place the egg yolks and sugar in a large bowl and whisk until very pale and fluffy. Drizzle the melted chocolate into the mixture and fold in together with the rum and heavy cream.

Place the egg whites in a separate large bowl and whisk until soft peaks form, then fold the egg whites into the chocolate mixture in 2 batches. Divide the mixture among 6 individual dishes and chill in the refrigerator for at least 2 hours.

To serve, decorate with a little whipped cream and marbled chocolate shapes.

Note: This recipe contains raw eggs.

1000 *Cappuccino soufflé desserts*

MAKES 6

butter, for greasing
2 tbsp superfine sugar, plus extra for coating
6 tbsp whipping cream
2 tsp instant espresso coffee granules
2 tbsp Kahlúa
3 large eggs, separated, plus 1 extra white
5½ oz/150 g semisweet chocolate, broken into pieces
unsweetened cocoa, for dusting

Preheat the oven to 375°F/190°C. Grease the sides of six ¾-cup capacity ramekins, coat with the extra sugar, and place on a baking sheet. Place the cream in a saucepan and warm gently. Stir in the coffee until dissolved, then add the Kahlúa. Divide the mixture among the ramekins.

Place the egg whites in a large bowl and whisk until soft peaks form, then gradually whisk in the sugar until they are stiff and glossy but not dry.

Place the chocolate in a heatproof bowl, set the bowl over a saucepan of gently simmering water, and heat until melted. Add the egg yolks to the melted chocolate, then stir in a little of the whisked egg whites. Gradually fold in the egg whites and divide the mixture among the ramekins. Bake in the preheated oven for 15 minutes, or until just set. Dust with cocoa and serve immediately.

1001 *Rich chocolate mousses*

MAKES 4

10½ oz/300 g semisweet chocolate, broken into pieces
5 tbsp superfine sugar
1½ tbsp butter
1 tbsp brandy
4 eggs, separated
unsweetened cocoa, for dusting

Place the chocolate in a heatproof bowl, set the bowl over a saucepan of gently simmering water, add the sugar and butter, and melt together, stirring continuously, until smooth. Remove from the heat and stir in the brandy, then let cool slightly. Add the egg yolks and beat until smooth.

Place the egg whites in a separate bowl and whisk until stiff peaks form, then fold into the chocolate mixture. Place a stainless steel cooking ring on each of 4 small serving plates, then spoon the mixture into each ring and smooth the surfaces. Chill in the refrigerator for at least 4 hours, or until set.

Remove the mousses from the refrigerator and carefully remove the cooking rings. Dust with cocoa and serve immediately.

Note: This recipe contains raw eggs.

Index

9-carrot gold cupcakes 32
24-carrot gold cupcakes 32

After-dinner coffee liqueur muffins 212
With espresso icing 212
Almond & raspberry jam drops 122
Almond & strawberry jam drops 122
Almond biscotti 153
Almond cherry cupcakes 23
Almond cookies with a cherry 66
Almond cookies with green tea cream 121
With almond cream 121
Almond croissants 263
Almond crunchies 122
With marzipan filling 122
Almond cupcakes 14
Almond macaroons 277
Almond madeleines 53
Almond slices 195
Almond stars 293
Almond truffles 289
Almond tuiles 125
With chocolate coating 125
Alphabet apple pie 297
Alphabet cookies 141
Anchovy & caper muffins 251
Angel ornaments 138
Animal lovers' cupcakes 37
Anniversary hearts 240
Anniversary muffins 240
Apple & cinnamon blondies 180
Apple & cinnamon muffins 204
Apple & cinnamon squares 52
Apple & cream turnovers 259
Apple & golden raisin danish 264
Apple & muesli muffins 217
Apple & walnut blondies 184
Apple danish 264
Apple gingerbread 58
Apple spice cookies 85
Apple streusel cupcakes 27
Apple streusel muffins 203
With apple brandy butter 203
Apple strudel with cider sauce 268
Apple strudel with sabayon sauce 268
Apple strudel with toffee sauce 268
Apple suns & pear stars 108
With apple icing 108
Apricot & almond clusters 275
Apricot & almond slices 285
Apricot & banana muffins 203
Apricot & chocolate slices 196
Apricot & hazelnut clusters 275
Apricot & pecan cookies 96
Apricot & pecan muffins 221
Apricot & pecan rugelach 283
Apricot & sunflower seed muffins 221
Apricot biscotti 156
Apricot brownies 172
Apricot cream cupcakes 31
Apricot danish 264
Apricot granola bars 186
Apricot petits choux 265
Apricot streusel cupcakes 27
Asparagus & sour cream muffins 253
With asparagus tip topping 253
Australian lamingtons 52

Baby meringues 295
Baby shower cupcakes with sugared almonds 43
Bagels 63
Bakewell slices 285
Baklava 281
Banana & butterscotch cupcakes 25
Banana & caramel cookies 106
Banana & chocolate cookies 149
Banana & chocolate cupcakes 25
Banana & coconut cookies 106
Banana & date cupcakes 25
Banana & pecan cupcakes 25
Banana & raisin cookies 106
Banana & sweet cream cookies 104
Battenberg cookies 134
Bedtime bears 111
With colored blankets 111
Berry tartlets 267
Berry-topped wedding muffins 240
Birthday muffins 243
Birthday party cakes 15
Bitter chocolate mint creams 286
Black forest brownies 166
Black pepper muffins 61
Black Russian brownies 165
Blackberry & apple muffins 202
Blackstrap molasses drizzles 129
Bleu cheese & walnut muffins 252
Bling & buy cupcakes 38
Blonde brownie hearts with raspberry sauce 179
With strawberry sauce 179
Blueberry & cranberry cinnamon cookies 86
Blueberry & pastry cream cookies 105
Blueberry cupcakes 35
Blueberry muffins 202
With chocolate topping 202
Blueberry orange cookies 86
Bourbon balls 77
Brandied peach galettes 55
Brandied peach muffins 205
Brandy & almond chocolate cups 286
Brandy & apricot muffins 206
With apricot brandy icing 206
Brandy snap cups 288
Brandy snaps 288
With coffee cream 288
With vanilla mascarpone cream 288
Brandy truffles 289
Brazil nut brittle 292
Breadsticks 161
With mixed seed coating 161
Brie & cranberry muffins 245
Brown sugar fudge 273
Brown sugar meringues 295
Brownie base cheesecake 168
Bursting berry blondies 184
Bursting cranberry blondies 184
Butterfudge blondies 180
Buttermilk & orange cupcakes 33
Buttermilk berry muffins 204
Buttermilk cranberry muffins 204
Butterscotch & peanut cupcakes 34
Buttery fork cookies 69

Camomile cookies 126
Canadian namaimo bars 189
Candy-topped chocolate cupcakes 15
Candy-topped vanilla cupcakes 15
Cappuccino brownies 165
Cappuccino cookies 127
With coffee bean topping 127
Cappuccino soufflé desserts 299
Caramel chip cookies 119
Caramelized onion muffins 245
Caramelized red onion muffin 245
Cardamom & chocolate cookies 81
Caribbean cookies 87
Caribbean rum & raisin muffins 206
With coconut icing 206
Carrot & cilantro muffins 246
Carrot & lemon cupcakes 23
Carrot & orange cupcakes 23
Carrot cake cookies 149
Carrot cake muffins 223
With carrot decoration 223
Carrot, cilantro & onion muffins 246
Carrot streusel brownies 174
Cashew nut & poppy seed cookies 123
Cashew nut cookies 123
Celery & cheese straws 160
Cheddar & caraway scones 62
Cheese & ham muffins 246
Cheese & herb scones 62
Cheese & mustard scones 62
Cheese muffins 61, 246
Cheese sables 160
Cheese straws 160
Cheesy palmiers 276
Checkerboard cookies 134
Cherry & almond biscotti 158
Cherry & almond crown 261
Cherry & almond danish 264
Cherry & chocolate diamonds 95
Cherry & coconut blondies 182
Cherry & coconut muffins 207
With coconut topping 207
Cherry & coconut triangles 285
Cherry & vanilla heart cupcakes 41
Cherry & walnut clusters 275
Cherry chocolate fudge 273
Cherry chocolate puff tarts 261
Cherry cupcakes 26
Cherry garlands 116
With cherry frosting 116
Cherry or cranberry & pecan cookies 96
Cherry refrigerator cookies 83
Cherry streusel cupcakes 27
Cherry Thanksgiving cookies 110
Chewy apricot crunchies 295
Chewy candied fruit cookies 87
With hazelnut topping 87
Chewy date crunchies 295
Chicken & corn muffins 247
Children's party muffins 243
Chile cornbread 62
Chinese fortune cookies 80
Choc & nut cupcakes 18
Choco mint stars 113
Chocodoodles 114
Chocolate & almond biscotti 154

Chocolate & apricot cookies 96
Chocolate & banana cream puffs 258
Chocolate & butterscotch brownies 167
Chocolate & cherry muffins 237
Chocolate & coffee whole wheat cookies 124
With ice cream filling 124
Chocolate & creamy cheese blondies 181
Chocolate & date brownies 164
Chocolate & hazelnut drops 89
Chocolate & hazelnut rugelach 283
Chocolate & orange biscotti 154
Chocolate & orange cookie sandwiches 107
With semisweet & white chocolate 107
With semiwseet chocolate 107
Chocolate & peanut muffins 242
Chocolate & peanut scones 51
Chocolate & raspberry brownies 166
Chocolate & vanilla creams 298
Chocolate almond petits fours 278
Chocolate blueberry brownies 166
Chocolate blueberry tarts 269
Chocolate brownie cupcakes 43
Chocolate brownies 164
Chocolate butterfly cakes 16
Chocolate buttons 78
Chocolate candied orange peels 270
Chocolate caramel shortbread 199
Chocolate carrot cupcakes 23
Chocolate cheesecake slices 197
Chocolate cherry cupcakes 28
Chocolate chile brownies 164
Chocolate chip & cherry brownies 174
Chocolate chip & cinnamon cookies 100
Chocolate chip & ginger blondies 181
Chocolate chip brownies 169
Chocolate chip cookies 66
Chocolate chip cupcakes 34
With fudge frosting 34
Chocolate chip granola bars 187
Chocolate chip muffins 225
Chocolate chunk muffins 242
Chocolate-coated Neapolitan cookies 81
Chocolate-covered raisin cookies 113
Chocolate cream & walnut cookies 147
Chocolate cream muffins 210
Chocolate creams 287
Chocolate cupcakes 14
Chocolate cupcakes with cream cheese frosting 24
With chocolate mascarpone frosting 24
Chocolate curl Easter cupcakes 39
Chocolate, date & pecan pinwheels 88
Chocolate daisies 70
Chocolate dinosaur cookies 111
Chocolate-dipped apple spiced cookies 85
Chocolate-dipped cookies 85
Chocolate-dipped madeleines 53
Chocolate-dipped nutty bars 185
Chocolate-dipped Viennese fingers 140
Chocolate dominoes 145
With black frosting 145
Chocolate Easter egg nests 280
Chocolate éclairs 260
Chocolate florentines 70
Chocolate fruit & nut bar 198
Chocolate fruit & nut crispy cakes 46
Chocolate fudge brownies 179
Chocolate fudge muffins 210
Chocolate fudge squares 85
Chocolate hazelnut petits fours 278
Chocolate ice cream bites 291
Chocolate ice-cream cone cupcakes 33
Chocolate liqueur balls 77
Chocolate liqueurs 289
Chocolate marshmallow fingers 197
Chocolate mendiants 277
Chocolate meringues 294
Chocolate mint cookie sandwiches 90
Chocolate mint sandwiches 147
Chocolate muffins 234
With chocolate topping 234
Chocolate nests 137
Chocolate nut butterfly cakes 16
Chocolate orange butterfly cakes 16
Chocolate orange cookies 92
With coffee frosting 92
Chocolate orange fudge 274
Chocolate orange langues de chat 79
Chocolate orange marbled cupcakes 45
Chocolate orange ravioli 284
Chocolate orange tarts 269
Chocolate palmiers 276
Chocolate peach cheesecake 168
Chocolate peanut butter cupcakes 21
Chocolate peanut butter squares 194
Chocolate pecan pie slices 195
Chocolate peppermint bars 190
Chocolate pistachio bars 189
Chocolate raspberry tarts 269
Chocolate refrigerator cookies 83
Chocolate rugelach 283
Chocolate rum pots 298
Chocolate sandwich cookies 91
Chocolate scones 51
Chocolate sparkles 297
Chocolate sprinkle cookies 150
Chocolate strawberry cupcakes 28
Chocolate temptations 109
Chocolate-tipped finger rolls 80
With white chocolate coating 80
Chocolate wholemeals 103
Chocolate whiskey cups 289
Chocolate zucchini cupcakes 45
Christmas angels 138
Christmas bells 138
Christmas cupcakes 40
Christmas holly muffins 239
Christmas snowflake muffins 239
Christmas tree decorations 139
Cinnamon & caramel cookies 127
Cinnamon & orange crisps 129
With white chocolate coating 129
Cinnamon & raisin bagels 63
Cinnamon churros 54
Cinnamon knots 259
Cinnamon palmiers 276
Cinnamon rolls 49
Cinnamon squares 52
Citrus almond party cakes 15
Citrus crescents 109
With lemon cream 109
Citrus drizzle slices 59
Citrus fruit muffins 207
Citrus rock cakes 59
Citrus scones 50
Classic oatmeal cookies 67
Classic saffron cookies 130
With sweet wine frosting 130
Clubs & spades 75
With jam filling 75
Cocoa, coffee & coconut panellets 78
Coconut & cherry bars 191
Coconut & cranberry cookies 88
Coconut & lime bars 191
Coconut & papaya cookies 88
Coconut bars 191
Coconut buttery fork cookies 69
Coconut cherry cupcakes 23
Coconut macaroons 277
Coconut mounds 293
Coconut paradise squares 194
Coconut refrigerator cookies 83
Coffee & cream muffins 211
With mocha cream topping 211
Coffee almond petits fours 278
Coffee cream & walnut cookies 147
Coffee cupcakes 14
Coffee éclairs 260
Coffee-frosted brownies 165
Coffee lovers' creams 287
Colored bells 138
Cookies & cream sandwiches 67
With strawberry filling 67
Corn muffins 219
Cornbread squares 62
Cranberry & almond muffins 208
With almond crunch topping 208
Cranberry & chocolate blondies 184
Cranberry & pastry cream cookies 105
Cranberry & pecan fudge 272
Cranberry cupcakes 26
Cranberry granola bars 186
Cranberry oatcakes 159
Cranberry orange & pecan muffins 238
Cranberry sour cream brownies 167
Cranberry streusel cupcakes 27
Cream & spice muffins 237
With spice butter topping 237
Cream-filled turnovers 259
Cream puffs 258
With strawberry coulis 258
Crispy bacon & spinach muffins 248
Crispy bacon muffins 248
Croissants 263
Crown loaf 261
Crumble-topped cheese & chive muffins 248
Crunchy muesli cookies 115
With nutty topping 115
Crunchy nut & honey sandwiches 118
Crunchy peanut butter muffins 224
With peanut frosting 244
Crunchy peanut cookies 134

Dark & white chocolate cookies 146
Dark & white fudge cakes 20
Dark chocolate & ginger muffins 214
With ginger buttermilk frosting 214
Dark chocolate & hazelnut cookies 146
Date & almond clusters 275
Date & lemon spirals 89
Date & nut clusters 275
Date & pecan pinwheels 121
Date blondies 183
Date granola bars 186
Dates & figs with an almond filling 271
Decadent chocolate dessert muffins 211
With Kirsch cherry topping 211
Devil's food cake with chocolate frosting 47
Dinosaur cookies 111
Double banana muffins 203
Double cheese muffins 246
Double choc éclairs 260
Double chocolate biscotti 154
Double chocolate brownies 167
Double chocolate cookies 84
Double chocolate muffins 224
Double chocolate swirls 56
Double heart cookies 140
Doughnuts 57
Dried apricot cupcakes 31
Dried fruit refrigerator cookies 83
Dutch macaroons 73
With white chocolate coating 73
Dutch speculaas 76

Easter animal cookies 139
Easter bunny cookies 136
Easter cupcakes 39
Easter eggs cookies 136
Easter fruit muffins 238
Easter muffins 238
Easter nest cookies 137
Easy bling cupcakes 38
English muffins 61
Extra ginger gingersnaps 133
Extra nutty chocolate swirls 56
Extra peachy cookies 101
Extra rocky muffins 244

Fairy faces 69
Farmyard friends 112
Feathered-iced coffee cupcakes 22
Feathered-iced chocolate cupcakes 22
Feathered-iced mocha cupcakes 22
Fennel & angelica cookies 128
Fennel, lemon & angelica cookies 128
Fig & almond clusters 275
Fig & rose water spirals 89
Fig & walnut pinwheels 88
Fig blondies 183
Figgy granola bars 186
Filo chocolate triangles 285
Filo Christmas crackers 281
Flower & bug cupcakes 36
Flower gems 131
Fluttering butterfly cookies 68
Fontina & pesto muffins 245
French beignets 282
With rum sauce 282
French galettes 55
Fresh berry tartlets 270
Fresh black cherry tarts 270
Fresh cranberry oat-topped muffins 220
Fresh croissants 263
Fresh flower muffins 208
Fresh orange muffins 209
Fresh peach muffins 209
Fresh raspberry cupcakes 35
Fresh strawberry & cream muffins 209
With sweet wine & strawberry topping 209
Fresh strawberry cupcakes 35
Frosted carrot cake cookies 149
Frosted chocolate orange muffins 205
With chocolate icing 205
Frosted cream cheese muffins 210
Frosted cupcakes 14
Frosted peanut butter cupcakes 21
Frozen blueberry cupcakes 26
Fruit & nut fudge 272
Fruit scones 50
Fruit wholemeal cookies 71
Fruity granola bars 187
Fruity rings 103
Fudge fingers 85

Galaktoboureko 282
German lebkuchen 72
With violets & ginger topping 72
Giant chocolate chip cookies 117
Giant chocolate chunk cookies 117
Ginger & chocolate diamonds 95
Ginger chocolate chip brownies 174
Ginger chocolate fudge 273
Ginger florentines 70
Ginger refrigerator cookies 83
Ginger wheat germ muffins 214
With ginger crunch topping 214
Gingerbread 58
Gingerbread ark 159
Gingerbread people 159
Gingersnaps 133
Glazed honey muffins 222
With honey ricotta topping 222
Gold & silver anniversary cupcakes 42
Golden apricot & almond tarts 279
Golden hazelnut cookies 118
With white chocolate coating 118
Golden raisin & walnut rolls 49
Golden raisin bran muffins 220
Golden raisin biscotti 156
Good-for-you wholemeal cookies 71
Gooey butterscotch muffins 223
With butterscotch topping 223
Gooey chocolate & cream cheese cupcakes 38
Gooiest chocolate cookies 148
Granola muffins 221
With extra chocolate 148
Grape tartlets 267
Grapefruit & apple mint cookies 90
Greek almond shortbread 151
Greek lemon shortbread 151
Greek pistachio shortbread 151
Greek shortbread 151
Gruyère sables 160

Halloween cupcakes 41
Halloween pumpkin muffins 239
With maple butter frosting 239
Halloween spiderweb cookies 137
Halloween spook cookies 137
Ham & cheese croissants 263
Hazelnut & almond tuiles 72
Hazelnut & coffee muffins 225
With hazelnut cream topping 225
Hazelnut & vanilla seed muffins 236
Hazelnut biscotti 152
Hazelnut chocolate bars 185
Hazelnut macaroons 277
Hazelnut slices 195
Hazelnut streusel brownies 174
Hazelnut whirly pinwheel cookies 71
Healthy oat & prune muffins 221
Hearts & diamonds 75
High-fiber muffins 216
High-fiber seed muffins 216
Honey & sesame biscotti 157
Honey & spice cakes 17
Honeycomb toffee 293

"I love you" vanilla hearts 135
With vanilla topping 135
Ice-cream cone cupcakes 33
Ice cream cookie sandwiches 147
Iced cherry rings 103
Iced coconut cherry cupcakes 23
Iced cupcakes 14
Iced marbled cupcakes 45
Iced queen cakes 19
Iced speculaas 76
Iced stars 141
Indulgent chocolate chunk cookies 117
Italian baked sweet ravioli 284
Italian chocolate salami 296
Italian chocolate truffles 290
Italian pesto muffins 249
With ricotta cheese topping 249
Italian ricciaretti 79

Jam blossoms 292
Jam doughnut muffins 226
Jam rings 91
Jewish oznei haman 74
With fruit filling 74
Jewish rugelach 283
Jumbo chocolate chip cupcakes 18
Jumbo oat & raisin chippers 124
Jumbo oat, apricot & prune chippers 124

Kiwi muffins 207
Kiwi tartlets 267

Ladies' kisses 294
Langues de chat 79
Lavender cookies 131
Lemon & cornmeal berry squares 55
Lemon & lime cookies 93
With chocolate topping 93
Lemon & poppy seed muffins 236
Lemon & raspberry cupcakes 46
Lemon & sesame seed cookies 93
Lemon & sweetie cookies 127
Lemon & thyme cookies 90
Lemon & vanilla shortbread 150
Lemon & white chocolate fingers 99
Lemon almond brittle 146
Lemon butterfly cakes 24
Lemon cheesecake cupcakes 39
Lemon cornmeal cookies 98
With Limoncello frosting 228
Lemon cornmeal muffins 228
Lemon cupcakes 14
Lemon drizzle squares 59
Lemon hearts & diamonds 75
Lemon refrigerator cookies 83
Lemon rings 91
Lemon scones 50
Lemon verbena cookies 126
Lime & coconut cupcakes 30
Lime & sesame seed cookies 93
London cakes 51

Low-fat banana cardamom brownies 170
Low-fat blueberry muffins 157
Low-fat cherry muffins 215
Low-fat muffins 215
Lucia saffron buns 54

Macadamia nut brittle 292
Macadamia nut caramel squares 193
Macadamia nut cinnamon cookies 86
Madeleine squares 52
Madeleines 53
Malted chocolate muffins 222
Mango & macadamia nut cookies 102
Mango, coconut & ginger cookies 94
Maple-glazed pecan brownies 170
Maple-glazed pistachio brownies 170
Maple pecan muffins 228
With maple crunch topping 228
Marbled biscotti 155
Marbled chocolate cheesecake brownies 177
Marbled chocolate cupcakes 45
Marbled chocolate muffins 231
Marbled chocolate orange brownies 177
Marbled coffee muffins 231
Marbled cookies 150
Marbled creamy brownies 177
Margarita cookies 97
With lime icing 97
Marshmallow daisies 70
Marshmallow muffins 242
Marshmallow s'mores 110
Marzipan & fruit cupcakes 40
Marzipan muffins 227
Marzipan rugelach 283
Marzipan stars 141
Marzipan stuffed dates & figs 271
Mega chip cookies 119
Melt-in-the-middles 114
Melting moments 76
With mascarpone cheese filling 76
Midnight cookies 82
With chocolate topping 82
Milk chocolate & pistachio brownies 176
Milk chocolate truffles 290
Mini bleu cheese & onion muffins 249
Mini bleu cheese & pear muffins 249
Mini florentines 296
Mini orange & cardamom muffins 229
With white chocolate frosting 229
Mini shrimp & dill muffins 250
Mini shrimp & parsley muffins 250
Mint chocolate chip muffins 229
With chocolate ganache 229
Mint cookies with white chocolate ganache 130
With mint ganache 130
Mint window cookies 145
Minted chocolate chip brownies 169
Mixed berry biscotti 158
Mixed berry muffins 202
Mixed cherry biscotti 158
Mixed fruit cookies 97
Mocha & macadamia nut brownies 178
Mocha biscotti 157
Mocha brownies 171
Mocha cupcakes 14
Mocha cupcakes with whipped cream 30
Mocha-filled langues de chat 79
Mocha fudge 274
Mocha muffins 212
With molten chocolate filling 212
Mocha walnut cookies 125
With mocha frosting 125
Mocha walnut cupcakes 30
Mocha walnut fudge 272
Mochachino brownies with white mocha sauce 171
With rich brandy sauce 171
Moist gingerbread muffins 230
With lemon frosting 230
Moist orange & almond muffins 230
With slivered almond topping 230
Moist pecan cupcakes 22
Moist walnut cupcakes 22
Mother's day breakfast muffins 241
With malted chocolate butter 241
Muesli muffins 217
Multicolored muffins 243

Name cookies 142
Naughty but nice cupcakes 44
Neapolitan cookies 81
Nice & naughty 44
No-bake chocolate & raisin cookie cake 199
No-bake chocolate fingers 198
Number crunchers 142
Nut & maple syrup sandwiches 118
Nut lovers' cookie brittle 146
Nutmeg & hazelnut cakes 17
Nutty chocolate clusters 275
Nutty chocolate wholemeals 103
Nutty cupcakes 14
Nutty drizzles 123
With nut chocolate topping 123
Nutty gingerbread 58
Nutty granola bars 185
Nutty granola squares 192
Nutty macaroons 115
Nutty meringues 295
Nutty palmiers 276
Nutty pecan cookies 126
Nutty walnut fudge brownies 179

Oat & cranberry muffins 220
Oatmeal & raisin cookies 67
Oaty chocolate caramel squares 193
Oaty golden raisin & walnut cookies 98
Oaty raisin & hazelnut cookies 98
Olive & walnut scones 60
Orange & chocolate fingers 99
Orange & lemon cookies 99
Orange butterfly cakes 24
Orange cheesecake cupcakes 39
Orange cupcakes 14
Orange jumbles 74
Orange queen cakes 19
Orange refrigerator cookies 83
Orange, walnut & rosemary muffins 231
Orangines 108

Pain au apricot 262
Pain au chocolat 262
Pain au chocolat et noisette 262
Painted butterflies 144
Panforte di siena 188
Papaya & cashew cookies 100
With cashew frosting 100
Parmesan & pine nut muffins 250
Parmesan & sage muffins 248
Party cookies 113
Peach daiquiri cookies 101
With peach icing 101
Peach, pear & plum cookies 101
Peaches 'n' cream cupcakes 31
Peanut & cherry bites 291
Peanut blossoms 292
Peanut butter & jam cupcakes 21
Peanut butter chip brownies 169
Peanut butter cookies 148
With banana filling 148
Peanut number crunchers 142
Peanut partners 119
With peanut brittle topping 119
Peanut sitting pretties 68
With hazelnut & chocolate topping 68
Pear & liqueur muffins 205
Pear & mint cookies 102
With pear liqueur icing 102
Pear & pistachio cookies 102
Pear & raisin danish 264
Pear galettes 55
Pear gingerbread 58
Pear, oat & nutmeg muffins 233
Pear strudel with cider sauce 268
Pecan & maple spice cakes 17
Pecan brownie muffins 226
With vanilla pecan topping 226
Pecan brownies 172
Pecan fudge cupcakes 20
Pepper & corn cornbread 62
Peppermint creams 286
Pepperoni & sun-dried tomato muffins 251
Persian almond rolls 280
Pesto & tomato palmiers 276
Petal gems 131
Pina colada cupcakes 29
Pine nut & lemon biscotti 155
Pineapple & ginger creams 94
With pineapple frosting 94
Pineapple, coconut & ginger cookies 94
Pink hearts 140
Pistachio & almond cookies 116
With pistachio cream 116
Pistachio & almond tuiles 72
Pistachio biscotti 152
Pistachio cookies 120
Plum & sweet cream cookies 104
Plum & white chocolate cookies 104
Prune blondies 183
Pumpkin-decorated cupcakes 41
Pure indulgence almond cupcakes 32

Queen's cakes 19

Rainbow cookies 87
Raisin bran muffins 220
Raspberry & golden raisin rugelach 283
Raspberry chocolate boxes 266
Raspberry cookies 99
Raspberry crumble muffins 232
With almond crunch topping 232
Raspberry lamingtons 52
Raspberry oat slices 196
Raspberry petits choux 265
Raspberry shortcakes 47
Really large coconut macaroons 115
Really rich chocolate tarts 271
Really chocolatey Easter cupcakes 39
Refrigerator cookies 83
Rhubarb, ginger & raisin muffins 213
With yogurt frosting 213
Rich apricot blondies 183
Rich chocolate fudge 274
Rich chocolate mousses 299
Rich ginger brownies with port cream 175
With brandy cream 175
Rich lemon tarts 271

Rich peanut & cream cookies sandwiches 120
With coconut & peanut cream 120
Ring doughnuts 57
Rock cakes 59
Rocky mountain cupcakes 42
Rocky road bars 192
Rocky road bites 291
Rocky road brownies 178
Rocky road chocolate muffins 244
Rose flower cookies 132
Rose petal cupcakes 19
Rose-topped wedding muffins 240
Rosemary cookies 131
Rosewater biscotti 153
Ruby wedding cupcakes 42
Rum & chocolate cups 286
Rum & raisin cookies with orange filling 133
With semisweet chocolate filling 133
Rum & raisin fudge 274
Rum truffles 289

Sacristons 276
Saffron-flecked biscotti 156
Saffron loaf 54
Savory oat crackers 161
Scented baby shower cupcakes 43
Scones 50
Seedy ginger squares 52
Shortbread 150
Shredded lemon cupcakes 30
Shredded orange cupcakes 30
Shredded vegetable & cheese muffins 251
Shredded vegetable muffins 251
Signature muffins 243
Simple cookies 84
Smiley faces 69
Smoked salmon & dill muffins 252
With caviar topping 252
S'mores 143
S'mores with banana 143
Snickerdoodles 114
Soft cheese & garlic muffins 252
Sour cream & pineapple muffins 232
With pineapple frosting 232
Sour cream brownies 176
Spanish almond cookies 73
Spanish buñuelos 56
Spanish churros 54
Spanish panellets 78
Spiced banana brownies 170
Spiced chocolate muffins 213
Spiced cookies 84
Spiced oat crackers 161
Spicy apple & oat muffins 233
Spicy chorizo & green olive muffins 253
Spicy chorizo muffins 253
Spicy Christmas cupcakes 40
Spicy dried fruit muffins 233
With brandy cream 233
Spicy nut biscotti 158
Spicy refrigerator cookies 83
Spiderweb cupcakes 41
Spinach & nutmeg muffins 254
Spring onion & goat cheese muffins 254
Springtime cupcakes 36
Stained-glass window cookies 145
Star-shaped cookies 139
Sticky citrus cookies 128
Sticky ginger cookies 128
Sticky gingerbread cupcakes 20
Sticky gingersnap cupcakes 20
Sticky orange & walnut cupcakes 22
Sticky pecan pie slices 195
Sticky toffee & banana squares 48
Sticky toffee & walnut squares 48
Sticky toffee apple squares 48
Sticky toffee muffins 234
Sticky toffee squares 48
Strawberry & almond blondies 182
Strawberry & amaretto muffins 227
Strawberry chocolate boxes 266
Strawberry chocolate slices 196
Strawberry petits choux 265
Strawberry pinks 105
With marmalade filling 105
Strawberry shortcakes 47
Strawberry tartlets 267
Sugar-coated chocolates brownies 164
Sugar-coated chocolates cupcakes 18
Sugar-coated midnight cookies 82
Sugared hearts 135
Sugared rose petal muffins 208
Sun-dried tomato & pecorino scones 60
Sun-dried tomato croissants 263
Sunflower seed muffins 216
With cheese topping 216
Super mocha brownies 178
Sweet cream doughnuts 57
Sweet walnut scones 50
Syrup drizzles 129

Tangy lemon jumbles 74
Thanksgiving cookies 110
Thanksgiving cranberry & orange muffins 238
Three grain muffins 219
With goat cheese topping 219
Thumbprint cookies 77
With lemon curd filling 77
Tiny chocolate cupcakes with ganache frosting 279
With milk chocolate ganache 279
Tiny coffee & hazelnut cupcakes 279
Toasted almond & apricot muffins 235
With apricot centers 235
Toffee apple cakes 49
Toffee chocolate puff tarts 261
Toffee nut chocolate puff tarts 261
Toffee pear cakes 49
Tomato & basil muffins 255
Tomato, basil & black olive muffins 255
Torrone molle 188
Traditional Easter cookies 136
Traditional oatcakes 159
Traffic lights 144
With jelly bean topping 144
Treasure chest gold bars 190
Triple chocolate chip muffins 227
Triple chocolate cookies 84
Triple chocolate cupcakes 34
Triple chocolate muffins 237
Tropical banana & passion fruit muffins 235
Tropical fruit cookie sandwiches 95
With coconut cream filling 95
Tropical fruit cookies 97
Tropical pineapple cupcakes 29
Tuna & olive muffins 255
Tuna, olive & caper muffins 255
Tunisian almond cigars 284
Tunisian hazelnut cigars 284
Tunisian pistachio cigars 284
Turkey & cranberry muffins 247
Tutti frutti cookies 141

Ultimate iced sugar cutouts 92
Upside-down pineapple brownies 173
Upside-down toffee apple brownies 173
Upside-down toffee pear brownies 173

Valentine heart cupcakes 41
Valentine heart muffins 241
Vanilla & almond biscotti 153
Vanilla & chocolate cupcakes 28
Vanilla & spice muffins 218
Vanilla butterfly cakes 24
Vanilla cream doughnut muffins 226
Vanilla fudge 274
Viennese pinks 140
Violet flower cookies 132
Walnut & apricot cookies 104
Walnut & cherry brownies 175
Walnut & cinnamon blondies 180
Walnut & cinnamon muffins 236
Walnut & fig pinwheels 121
Walnut & honey triangles 278
Walnut & romano scones 60
Walnut & rosemary biscotti 155
Walnut brownies 172
Walnut refrigerator cookies 83
Warm molten-centered chocolate cupcakes 28
Warm peach cupcakes 29
Warm rasberry cupcakes 29
Warm spiced apple pie cupcakes 44
Warm strawberry cupcakes baked in a teacup 29
Wheat germ, banana & pumpkin seed muffins 217
With crunchy topping 217
Whirly pinwheel cookies 71
White & dark chocolate truffles 290
White chocolate & raspberry boxes 266
White chocolate & raspberry muffins 225
White chocolate & spice cookies 100
White chocolate brownie cheesecake 168
White chocolate brownies 176
White chocolate butterfly cakes 16
White chocolate-centered cupcakes 28
White chocolate chip cookies 66
White chocolate cookies 81
White chocolate cupcakes 24
White chocolate truffles 290
White heart muffins 241
White mint stars 113
White s'mores 110
White sugar hearts 135
Whole wheat banana muffins 218
With banana topping 218

Xmas alphabet cutouts 92

Yogurt & spice muffins 218
Yogurt-topped brownies 176

Zebra cookies 132
With zebra icing 132
Zesty lemon biscotti 152
Zesty orange & walnut biscotti 152
Zoo animal cupcakes 37
Zucchini & feta cheese muffins 247
Zucchini & sesame seed muffins 247